MICROPOLITICAL THEORY

HANDBOOK OF POLITICAL SCIENCE

Volume 2

MICROPOLITICAL THEORY

Edited by
FRED I. GREENSTEIN Princeton University
NELSON W. POLSBY University of California, Berkeley

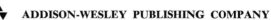 **ADDISON-WESLEY PUBLISHING COMPANY**

Reading, Massachusetts
Menlo Park, California · London · Amsterdam · Don Mills, Ontario · Sydney

This book is in the
ADDISON-WESLEY SERIES IN POLITICAL SCIENCE

ISBN 0-201-02602-3
ABCDEFGHIJ-HA-798765

PREFACE

Early in his career, the fledgling political scientist learns that his discipline is ill-defined, amorphous, and heterogeneous. This perception will in no way be rebutted by the appearance of a presumably encyclopedic eight-volume work entitled *The Handbook of Political Science*. Indeed, the persistent amorphousness of our discipline has constituted a central challenge to the editors of the *Handbook* and has brought to its creation both hazards and opportunities. The opportunities were apparent enough to us when we took on the editorial duties of the *Handbook;* the hazards became clearer later on.

At the outset, it seemed to us a rare occasion when a publisher opens quite so large a canvas and invites a pair of editors to paint on it as they will—or can. We immediately saw that in order to do the job at all we would have to cajole a goodly number of our colleagues into the belief that our canvas was in reality Tom Sawyer's fence. We did not set out at the beginning, however, with a precise vision of the final product—i.e., a work that would be composed of these particular eight volumes, dealing with the present array and number of contributions and enlisting all the present contributors. Rather, the *Handbook* is the product of a long and in some ways accidental process. An account of this process is in order if only because, by describing the necessarily adventitious character of the "decisions" that produced this work, we can help the reader to see that the *Handbook* is not an attempt to make a collective pronouncement of Truth chiseled in stone, but rather an assembly of contributions, each an individual scholarly effort, whose overall purpose is to give a warts-and-all portrait of a discipline that is still in a process of becoming.

We first became involved in discussions about the project in 1965. Addison-Wesley had already discussed the possibility of a handbook with a number of other political scientists, encouraged by their happy experience with a two-volume compendium of highly respected review essays in social psychology (Lindzey, 1954), which has since been revised and expanded into a five-volume work (Lindzey and Aronson, 1968–69).

Of the various people to whom Addison-Wesley aired the handbook idea, we evidently were among the most persistent in encouraging such a project. No doubt the reason was that we were still close to our own graduate work in a department where a careful reading of many of the chapters in *The Handbook of Social Psychology* was in some ways more fundamental to learning our trade than a comparable exposure to many of the more conspicuous intellectual edifices of the political science of the time. Gardner Lindzey, in writing his introductory statement to the first edition of *The Handbook of Social Psychology* (reprinted in the second edition), described *our* needs as well as those of budding social psychologists in saying that

> the accelerating expansion of social psychology in the past two decades has led to an acute need for a source book more advanced than the ordinary textbook in the field but yet more focused than scattered periodical literature. . . . It was this state of affairs that led us to assemble a book that would represent the major areas of social psychology at a level of difficulty appropriate for graduate students. In addition to serving the needs of graduate instruction, we anticipate that the volumes will be useful in advanced undergraduate courses and as a reference book for professional psychologists.

With the substitution of "political science" in the appropriate places, Lindzey's description of his own purposes and audiences reflects precisely what we thought Addison-Wesley might most usefully seek to accomplish with a political science handbook.

In choosing a pair of editors, the publisher might well have followed a balancing strategy, looking for two political scientists who were poles apart in their background, training, and views of the discipline. The publisher might then have sought divine intervention, praying for the miracle that would bring the editors into sufficient agreement to make the planning of the *Handbook*—or *any* handbook—possible at all. Instead they found a pair of editors with complementary but basically similar and congenial perspectives. We were then both teaching at Wesleyan University and had been to graduate school together at Yale, at a time when the political science department there was making its widely recognized contribution to the modernization of the discipline. Each had recently spent a year in the interdisciplinary ambience of the Center for Advanced Study in the Behavioral Sciences. Moreover, we were both specialists in American politics, the "field" which in 1973 still accounted for three-quarters of the contributions to *The American Political Science Review*. There were also complementary divergencies. Within political science, Polsby's work and interests had been in national politics and policy-making, whereas Greenstein's were more in mass, extragovernmental aspects of political behavior. Outside political science, Polsby's interests were directed more toward sociology and law, and Greenstein's tended toward psychiatry and clinical and social psychology.

To begin with, neither we nor the publisher could be sure without first gathering evidence that the discipline of political science was "ready" for a handbook comparable to the Lindzey work. We were sure that, if it was at all possible for us to bring such a handbook into being, we would have to employ the Aristotelian tack of working within and building upon existing categories of endeavor, rather than the Platonic (or Procrustean) mode of inventing a coherent set of master categories and persuading contributors to use them. First, at our request the publisher inquired of a number of distinguished political scientists whether they felt a need would be served by a handbook of political science similar to *The Handbook of Social Psychology*. This inquiry went to political scientists who had themselves been involved in extensive editorial activities or who were especially known for their attention to political science as a discipline. The responses were quite uniform in favoring such a handbook. The particular suggestions about how such a handbook might be *organized,* however, were exceptionally varied. But fortunately we had asked one further question: What half-dozen or so individuals were so authoritative or original in their contributions on some topic as to make them prime candidates for inclusion in any political science handbook, no matter what its final overall shape? Here agreement reemerged; the consultants were remarkably unanimous in the individuals named.

Seizing the advantage provided by that consensus, we reached the following agreement with the publisher. We would write the individuals who constituted what we now saw as a prime list of candidates for inclusion as authors and ask whether they would be willing to contribute to a handbook of political science, given a long lead time and freedom to choose the topic of their essay. (We did suggest possible topics to each.) It was agreed that unless we were able to enlist most of those with whom we were corresponding as a core group of contributors, we would not proceed with a handbook. Since all but one of that group indicated willingness to contribute, we signed a publishing agreement (in September 1967) and proceeded to expand our core group to a full set of contributors to what we then envisaged as a three-volume handbook, drawing on our core contributors for advice. Our queries to the core contributors were a search not so much for structural and organizational suggestions as for concrete topics and specific contributors to add to the initial list.

The well-worn term "incremental" suggests itself as a summary of how the table of contents of *The Handbook of Political Science* then took shape. As the number of contributors increased, and as contributors themselves continued to make suggestions about possible rearrangements in the division of labor and to remark on gaps, the planned three volumes expanded to eight, most of which, however, were shorter than the originally intended three. Throughout, Addison-Wesley left it to us and the contributors, within the very broadest of boundaries, to define the overall length of the project and of the individual contributions. And throughout, we urged the contributors not to seek intellectual anonymity in the guise of being "merely" summarizers—or embalmers—of their fields but rather to endeavor to place a distinctive intellectual stamp on their contributions.

A necessary condition of enlisting the initial group of contributors was a production deadline so far in the future as to dissolve the concern of rational individuals about adding to their intellectual encumbrances. As it turned out, our "safely remote" initial deadline (1970) was in fact a drastic underestimation of the number of postponements and delays.* Along with delays there have been occasional withdrawals, as individual contributors recognized that even with a long fuse the task of preparing a handbook article would be a major one and would inevitably preempt time from other projects and interests. Departing contributors were often helpful in suggesting alternatives. Both through the late enlistment of such substitutes and through the addition of collaborators taken on by invited contributors, we feel we have been spared a table of contents that anachronistically represents only the cohort of those individuals who were responsible for the shape of political science circa 1967.

Whether one builds a handbook table of contents a priori or ex post facto, *some* basis of organization emerges. We might have organized a handbook around:

1. *"political things"* (e.g., the French bureaucracy, the U.S. Constitution, political parties);

2. *nodes or clusters in the literature* (community power, group theory, issue voting);

3. *subdisciplines* (public administration, public law, comparative government, political theory, international relations);

4. *functions* (planning, law-making, adjudication);

5. *geography* (the American Congress, the British Cabinet, the politicoeconomic institutions of the U.S.S.R.);

6. or any combination of the above and further possibilities.

Any of our colleagues who have tried to construct a curriculum in political science will sympathize with our dilemma. There is, quite simply, no

---

* For the comparable experience of *Handbook of Social Psychology* editors with delays, see Lindzey, 1954, p. vii, Lindzey and Aronson, 1968–69, p. ix.

sovereign way to organize our discipline. Although much of our knowledge is cumulative, there is no set beginning or end to political science. Apart from certain quite restricted subdisciplinary areas (notably the mathematical and statistical), political scientists do not have to learn a particular bit of information or master a particular technique at a particular stage as a prerequisite to further study. And the discipline lacks a single widely accepted frame of reference or principle of organization. Consequently, we evolved a table of contents that to some extent adopted nearly *all* the approaches above. (None of our chapter titles contains a geographical reference, but many of the chapters employ one or more explicitly specified political systems as data sources.)

The protean classifications of subspecialization within political science and the ups and downs in subspecialty interests over the years are extensively reviewed by Dwight Waldo in his essay in Volume 1 on political science as discipline and profession. A further way to recognize the diversity and change in our discipline—as well as the persisting elements—is to note the divisions of disciplinary interests used by the directories of the American Political Science Association, the membership of which constitutes the great bulk of all political scientists. A glance at the three successive directories which have been current during our editorial activities is instructive.

The 1961 *Biographical Directory of the American Political Science Association* (APSA, 1961) represents a last glimpse at a parsimonious, staid set of subdisciplinary categories that would have been readily recognizable at the 1930 Annual Meeting of the Association.

1. American National Government

2. Comparative Government

3. International Law and Relations

4. Political Parties

5. Political Theory

6. Public Administration

7. Public Law

8. State and Local Government

In the next *Biographical Directory* (APSA, 1968), there appeared a categorization that was at once pared down and much expanded from the 1961 classification. A mere three "general fields" were listed. The first was "Contemporary Political Systems." Members electing this general field were asked to specify the country or countries in which they were interested, and those countries were listed parenthetically after the members' names in the subdisciplinary listing, presumably out of a desire to play down the importance of "area studies" as an intellectual focus and to accentuate the importance of functional or analytic bases of intellectual endeavor. "International Law, Organization, and Politics" was the second general field, and "Political Theory and Philosophy" was the third. But the 26 categories in Table 1 were provided for the listing of "specialized fields." They included some venerable subdivisions, perhaps in slightly more fashionable phrasing, and other distinctly nonvenerable subdivisions, at least one of which (political socialization) did not even exist in the general vocabulary of political scientists ten years earlier. In this *Handbook*, the 1968 categories have many parallels, including the general principle of organization that excludes geography as a specialized field criterion while at the same time recognizing that political scientists can and should study and compare diverse political settings. Diplomatically avoiding the presentation of a structured classification, the editors of the 1968 *Directory* relied on the alphabet for their sequence of specialized fields.

TABLE 1 Subdisciplinary categories used in *Biographical Directory* of the American Political Science Association, 1968

1. Administrative law
2. Administration: organization, processes, behavior
3. Budget and fiscal management
4. Constitutional law
5. Executive: organization, processes, behavior
6. Foreign policy
7. Government regulation of business
8. International law
9. International organization and administration
10. International politics
11. Judiciary: organization, processes, behavior
12. Legislature: organization, processes, behavior
13. Methodology
14. Metropolitan and urban government and politics
15. National security policy
16. Personnel administration
17. Political and constitutional history
18. Political parties and elections: organizations and processes
19. Political psychology
20. Political socialization
21. Political theory and philosophy (empirical)
22. Political theory and philosophy (historical)
23. Political theory and philosophy (normative)
24. Public opinion
25. Revolutions and political violence
26. State and local government and politics
27. Voting behavior

Even with this burgeoning of options, many members of the discipline evidently felt that their interests were not adequately covered. Goodly numbers took advantage of an opportunity provided in the questionnaire to the APSA membership to list "other" specialties, referring, for example, to "political sociology," "political behavior," "political development," "policy studies," "communication," "federalism," and "interest groups."

The 1973 *Biographical Directory* (APSA, 1973) attempted still another basis of classification, a revised version of the classification used in the 1970 *National Science Foundation Register of Scientific and Technical Personnel.* Braving a structured rather than alphabetic classification, the authors of this taxonomy divided the discipline into nine major classes and a total of 60 specialized classifications, with a return to the antique dichotomy of foreign versus U.S. politics. The specifics of the 1973 listing are given in Table 2.

TABLE 2 Subdisciplinary categories used in *Biographical Directory* of the American Political Science Association, 1973

I   Foreign and Cross-National Political Institutions and Behavior

1. Analyses of particular systems or subsystems
2. Decision-making processes
3. Elites and their oppositions
4. Mass participation and communications
5. Parties, mass movements, secondary associations
6. Political development and modernization
7. Politics of planning
8. Values, ideologies, belief systems, political culture

II   International Law, Organization, and Politics

9. International law
10. International organization and administration
11. International politics

III   Methodology

12. Computer techniques
13. Content analysis
14. Epistemology and philosophy of science
15. Experimental design
16. Field data collection
17. Measurement and index construction
18. Model building
19. Statistical analysis
20. Survey design and analysis

IV   Political Stability, Instability, and Change

21. Cultural modification and diffusion
22. Personality and motivation
23. Political leadership and recruitment
24. Political socialization
25. Revolution and violence
26. Schools and political education
27. Social and economic stratification   (continued)

As will be evident, the present *Handbook* contains articles on topics that appear on neither of the two recent differentiated lists and omits topics on each. Some "omissions" were inadvertent. Others were deliberate, resulting from our conclusion either that the work on a particular topic did not appear ripe for review at this time or that the topic overlapped sufficiently with others already commissioned so that we might leave it out in the interests of preventing our rapidly expanding project from becoming hopelessly large. There also were instances in which we failed to find (or

keep) authors on topics that we might otherwise have included. Hence readers should be forewarned about a feature of the *Handbook* that they should
know without forewarning is bound to exist: incompleteness. Each reviewer
will note "strange omissions." For us it is more extraordinary that so many
able people were willing to invest so much effort in this enterprise.

It should be evident from our history of the project that we consider the
rubrics under which scholarly work is classified to be less important than the
caliber of the scholarship and that we recognize the incorrigible tendency of
inquiry to overflow the pigeonholes to which it has been assigned, as well as
the desirability that scholars rather than editors (or other administrators)
define the boundaries of their endeavors. Therefore we have used rather
simple principles for aggregating essays into their respective volumes and
given them straightforward titles.

The essays in Volume 1 on the nature of political theory which follow
Waldo's extensive discussion of the scope of political science are far from
innocent of reference to empirical matters. This comports with the common
observation that matters of theoretical interest are by no means removed
from the concerns of the real world. And although we have used the titles
Micropolitical Theory and *Macropolitical Theory* for Volumes 2 and 3, we have
meant no more thereby than to identify the scale and mode of conceptualization typical of the topics in these volumes. Here again the reader will find
selections that extensively review empirical findings.

Similarly, although the titles of Volumes 4, 5, and 6 on extragovernmental, governmental, and policy-output aspects of government and politics
may appear to imply mere data compilations, the contents of these volumes
are far from atheoretical. This is also emphatically true of Volume 8, which
carries the title *International Politics*, a field that in recent decades has continuously raised difficult theoretical issues, including issues about the proper
nature of theory. Volume 7 carries the title *Strategies of Inquiry* rather than
Methodology to call attention to the fact that contributors to that volume have
emphasized linking techniques of inquiry to substantive issues. In short, contributions to the eight volumes connect in many ways that can be only
imperfectly suggested by the editors' table of contents or even by the comprehensive index at the end of Volume 8.

It can scarcely surprise readers of a multiple-authored work to learn
that what is before them is a collective effort. It gives us pleasure to acknowledge obligations to five groups of people who helped to lighten our part of
the load. First of all, to our contributors we owe a debt of gratitude for their
patience, cooperation, and willingness to find the time in their exceedingly
busy schedules to produce the essays that make up this *Handbook*. Second, we
thank the many helpful Addison-Wesley staff members with whom we have
worked for their good cheer toward us and for their optimism about this
project. Third, the senior scholars who initially advised Addison-Wesley to

undertake the project, and who may even have pointed the publishers in our direction, know who they are. We believe it would add still another burden to the things they must answer for in our profession if we named them publicly, but we want to record our rueful, belated appreciation to them. Fourth, Kathleen Peters and Barbara Kelly in Berkeley and Lee L. Messina, Catherine Smith, and Frances C. Root in Middletown kept the paper flowing back and forth across the country and helped us immeasurably in getting the job done. Finally, our love and gratitude to Barbara Greenstein and Linda Polsby. And we are happy to report to Michael, Amy, and Jessica Greenstein, and to Lisa, Emily, and Daniel Polsby that at long last their fathers are off the long-distance telephone.

Princeton, New Jersey   F.I.G.
Berkeley, California   N.W.P.

REFERENCES

American Political Science Association (1961). *Biographical Directory of The American Political Science Association,* fourth edition. (Franklin L. Burdette, ed.) Washington, D.C.

American Political Science Association (1968). *Biographical Directory,* fifth edition. Washington, D.C.

American Political Science Association (1973). *Biographical Directory,* sixth edition. Washington, D.C.

Lindzey, Gardner, ed. (1954). *Handbook of Social Psychology,* 2 volumes. Cambridge, Mass.: Addison-Wesley.

Lindzey, Gardner, and Elliot Aronson, eds. (1968–69). *The Handbook of Social Psychology,* second edition, 5 volumes. Reading, Mass.: Addison-Wesley.

CONTENTS

CONTENTS OF OTHER VOLUMES IN THIS SERIES

MICROPOLITICAL THEORY

1
PERSONALITY AND POLITICS

FRED I. GREENSTEIN

1. INTRODUCTION

Did Lyndon Johnson's personal psychological proclivities contribute to the American escalation of the Vietnam conflict? Was Woodrow Wilson unable to achieve Senate ratification of the Versailles Treaty for reasons stemming from the way he was constituted as a human being? Have the personalities of such individuals as Richard Nixon and Henry Kissinger been consequential for their political behavior in and out of office? Do "the French" (Russians, Japanese, Germans, Americans, etc.) differ in typical personality traits from members of other national or subnational groups, and if so, are the differences politically consequential? Are there distinctive personality syndromes that are sufficiently resonant with aspects of political behavior to produce personality-based political types—for example, individuals with the need to differ or to rebel against authority, or to hold rigid or flexible belief systems?

These are examples of specific, substantive questions that have led to the diverse array of empirical and theoretical work reported in what can be loosely labeled "the personality-and-politics literature." The tradition in this area—if there can be said to be anything as stable as a tradition—is ragged in the extreme:

1. Many writings seeking to connect personality and politics have appeared over the years.

I am indebted to the following commentators on the first draft, none of whom are culpable for the final product: James David Barber, Alexander L. George, Paul M. Sniderman, M. Brewster Smith, and Robert C. Tucker. Copyright © 1975 Fred I. Greenstein.

2. Much of this work has been generated not by academic students of politics but rather by nonscholars, such as journalists, or by psychologists, culture-and-personality anthropologists, and psychiatrists.

3. If there has been a considerable volume of work on personality and politics, there has also been a remarkable quantity of criticism of that work, both by scholars and, to the extent that personality-and-politics writings have come to their attention, by lay intellectuals. Pervasive skepticism, extending even to the question of whether *in principle* systematic personality-and-politics inquiry is feasible, has been evident in the reception of this genre of work within its principal parent disciplines of psychology, anthropology, and psychiatry, and skepticism has been even more evident in the reactions of political scientists. Still another behavioral science, sociology, was virtually erected on a cornerstone of resistance to "psychologizing" about social, and hence political, phenomena. It is noteworthy, however, that Durkheim's admonition that society be explained "at the social level" (Durkheim 1895, 1897) has not prevented sociologists from being among the principal users of attitude surveys, nor has it precluded the development of a subfield of personality and social structure with problems directly cognate to those in personality-and-politics inquiry.

4. In spite of the prevailing skepticism toward their endeavors, the impulse of at least some students of politics to continue to examine personality-and-politics connections seems irrepressible. There is a modest but not minuscule cadre of personality-and-politics students in all the disciplines referred to above, including sociology, although it is rare to see an entire research career devoted to work in this vein. The cadre continues to be renewed with additional recruits. Finally, there are a good many workers on cognate, nonpolitical aspects of personality and social structure, and their contributions often are more or less directly applicable to the study of human aspects of politics.

Why should there be a persistent interest in a "messy," controversial nexus of research? I submit that the most important single reason is the prima facie evidence of day-to-day political experience that personal qualities *do* make a difference—often a critical difference—in determining political outcomes. Let us consider two illustrations—a specific one from governmental politics and a more general one from the politics of the immediate environments of many of the readers of this chapter. Each example could easily be embellished, and a very much larger list of examples could be furnished.

A striking recent historical example is referred to in the first sentence of this chapter: the impact of Lyndon Johnson's personality on the escalation of the Vietnam war. Even a selective reading of the many firsthand reports by participants in and direct observers of the Johnson and Kennedy administrations compellingly suggests that if Kennedy had remained in office, the Vietnam conflict, even if it would not have been terminated, would certainly not have expanded so drastically, both in Southeast Asia and as a bitterly divisive domestic issue.

Psychological differences between Johnson and Kennedy are highly relevant to understanding Johnson's personal contribution to the 1964–1968 military escalation. The two men differed in terms of cognitions and attitudes of the sort political scientists usually do *not* have in mind when they refer to "personality": for example, explicit and implicit beliefs about means-and-ends relationships in national and international politics, assumptions about the relative efficacy of military and political solutions, and beliefs about the capacities and legitimacy of the various political groupings in Vietnam. Without accepting the premise that excludes such factors from the domain of "personality," one can convincingly argue that there were still further, perhaps more intractable, differences between the two presidents *qua* persons that help to account for the Vietnam escalation. These include Johnson's intensely personal power needs, which appear to have contributed to his inarticulate major premise that failure to preserve the Saigon government could only be defined as an American—and a *Johnson*—defeat. A further and perhaps more important personal difference between the two men was Johnson's corrosively aggressive, domineering style of dealing with subordinates, which had the effect of progressively surrounding him with a claque of uncritical supporters of his policy of self-defeating perseveration.

Kennedy, on the other hand, who in many respects was indistinguishable from Johnson in basic ideological commitments, was not the sort of individual who would perceive an issue in either-or terms. Nor was he disposed to pour good resources into a bad investment—as is evidenced by his prompt withdrawal from the Bay of Pigs, as well as by his remarkable capacity to accept personal responsibility for that abortive invasion and to put policy failure behind him without lamentations and recriminations. And far from insulating himself from criticism, he positively encouraged tough-minded, egalitarian give-and-take with his advisers. The most striking example of this also is connected with Cuba—namely, the free-wheeling Excom sessions Kennedy set in motion in order to devise a response to the surprise installation of Soviet missiles in Cuba. (See the analyses of Johnson and Kennedy in Barber, 1972a.)

The regular ups and downs of administrative politics in any academic institution provide an everyday-life example of how "personality factors," as difficult as they may be to analyze, nevertheless press themselves inescapably on the political observer. University instructors who are several years beyond graduate school and who have an average awareness of administrative politics in one or more universities will, if they reflect on their experience, have a strong sense that "it makes a great difference" who occupies such positions as chairmanships, deanships, and presidencies. They will further recognize that "the difference" far exceeds differences in administrators' positions on the standard educational policy issues dividing university faculties and administrators, as well as that administrators' behavior is far from being a mere product of the "role requirements" of their offices. It is not that the official roles university administrators occupy are unimportant in accounting for their behavior but, rather, that the actor *makes* his role *as well as* responding to preestablished expectations about his official responsibilities.

Political actors themselves incessantly take account of the personal properties of their counterparts. And the closer the political analyst's vantage point is to events and the more painstaking and detailed his account is of the precise specifics of who did what and when, the greater the analytic necessity of taking account of "the personalities involved." Consider, for example, the impossibility of an investigation of the 1972 Watergate affair and its complex aftermath that simply treated all participants as if their personal properties were identical. The following statement by Allison (1969, p. 709) on the basis of his intensive case study and theoretical analysis of the Cuban missile crisis is instructive. Referring to the level of political behavior at which the pulling and hauling among bureaucratic actors occurs, he notes:

> The core of the bureaucratic politics mix is personality. How each man manages to stand the heat in his kitchen, each player's basic operating style, and the complementarity or contradiction among personalities and styles in the inner circles are irreducible pieces of the policy blend.

It is precisely at the point of Allison's analysis where he deals with the specific, detailed sequence of activities during the missile crisis that he arrives at this observation.

In this chapter I suggest ways to improve on intuitive, anecdotal "demonstrations" about connections between personality and politics of the sort presented in the foregoing paragraphs. The mission of contributors to this volume of *The Handbook of Political Science* is to discuss theoretical aspects of micropolitics. I interpret my theoretical assignment broadly to include discussion of basic problems of conceptualizing overarching methodological issues that bear on the task of thinking clearly about personality and politics, as well as exposition of selected empirical findings that bring out theoretically interesting points. My purpose is to suggest how the typical substantive problems faced by analysts of personality and politics can be framed in ways that minimize the standard difficulties of the existing literature. By and large, I proceed at a level of generality that precludes discussion of measurement mechanics.

Much of the argument that follows can be found in an expanded form in Greenstein (1969), although at various points I have reorganized, rephrased, or changed my assertions in hope of arriving at a clearer and more comprehensive formulation and one that would respond to points made by reviewers.[1] Many basic writings on personality and politics drawn on both in that work and in this chapter are reprinted with critical introductions in Greenstein and Lerner (1971). Also see the comprehensive bibliographical essay by Lerner

(1969) and the several literature reviews in Knutson (1973) . For an important source of parallel work on nonpolitical aspects of personality and social structure, see Smelser and Smelser (1970) .

The elements of this chapter are:

1. A conceptual exposition of how psychological and environmental factors converge to determine behavior; of types of psychological antecedents of behavior; of the relationship between social background influences, psychological inferences, and behavior; and of how macrosystemic influences connect with individual political behavior and its immediate antecedents (Part 2) .

2. A problem-clarifying, problem-dissolving discussion of a series of considerations that are sometimes viewed as obstacles to the study of personality and politics but that by and large turn out to be first-approximation insights into the complexities of studying phenomena that are themselves likely to operate in highly complex ways (Part 3) .

3. A rough classification of kinds of personality-and-politics literature and a selective review of literature falling under the headings of the classification, with attention to delineating past difficulties and suggesting how they might be remedied in future inquiry (Parts 4–8) .

4. Brief concluding remarks (Part 9) .

2. BASIC CONCEPTUAL DISTINCTIONS

The distinctions I shall introduce are derived from M. Brewster Smith's lucid "A Map for the Analysis of Personality and Politics" (1968a and b) . Following Smith's lead, I first present and discuss certain of the components of the map and then combine the elements in a summary figure. In essence, what follows is a skeletal and theoretically eclectic set of basic categories, which might appear in a textbook discussion of personality and social structure, with special emphasis on charting the typical chains of causal linkage. The resulting overall map constitutes a basic set of analytic distinctions useful for guiding inquiry, not a set of "real" structures (Ryle, 1949; Wood and Pitcher, 1970) . Since such charting exercises are inevitably arid, the reader is advised to examine this section briefly and then refer to it from time to time as distinctions in the map are drawn on to deal with specific issues.

2.1 The E→P→R Paradigm

The most convenient starting place in charting the typical kinds of behavioral antecedents and their links is the venerable formula central in Kurt Lewin's work (e.g., Lewin, 1936, pp. 11–12; see also J. C. Davies, 1963, pp. 1–6) that "behavior or any kind of mental event . . . depends on the state of the person and at the same time on the environment"; in summary, $B = f$ (PE). Lasswell and Kaplan (1950, pp. 4–6), whose usage I follow, make the same distinction, using the terms environment, predisposition, and response, and they place the $E \rightarrow P \rightarrow R$ paradigm at the base of their edifice of terminology for political analyses.

This formula, which is of course also equivalent to the often used stimulus→organism→response paradigm, may seem totally noncontroversial to the point of truism. Yet in fact there *are* a number of controversies and qualifications. Perhaps the most fundamental, if not the most substantive, controversy results from the radical behaviorist claim that the very use of "mentalistic" concepts such as personality is scientifically inadmissible. Behaviorist psychologists like B. F. Skinner (1953, 1971) stress that only environmental variables are observable and hence measurable as concomitants of behavior. Chomsky's (1959) searching critique of Skinner's *Verbal Behavior* makes it clear that there is ample scientific precedent for positing the structures of an organism on the basis of what is known about the inputs into it and its outputs, and that in studying human beings doing so is necessary, given the extremely complex quality of the organism's contribution to action. (Also see Scriven, 1956, on Skinner; Fodor, 1968, on behaviorist psychology in general; and Hempel, 1965, on the scientific status of unobservable constructs.) Thus it does seem appropriate to use terms describing predispositions, of which I shall introduce a number shortly—although I shall use only a small fraction of the 80 terms cited in Donald Campbell's comprehensive discussion of the terminology referring to predispositional variables (Campbell, 1963).

In a sense the individual's inner predispositions not only need to be taken account of but also can be thought of as "overflowing" into the environment, in line with the well-recognized adage that behavior—or at any rate, motivated behavior—is influenced by *the environment as perceived* rather than that elusive entity the "real" environment. In addition, the "objective" environment of political behavior is heavily psychological in that some of its most politically consequential elements are the norms, beliefs, and expectations of other actors in the political system.

Just as we cannot eliminate predispositions from the equation, so we cannot solipsistically ignore the "real" external environment simply because it has so many psychological components.[2] Perceptions of reality have a grounding in brute events that are independent of the perceiver. Further, an important if underutilized research strategy consists of comparing actors' perceptions of their environment with independent observations of the environment. And the environment *can* have effects without psychological mediation—as when lightning strikes!

The Lewinian precept that behavior be considered *jointly* in terms of the environmental situation and the actor's predisposition cannot be overstressed.

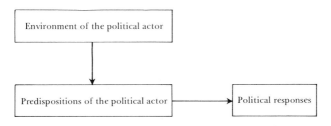

Fig. 1. Basic Antecedents of Political Behavior: $E \to P \to R$

Situational variables do not merely "dampen" the effect of psychological variables on behavior and vice versa. In each case the result of the interplay between inner and outer forces may even reverse effects that would otherwise be expected. For example, an external threat of the sort that would lead most people to retreat may spur a brave or reckless person to advance; bigoted authoritarians may discriminate against minority-group members in environments that support their prejudices but may, as the interesting research of Katz and Benjamin (1960) shows, sometimes actually lean over backward to be nondiscriminatory in environments where liberal norms prevail. These simply are extreme examples, moreover, of the much more pervasive tendency for environmental and predispositional forces to interact in ways that make the typical connections between personality and political (or other) behavior complex and contingent rather than direct and linear—a point to which I shall return several times in this essay.

Figure 1, summarizing the $E \to P \to R$ relationship, presents the E impinging from above on the P by way of preparation for an expanded figure that takes account of past and future states of E and P. But first, continuing to conceive of a single act at a single point in time, we need to "look into" the predispositional panel, remembering that terminology about inner states is analytic rather than directly observational and is based on inferences from outer manifestations.

2.2 A Conceptualization of Predispositional Variables

Figure 2 expands the predispositional panel of Figure 1, providing the scaffolding for a drastically simplified summary of certain standard distinctions made in most personality theories (Hall and Lindzey, 1957, 1970).

The portion of the predispositional panel in closest touch with the environment is labeled "perceptions of the environment." So locating this analytic category helps emphasize the primacy for political psychology of establishing precisely how actors view the politically relevant environment that surrounds them—where they focus their attention, how they absorb and process information, what information they seek, and what categories they use. Relevant here is the formal, physically grounded literature on perception, the literature on

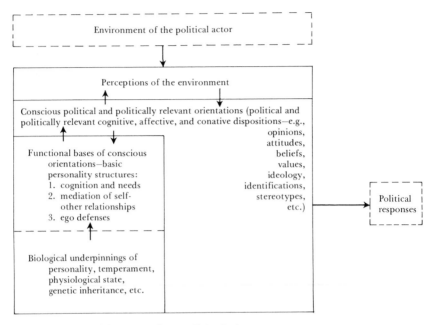

Fig. 2. Predispositions of the Political Actor

social perception, and various cognitive literatures on the "natural categories" into which people consciously or more often without much self-consciousness organize their experience. Among the relevant intellectual emphases are "ethnomethodology" and "symbolic interactionism" (Denzin, 1969), cognitive anthropology (Tyler, 1969), and the extensive literature on selective exposure and perception (Freedman and Sears, 1965).

The perceptual aspect of predispositions can be thought of as shading continuously into conscious political and politically relevant psychological orientations. These are the direct mediators of political behavior, although it should be stressed that much behavior is preceded by little if any explicit self-conscious reflection, and in the specialized case of unconscious motivation as described in the psychoanalytic literature, the conscious "reason" for an individual's behavior is self-deceptive.[3]

One working definition of "conscious political and politically relevant orientations" characterizes them as the orientations that are more or less directly accessible via appropriately sensitive interviewing and questionnaire-administration procedures. In this segment of the panel I have included, without pausing to define them, an array of the terms commonly used in reporting such data—opinion, attitude, belief, values, ideology, identification, stereotype, etc.—as well as the three venerable, mutually exclusive and exhaustive terms used to describe psychological content: cognitions (information), affect (feeling, including the emotional content of evaluations), and conations (orientation about how to act under varied circumstances). In referring to conscious political orientations, I do not assume that they are stable or well developed. See Converse (1970) for evidence of the weakness of political cognition and affect in general populations. The closer one moves to the stage of politics, however, the more one is likely to encounter actors with highly formed political orientations, not only on matters of political preference but also vis à vis the nature and operating principles of the political process itself. Hence the great value of the intellectual emphases pioneered by Leites (1951, 1953, 1959) and explicated by George (1969) of seeking to ascertain the explicit and implicit assumptions in the "operating codes" of political leaders.

Much of the data typically used in political psychology (e.g., in studies of public opinion, voting, and political participation) are derived from measurement procedures designed to elicit "conscious orientations." The words "designed to" should be emphasized since there continue to be major, unresolved problems posed by the task of actually eliciting and categorizing political orientations. Some of the most analytically powerful political psychological categories—e.g., "party identification" (Campbell, Converse, Miller, and Stokes, 1960) —are disturbingly difficult to distinguish from the fixed-choice questionnaire items used to measure them, even though "actual" subjective orientations do not take the form of such questionnaire response categories as "agree, agree strongly, disagree, disagree strongly, no opinion" (Greenstein and Tarrow, 1970, pp. 504–505) .

The segment of the representation of major predispositional categories in Figure 2 farthest from the environment and the response refers to genetic and psychophysical influences on predispositions behavior and to the concerns that distinguish this chapter from the other *Handbook of Political Science* chapters dealing with psychological issues—"functional bases of conscious orientations" and "basic personality structures." Here I continue to paraphrase Smith (1968a and b), drawing also on other work that takes a "functional" approach to analyzing the connections between personality, opinion, and behavior (Smith, Bruner, and White, 1956; Katz, 1960). The chart conceives of three underlying "functional bases of conscious political orientations" or, synonymously, "basic personality structures." These are patterned, ongoing psychic processes performing basic adaptive tasks required for the functioning of all individuals, albeit performing them in different ways and with different degrees of prominence from person to person. There is no implication that these processes are functional in the sense of having consequences that either the individual or society will positively value—only that they are causal elements in processes through which individuals manage their inner economies and cope with their environments. The three structures or functional tasks are:

1. *Cognition*:   the acquiring, storing, processing, and using of information.

2. *Mediation of self-other relations*:   the needs and processes giving rise to

dispositions bearing on how the individual relates to others, including identifications, loyalties, positive and negative reference-group attachments, etc.

3. *Ego defenses*:   adaptations to inner emotional conflict, including mechanisms of creative integration, as well as the more standard symptomatology this term evokes.

The elements in this trichotomy are present with varying degrees of emphasis in most personality theories, although Gestalt and other cognitive psychologists have particularly stressed the first category, social psychologists the second, and clinicians the third. The three categories roughly parallel Freud's terms ego, superego,[4] and id. The shift within psychoanalysis in the 1930s from Freud's emphasis on repression, the unconscious, and symptom formation to the increased concern with conscious, adaptive processes by such ego-psychology psychoanalysts as Anna Freud, Hartmann, and Erikson can be translated in terms of Figure 2 as an expansion from almost exclusive emphasis on the third functional category to simultaneous interest in the first and the third. (For a critical review of developments in psychoanalytic ego psychology, with references to basic bibliographical sources, see Leites 1971.) Both ego-psychology and more orthodox id-centered psychoanalysts employ a basically similar account of the personality functioning. In each case it is assumed that the basic task of the ego is to respond to the demands of external reality while simultaneously dealing with two often highly contradictory sources of inner pressure —the restrictive prescriptions of the superego and the primitive, typically unconscious, id impulses toward immediate emotional gratification. The mechanisms of ego defense (projection, displacement, identification with the aggressor, etc.) are means of giving "safe" expression to unacceptable impulses.

In the concluding chapter of each edition of their magisterial summary of major types of personality theory, Hall and Lindzey (1957, 1970) present an extended list of the possible elements and emphases in personality theories. Two of the elements on their list more or less directly parallel the second and third of the functional bases noted in Figure 2: "unconscious determinants" (which connects with the ego-defensive function) and "group membership determinants" (which parallels the mediation of self-other–relationships function) .

As Hall and Lindzey note, some personality theories, such as those of Jung, Horney, Murray, and of course Freud, place a high emphasis on unconscious determinants whereas others, such as those of Lewin, Allport, and Rogers, place little if any emphasis on unconscious determination as a key aspect of motivation—or at least of the motivation of "normal" individuals. On the matter of whether orientations to the group are a key behavioral determinant, Hall and Lindzey note the high emphasis on this source of behavior in theories such as those of Sullivan, Fromm, and Lewin and the relative absence of interest in the mediation of self-other relationships as a personality function in the writings of Jung, Sheldon, and Skinner. (See also Campbell, 1965, for a discussion of the importance of "altruistic" or other-oriented motivations and sentiments in social behavior.)

In addition to the work more conventionally thought of as personality theories and therefore appearing in the Hall and Lindzey volume, there is of course a long-standing tradition of psychological theory and inquiry emphasizing cognition and cognitive needs as a central source of behavior (Neisser, 1967), and there has been important recent movement in the direction of recognizing the interdependence of cognitive styles and underlying noncognitive motivational patterns (Kagan, Moss, and Sigel, 1970; Breger, 1969). In general, although separate personality functions and even individual traits can be identified in isolation and their connection with political behavior established, it is also possible to search for interdependencies among traits and functions. Individuals with particular kinds of ego-defensive patterns may tend to orient themselves to others in distinctive ways—e.g., tending to be conformist or anticonformist—and even to exhibit distinctive cognitive patterns.

As Hall and Lindzey (1970, p. 588) note, the tendency to conceive of psychic elements as part of an interdependent personality system is itself still another dimension of variation among personality theories. At a minimum, the emphasis on personality holism calls for an approach to conceptualizing personality that is "complex, multivariate, and include[s] reference to the situation within which a behavior event occurs, as well as to other behavioral events of the actor." At a maximum, such an emphasis may also suggest the uniqueness of the way each individual is "cemented together" and may therefore make idiographic analysis of individual actors a necessary part of psychological inquiry.

The merit of the functional approach is its theoretical ecumenicism and its openness to "complex, multivariate" analyses. Unlike both the older and the newer psychoanalytic approaches, the functional approach does not take for granted that particular conscious political orientations or behavioral acts are "bound" to be influenced by ego defenses and unconscious psychodynamic forces. But unlike formulations with no dynamic element, it does not *preclude* this possibility, which after all seems necessary at a minimum to deal interpretatively with extreme intrusions of psychopathology into politics—e.g., the several cases of emotionally disturbed assassins in the history of American politics. (See Hastings, 1965a, b, c, and d; Rothstein, 1964, 1966; Weisz and Taylor, 1969.) There is no question that defense mechanisms and other aspects of psychiatric symptomatology are present in the behavior of the Lee Harvey Oswalds and Arthur Bremers. Whether and to what degree similar patterns are evident in other more mainstream political actors is an empirical question that can be dealt with only if conceptual distinctions are used that leave the question open. (On the shortcomings of conceptualizations that take account of only cognitive factors in seeking to explain behavior in institutional contexts, see Argyris, 1973.)

For any conscious political orientation or act the functionalist assumption is that it *may* be an outward ego-defensive manifestation of an inner conflict. But alternatively it may be rooted in social needs—e.g., the need to be a member of the crowd or to stand out from the crowd (mediation of self-other relations). *Or* it may be a rational act (rather than a rational*ization*), which is not to say that it is necessarily accurately grounded in factual premises but merely that it is a function of cognitive learning and of inner needs, whether instrumental or intrinsic, to screen and canvass the environment. Finally, it may be "overdetermined"—i.e., based on some interconnected pattern of these functional needs.

The most conveniently available attitude area from which to choose an illustration of how these functionalist notions can be used is the one in which functional analyses were first developed—racial and ethnic relations. Individual A may be racially prejudiced because he is a southerner and simply has never been exposed to any alternative information about blacks. For Individual B, the "same" attitude may have its roots in a need to be like his peers, whereas C may be a classical emotional bigot, channeling repressed aggressive and sexual impulses into obsessive racial bigotry. And Individual D may reflect some combination of the foregoing functional bases for his conscious sociopolitical orientations, whether in the realm of racial orientations or elsewhere (Pettigrew, 1958).

Depending on the actor's functional type, the circumstances vary under which his political orientations will develop, be aroused, or change, and under which he will act on them. Informational stimuli will tend to be effective with individuals whose orientations serve cognitive functions, but the same messages may boomerang drastically when directed at individuals whose orientations serve to bolster ego defenses. The latter will be moved, if at all, by irrational procedures, such as authoritarian suggestion (if their ego defenses take an appropriate form), or by procedures of a quasi-psychotherapeutic sort that provide them with inner insight, thus demonstrating to them that the source of their orientation is inner rather than in the external object to which they have been directing affect. Procedures of this sort—insight, authoritarian suggestions, etc.—are in turn not likely to affect individuals whose orientations serve cognitive needs. And individuals whose orientations largely have a social basis must change either their reference groups or their social environments in order to change their orientations. Sniderman (1974) and Sniderman and Citrin (1971) provide good examples of analyses in which classification of the psychological underpinnings of beliefs enables the investigator to predict their properties.

There follows from this primer sketch of the functional approach another reason (in addition to the interplay of inner and outer factors) for expecting contingent and interactive rather than general and linear personality-and-politics connections. Not only may the same sociopolitical orientation serve different functional needs for different individuals; different orientations may serve the same needs. The classic instance is the left-wing ideologue who undergoes an emotional conversion and becomes a right-wing ideologue. In each case his rigid adherence to a dogmatic ideology presumably serves the same personality needs. The "functional approach" encourages the analyst to search for such connections rather than mechanically seek correlations between the manifest content of political orientations "in general" and underlying personality structures "in general."

The distinctions in Figure 2 make it possible to pin down a simple difference in usage that generates certain false disagreements about whether "personality" factors are a major cause of political behavior. Psychologists like Smith, Bruner, and White (1956, p. 24) treat personality as a comprehensive term referring to *all* patterned predispositional tendencies. They think not only of the "functional bases" but also of "conscious political or politically relevant orientations"—such as party attachment, isolationism, internationalism, sense of political alienation, etc.—as aspects of personality. "Personality," Henry Murray (1968) observes, "is the most comprehensive term we have in psychology."

Political scientists have no difficulty recognizing the causal influence of conscious political orientations. Survey research in which these orientations are the principle classes of variable has been a virtual defining characteristic of contemporary political science. The referent that political scientists are likely to have in mind when they ask "whether personality is important" is the lower left area of Figure 2—the functional bases. In fact, for many political scientists the term has an even more restricted meaning, referring only to *one* of the functional bases—ego-defensive personality functions—since these are the main focal points of personality-and-politics writings such as the early psychobiographies and Lasswell's *Psychopathology and Politics* (1930).

Obviously, as long as one's referents are clear, usage makes no difference, particularly since the concern in actual inquiry is not with a reified entity called "personality" but rather with particular psychological variables. But it is necessary to be aware of this particular difference in usage in order to avoid one of the most "merely semantic" of the false disagreements in a false-disagreement-ridden literature.

2.3 *Adding the Time Dimension and Systemic Factors*

Figure 3 completes the conceptualization by adding two elements to the basic formula presented in Figure 1 and elaborated on in Figure 2—namely, changes over time in the state of the environment and the actor's predisposition and a distinction between the microscopic, immediate aspects of the environment of political action and the macroenvironment.

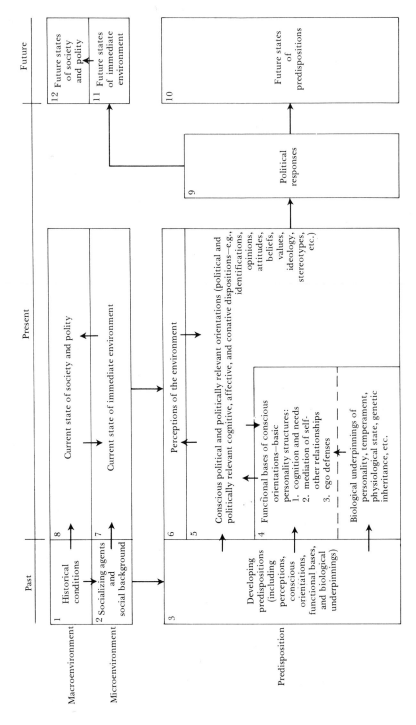

Fig. 3. A Comprehensive Map for the Analysis of Personality and Politics

Introduction of the time dimension directs us from an atomized, response-at-a-time conception of $E \rightarrow P \rightarrow R$ to a recognition of the endless chain of political experience and predispositional modification. Immediately contiguous in the figure to the present environment of political behavior and the present predispositions of actors is the previously developing (from early childhood through yesterday) predispositional states of the actor and the actor's background environments. Social backgrounds, socialization, and learning are continuous with current environmental and predispositional determinants of behavior. The historical antecedents of course cannot act *directly* on contemporary behavior; therefore it is in principle true that if we know "all there is to know" about the current environment of action and the current predispositions of actors, we do not need background data in order to explain contemporary behavior. Yet, as we shall see, in practice there are a variety of reasons why developmental and socialization inquiry is valuable to political psychologists.

Figure 3 continues its representation of the chain of experience and predispositional change into the future, representing the constant feedback of actors' behavior on their own environments and on their own predispositional states. One reason political and other actors are not mere creatures of their environments is that to varying degrees they manage to shape and modify the very setting within which they operate, as well as opting to act within settings they find congenial. And as the extensive literature on cognitive balance and consistency makes clear (Abelson *et al.*, 1968), one of the more persistent influences on an individual's orientations at any time arises out of the propensity to make one's dispositions, both cognitive and affective, consistent with one's own previous behavior.

The past, present, and future environmental panels in Figure 3 are horizontally divided to distinguish between immediate environmental and larger environmental determinants of behavior. According to the figure, past and present macroenvironmental influences have their impact on past and present predispositions via the mediation of immediate environmental agents and stimuli—i.e., wars, revolutions, social institutions, larger political structures, and the like are not conceived of as being directly influential but rather as having to reach into the individual's face-to-face environment. This, however, is simply a point of expositional tidiness: the portions of the wider environment that actually impinge on an individual in doing so by (the present) definition become part of the immediate environment.

In carrying the chain of causality forward into the future, the arrows in Figure 3 flow upward, indicating the aggregation of whatever affects the actor's behavior has on his immediate environment into future states of the macrophenomena that surround him—his society and polity (cf. Elder, 1973). Individual behavior does not aggregate in a simple additive manner, of course. Compare the impact of the simple act of voting on the part of a single voter with, say, the act of an American president giving the order to discharge his nation's nuclear armaments system. Some of the issues that arise in the analysis of such aggregative effects will be discussed in Part 7. Figure 3, of course, could be infinitely extended to show the continuing play of wider environmental influence on immediate environments and of the latter on predispositions as the actor responds over time. Note, however, that much action is not in response to immediately antecedent stimuli.

2.4 An Overview of the Conceptualization

Looking now at Figure 3 as an overall summary and following its panels in the sequence of their numbering, we arrive at an expansion of the $E{\rightarrow}P{\rightarrow}R$ paradigm which can be stated as a run-on sentence keyed to panel numbers, to which I shall be referring from time to time in the remainder of the chapter.

1. Historical larger-society sociopolitical structures shape
2. immediate environment socialization practices, which contribute to
3. the developing psyche and, eventually, to
4. contemporary functional predispositions,
5. conscious sociopolitical predispositions, and
6. perceptions of the environment, as stimulated by
7. immediate environment phenomena
8. and contemporary larger-society phenomena to produce
9. present political behavior (of individuals and types of individuals) which affects future states of the
10. political actor,
11. the actor's immediate environment, and
12. the larger society.

This overall "mapping" formulation is heuristic—that is, designed to foster thought and inquiry—rather than true or false and therefore empirically testable. By exposing the student of personality and politics to a comprehensive panorama of types of variables and the ways they impinge on one another, such a map can encourage the design of inquiries, which, even if they themselves are not fully contextual in the sense of taking account of the broad range of behavioral determinants and consequences, are at least intellectually in touch with larger contexts.

The intellectual perspective so provided can in turn lead to proper attention to the sorts of interactive, context-related relationships that seem to prevail in political affairs and in human affairs more generally. The stress on the likelihood of contingent rather than general relations between personality factors and behavior is applicable not only to politics, needless to say. Consider the following statement by McGuire (1968, p. 1139) about the connections between personality and susceptibility to influence.

It is highly likely that personality factors will interact with various other classes [of factors] . . . in affecting influenceability. Hence, although we should seek the most general relationships in mapping the domain of personality-influenceability interrelations, it is likely that these will tend to be interaction effects rather than condition-free main effects of single personality variables.

The following similar statement was made by Fiedler (1971, p. 15) in his review of the leadership literature.

We can now see quite readily why leadership traits will not predict leadership effectiveness. If any one can be an effective leader in some situations and not in others, it is obvious that a single leadership trait or a combination of traits will not enable prediction in all situations. Such a trait or combination of traits may well predict performance in certain situations that can be specified, and this is what the contingencies model [that Fiedler presents] shows.

As Morris Rosenberg has commented (personal communication), this point has broader implications for the study of human behavior. "In a certain sense, all relationships are conditional ones. If we look at the relationship between X and Y, it is extremely unlikely that it will be identical for all class, sex, race, age, etc., categories, as well as under all social conditions. Conditional relationships are norms rather than exceptions. Unfortunately, some researchers seem to treat them as irritants rather than meaningful findings of significance." (See also Rosenberg, 1968, Chapters 5 and 6.)

For an extensive literature review that takes the same general position as these assertions and that systematically criticizes the recent claims by Mischel (1968, 1969) of the lack of connection between personality and behavior, see Henry Alker's (1972) essay, "Is Personality Situationally Specific or Intrapsychically Consistent?" For a broader discussion of the general importance of interactive effects, see Sonquist (1970).

In addition, by providing a frame within which to assemble and reconcile diverse findings and observations from diverse inquiries, such a map can contribute to the cumulation of knowledge. (Later I shall seek to illustrate this assertion by showing that seemingly contradictory findings in the extended empirical literature of the late 1960s and early 1970s on campus activism can be reconciled by making use of such an overall scheme.) Finally, simply by providing working definitions of analytic terms widely used in highly diverse ways and by tracing the causal links among the phenomena to which the terms refer, such a map may be used in efforts to dissolve or reformulate controversies of the sort discussed next.

3. OVERALL THEORETICAL ISSUES

There exists what might be called a "metaliterature" on personality and politics, a literature concerned less with the nature of specific connections and nonconnections between diverse aspects of personal psychological functioning and politics than with the *possibility* of establishing such connections. Interestingly, there appear to be cognate metaliteratures in other disciplinary contexts where efforts have been made to establish connections between personal predispositions and individual and aggregate behavioral patterns—for example, in sociology and anthropology. With respect to politics, some of the more influential metawritings taking the position that efforts to explain politics in personality terms are *not* likely to be very fruitful are Bendix (1952), Shils (1954), and Verba (1961). The opposite position—that personality factors are politically consequential—has been argued by Goldhamer (1950), Levinson (1958), Lane (1959c, pp. 99–100), and Greenstein (1967b, 1969, 1971).

These ostensibly opposed writings have an important common characteristic. On neither side is the position typically argued without qualification, and in many cases the specific qualifying points made on the two sides of the debate in fact converge and form a variegated fabric of theoretical observations about contingent relationships of precisely the sort discussed in Part II, Section 4. One of my purposes here in Part III is to distill from these discussions a common theoretical ground that could usefully serve to guide inquiry rather than to fuel argumentation. Another purpose is to dissolve those controversies not susceptible to empirical solution because they result from faulty conceptualization—for example, the controversies noted above about the scientific admissibility of "mentalistic" language and controversies based on nothing more than the different referents used by political scientists and psychologists for "personality."

Drawing on the metaliterature, we can identify, among others, the following problems for solution by redefinition or dissolution by clarification.

1. The problem of reconciling personality and situational explanations of political behavior.
2. The problem of whether ego-defensive aspects of personality are politically consequential.
3. The problem of reconciling personality and role explanations of political behavior.
4. The problem of reconciling personality and cultural explanations of political behavior.
5. The problem of whether individuals' social characteristics rather than their personality characteristics determine their political behavior.

6. The problem of whether personality can influence political events and outcomes and, conversely, of whether "individual personalities" are products of their societies and times.

3.1 The Problem of Reconciling Personality and Situational Explanations of Political Behavior

Perhaps the most pervasive of the reasons given for pessimism about the likely fruitfulness of personality-and-politics inquiry is one that follows both from Durkheimian sociology and from behaviorist psychology: that situational (environmental) rather than predispositional influences determine political behavior. This, of course, is the reciprocal of the psychologizing tendency to explain political behavior exclusively in terms of predispositions evident in some personality-and-politics literature.[5]

The viewpoint summarized in Figure 1—that behavior needs to be examined as a *joint* function of environment and predispositions—is in fact what emerges from the writings pro and con on this issue, once the qualifications on each side are noted. These qualifications provide an inventory of contingent propositions about circumstances under which it will be more or less imperative to have information about the predispositions of political actors in order to account for the way they vary in political behavior.

It is possible to study psychological aspects of any behavior, since behavior is invariably psychologically mediated. But the standard correlational procedures used by behavioral scientists discourage interest in factors that do not vary with the dependent variable being explained. Hence, if there are contingencies under which individuals of diverse personal properties nevertheless engage in uniform behavior, it will not be *necessary* (though, as we shall see, it may be possible or desirable) to analyze their personalities. Conversely, however, there are contingencies that *do* make it imperative to search for predispositional determinants of variation in political behavior. The following list of propositions, culled from the metaliterature, is identical, with one exception, to the list in Greenstein (1969, Chapter 2), where sources and more extended glosses of each assertion are given. Each proposition takes the form of an answer to the following question.

> Given a common environmental stimulus, what other factors, whether environmental, predispositional, or in the nature of the response itself, lead individuals of different dispositions to behave uniformly, and what factors contribute to the expression of personal variability through differences in behavior?

1. *Ambiguous situations leave room for personal variability to manifest itself.* The prototype of situational ambiguity, the Rorschach inkblot test, is devoid of cognitive context. There are vast variations in the stories different

individuals tell about the same inkblot. Ambiguous political and other situations often have one or more of three characteristics: newness, complexity, and contradictoriness of elements in the situation.[6]

2. *The opportunities for personal variation are increased to the degree that political actors lack socially standardized mental sets that might lead them to structure their perceptions and resolve ambiguities.* This is the predispositional counterpart of proposition 1. (Of course, the very tendency not to share in prevailing belief systems may itself be a result of variable personality factors. See Di Palma and McClosky, 1970.)

3. *The impact of personal differences on behavior is increased to the degree that sanctions are not attached to certain possible alternative courses of behavior.* An extreme illustration of the presence of sanctions would be a situation in which all occupants of a building were credibly informed that failure to evacuate the building would mean certain death within a stipulated period of time. There might be variations in the mode of departure (see proposition 10), but ordinarily there would be perfect uniformity in the actual act of leaving the building.

4. *Intense dispositions in an opposite direction from the prevailing sanctions increase the likelihood that personal characteristics will affect behavior.* This is the predispositional counterpart of enviromental proposition 3.

5. *To the degree that individuals are placed in a group context in which what they do is visible to others, personal variation is likely to be reduced.* This proposition is derived from the research on conformity to group pressures (Asch, 1952; Milgram, 1961).

6. *Intense needs to take one's cues from others will tend to reduce the effects of personal variation.* The psychological counterpart to proposition 5. "Compulsive conformity" is itself a psychological variable, of course, but by encouraging the individual to blend with his environment, this predisposition reduces the effect of other psychological variables on behavior. (Again see Di Palma and McClosky, 1970.)

7. *The greater a political actor's affective involvement in politics, the greater the likelihood that other of his psychological characteristics in addition to political involvement will be exhibited in his behavior.* Highly involved political actors stand in contrast to the many apolitical individuals whose conceptions of politics are so barren, vague, and inarticulate that their political dispositions have no imprint on their political behavior, except in random and haphazard ways.

8. *The more demanding the political act—the more it is one that calls for an active investment of effort—the greater the likelihood it will be influenced by*

personal characteristics of the actor. This proposition, which is directed not to environmental or predispositional antecedents but to behavior itself, is a counterpart of proposition 3 on sanctions and proposition 4 on intensity of dispositions.

9. *On the other hand, variations in personal characteristics are also likely to be exhibited in spontaneous behavior—that is, behavior which proceeds from personal impulse, without effort or premeditation.*[7] (But whether these are patterned and predictable may depend on whether the individual has a sufficiently stable and effectively grounded set of political orientations. See proposition 7.)

10. *Even when there is little room for personal variability in the instrumental aspects of actions, there is likely to be variation in their expressive aspects.* This point is suggested in the gloss on proposition 3. Whether the stylistic variation in otherwise uniform behavior warrants analysis depends on the interests of the analyst. There is no evident reason for seeking to differentiate among various styles of pulling the lever in the voting booth on election day (sharply, diffidently, etc.). But shades of American presidential response to the nuclear missile command devices that follow the President everywhere are of enormous interest. To paraphrase Shakespeare: "Nuances in great ones should not unwatched go."

11. *Personality variations will be more evident to the degree that an individual occupies a role for which the expectations are undefined or are intentionally left at the discretion of the role incumbent.* Each of the previous propositions is addressed to one of the three panels of Figure 1. Propositions about roles, as we shall see, can relate to any or all of the three panels, depending on which of the several referents of "role" one chooses to employ. Willcox (1964, pp. ix–x) argues that military leadership roles leave a great deal up to the leader's definition of the situation, although this is probably less true in bureaucratized modern armies than in the military of the eigthteenth century, the period about which Willcox writes. In general, certain historical settings appear more likely than others to have roles fitting the stipulations noted above. Cantor (1967, p. 136), for example, comments that in medieval England "government was always heavily dependent on the King's personality and that without an intelligent, energetic monarch the effectiveness of royal administration and laws was bound to be diminished. On the other hand, a king of great qualities could have a profound impact on the expansion of royal authority." Crozier (1964, p. 192) provides interesting illustrations of how under some bureaucratic circumstances it can be subordinates rather than superiors who have very great discretionary powers.

A list of eleven propositions (why not twelve?) lacks any obvious symmetry. This list is simply the most careful ordering I can manage of a much larger range of not invariably consistent qualifying assertions in the metaliterature. None of the propositions is stated with the detail of testable hypotheses, although by and large they could be so specified. In this respect they take the form of what Lasswell and Kaplan (1950, pp. xxii–xxiii) call "hypotheses-schema": "statements which form hypotheses when specific indices relate them to the conditions of a given problem."

Apart from their function as possible sources of testable hypotheses, these propositions can be used in the same heuristic fashion as the categories in Figures 1 to 3—as sensitizers. In stressing determinants of variations in political behavior, they are reminders of the *necessary* and not of the *sufficient* conditions for studying the predispositions of political actors. If political psychological factors were studied only for behavior that varied, political psychology would be in danger of being applicable more to deviant behavior than to the full range of political behavior, and there would be a particular danger of failure to study behavior that exhibits a high degree of uniform conformity even though such behavior might in fact be both politically important and psychologically rich. (For an expansion on this point, see Greenstein, 1973, pp. 445–446.)

3.2 The Problem of Whether Ego-Defensive Aspects of Personality are Politically Consequential

The foregoing list of necessary conditions for taking account of the way political actors vary in their personal predispositions gives no indication of *what kind* of predispositional variations may be politically consequential. The variations may be in any of the types of psychological structures listed in the predispositional panels of Figures 2 and 3. Often, however, when it is argued in the metaliterature that "personality" is not politically consequential, the implicit definition of "personality" excludes conscious orientations. The implicit definition sometimes does not even include the full array of functional processes and structures summarized in the tripartite personality classification of cognitive needs, mediation of self-other relationships, and ego defenses. Rather, it conceives of the term as referring only to the ego-defensive level of psychic functioning.

Without accepting this implicit equation of personality with its psychodynamic aspects, we can again adopt the mode of distilling contingent propositions from the various qualifying assertions in the literature. Here, then, our concern is not with personality explanations in general but rather with the class of personality explanations that has monopolized so much attention in the personality-and-politics literature as a result of the pervasive influence of psychoanalysis on such seminal works as Lasswell's *Psychopathology and Politics* (1930) and Fromm's *Escape from Freedom* (1941). Earlier I noted that pathological presidential assassins serve as a limiting case, demonstrating that *some* ego-defensiveness finds its way into politics. More broadly, we may note the following three very general environmental, predisposition and response circumstances likely to increase the chances that politics will serve as an outlet for ego defenses. Each one is of course in addition to the eleven general conditions just noted for the expression of *any kind* of predispositional variable, and each is open to further qualification in terms of the ways that *specific kinds* of ego defenses are likely to affect political behavior.

1. *Certain types of environmental stimuli appear to have a greater "resonance" with ego defenses and the deep inner conflicts with which they cope than do other stimuli.* Lane and Sears (1964, p. 76) suggest that such stimuli are often "topics dealing with material commonly repressed by individuals. Obvious examples are war or criminal punishment (both dealing with aggression) and birth control or obscenity legislation (both dealing with sexuality) ." Lane and Sears also suggest that opinions connected with individuals or groups are more capable of eliciting "irrational thought" than those dealing with certain kinds of substantive issues, such as economic issues.[8]

2. *The likelihood that ego-defensive needs will affect political behavior is also related to the degree that any stipulated actor or actors have ego-defensive needs.* A common empirical assumption is that ego-defensive needs are not widespread and that there is little continuity between the personality dynamics of highly disturbed, institutionalized individuals and most individuals in general populations. Thus, for example, Burwen and Campbell (1957, p. 30) , on finding a lack of association between questionnaire data on individuals' orientations toward their parents and toward other authority figures, comment that

> although this kind of symbolic equivalence or stimulus generalization is appropriate to the autistic thought processes in normal dream states and in the waking states of extreme neurotics and psychotics, it does not interfere with the waking perceptions of normal individuals.

But there are contrary observations. A number of epidemiological studies report a substantial incidence of neurotic symptomatology in general populations (Srole *et al.*, 1962; Manis *et al.*, 1964; Leighton, 1967) . Tucker (1965) argues that certain kinds of leadership roles, notably those at the head of totalitarian one-party systems that have evolved out of "fighting" revolutionary parties, tend to recruit individuals with certain types of psychic disturbance—especially paranoia. He further suggests that the nature of totalitarian social and political systems is such that the symptomatology of the dictator finds its way into policy through the acts of compliant subordinates, contributing, for example, to certain of the more extreme excesses found in totalitarian politics (reigns of terror, purges, etc.) . Rutherford (1966) , drawing on Tucker's formulations, studied patients in a state mental hospital to see if there was any association between symptom type and political activity before commitment and in the mental hospital's patient–self-government institutions.

Very striking associations were found between paranoid symptomatology and participation in both of these settings.[9]

3. Finally, *certain types of response undoubtedly provide greater occasion for deep personality needs to find outlet than do others*—for example, such responses as affirmations of loyalty in connection with the rallying activities of mass movements and the various other types of response deliberately designed to channel affect into politics.

3.3 The Problem of Reconciling Personality and Role Explanations of Political Behavior

"Role theory" is widely viewed in a number of the behavioral science disciplines as an important competitor to motivational and other psychological approaches to the explanation of behavior. Since official and unofficial but generally recognized statuses are so important in political systems and processes, it is not surprising that role explanations present themselves as possible alternatives to personality explanations of political behavior.

We can see why roles are important and yet do not eliminate personality effects by returning to the source of the metaphor—the theater. Actors with possibly quite different personal qualities—say, Alec Guinness and John Gielgud—may well converge in their behavior when cast in a common role, for example, that of the Prince of Denmark. But imagine the Hamlet of an actor whose personal qualities are substantially different from those of Guinness and Gielgud—say, John Wayne or Woody Allen. Further, political roles imperfectly parallel the scripted roles of traditional drama. As noted in the eleventh proposition on circumstances of individual variability, many political roles are more or less unconstrained, and even Guinness and Gielgud might well diverge sharply in the improvisatory theater.

As Levinson (1959) points out, "role" is used by different commentators in three general ways, which again bring us back to $E{\rightarrow}P{\rightarrow}R$.

1. In some usages, "role" refers to a personal predispositional variable—the individual's own cognitive and affective orientations toward a position he occupies (his notions of what is expected of him as lawyer, doctor, or President of the United States) as well as of how he himself feels he *should* behave as a role incumbent.

2. In some usages, "role" has its referent in the environment of the political actor—namely, in the psychological expectations of other political actors about how the role incumbent will, can, and should behave. Thus an ingredient in "the American presidential role" is that immediately on assuming office, the President is no longer called "Harry" or "Lyndon" or "Dick" by his associates; he becomes "Mr. President."[10]

3. Finally, some uses of the term simply refer to what an actor actually does—his pattern of responses.

Any particular usage may be more or less explicit about its referents and may employ more than one of the three kinds of referents. Whatever the circumstances, there is much to be said for explicitly identifying the *E, P,* and *R* components of the usage. Doing so not only adds to precision of expression but also immediately raises substantive social psychological questions challenging the dubious assumption in some of the literature on roles that all these elements are congruent. In short, role analysis and dispositional (cum situational) analysis proceed hand in glove.

3.4 The Problem of Reconciling Personality and Cultural Explanations of Political Behavior

The assertion that "culture" is more important than "personality" as a determinant of behavior was sometimes encountered in the heyday of personality-and-culture research in anthropology. Such assertions led Melford Spiro to write a seminal paper entitled "Personality and Culture: The Natural History of a False Dichotomy" (1951). Much the same assertion has latterly found its way into political discourse. The term "political culture" was borrowed from anthropology by political analysts seeking an intellectually solid means of addressing the comparative political psychology issues raised in the older, controversial, national-character literature (Verba, 1965). Typically, a culture-*versus*-personality assertion takes the form of reinterpreting some behavior or trait pattern previously explained in terms of personality dynamics and arguing that the problematic pattern is in fact a cultural convention rather than an outward manifestation of an inner dynamic. Three examples follow.

Example 1. A high score on the traditional authoritarianism scales results from positive response to questionnaire items designed to ascertain whether the respondent is deferential to superiors, punitive to inferiors, prone to stereotyped thinking, reluctant to canvass his own inner feelings, fascinated with power and toughness, preoccupied with the alleged sexual goings-on of others, etc. These traits were interpreted by Adorno *et al.* in *The Authoritarian Personality* (1950) as the outward manifestations of inner psychic conflicts—and in particular as reaction formations to repressed needs to defy authority. But subsequent writers argued that such patterns of response are typical of the cultural or subcultural orientations of individuals of low education and low socioeconomic status. (For example, see Hyman and Sheatsley, 1954; Hyman, 1959, pp. 29–36.) This argument has been couched by some commentators, though not by Hyman and Sheatsley, in culture-versus-personality terms. Their assertion is that *F*-scale scores are reflections of cultural rather than personality influences.

Example 2. In Freud's disquisition on Leonardo (1910), an elaborate psychodynamic explanation is given of the painter's motivation for endowing the

Mona Lisa with her famous enigmatic smile. Meyer Schapiro (1956) has shown that the smile was in fact conventional for its time—that books of the day on comportment provided detailed instructions on how to affect "the Mona Lisa smile."

Example 3. American blacks typically receive more "pathological" ratings than American whites on the widely used Minnesota Multiphasic Personality Inventory, but Gynther (1972) convincingly argues that the black scores result not from psychodynamic sources but rather from a subculturally typical cynicism and distrust for society (also see Cole and Bruner, 1971).

Like the "role-versus-personality" disagreement, "culture-versus-personality" is precisely what Spiro suggested—a false dichotomy in need of dissolution. The three examples above show the actual points of reference of this false antithesis. In effect, such assertions make claims about alternative possible functional bases of attitudes and behavior. In each example it is argued that a particular conscious orientation or response pattern has its motivational basis in cognitive, and perhaps also social, needs rather than in ego-defensive needs. The evidence for this assertion is taken from environmental rather than predispositional data—namely, the observation that the item in question is typical in the individual's social environment and therefore is likely to have been absorbed through modeling and other basically cognitive learning modes rather than out of a symptomatic need emerging from an inner conflict.[11]

There is no special provision in the predispositional panels of Figures 2 and 3 for "cultural predispositions," just as there is no provision in the figures for "role." The term "culture" is of such consummate ambiguity that Kroeber and Kluckhohn (1952) devoted a book to explicating its meanings. With Wallace (1961), I would relegate "culture"— or at least the nonmaterial aspects of culture—to collective rather than individual patterns. "Culture" is a collective counterpart to "personality" in its broadest usage by psychologists. As so defined, culture is a key part of the past and present environments in which personality formulation and behavior occur, but like situations and roles, "culture" does not refer to processes that compete with personal predispositions as a cause of behavior.

3.5 The Problem of Whether Individuals' Social Characteristics Rather Than Their Personality Characteristics Determine Their Political Behavior

Here we have still another of the inordinate number of false controversies based at least partly on semantics that have kept so much of the personality-and-politics literature fixated on meta-issues.[12]

A prototypical imputation of conflict between personality and social background variables can be found in the literature on American college-student activists. Lipset (1968) deprecates explanations of activism in terms of activists' personalities. Some research reports had pointed to unusually "healthy" personalities and strong cognitive capacities on the part of activists; others had pointed to ego-defensive correlates of at least some kinds of activism. The "real" determinant of activism, Lipset argued, was that activists came disproportionately from Jewish backgrounds (although very few of them were practicing, theistic participants in denominational Judaism) and consequently exhibited the kind of behavior to be expected of individuals from their particular specialized social backgrounds.

As Block, Haan, and Smith (1969, pp. 170–173) point out, social background variables and personality-disposition variables are in no sense exclusive of each other. Rather, it is background (cum biological) factors that *produce* personality predispositions, a sequence described by panels 2 through 6 of Figure 3. These panels make it possible to visualize the fallacy in Lipset's formulation about student activists and other assertions of false antinomies between social and psychological characteristics. Such formulations erroneously place in opposition causal factors from panel 3—background social environment—and factors from panels 4 through 6—current predispositions. The alternative to such false antitheses is research that actually traces the flow of causality from social background through social development to current dispositions and environment. Further, there needs to be greater awareness of the shortcomings of analyses that implicitly *infer* psychological disposition from such social characteristics as age, region, and socioeconomic background. (Compare Block's [1971, pp. 271–274] discussion of "the necessity of psychologizing the notion of social class.")

Confusion is increased by the ambiguity of reference of the standard survey indicators of political variables, many of which simultaneously relate to factors in both the past and present environments and predispositions of actors. Often data of this multiply ambiguous sort are submitted to the traditional multivariate analysis procedures which "soak up" variance without regard to causal structure, with little if any sensitivity to the problem of multicolinearity (Blalock, 1963, 1964; Farrar and Glauber, 1967). Such a procedure makes it possible even to emerge with a spurious statistical "demonstration" that personality factors are unimportant because a seeming relationship between a psychological variable and a political variable is controlled. Examples of this misleading procedure are White's (1968) argument that class is not an important determinant of political socialization, because controls for IQ eliminate the association of class with political information (cf. Jackman, 1970; Greenstein, 1970c), and Bronfenbrenner's conclusion for similar reasons that "personality" is not important for social participations. Fortunately, there are now newer approaches to multivariate analysis, notably path analysis and related procedures (Duncan, 1966; Sonquist, 1970) which *are* appropriate for untangling causal relationships.

3.6 The Problem of Whether Personality Can Influence Political Events and, Conversely, of Whether "Individual Personalities" Are a Mere Product of Their Societies and Times

A final set of metaproblems relates to the impact of systemic influences on individuals and vice versa. Three rather different but complementary claims are worth noting.

1. Individuals are not consequential because they are creatures of their societies.

2. Single individuals are so circumscribed by their environment—their contributions are so "dampened" by the influence of others or by the refractory nature of sociohistorical process and events—that outcomes cannot be attributed to individual inputs.

3. Individuals are not personally consequential, since personality types tend to be randomly distributed in social roles.

The first of these claims parallels the claim that social characteristics are more important than personality characteristics, and it is fallacious for the same reasons. In effect, such claims impute exclusive causality to a link in the causal chain shown in Figure 3. It is inappropriately elliptical to argue, for example, as Erich Fromm (1941, pp. 286–287) does, that family socialization processes and their distinctive psychological sequels are not important because character structures are responses to such societal needs as the role requirements of industrialized societies. *Both* overarching historical processes *and* immediate environment socializing agents are likely to influence developing personal predispositions. Or if the family *is* merely a conveyor belt from the larger society, the absence of family-induced variation in predispositions must be demonstrated empirically.

The second claim, that single actors cannot influence events, has an ancient lineage and was the object of an ill-defined debate by nineteenth-century historiographers on the role of "great men" in history. Sidney Hook's *The Hero in History* (1943) provides a still useful expansion of the nineteenth-century literature. Historical actors such as leaders are dependent on the presence of appropriate historical circumstances in order to have an impact, that literature argued. Hence it is historical circumstance, not the individual, that deserves attention. What effect could even a Napoleon have had if born in a peasant hut during the Middle Ages?

The problems raised by assertions of this sort are *not* artificial. After all, most individuals leave little if any imprint on history. But what about the individuals who do leave an imprint, whether large or small? Clearly this is another of the claims that can be restated in ways that take account of contingency. The following three propositions[13] summarize some of the standard assertions about when single individuals are and are not likely to have an impact on historical outcomes.

1. *The likelihood of personal impact increases to the degree that the environment admits of restructuring.* Some historical periods are "ripe for change." Others appear to be locked into a self-reinforcing pattern and are not readily manipulable. Environments that admit substantial restructuring on the basis of modest interventions are unstable in the sense of being in precarious equilibrium. A physical example is a massive rock formation at the side of a mountain held in place by a single keystone.

Stability in the sense of firm equilibrium is by no means synonymous with immobility: An avalanche in motion exhibits an extraordinarily steady state in that even very substantial attempts to influence it are not likely to keep it from running full course. This example suggests a characteristic of stable equilibrium—namely, that *a large number of simultaneous forces are pressing toward the same outcome* and therefore the actions of any single actor when they are directed toward the likely outcome will be simply submerged; when they are directed against it, they will be crushed.

Hook treats the outbreak of World War I as an outcome determined by a host of converging forces and therefore not manipulable by individual inputs; on the other hand, he treats the period preceding the October Revolution as unstable in the sense of being susceptible to substantial alteration as a result of small "triggering" interventions. Obviously such analyses present severe methodological problems in that it is tautological to characterize a historical situation as unstable ex post facto simply *because* substantial changes occurred thereafter. Independent indicators are needed.

2. *The likelihood of personal impact varies with the actor's location in the environment.* Russia in October 1918 was manipulable from the vantage point of an actor with Lenin's information resources and leadership role. Few other Russians of the day were comparably positioned.

3. *The likelihood of personal impact varies with the personal strengths or weaknesses of the actor.* The game of pool provides a convenient analogy to the conditions under which political actors can have an impact. The number of balls that can be cleared from the table is a function of the initial location of balls after the break (manipulability of the environment), the location of the cue ball (position of the actor), *and* a third factor—the skill of the player. Lenin's example continues to be instructive. It is generally agreed that few if any of his counterparts had the personal qualities appropriate for bringing the October Revolution to its conclusion.[14]

The third claim—that individuals are distributed randomly in roles and therefore cannot influence events—asserts not only that single individuals cannot directly influence future states of their society and polity but also that the *collective effects* of individuals on their immediate environments are without consequence for the larger environment.

In fact, there is no reason to believe that personal predispositions *are* randomly distributed in roles. Furthermore, as Inkeles (1963) points out, even if this were true, random distribution would mean that any particular role— e.g., the American presidency—might be filled by a full normal distribution of personality types and might therefore be performed in highly varied ways. Personality factors, rather than being canceled out, would warrant systematic observation and inclusion in any attempt to account precisely for institutional functioning, although, as we shall see in the discussion below on aggregation, it is by no means simple to establish the links from personalities to institutions.

4. A CLASSIFICATION OF THE PERSONALITY-AND-POLITICS LITERATURE

As Kluckhohn and Murray (1953) put it in their widely cited discussion of the nature and determinants of personality:

> Every man is in certain respects
>   a. like all other men,
>   b. like some other men,
>   c. like no other men.

A number of years later Milton Singer (1961) made effective use of this threefold distinction to review the literature on culture and personality in terms of work dealing with the relationship between a society's culture and those personal properties that are shared by (a) *all* people, i.e., human nature; (b) *some* people, i.e., people similar to one another in terms of any of the numerous possible classifications of personality types; and (c) *no* individuals—i.e., the properties are idiosyncratic. Within political science, as in the behavioral sciences generally, it is difficult to find satisfactory analytic leverage for studying invariant universals ("human nature"), although Singer notes a few anthropological discussions of the topic, and the political scientist James C. Davies (1963) has borrowed the title of Graham Wallas's early (1908) work, *Human Nature in Politics,* in his commendable effort to explore the political significance of basic human needs and propensities.

The difficulty of studying that which is general to *all* human beings stems from the absence of variation that can be explained by standard correlational or experimental means. Witness the continuing lack of a widely accepted explanation of the virtually universal, if culturally variable in its marginal details, phenomenon of the incest taboo. Also see the various recent attempts to establish a field of "biopolitics," which studies the political implications of the biological "stuff" from which psychological dispositions emerge, in interaction with environmental influences (Somit, 1972) .

Under the "human nature" heading we may note the continuing production by theorists of broad, almost metaphysical accounts of society in terms of the human "stuff" of society. Analyses of this sort, many of them highly stimulating, often have a short citational half-life. They receive attention for a number of years; perhaps to some limited extent they are mined by empirical workers for testable hypotheses; then they tend to be replaced by a new generation of works of a similar sweeping character. Comprehensive overviews of personality and society by earlier generations of commentators include Ranyard West's *Conscience and Society* (1945) and R. E. Money-Kyrle's *Psychoanalysis and Politics* (1951), as well as Freud's *Civilization and Its Discontents* (1930) and the final chapter of Lasswell's *Psychopathology and Politics* (1930). Later entries are Norman O. Brown's *Life Against Death* (1959), Alexander Mitscherlich's *Society Without the Fathers* (1969), Herbert Marcuse's *Eros and Civilization* (revised edition, 1969), and Weinstein and Platt's *The Wish to be Free* (1969) and *Psychoanalytic Society* (1973).

In the remainder of this chapter I shall leave "human nature" as an intractable if undoubtedly highly important congeries of issues and borrow the remaining Kluckhohn-Murray distinctions to identify two major kinds of personality-and-politics research: analyses of *individual* and of *typical* qualities in populations of political actors. Individual analyses and typological analyses do not exhaust the concerns of students of politics, however. Like sociologists, political scientists are concerned with more than isolated human entities. They are concerned with the functioning of political collectivities. Analyses of political systems or processes that draw on individual or typical properties of those who compose the larger entities can be conveniently labeled *aggregative* analyses. Here I have in mind both studies of aggregates of political actors and studies of individuals that deal with the impact of strategically placed individuals, such as leaders on collectivities (e.g., Tucker, 1965).

In practice, any particular investigation is likely to involve more than one of these modes. And it can readily be shown that the logic of inquiry leads from each mode to the other two. Data on individual political actors (for example, leaders) and typical political actors (for example, characteristic psychological groupings in the leaders' polities) are building blocks of aggregative analyses. Aggregate phenomena (sociopolitical institutions) provide the environmental contexts within which individuals and types behave and are socialized. What is distinctive about an individual can be established only via at least implicit reference to what is typical for such an individual. And since typologies never exhaust the personal properties of the individuals classified in them, classification is often a step toward individual diagnosis. Therefore it is often neither feasible nor desirable to work within one of these analytically distinguishable investigative modes without also drawing on either or both of the others. Nevertheless, in spite of the interdependence of the three modes, each presents sufficiently discrete problems to be discussed separately.

5. CASE STUDIES OF INDIVIDUAL POLITICAL ACTORS

5.1 Why Case Studies?

Rae Carlson (1971) has surveyed the contents for a representative recent year of the two leading "mainstream" academic psychology journals that report personality research (*Journal of Social and Personality Psychology* and *Journal of Personality*). Her article, which is of great interest to political scientists seeking to find their way through the labyrinthine literatures of psychology and psychiatry, is entitled "Where is the Person in Personality Research?" One of her most striking findings was a total lack of interest in the ways in which each man is "like no other men": "the analysis revealed that *not a single published study attempted minimal inquiry into the organization of personality variables within the individual*" (Carlson, 1971, p. 209, italics in original).

Within psychology there has been considerable discussion over the years about the problem, in Gordon Allport's (1962) words, of "the general and the unique in psychological science." Allport took the view that one of the persisting tasks of psychologists ought to be the systematic charting of the unique constellations of individual personalities. (Also see Holt, 1967.) Among non-clinicians Allport's view has been far from dominant. Typically, investigators of personality and social psychology argue that single-case analyses are at best illustrative and that they do not directly connect with the overriding purpose of psychological inquiry—the establishment of general laws applicable to multiple cases. (On the current debate among philosophers of social science about the overall merits of a natural-science-based "general laws" approach to social inquiry, see Moon's chapter in Volume 1 of this *Handbook*.)

Whatever one may feel about the appropriateness of case studies for psychology, it is difficult to see how they can be exorcised from political science, where both individual actors and individual constellations of events (the Cuban missile crisis, the Russian Revolution, etc.) are often of overriding substantive interest. (On case studies in general, see Eckstein's contribution to Volume 7 of this *Handbook*.) The student of the modern American institutionalized presidency, for example, had at the time of this writing only seven available cases—Franklin Roosevelt, Truman, Eisenhower, Kennedy, Johnson, Nixon, and Ford.

Two qualities of political interaction and behavior—both of them deducible from the discussion above of the metaliterature—increase the likelihood that an intensive psychological analysis of a single political actor will be necessary. The first occurs when the actor is placed in circumstances under which behavior is in principle not likely to be explicable in situational terms. The eleven propositions on pages 19–21 are to the point here. The second occurs when the circumstances hedging the actor make it likely that his behavior will have sociopolitical consequences (page 28). The more that behavior is likely to be consequential, the greater the interest in intensive analysis of the actor, even if his behavior *does* seem "largely" explicable in situational terms. But *any* political actor can be studied intensively. As noted above, if personality analysis were confined to the necessary occasions for such inquiry, political psychology would tend to be relegated to a source of residual explanations of deviant behavior.

The political psychology literature includes two kinds of case studies: those of individual actors in larger populations—"faces in the crowd," in the title phrase of Riesman and Glazer's (1952) book—and psychobiographies of public figures, past and present. The differences between these modes are less in their basic requirements for evidence, inference, and conceptualization than in the typical uses to which they are put and various practical considerations that bear on them.

Case studies of individuals in the general population are more likely to draw on extended direct contact by the investigator with the subject and on orthodox clinical data-gathering procedures than are studies of public figures and, perforce, studies of figures from periods long past. Nevertheless, clinicians have sought to diagnose persons they did not have "on the couch." Psychobiographers of contemporary figures sometimes are able to conduct clinically instructive interviews with their subjects or with individuals who have known their subjects. And there sometimes exists clinically informative archival material on historical subjects—diaries, intimate letters, fantasy materials, and even dream reports.

Although it is sometimes assumed that the clinician has a fundamental advantage over the psychobiographer in that he can "test" his hypotheses by directing appropriate questions and other information-eliciting stimuli to his subject, clinical practice does not depend on this capacity (witness clinical-case conferences.) And the psychobiographer at least cannot be suspected of having "imposed" through psychotherapy the very psychological patterns he observes in the subject of his case study. Moreover, the biographer of a public figure often has a far larger set of reports by multiple observers on his subject's behavior over time, a greater opportunity to draw on documents that have accrued in the subject's lifetime, and a record of the subject's behavior in a variety of settings which is not dependent on the subject's reports. Finally, the psychobiographer is not likely to be using his material for "mere illustration," and he is not required to conceal identifying life-history details along with the subject's name. In short, both kinds of case study have compensating practical advantages.

5.2 The Case-Study Literature on Individuals in General Populations

Studies focusing on the personalities of individuals in the general population represent a long-standing investigative tradition in the behavioral sciences, especially in clinical psychology and anthropology, although anthropological life histories often serve to illustrate cultural specimens rather than to explicate the inner functioning of their subjects (Dollard, 1935; Allport, 1942; A. F. Davies, 1967; Mandelbaum, 1973). Case studies of members of the general population usually present their subjects pseudonymously and disguised. Both the usual purposes of such studies (illustration of theoretical points and exploratory analysis of possible links among variables) and the need to alter details tend to make the issue of precise causal inference less pressing than in psychobiography, except when there is a psychotherapeutic interest in diagnosis, treatment, and prognosis.[15]

Although there have been few intensive political psychological analyses of members in the general population, in spite of the obvious availability of subjects, several of the studies that *have* been reported are influential and widely quoted. This suggests that important scholarly—or at any rate, pedagogical—needs are served by such case studies. An indication of the presence of a "market" for well-executed general-population case studies is the continuing intellectual viability of a set of case studies reported in 1956 by three distinguished psychologists: Smith, Bruner, and White's *Opinions and Personality*, which reports the results of a roughly 30-hour sequence of interviewing and testing of 10 male members of the general population conducted in 1947. The specific data Smith and his associates acquired included extensive life histories, personality observations, and a broad range of information about their subjects' political orientations, with special emphasis on their attitudes toward the Soviet Union. (Since the authors also used their case materials to inform a broad conceptual analysis of how opinions contribute to an individual's psychological functioning, the enduring interest in their work cannot be attributed only to the case studies. But the latter have clearly contributed to the landmark reputation of *Opinions and Personality*.)

Smith, Bruner, and White present case material on all ten of their subjects, but they concentrate on very detailed discussions of the three subjects who seem to exemplify the categories of their classification of functional bases of opinions. Their rational, problem-oriented law student, "John Chatwell," exemplifies "object appraisal"—i.e., cognitions and reality-testing processes. "Charles Lanlin," a lower-middle-class salesman and small-time property holder, represents social needs—the mediation of self- and other-relationships functions noted in Figures 2 and 3. Finally, the anxiety-ridden "Hilary Sullivan," a self-taught closet Communist, represents the ego-defensive, psychodynamic needs that sometimes can be served by opinions. Because these three cases are the most extended published general-population case studies in the political psychology literature, they provide an excellent basis for asking what can be learned from a profusely documented clinical case study of an individual. Interestingly, the plenitude of what in part is atheoretical descriptive detail in the *Opinions and Personality* case studies suggests a theoretical conclusion. One infers from such detailed presentations of individual case data that there are many links between personal psychological predispositions and political behavior that are too idiosyncratic to be identified in multi-case typological analyses. Such links may have profound political consequences if they occur in strategically placed political actors. But that they exist at all often can be shown only in studies of political nonentities who therefore are available for direct interviews and observation.

Consider the Smith-Bruner-White subject "Charles Lanlin." Lanlin's need to be in a dependent relationship to authority figures is the *leit-motif* of the case presentation on him. This theme is so ubiquitous in his open-ended life history data that it cannot be mistaken for artifacts of the interview procedure or an interpretative imposition by the authors. Lanlin is an only child who deferred to his father to a striking degree and who, in discussing his childhood, stresses with somewhat ambivalent pride his willing subordination to his parents. He makes a point, for example, of describing his own childhood docility in terms of the general desirability that a child learn to yield to superior authority. When Lanlin is asked to describe and comment on the Soviet Union and Soviet-American relations, the anti-Soviet *direction* of his assertions is largely what might be expected from his lower-middle-class New England Catholic background. The specific *imagery* he uses and his embellishments seem obviously linked to his own personality needs and in ways that are likely to be applicable to too few other individuals to be well described in terms of universal propositions—even propositions about the political imagery of people with dependency needs. He "chooses" to perceive of Russia as an "unruly child" in need of discipline and as "dependent on" the United States rather than in terms of the numerous other "available" images at the time he was studied—for example, the image of Soviet aggressiveness.

Such case-study observations contribute to an expansion of the point made earlier that relationships between personality characteristics and political behavior are more likely to be complex and contingent than simple and universal. Idiosyncratic personality-politics connections of the sort one finds in the Smith-Bruner-White data help show how personality factors can be politically consequential in more ways than are likely to be documentable even through much more subtly designed, large sample, multi-case correlational analyses than are presently available. There evidently are connections "in the real world" between personal disposition and political behavior that are too segmental and varied to be trapped in the form of measured general relationships.[16] (Compare Converse's remarks on this point in Volume 4 of this *Handbook.*)

Another influential study of single actors, which built directly on the procedures and approach of the *Opinions and Personality* study, is Lane's 1957–58 sequence of intensive interviews with 15 working-class men from the New England industrial city of "Eastport." Lane made less use than did Smith, Bruner, and White of technical procedures from the armamentarium of clinical psychology, such as projective tests, gathering much of his personality data from life-history interviews. (Smith *et al.* had found their life-history interviews more useful than test data.) Rather than mainly examining political beliefs in one issue area, Lane broadened his compass to a fairly comprehensive interview schedule on the individual's political orientations and participation patterns.

Lane reported his work in articles that hewed rather closely to findings in his case-study data (Lane, 1959a, 1959b) and then incorporated the articles in a major book (1962) that to a considerable extent goes beyond our concern here with single-case analysis in that it reviews the standard assertions in the literature on American national character and goes on to enunciate an original typological construct of "democratic character." Lane's cases suggest a number of the uses, as well as problems, of single-case analyses.

Lane's detailed quotations from his interview protocols have the same vividness and are as thought-provoking as the open-ended case materials presented by Smith, Bruner, and White. One value of such case presentations is that they exhibit "natural" categories of political thought and expression, rather than the preprocessed categories provided by the fixed-choice questionnaire items so common in survey research. Surveys, of course, also use open-ended questions, but the survey approach is intrinsically multi-case; it permits neither the sort of semistructured exploration Lane practiced in bringing out his respondents' beliefs and thought categories nor the detailed expository attention he was able to lavish on individual respondents. Perhaps the best example of how Lane's procedure elicits categories of thought and expression in terms of the respondents' own frame of reference rather than the analyst's is "The Fear of Equality" (1959b), which describes a "texture" of working-class ambivalence toward authority which would not be readily captured in conventional attitude scales.

Lane's case materials also provide many illustrations of the fertility of such expositions as a way of coming forth with hypotheses about and even preliminary evidence about general (as well as idiosyncratic) relationships among underlying personality and political dispositions. The individual Lane calls Sokolsky in *Political Ideology,* for example, has a deeply etched cynicism toward politics that goes well beyond the conventional negativism toward politics that one would expect in an individual of comparable social background. Lane's emphasis in *Political Ideology* was not on case-by-case presentation, but he has preserved his individual protocols (which average 200 pages in length) for the use of other investigators. As we shall see below, one of the hypotheses about the ego-defensive authoritarian type is that in such individuals the same personality needs that encourage especially intense interest in and selective perception of the corrupt nature of politics—and human nature in general—also encourage a prurient fascination with sexual "goings on." One finds in the transcript of Lane's extended, sensitively conducted, semistructured interview with Sokolsky something very much like the linkages that occur in psychoanalytic free associations at the precise point that might have been expected on the basis of authoritarian personality theory: After an extended, luxuriant sequence of ruminations on the ubiquity of corruption among politicians, Sokolsky immediately and equally spontaneously launches into a set of reflections on a recent Hollywood sex-violence scandal. The functional connection between his two disquisitions may be difficult to document, but it is highly convincing in the context of Lane's interview.

Lane also was sometimes able to treat his small sample quantitatively, doing finely honed typological analysis. Here he was helped by the richness of his data in that he could use a number of different kinds of indicators to categorize his respondents, as in his approach to identifying damaged father-son relationships (Lane, 1959a). Lane identifies four respondents who in different senses which might not readily be identified and pooled via psychometric techniques can be said to have had difficult father-son relations. He compares them with his other respondents on such abstract orientations as beliefs about whether the conditions of life are improving or worsening and capacity to envisage a utopia. There was a strikingly more pessimistic, less utopian set of orientations on the part of men whose relations with their fathers were unsatisfactory.[17]

Since there are so few published intensive single-case analyses of individuals in the general population, the investigators considering exploiting this approach should consult two careful, clinically sensitive studies reported as unpublished doctoral dissertations. The first reports on a series of interviews Parenti (1962) conducted with immigrant grandfathers, their assimilated, upwardly mobile second-generation sons, and their grandsons in four Italian-American families. Parenti extracts intriguing insights into the interplay of sociocultural assimilation and personality development from his protocols. The second is by Lerner (1970), who conducted three extraordinarily extended case studies of undergraduate student leaders on which he lavished detailed, virtually James Joycean, interpretative attention. A valuable feature of Lerner's analysis is the "blind" diagnosis of each of his subjects by a clinical psychologist which is juxtaposed with Lerner's own conclusions based on his extended life-history interviews.

Also warranting attention is a slim Australian book by A. F. Davies, *Private Politics: A Study of Five Political Outlooks* (1966), which falls in the promising terrain between the case study of a face in the crowd and that of the eminent public figure. Davies's five case studies are of middle-level Australian political and governmental participants—a party organizer, a town planner, a state M.P., a public servant, and a union member. He interviewed these individuals for a total of from 12 to 30 hours over a period of several months. Both his interview technique and his interpretative mode are unabashedly unstandardized. In departing from orthodox canons, Davies adds an ingredient that is invariably important for single-case analysis: artfulness. Each of his cases is an exquisite mosaic of observational detail. Shortly before the end of the presentation of each case, he indicates, after the fashion of Ellery Queen, that he has now provided the wherewithal for his interpretation. The interpretations are elliptical. Davies barely pauses to hint at his inferential criteria. His implicit method combines psychoanalytically informed close analysis of symbolic meanings underlying everyday-life phenomena, as in Freud's *Interpretation of Dreams* (1900) and his *Psychopathology of Everyday Life* (1901), with the close textual analysis used by Kenneth Burke (1945, 1950) to deal with literary and other symbolic products. (For a literary critic whose technique resembles that of Davies, see Holland, 1968. For a further discussion of Davies's work, see Greenstein, 1967a. Also see the sensitively presented and discussed set of psychopolitical case studies of three Australian university students by Little, 1973.)

5.3 The Psychobiographical Literature on Public Figures

Both psychological case studies of members of general populations and psychobiographies based on the public record of celebrated individuals have their origins, if not all their sources of inspiration, in the basic body of psychoanalytic writing set down by Freud during the first decade of this century. Seven decades later, psychoanalytic personality theory continues to have a remarkable influence, in spite of the blatantly "unscientific" [18] form in which Freud enunciated it. Outside psychiatry, the direct contemporary influence of Freud's contributions is less in psychology than in the humanities, including history. (Many historians who work on biography and on cultural history have found their inspiration in psychoanalysis.) But *indirectly,* Freud's thinking, apart from its incalculable influence on many workaday aspects of modern mores, informs some aspects of most personality theories. Furthermore, Freud's own clinical facility and his high literary powers make it still to the point for students of personality and politics to read his case studies. His pseudonymous early case subjects—e.g., "Dora" (1905), "Little Hans" (1909a), "Rat Man" (1909b), and "Wolf Man" (1918)—have no doubt been more often read about and written on by subsequent commentators than many "real" historical actors of consequence.

In 1910 Freud briefly directed his torrential energies to psychobiography, choosing the enigmatic figure of Leonardo da Vinci (1910), about whom there is the most fragmentary of historical records, to render a psychodiagnosis. Freud did not return to psychodiagnosis of public figures in his published writings again until *Moses and Monotheism* (1938), which is less a psychobiography than an attempt at advancing an interpretation of the collective history of the Jews. Evidently he did, however, spend many years in intermittent collaboration with the American diplomat William C. Bullitt on a manuscript on Woodrow Wilson. This manuscript was published in 1967, well after the deaths of both authors and under circumstances that left ambiguous the exact nature of Freud's contribution to it (Freud and Bullitt, 1967).

But Freud's influence on the craft of biography is not mainly a result of his own occasional interpretations of public figures. As "Freudianism" began diffusing just before World War I and then in a much accelerated way in the 1920s, there was an explosion of psychobiography of public figures of all types —explicitly political actors, such functionally equivalent political actors as the leaders of religious movements, and figures from walks of life remote from politics, such as writers and artists. Psychoanalysis seemed to a few historians, many popular writers, and many more individuals writing from within "the psychoanalytic movement" to be the philosopher's stone for historical analysis.

By the late 1920s enough such writings had appeared to permit an extended bibliographical review of the literature (Fearing, 1927). By that time some of this work had begun to find recognition within political science, although only by the few political scientists who had taken an interest in psychoanalysis— most notably Harold D. Lasswell. In addition to assembling case materials on psychiatric patients in connection with the typological analysis reported in his *Psychopathology and Politics* (1930), Lasswell took an interest in the work of such psychiatrists as the Lincoln biographer L. Pierce Clark (1921, 1933).

The early psychoanalytic biographies had a number of shortcomings so glaring that it is less wonder that they were widely maligned than that they received a good bit of interested attention. The difficulties identified by critics of these early works can readily be seen to converge with many of the standard problems of personality-and-politics metatheory. The critics suggested that such biographies often

1. tended to see adult character as immutably fixed by early childhood experience;
2. were preoccupied with inner conflict arising out of sexuality as a singular source of character formation;
3. equated character with pathological tendencies and unconscious forces and in general underplayed characterological sources of strength and conscious adaptive capacities;
4. underplayed situational determinants of behavior;
5. made diagnoses, often on the basis of fragmental data, without explicating standards of evidence and inference.

There was a decline in interest in psychobiography in the 1930s, but the genre was revived in the postwar period, partly because of interest in explaining egregious irrationality occasioned by Nazism. Of the psychological case studies of public political actors that appeared during the post–World War II years, few are as fundamentalistically and exclusively psychoanalytic as the early psychobiographies. Conversely, most of them seek more or less self-consciously not to fall into the difficulties of the older psychobiographies. There are a number of notable contributions to this second wave of psychological analysis of public political actors: Erikson's two works on politico-religious leaders, *Young Man Luther* (1958) and *Gandhi's Truth* (1969) ; George and

George's brilliantly measured treatment of Woodrow Wilson (1956), which paradoxically draws on Freudian insights but is more successful as a psycho-diagnosis than the Freud-Bullitt effort; Edinger's (1965) careful personality analysis of the German Socialist leader Kurt Schumacher; and Tucker's (1973) account of Stalin's formative years and rise to power. The study by Rogow (1963) of Forrestal and the one by Glad (1966) of Charles Evans Hughes are somewhat more straightforwardly political biographies. These works defer psychological interpretation to the final chapters, but in each the author's full historical narrative is informed by an overall psychological conception of the subject.

Psychobiographies by political scientists tend to make explicit reference to clinical literature and to the logic of the biographer's inferences. Historians using this mode tend simply to introduce their diagnostic conclusions in the course of unfolding their historical narrative. Even when historians engage in under-the-table clinical interpretation, simply using their analyses to inform their exposition, their work can profit from the clinical exposure. This point is illustrated by a comparison of the motivationally convincing biography by Fawn Brodie (1959) of a complicated, tormented nineteenth-century American, Thaddeus Stevens, with David Donald's (1960, 1970) work on a similarly complex figure from the same historical period, Charles Sumner. The latter work, as painstaking as it is, lacks an implicit (much less, an explicit) model of the protagonist's inner dynamics. As a consequence, Donald's Sumner seems merely to be contradictory and inscrutable, whereas there is a motivational coherence to Brodie's portrait of Stevens.

Some works include both single-case and typological analysis: Wolfenstein, in a rather orthodoxly psychoanalytic treatment, presents sketches of the life, character, and personal development of Lenin, Trotsky, and Gandhi (1967).[19] Interestingly, Wolfenstein, a political scientist, has been criticized by Erikson (1968), a psychoanalyst, for overmechanical use of Freudian interpretative techniques. Barber's *The Presidential Character: Predicting Performance in the White House* (1972a) develops a typology, discussed below, of political leaders and presents psychobiographical sketches of the American presidents from Taft through Nixon. Barber avoids "deep" psychodynamic interpretations but clearly draws for background insight on depth-psychological notions.[20]

5.4 Evidence and Inference in Single-Case Analysis of Political Actors

Even though the more recent psychobiographies tend to avoid the excesses of the earlier works, psychobiographies and individual case studies generally suffer from the absence of explicit canons for data presentation, analysis, and interpretation. Single-case psychological analyses of political actors and, in particular, psychological biographies of public actors seem at once to be an inescapable enterprise and one that raises profound empirical problems. It is by no means clear how one can assess the truth value of single-case diagnoses.

Some single-case analyses *are* clearly more satisfactory than others. By extracting standards from the more satisfactory studies, one can suggest a program of incremental improvement of the rigor of evidence and inference in single-case analyses. The distinctions that follow are largely an elaboration on some of Alexander George's discussions (e.g., 1968, 1971). They also are applicable to the construction and validation of political personality typologies.

Psychodiagnosis entails three analytically distinguishable, if empirically overlapping, tasks, the simplest of which is the delineation of what might be called the "presenting characteristics" of the subject of diagnosis. These are an individual's more readily observable traits, perceptions of his environment, conscious political orientations, and the regular pattern of his actions under varied environmental stimuli. (See panels 5, 6, and 9 of Figure 3.) This first-order level of descriptive data I have elsewhere (Greenstein, 1969, Chapter 4) called *phenomenology*. The actor's phenomenology cannot be discussed in a conceptual void, but by and large it *can* be discussed in terms of conceptualizations that are widely shared by investigators of such diverse psychological persuasions as radical behaviorism and psychoanalysis.

In perhaps the most systematic of the psychobiographies, the George and George (1956) analysis of Woodrow Wilson, the following descriptive elements can be located under the heading of "phenomenology": rigidness, self-righteousness, pedantry, stubbornness, reluctance of compromise under at least some circumstances. As a descriptive account of traits becomes more detailed and more closely tied to the way these traits manifest themselves under different circumstances, various interpretative problems arise. For example, it may turn out that a seemingly well-developed trait does not manifest itself under some circumstances, or even that under some circumstances the individual behavior seems quite inconsistent with what appears to be a well-established trait.

Thus Wilson's rigidity and reluctance to compromise on points of principle, which seemed so pronounced in his obdurate behavior during the crisis over adoption of the Versailles Treaty by the Senate, and his earlier conflict as college president with his Princeton adversaries over location of the graduate school, seem dramatically absent under other circumstances. Wilson did an extraordinary about-face during the first decade of the twentieth century, shifting from the conservative to the progressive wing of the Democratic party and systematically ingratiating himself with a man for whom he had earlier expressed contempt, William Jennings Bryan. During his initial periods in office as Governor of New Jersey and President of the United States, he was reasonably prone to compromise his aims.

Such inconsistencies call for explanation, as does the overall juxtaposition of character traits in the individual. This need for explanation leads to a second, more refractory class of diagnostic operation—namely, analysis of the *dynamics* of a personality trait. Dynamic analysis at its simplest need involve no more than an expansion of the descriptive account of traits-in-action, moving as it were from successive slides to a motion picture. But the term "dynamics" is systematically ambiguous, also referring to "inner dynamics." An attempt can be made to specify what inner processes, structures, and needs during the contemporaneous functioning of the individual are responsible for his outward phenomenological manifestation. In the language of Figure 3, dynamic analysis focuses on the functional bases of conscious orientation (panel 4).

Once psychological discourse begins positing more or less "deep" inner psychic structures, interpretative disagreement is inevitable. Not only are there disagreements within psychology of the sort summarized earlier about the usefulness of *all* concepts that refer to intrapsychic states; there also are disagreements among personality theorists about the significance and appropriate conceptualization of "deep" psychic structures and ego defenses.[21] The Georges' dynamic account of Woodrow Wilson includes such relatively uncontroversial elements as a contingent analysis of the circumstances under which he was and was not willing to compromise. He was willing to compromise in order to *obtain power;* he was much less willing to compromise once he *held power,* except in areas which he had not initially defined as part of his leadership "mission." More controversially, the Georges argue that underlying Wilson's need to dominate was the predispositional condition Lasswell had identified (1948) as a source of power-seeking motivation—a damaged self-esteem. *Most* controversially, they link the latter to repressed hostility to his father manifesting itself in a strong resistance to being dominated by other males, especially those whom Wilson could readily perceive as analogous to Wilson's father in their manner of relating to Wilson.

The dynamic interpretation of the continuing influence of Wilson's conscious and unconscious memories of his father on the adult Wilson points to the need for the third set of analytic tasks in psychodiagnosis: a developmental account of the genesis of the individual's adult patterns (panels 2 and 3 of Figure 3). What in fact *were* the developmental experiences of the political actor in question? There need be no implication that developmental experiences should be looked at exclusively in terms of psychogenetic hypotheses. "Social learning" theory (Bandura and Walters, 1963) can apply particularly well here. This theory employs as one of its key developmental concepts "modeling," which overlaps to some extent such psychoanalytic terms as identification.

Just as dynamic analyses are less likely to be universally convincing than phenomenological analyses, developmental analyses tend to be less convincing than dynamic analyses, especially the less theory-based dynamic analyses. Developmental analyses are least convincing, partially because of the sparsity of information about critical periods in the lives of most historical actors likely to concern the political analyst. In addition, the complexity of psychic development and the weakness of the general theoretical and empirical resources at the disposal of behavioral scientists for testing hypotheses about human development make psychogenetic interpretations highly uncertain. Fortunately, from the standpoint of political analysis, developmental interpretations deal with the phenomena furthest in time and in causal linkage from the actual behavioral outcomes political analysts seek to explain. The intrinsic difficulty of this aspect of psychodiagnosis is not fatal to the entire enterprise.

With Wilson, the Georges were fortunate in having a subject whose early years were remarkably well documented by a family that kept records and a biographer who collected extensive depositions from family members and friends who knew the young Wilson. The Georges, partly as a result of the questions raised by their dynamic hypotheses, were led to identifying a series of developmental experiences that had not been emphasized by other Wilson biographers and that help support their dynamic interpretations. They noted the extremely close, emotionally charged, tutoring relationship between Wilson and his father; Woodrow's stubborn early failure to acquire the verbal skills that his father valued so highly, and that Woodrow was later to emphasize so strongly in his political behavior; the elder Wilson's caustic mode of chastising his son in the presence of others. These early experiences, the Georges argued, appear to be part of a pattern in which Wilson repressed his substantial grievances against his father, reactively idealized his father, and was fatally drawn into intense conflict with certain kinds of male counterparts.

With the three tasks of phenomenological, dynamic, and genetic explanation in mind, the following five schematically stated steps seem promising ways into a program of systematizing evidence and inference in single-case analysis.

1. So far as possible, there should be explicit formulation of hypotheses about at least the first level and ideally all three levels of the subject's psychological functioning. By and large, these are not likely to be *a priori* hypotheses, given the iterative nature of research as the investigator dips into the available sources on his subject. But so far as possible, the analyst's assumptions about phenomenological patterns, underlying dynamics, and developmental relationships ought to be stated in potentially falsifiable form.

2. Interpretations should be kept distinct from the observational data on which they are based. Interpretations are bound to be more controversial than their observational basis, although it must be recognized, that observations are never "theory-free" in the sense of existing in a total absence of interpretive interests.

3. Specific operational criteria should be established for the various terms in the observational statements.

4. In single-case analysis, as in multi-case analysis, it is possible to focus in an organized way the tasks of establishing *reliability*. In this respect, it is helpful to realize that, although the single-case analyst is dealing with only one actor, he is dealing with a large universe of observations connected with that actor. In clinical psychology, progress has been made toward the quantitative treatment of the many items of data on each subject of a single-case analysis (Davidson and Costello, 1969; Barlow, 1973; S. R. Brown, 1974). Similar efforts are possible for single-case analyses of political actors, though there would be an obvious danger of substituting ineffective scientism for effective clinical imagination.[22] In general, reliability can be explored by separating descriptive from interpretative data, explicating interpretative criteria, and employing (not necessarily in a narrowly quantitative fashion) panels of judges.

5. Finally, it is necessary to go beyond reliability to a consideration of the *validity* of one's single-case interpretations. Here the basic problem entails grounding single-case analyses in empirically supported theoretical propositions—propositions which themselves are grounded in multi-case research. (For an expansion, see Greenstein, 1969, Chapter 3. For up-to-date summaries of current thinking in psychology about the problem of assessing validity, see Fiske, 1971 and 1973.)

6. TYPOLOGICAL MULTI-CASE STUDIES OF POLITICAL ACTORS

6.1 The Literature on Political Typologies

Under the typological heading I include the entire range of explicit or implicit multi-case analyses that employ classifications. Typology, thus, is here used as an umbrella term encompassing the range of possibilities from such straight-forward classifications as divisions of a population into the categories of a single trait—e.g., high or low sense of self-esteem, ego strength, etc.—to elaborate "syndrome" classifications that identify interdependent constellations of traits with distinctive origins, dynamics, and behavioral links—e.g., the authoritarianism typology—although the traditional uses of the term make it less than perfectly applicable to categorizations of single continuous variables.

For a reminder that political personality typologies do not begin with Freud, one need only note Plato's accounts in the eighth and ninth books of *The Republic* of the aristocrat, the democrat, the timocrat, and the tyrant—political types that had their origin in an intergenerational dialectic of reactions of sons to the shortcomings of their fathers. (A latter-day gloss on this aspect of *The Republic* is provided by Lasswell, 1960. On the history of psychological classifications, see Eysenck and Eysenck, 1969, Chapters 1–6.)

In psychiatry, Kraepelin's classification of the psychoses (Eysenck, 1968) although of nineteenth-century vintage, continues with modifications to be a basic source for categorizing regularities in deviant character structures—regularities that are commonly assumed to have their analogies in nonpsychotic personalities. Freud's clinical concerns, which were largely with neurotics rather than psychotics, led him to identify a number of personality syndromes, the most notable being the oral, anal, and phallic types. Of these, the anal, which is marked by three interdependent central traits—obstinacy, stinginess, and orderliness—in particular has been subject to reasonably convincing confirmatory research (Kline, 1972, Chapter 3).

Another major tradition in twentieth-century personality psychology arises out of personality testing—namely, psychometric classification. Such classification may be based on more or less eclectic inventories of psychological traits or on tests that have their basis in the various personality theories. The 1970 volume edited by Alvin Mahrer, *New Approaches to Personality Classification,* provides a convenient guide to the pluralistic diversity of contemporary classification practice, as, at a more mechanical extreme, do the detailed "official" American Psychiatric Association (1968) codifications of types of "mental disorders." (For a good recent discussion of problems in personality typologies, see Dahlstrom, 1972.)

Within political psychology, the pioneering classificatory work of Harold D. Lasswell had its primary inspiration in psychoanalytic interpretations of neurotics, although Lasswell also viewed with interest the early glimmerings of psychometric political research and made use of psychiatrists' diagnoses of psychotics as well. Lasswell's purpose in his somewhat misleadingly titled book *Psychopathology and Politics* (1930) was not so much to show that personal pathology influences politics as to argue that the "clinical caricature" of psychosis provides the political analyst with "pure"—i.e., intensified—versions of personality traits that are present but more difficult to observe in nonpsychotics. For this reason and because of the detailed records available on patients, Lasswell felt that mental patient populations were a promising source for research on personality and politics. His suggestion was picked up many years later in Rutherford's (1966) study of patients in Illinois's Elgin State Hospital, which produced sufficiently striking, strong correlations between psychiatric diagnostic categories and political dependent variables to suggest that this strategy might profitably be pursued further. As noted above, Rutherford found very high rates of participation in both the patient self-government system of the hospital and in "real world" politics during remitted periods by patients diagnosed as paranoid. (For important qualifications and an extension to a nonpatient population, see Alker, 1971.)

Lasswell's own contribution to political typology was his introduction of a threefold classification of political leaders and other activists—agitators, administrators, and theorists. Any single political actor might fit into only one of these typologies, or he might be a mixed type. There is an explicit logic for developing and validating typologies underlying Lasswell's array of types—an array that Lasswell later embellished and added to in his 1948 *Power and Person-*

ality and his 1951 "Democratic Character." A recent monograph by A. F. Davies (1973) provides the "last word" (to date) on Lasswell's typologies, carefully summarizing his initial formulations and juxtaposing them with subsequent empirical findings. Lasswell (1930, Chapter 4, and 1968) suggested that the nosologist of character should begin with a *nuclear* typology—one revolving around some central variable or relationship of variables. The concomitants of this nuclear type could then be systematically established. Lasswell described the resulting syndromes as *co-relational* types. This analysis of contemporary aspects of the character type would then be expanded to a developmental analysis of the life-cycle (*genetic*) antecedents of the character type.[23]

Many of the political or politically relevant typologies that have been advanced since the publication of Lasswell's work have not in fact been subjected to systematic explication and validation. For example, Riesman's famous triad of tradition-, inner-, and other-directed characters (Riesman, Glazer, and Denney, 1950), as Riesman later acknowledged (1953), is as much concerned with an individual's social behavior as with his inner orientations. The Riesman typology does not dwell on inner psychological dynamics, although there have been interesting empirical efforts to expand on the psychological aspects of Riesman's formulations and to develop empirical measures of the inner-other directedness continuum. (See the various contributions to Lipset and Lowenthal, 1961, especially Sofer. See also the earlier typology presented in Fromm, 1947, from which Riesman's typology is derived.)

By far the most often discussed and the most complexly controversial of the political psychology typologies is that of the authoritarian personality. Some of the aspects of this typology developed in the 1930s and 1940s seem anachronistic in the context of the prevailing 1970s assertions about the rise of new generations of individuals free of rigid characterological trends (Sanford, 1973). But as recently as 1972 Wilkinson was able to use the authoritarianism typology for a wide-ranging survey of political trends. For our purposes here the question of whether authoritarianism is an important contemporary syndrome is beside the point. The proliferated nature of the authoritarianism literature and the numerous controversies attendant on it make that literature perhaps the most fertile single source of illustrating the problems of studying personality and politics.

Although there is no single "official" delineation of "the authoritarian personality type," virtually all discussions of the typology agree on the nuclear defining characteristics of the typology. Individuals with authoritarian personalities are disposed to defer to those whom they perceive as superiors and to seek to dominate perceived inferiors. The notion that individuals vary in deference-dominance tendencies and that these tendencies might be rooted in personality structure is probably a stock ingredient in common-sense folk psychology. This notion acquired the status of a formal intellectual construct in the 1930s as a result of the understandable compulsion of scholars to seek explanations for the rise of totalitarianism, and especially German national socialism,[24] and for the striking psychological qualities of leadership and followership in such political systems.

In seeking to explain such *collectively* irrational phenomena as the authoritarian practices of Hitler Germany, the massive public acts of obeisance to Hitler, and the Nazi doctrines of racial superiority and inferiority, psychologically oriented scholars found it natural to draw on an intellectual framework developed to explain *individual* emotional disturbance—notably psychoanalytic theory. A further element in 1930s and early 1940s delineations of the authoritarian type (especially Fromm, 1941) was the reliance on Marxist notions to link the individual and societal levels. Fromm saw authoritarianism as a surrogate for Weber's Protestant Ethic and considered that such character types were a consequence of and a functional necessity for the operation of a capitalist economy. Later writers on authoritarianism, notably the authors of *The Authoritarian Personality* (Adorno *et al.*, 1950), tended to envisage nonsocialist industrial societies as being potentially in danger of succumbing to right-wing totalitarianism because of the widespread authoritarian needs of their citizens.

These currents of thought plus social psychological-measurement techniques were drawn on in the so-called Berkeley Project, which was reported in *The Authoritarian Personality*. That massive volume contained a heterogeneous array of exploratory studies of anti-Semitic attitudes and their psychological correlates. By far the most immediately influential aspect of the study was the F scale, a set of ostensibly nonpolitical, nonideological questionnaire items. The face content of the F scale avoids politics and ethnic prejudice and instead deals with such matters as the desirability of obedience in children, how society should deal with sexual deviance, superstition, one's attitudes toward one's own feelings, etc. Items with this manifest content, it was argued, are indicators of an underlying personality syndrome that fosters emotionally based ethnic prejudices and deference-dominance needs. (The "F" in F scale was originally introduced to refer to personality trends that would incline one to support fascism.)

The publication in 1950 of *The Authoritarian Personality* was an extraordinary catalyst for psychological research. By 1958, an admittedly incomplete bibliographical article by Christie and Cook of the literature through 1956 listed 260 authoritarianism studies. By 1967, Kirscht and Dillehay found it necessary to employ a monograph to summarize the authoritarianism literature. Unfortunately, much of that research mechanically used the F scale, and little of it drew explicitly on the personality-based construct of authoritarianism that was rather unsystematically scattered through that work. The most succinct summary of the Adorno *et al.* study's theoretical assumptions by one of the original authors was published well after the original volume (Sanford, 1959).

As early as 1954, however, the initial uncritical enthusiasm for what might be accomplished through the study of authoritarianism had faded. There appeared in that year a highly influential volume of critical *Studies in the Scope and Method of "The Authoritarian Personality"* (Christie and Jahoda, 1954), many of which were in themselves fundamental contributions to the analysis of personality and sociopolitical behavior. In particular, the critics of *The Authoritarian Personality* made the following points that relate broadly to the problem of conducting satisfactory personality-and-politics inquiry, typological or otherwise.

1. There was insufficient evidence that the F scale in fact tapped a personality syndrome, much less the particular pattern of surface traits, unconscious personality dynamics, and developmental experiences posited by the authors of *The Authoritarian Personality.*

2. Writers on authoritarianism tended to focus exclusively on right-wing authoritarianism, in effect equating left-wing orientations with psychological health.[25] There was insufficient appreciation (a) that a personality disposition can vent itself in diverse ways—e.g., in left-wing as well as right-wing authoritarianism—and (b) that the same or a similar belief system can be held, perhaps with differing degrees of force and persistence, by individuals with different underlying personality structures.

3. Finally, writers on authoritarianism tended too facilely to extrapolate from *individual* authoritarianism to the proclivity of political *systems* populated by such individuals to be authoritarian.

To the difficulties discussed by contributors to *Studies in the Scope and Method of "The Authoritarian Personality"* there was soon added another complexly unraveling controversy over the possibility that "response set" may have been responsible for some of the principal findings by students of authoritarianism. In 1967 Samelson and Yates presented an extensive array of sources on the skein of inquiry that still continued to explore this possibility. (For the latter-day extension of this controversy into personality testing in general, see Bentler, Jackson, and Messick, 1971, and Block, 1972, and the sources there cited.)

In essence the problem of response set in authoritarian studies takes the following form. Much of the seeming statistical support for the early authoritarianism research is based on positive correlations between test scales composed of the widely used "agree-disagree" Likert scale format. Individuals scoring high on the F scale tend also to score high on such other measures as the anti-Semitism (A-S) and on the politicoeconomic conservatism (PEC) scales. But it was later noted that all these factors also co-vary with socioeconomic and educational status; the lower one's socioeconomic status (SES) and educational level, the higher one's F, A-S, and PEC scores.

Evidently much of the co-variation of the original scales resulted from an artifact of the tests used to measure authoritarianism. All the items in the various scales were worded positively so that an "agree" response contributed to a high-scale score. Some individuals—particularly those of lower SES and educational levels—respond not so much to the *content* of the test items as to such extraneous considerations as the aura of the testing situation. They more or less automatically check "agree," out of a general disposition to be impressed by vague, pontifical-sounding aphorisms of the sort that appear in test items. In short, the tendency of people of lower SES and education to score high seemed heavily if not exclusively to be a function of "agreeing response set." Therefore it was possible for the survey researchers whose work is reported in *The American Voter* (Cambell *et al.*, 1960, pp. 512–515) simply to reverse the wording of the F scale so that "disagree" responses produced high authoritarian scores and to come up with findings directly opposite to the standard finding. In their survey, respondents with lower SES and education were *lower* in "authoritarianism." Evidently many of the same people who checked "agree" when posed with some typical F scale assertion such as "Obedience and respect are the most important virtues children should learn," or "No sane, normal, decent person could ever think of hurting a close friend or relative," were equally ready to check "agree" when posed with denials of these assertions.[26] That people might be willing to agree with diametrically opposed statements becomes credible if one considers the great vagueness and oracular generality of such questionnaire items.

As a result of the response-set controversy, a variety of revised, reversed, and mixed F scales have been developed (Titus and Hollander, 1957; Christie, Havel, and Seidenberg, 1958; R. Brown, 1965, Chapter 10; Samelson and Yates, 1967). In the 1970s, a quarter century after the earlier research reports from the Berkeley Project, studies using variants on these scales still were being reported and attempts were being made to reconcile and explain the diverse findings. A listing of reports of authoritarianism research published in 1972 alone (Greenstein, 1973, p. 451) notes seven articles in well-known journals that apply their principal focus to authoritarianism, the F scale, and related issues. Evidently there seemed to investigators to be an inescapable core of empirical reality in the authoritarian typology, but what this was could not be readily agreed upon.

This summary of the tangled history of theory and research on the authoritarian typology serves to illustrate a variety of the pitfalls, problems, and prospects of typological inquiry, especially when that inquiry is insufficiently clearly and explicitly conceptualized in the first instance and when it mechanically relies on a restricted range of convenient but artifact-prone psychometric procedures. On the matter of measurements, Samelson's comment is to the point, but his view is too little heeded.

> . . . it seems to this author that Likert scale data are inadequate to produce a satisfactory solution to the content-versus-response-set problem on the F scale since with unscaled items and multiple-choice responses too much

of the information required must be imposed on the data in the first place. As others have said before, perhaps we should give fewer questionnaires and study the attitudes in more detail and depth. (Samelson, 1964, p. 342)

One offshoot of the authoritarian personality studies was the interesting array of studies of "dogmatism" reported by Rokeach in *The Open and the Closed Mind* (1960). Rokeach sought an alternative typological formulation and measuring procedure that would be free of ideological content and therefore not open to Shils's (1954) criticism that the research reported in *The Authoritarian Personality* had been insensitive to left-wing authoritarianism. Unfortunately, Rokeach's key demonstration of the efficacy of his instrument as a means of identifying rigidly held beliefs, irrespective of where the subjects stand on the political spectrum, relies on a single far-left comparison group of 13 English Communists. Rokeach carefully presents, in an appendix to *The Open and the Closed Mind,* an item-by-item listing of the dogmatism scores for the left- and right-wing groups he used to establish the ideology-free status of the dogmatism scale. In a number of instances his two extreme ideological groups seem to have achieved high scores by responding positively to different items on the scale, and some of these items seem suspiciously close to the likely manifest ideologies of the comparison groups. Thus the possibility arises that Rokeach's scale, which is designed to measure an inner personality dynamic, is in fact eliciting conscious political orientations and attitudes. Nevertheless Rokeach's many other research findings on such matters as the problem-solving ability of low and high scores on dogmatism suggest the general potentiality of dogmatism as a typology of interest to political analysts.

Another politically fascinating typology "spun off" the early interest in identifying ideology-free political personality patterns is Christie's intriguing notion of the Machiavellian type. Forewarned by the measurements problems in the authoritarianism literature, Christie delayed publication for many years, perfecting successive versions of his "Mach" scale that included a forced-choice version not susceptible to the agree-disagree response set problem and conducting numerous validational and other empirical studies (Christie and Geis, 1970; Guterman, 1970). As the reference to the author of *The Prince* suggests, the Machiavellianism scale is designed to identify individuals disposed to fill manipulative social and political roles—individuals low in affect invested in interpersonal relationships, concern with conventional morality, and intensity of ideological commitment and sufficiently lacking in "gross psychopathology" to use these permissive proclivities to act as "operators" or manipulators.

Christie's research appears to have profited greatly from the extended maturation period during which early measurement artifacts were dealt with and a carefully conceived and orchestrated array of experimental investigations was conducted as efforts were made to explain seemingly contradictory findings.

The approach taken in *Studies in Machiavellianism* (Christie and Geis, 1970) to resolving the points of apparent contradiction among studies is wholly congenial to the emphasis in this chapter on interactive personality-and-politics relationships. In situations in which high and low Machs did and did not differ in response to experimental stimuli, there turned out to have been three "moderator variables"—i.e., "characteristics of the situation that may either facilitate or mask the dispositional differences." These characteristics concerned whether the situation called for face-to-face interaction, whether it allowed latitude for improvisation, and whether it was one that introduced "irrelevant affect" that might distract the non-Machiavellians from the various tasks Christie and Geis asked their subjects to perform (Christie and Geis, 1970, pp. 285–294).

The three quantitative typological literatures just discussed dealing with authoritarianism, dogmatism, and Machiavellianism, have produced more in the way of substantively interesting and credibly patterned findings than the scattering of early psychometric studies in which standard personality and political-attitude inventories simply were rather uncritically administered, usually in the archetypical population of college sophomores, and intercorrelated. Describing these as "trait-attitude correlation studies" in their review of the personality-and-politics literature, Smith, Bruner, and White (1956, Chapter 2) point to the low and inconsistent correlations in the early research comparing, for example, radicals and conservatives on such continuums as introversion-extroversion.

We can readily see from the response-set controversy one reason why these early studies failed to cumulate. They too often used unsatisfactory measures of both the independent and the dependent variables, both overly "weak" measures that fail to tap personality and attitude dimensions and overly "strong" measures of the sort that artifactually inflate correlations. In addition, by failing systematically to introduce observations on situational determinants of attitudes and behavior, trait-attitude students condemned themselves to inconsistency by failure to build moderator variables into their inquiries.

By and large, these are difficulties that can be substantially mitigated if not eliminated by satisfactorily designed research. For models of carefully designed, rigorously conceptualized psychometric studies, the reader should examine the important series of papers reported over the years from Herbert McClosky's late 1950s studies of national and Minnesota samples of citizens and of political leaders. These well-designed, large-sample studies made use of the best-validated available personality-and-attitude scales and have since been carefully mined by McClosky and his associates (McClosky, 1958, 1967; McClosky and Schaar, 1965; Di Palma and McClosky, 1970; Sniderman, 1974; and Sniderman and Citrin, 1971). The forthcoming book-length presentation of McClosky's overall findings promises to have the same sort of variegated responsiveness to the real-world complexity of personality-and-politics connections that marks the summary report of Christie's work on Machiavellianism. Among the elements that have emerged to date are the following.

1. The development and validation of an omnibus questionnaire by Mc-Closky (with the collaboration of Paul E. Meehl, and Kenneth E. Clark) capable of assessing at one administration a host of political attitudes (e.g., isolationism); ideological orientations (e.g., classical conservatism); social attitudes (e.g., chauvinism); extremist political attitudes; opinions on issues of the day (e.g., reliance on the United Nations); attitudes toward the party system (e.g., the use of primaries); reference group identifications; commitment to democratic values and civil liberties; indicators of social and personal adjustment (e.g., anomie); a variety of clinical psychological traits (e.g., intolerance of ambiguity, hostility); and, of course, the whole array of standard sociodemographic indicators. This questionnaire remains unique in at least two respects: (a) it represents the most ambitious attempt to develop a multifaceted assessment of the political beliefs and behavior of Americans; and (b) it represents the most sophisticated and rigorous development of survey measures, eschewing the use of indicators based on only one or two items and developing multi-item scales cross-validated in a continuing series of studies.

2. McClosky's pioneer study on ideology and personality (1958), demonstrating the strong psychological roots of a prominent facet of conservatism—classical conservatism or orientations toward change.

3. McClosky and Schaar's original analysis of the psychology of anomie. Previously anomie had been understood as a sociological phenomenon, but McClosky and Schaar developed a complementary psychological model, persuasively showing how a variety of personality characteristics contributed independently to the development of anomie.

4. McClosky's (1967) fine-grained analysis of the psychology of isolationism, which showed the strong links between isolationist attitudes and a number of aversive personality characteristics such as inflexibility and hostility among both ordinary citizens and political influentials.

5. Sniderman and Citrin's analysis of the relationship between personality and isolationism (1971), which demonstrated that the network of beliefs which isolationist attitudes belonged to depended on whether isolationism was personality-derived or not. The psychological roots of political attitudes thus appear to be an important subject for study because those whose political views, at least on foreign policy, are partly derived from their personal needs are likely to take very different positions on other political questions from those whose foreign policy orientations are derived from some other source (e.g., social learning).

6. Sniderman's (1974) analysis of self-esteem illustrates the importance of disaggregating global (and often loosely defined) personality traits. Self-esteem was broken down into three more specific facets—a sense of personal unworthiness, a sense of social inferiority, and a sense of interpersonal competence. Only the third facet of self-esteem was of consequence in determining whether individuals became politically active or political leaders.

7. Di Palma and McClosky's (1970) analysis of the psychological dynamics of conformity showed how the same personality characteristics (e.g., low self-esteem) that lead to conformity in the laboratory lead to deviance outside it. They made extensive use of education as a moderator variable in studying relationships between personality factors and the holding of atypical political attitudes. (Psychopathology is more likely to be associated with political deviance among the uneducated than among the educated.)

8. Sniderman's (1974) study of the connection between personality and political leadership underlines the importance of moving from trait analysis to profile analysis. Specifically, though low self-esteem generally inhibits the tendency to participate in politics as do several facets of the inflexibility syndrome, those who are both low in self-esteem and high in, say, rigidity are markedly *more* likely to be politically active than are those who are low in self-esteem and low in rigidity. In short, two traits which, taken separately, inhibit involvement contribute to it when combined. This specific finding emphasizes a more general principle: the importance of studying not only the interaction of personality and the situation but also the interaction of personality traits themselves.

A political personality typology that derives directly from behavior in the political arena rather than from psychological scales is Barber's fourfold classification of political leadership types. Barber has persistently sought to develop characterological criteria for predicting and evaluating the behavior of public officials. His categories arise from a cross-classification of a pair of dichotomous variables, each of which could also be treated as points on a continuum. The variables, which he specifies and operationalizes somewhat differently in his two studies, relate to an individual's *level of activity* and his *affect* toward politics and life more generally.

Barber's first study (1965) was of freshman Connecticut state legislators elected in 1958. Barber had administered questionnaires to his respondents and also had conducted extended, tape-recorded interviews with a subset of them. He arrived inductively at a classification of his respondents in terms of high versus low levels of activity in the legislature, as measured by a variety of objective indicators such as number of speeches given, and in terms of positive versus negative affect toward their legislative role, as indicated by the legislator's report of willingness or lack of willingness to serve for a number of additional terms. Barber's four resulting groups—lawmakers, advertisers, spectators, and reluctants—had the distinctive social and psychological characteristics summarized in Figure 4.

Barber was initially struck by the incidence of each of his four types. If political participation were simply a function of positive orientations toward politics, it would follow that most legislators would fall into the high-participation, positive-affect (Lawmaker) category, with most of the remainder falling into the low-negative (Reluctant) category. In fact, however, there was a roughly equal concentration in all four cells. Why, Barber wondered, would an individual who dislikes a role nevertheless seek to carry it out actively? Conversely, why would one who likes a role fail to be active in pursuing it? The answers suggested by Barber's data are briefly suggested in Figure 4: The active-negative-affect Advertisers seek visibility to advance their careers and also seem to be displacing various hostile-aggressive impulses into the political arena. The inactive-positive Spectators derive a sense of worth from political recognition. Like the Advertisers, they are asking what politics can do for them rather than vice versa.

Barber (1965, pp. 219–233) goes on to argue that active political participation tends to recruit emotionally deviant types from the general population. Politics, as a late-entry and not widely respected profession, has a high psychological entry threshold. It takes exceptional motivational push to rise beyond the local activist level and run for office. This motivation, Barber argues, can come either from dissatisfactions and tensions (as appears to be true of the Advertisers, Spectators, and perhaps to some extent, the Reluctants). Or it can come from opposite capacities—needs for mastery, problem-solving, and challenge (as for the Lawmakers). Thus office-seeking politicians would tend to cluster bimodally when compared with the larger population in terms of such personality variables as sense of self-esteem.

Barber's emphasis on motivational diversity is an important departure from the misleading search by some students of political personality for a unitary constellation of personality traits characterizing *all* politicians. As Lasswell long ago noted (1930, Chapter 4), the individuals in the real world who happen to fill what are conventionally defined as political roles simply are too varied to have uniform qualities. For this reason Lasswell sought to identify "functionally" homogeneous roles—such as power-seeking—that were performed in varying conventionally labeled social contexts—for example, the church and business as well as government and politics. The multimodal nature of motivation in government and politics makes it less than useful to follow the procedure of administering personality inventories to politicians and seeking a *single* set of personality characteristics that distinguish politicians from nonpoliticians, as do Hennessey (1959), Schwartz (1969), and Di Renzo (1967). See Greenstein (1970b and 1973, pp. 456–457).

Following his study of state legislators, Barber went on to apply his

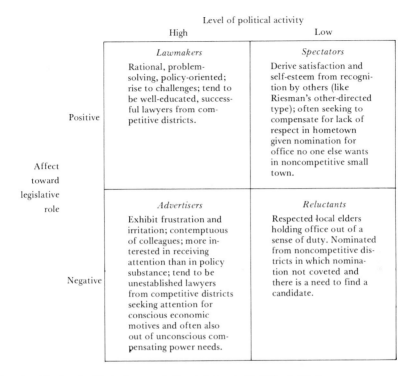

Level of political activity

	High	Low
Positive	*Lawmakers* Rational, problem-solving, policy-oriented; rise to challenges; tend to be well-educated, successful lawyers from competitive districts.	*Spectators* Derive satisfaction and self-esteem from recognition by others (like Riesman's other-directed type); often seeking to compensate for lack of respect in hometown given nomination for office no one else wants in noncompetitive small town.
Negative	*Advertisers* Exhibit frustration and irritation; contemptuous of colleagues; more interested in receiving attention than in policy substance; tend to be unestablished lawyers from competitive districts seeking attention for conscious economic motives and often also out of unconscious compensating power needs.	*Reluctants* Respected local elders holding office out of a sense of duty. Nominated from noncompetitive districts in which nomination not coveted and there is a need to find a candidate.

Affect toward legislative role

Fig. 4.   Barber's Typology of Legislators' Political Styles

classification to twentieth-century American presidents, drawing on biographical sources. His conclusions are reported in *The Presidential Character: Predicting Performance in the White House* (1972a) and several earlier reports (Barber, 1968a, 1968b, 1971). The presidents are easily classifiable on an active-passive dimension. Calvin Coolidge was notable for his passivity, which extended to 12 hours of nightly sleep and afternoon naps. His personal motto was "Let well enough alone." Coolidge's passivity was far in excess of his go-slow governmental philosphy. His successor, Hoover, shared Coolidge's conservative political philosophy but was clearly an active type. Hoover was constantly at work and otherwise in action from his early morning calisthenics through post-midnight sessions at his desk.

The affective dimension is more difficult to measure at the presidential than at the state level. The rigors of political recruitment are likely to screen out those with an out-and-out distaste for the presidential role. Barber suggests that a somewhat different positive-negative affect dimension *is* evident in the historical record left by the 12 presidents he has studied—Taft through Nixon plus Andrew Johnson. (On the latter, see Barber, 1968a.) This dimension is "general outlook on life." Barber's specific statements of his criteria refer to how the leader "feels about what he does. Relatively speaking, does he seem to experience his political life as happy or sad, enjoyable or discouraging, positive or negative, in its main effect . . . is he someone who, on the surfaces we can see, gives forth the feeling that he has *fun* in political life?" (Barber, 1972a, p. 42) "And how does he feel about his experience—is his effort in life a burden to be endured or an opportunity for personal enjoyment?" (Barber, 1972a, p. 495).[27]

Some of the presidents plainly are optimistic, outgoing, sanguine individuals—for example, that incorrigibly bouncy optimist, Harry S Truman. Others plainly have a more negative characterological cast—the dour Calvin Coolidge is an obvious example. Barber's four presidential types exhibit essentially the same psychological patterns as the four types he identified at the state legislative level, although his second typology is relabeled in terms of the combinations of the two dichotomous defining variables—active-positive, active-negative, passive-positive, and passive-negative. Figure 5 shows the 12 presidents Barber has studied within the categories of his two-by-two classification.

Alexander George (1974) in an extended review article on *The Presidential Character* has raised a variety of searching questions about whether and to what degree Barber has validated his typology and about his specific assignments of presidents to its categories (also see Katz, 1973). Some of George's points suggest refinements implicit in Barber's typology: His two defining variables can usefully be treated as continuous rather than dichotomous, and it would be possible to modify the positive-negative dimension to take account of mood swings and ambivalence of the sort that probably could emerge from clinical studies of Lincoln and Roosevelt. Other of his points seem to demand a more complex and theoretically explicit typology, such as the one illustrated in the theoretical reconstruction of the authoritarian typology in the next section. Barber has subsequently (1974) made more explicit his methodological procedures and the rationale and history of his continuing work on types of leaders.

6.2 Evidence and Inference in the Study of Types of Political Actors

Single-case analysis is widely assumed to be without standards of evidence and inference. In contrast, the psychometric standard operating procedures for multi-case typological research are, if anything, hypertrophied.[28] Yet it is within the well-developed empirical mode of quantitative typological research that some of the most gnarled controversies have occurred, the most striking example of course being the tangled history of authoritarian personality inquiry. Many of the difficulties that arose in the course of authoritarianism research result from what Smelser (1968) calls problems that are "methodological in a theoretical rather than an empirical sense." Even the response-set controversy is not wholly over a matter of measurement mechanics, in that the controversy might have been avoided if adequate conceptualization had oc-

	Active	Passive
Positive	Active-positive (lawmakers) 1. Franklin D. Roosevelt 2. Harry S. Truman 3. John F. Kennedy	Passive-positive (spectators) 9. William H. Taft 10. Warren G. Harding
Negative	Active-negative (advertisers) 4. Andrew Johnson 5. Woodrow Wilson 6. Herbert Hoover 7. Lyndon B. Johnson 8. Richard M. Nixon	Passive-negative (reluctants) 11. Calvin Coolidge 12. Dwight D. Eisenhower

Fig. 5. Barber's Classification of Presidential Style

curred initially. By way of illustration of how adequate conceptualization might eliminate many of the difficulties that plagued authoritarian research, it is informative to reconstruct the authoritarian typology in terms of the phenomenology, dynamics, and psychogenesis of distinctions introduced in Part 3. Such a reconstruction suggests a systematic program of examination of precisely the issues that have led critics and defenders of the validity of the authoritarianism construct to pass each other in the dark.

At the level of phenomenology ("presenting characteristics") a reconstruction of the (hypothesized) typology that was geared to the interests of political psychology might usefully treat as its nuclear traits the pair that Adorno and his associates described as "authoritarian aggression" and "authoritarian submission"—the tendency of the authoritarian to bow to those above him and to seek to dominate those he perceives to be his inferiors. On the basis of their clinical interviews with ethnically prejudiced and nonprejudiced Californians in the 1940s, and to some unknown degree on the basis of earlier clinical writings of Fromm and others, the authors of *The Authoritarian Personality* went on to elaborate a series of further traits that they felt cohered, forming the syndrome they sought to measure in the F scale. These additional aspects of the phenomenology of authoritarianism include the tendency to perceive interpersonal relationships in power terms, stereotypical thinking, "intolerance of ambiguity," and compulsive adherence to the standards of one's social group.

To this constellation of traits there is appended a further, less "obvious" set of traits, seemingly not closely tied to one another but in fact important for the psychodynamic explanation of authoritarianism implied by the authors of *The Authoritarian Personality*. The traits, which are the probable indicators of what I shall call "ego-defensive authoritarianism," include superstition, preoccupation with virility, "hardboiled" toughness in males (the counterpart in women being "pseudofemininity"—adherence to the soft, clinging aspects of a conventionally defined female role). The authoritarian's assumption about human nature tends to be pessimistic and cynical; he believes that "wild and dangerous things go on in the world" and that "the world is a jungle." He shows a prurient concern with the sexual goings-on of others and a punitive interest in seeing that sexual miscreants are punished. Finally, he exhibits "anti-intraception," described as "an attitude of impatience with an opposition to the subjective and the tender-minded," which particularly revolves around an inability to introspect and to acknowledge his feelings and fantasies.

The exposition of the pattern authoritarian traits—i.e., their phenomenology—in *The Authoritarian Personality* tends not to make sharp distinctions between the description of observable surface characteristics and interpretative assertions about underlying psychodynamics. Indeed, one of the traits presented in that exposition, which I have *not* listed as a part of the hypothesized phenomenology of authoritarianism, is "projectivity." This reference to an inner mechanism of defense might better be formulated as a dynamic-level explanation of such outer manifestations as the tendency to perceive hostile agents in the environment.

Even after more than two decades of authoritarianism research, there have been too few systematic empirical efforts to clarify the descriptive traits that are said to constitute the authoritarian type and its various subtypes. Much of the work that has sought to identify naturalistic patterns—e.g., via factor analysis—has relied on the F scale with all its imperfections. An important exception is the study in which Smith (1965) reports a revised questionnaire measure of authoritarianism, corrected through item reversals to take account of response-set tendencies, and validates the revised measure against quantitative scores derived by coding open-ended psychiatric interviews with the same subjects. Neither the psychiatrists who conducted the original interviews nor the psychologists who converted the psychiatric reports to quantitative personality assessment scores were aware of Smith's theoretical interest in the phenomenology of authoritarianism. Nevertheless, these psychiatrist-psychologist teams produced clinical profiles of a number of the subjects that mesh with the characterological portrait set forth in *The Authoritarian Personality*. Smith's success in measuring authoritarianism by an additional, nonquestionnaire procedure is an important demonstration that a real syndrome underlies the psychometric ambiguities of previous research.

In typological as in single-case analysis, the attempt to explain the less "obvious" elements, the apparent inconsistencies, and the distinctive configurations in the phenomenological pattern leads to dynamic interpretation. As we have seen, much of the debate in the authoritarianism literature has been over whether *The Authoritarian Personality* authors' psychodynamic explanation of their research findings was appropriate or whether, in fact, their measurements were simply differentiating between individuals of differing levels of education and conceptual sophistication. Employing distinctions introduced above, one can state *both* of these interpretations in a potentially testable form, leaving open as an empirical question whether either, neither, or both kinds of authoritarianism exist.

The Authoritarian Personality posits what might be called *ego-defensive authoritarianism.* The ego-defensive authoritarian syndrome is the outward manifestation of inner conflicts revolving around repressed hostility to authority figures of the sort that the Georges feel must have been present in Woodrow Wilson. The ego of such an individual defends itself from awareness of potentially threatening insight into such hostilities by the drastic defense mechanism of reaction formation. Thus the ego-defensive authoritarian's attitudes toward authority, which on the surface are highly positive, are in fact ambivalent, with the negative component outside conscious awareness.

Consistent with the Freudian principle of "the return of the repressed," the ego-defensive authoritarian is unable to escape the effect of his powerful though unacknowledged hostile impulses. These have their primary outlet, via projection and displacement, in hostility toward inferiors, socially despised groups, foreign nations, etc. The authoritarian projectively perceives such categories of people as being antagonistic to him; they therefore become legitimate objects for expression of hostility. Simultaneously, there is a generalized diffusion of hostile and negative affect through other aspects of the authoritarian's perceptual and cognitive makeup. The massive energies ego-defensive authoritarians need to invest in repression have further basic cognitive and affective consequences in their general uneasiness with feelings and their reluctance to engage in introspection.[29]

The prevailing alternative theory of the source of authoritarianism can be conveniently labeled the *cognitive authoritarianism* typology. Descriptions of this syndrome, as presently elaborated in the literature, are scarcely detailed enough to warrant the label "typology." Essentially it is argued that the life circumstances of some classes of individuals encourage them to think in the simplistic terms in which the various assertions of the F scale are couched. What ensues in most discussions of cognitive authoritarianism is less a detailed analysis of psychological functioning than a discussion of the prevailing social norms and life circumstances in the populations (for example, lower education groups) believed to be characterized by this kind of authoritarianism. For an extended effort to treat F-scale findings in cognitive terms, see Selznick and Steinberg (1969).

How would one distinguish between ego-defensive and cognitive authoritarians? In terms of the various analytic notions I have been setting forth, the research task would be to establish which aspects of the phenomenological presenting characteristics of authoritarians are associated with differing functional bases. I have already suggested one possibility: that cognitive authoritarians would exhibit the first "more obvious" cluster of phenomenology indicated above but not the "less obvious" traits, such as resistance to introspection. The motivational basis also might be established by administering other measures of the individual's contemporaneous personality to assess basic levels of ego-defensive need and cognitive capacity. Motivation can also be illuminated by developmental data and by information about the behavioral consequences of holding authoritarianism-based attitudes. As we saw in the discussion of the functional bases of opinions, beliefs with differing functional underpinnings seem to have different arousal and change properties.

The psychogenetic elements of the cognitive model stress simple acquisition of the prevailing norms in one's environment. An example of this sort of reasoning can be found in Pettigrew's (1958) ingenious argument that cognitively based racial prejudice is more common in the American South, where prejudice is a learned cultural norm, than in the North. In the North bigotry is more likely to have an ego-defensive basis. The psychogenesis of ego-defensive authoritarianism is described by Frenkel-Brunswik (1954). In very brief summary, children are likely to acquire such a character structure if they are raised in ways that at the same time exacerbate their impulses—for example, to strike out at the authorities in their life—and inhibit expression and even conscious awareness of these very same impulses.

7. AGGREGATIVE ANALYSES OF PERSONALITY AND POLITICS

By "aggregation" I refer to the effects of individual and typical political actors on political collectivities, ranging from ephemeral two-person subsystems (e.g., temporary work groups in administrative bureaus) all the way through stable systems of international political interactions (e.g., consortiums of militarily allied nations). Aggregative analysis is problematic because when two or more individuals operate in concert, the result of their activity is rarely a simple arithmetic sum. Individual A may be a dictator and B a minor subordinate; an individual added to a group may *reduce* rather than increase group productivity. These, of course, are the issues alluded to in the final sections of Parts 2 and 3. (For a general empirical effort to connect individuals with collectivities, see the selections in Section III of Lazarsfeld *et al.,* 1972.)

7.1 The Literature on Aggregation

In especially the older personality-and-politics literature there is a widespread failure to recognize that extrapolations from personal-level data to system-level explanations *are* problematic. Inkeles and Levinson (1954, p. 977) point out in their classic review essay on "modal personality," for example, that many of the early writings on national character, such as Ruth Benedict's *Patterns of Culture* (1934), tended not to make "a clear conceptual distinction between the sociocultural system and the personality." Instead it appears to have been "assumed that the individual personality was isomorphic with the psychological coherence of the culture." Obviously it is not. Yet even the most stringent critique of "reductionism" does not gainsay the possibility that individual dispositions will make *some* contributions to larger sociocultural phenomena (cf. Webster, 1973). It is difficult to preclude the possibility that *how* institutions work is in some way connected with *who* works them.

One example of an aggregative analysis at the subnational level is Barber's speculative account in *The Lawmakers* on how each of his four types fits into the functioning of a legislature. The Lawmaker type invests the necessary energy and disciplined rationality for the work of hammering out policies; the Advertiser provides some of the emotional fervor that elicits political interest on the part of wider audiences; the Spectator is a potential mediator and loyal supporter; the Reluctant can serve as custodian of the rules. But Barber's suggestions await empirical testing.

By far the best known, if not the best respected, attempts to argue from psychological data to political-system characteristics are in the national-character literature, which is a more or less linear antecedent of present work in "political culture" (Verba, 1965). Beginning roughly in the 1930s, a number of anthropologists sought to explain the cultural patterns of simple, preliterate societies in psychodynamic terms, with particular attention to how child-rearing practices generate certain typical personality structures. (For a historical summary of culture-and-personality studies, see Singer, 1961.) During World War II the same analytic lenses were applied to advanced, complex societies by scholarly consultants to the allied powers. As might be expected, there was a particular emphasis on studies of the Germans and Japanese, as in Benedict's *The Chrysanthemum and the Sword* (1946) and Dicks's "Personality Traits and National Socialist Ideology" (1950), both of which appear to have had a prepublication life as background documents for allied leaders. (Also see Kecskemeti and Leites, 1948a, b, c). In addition, there were inter-allied analyses such as Margaret Mead's (1942) effort to explain the Americans and English to each other. National-character writings continued to flourish during the early cold-war years, with the attention shifting to new adversaries (e.g., Gorer and Rickman, 1949; Dicks, 1952; Solomon, 1971).

By 1950 the national-character literature was as controversial and critique-ridden as the authoritarianism literature became a few years later. Critics pointed to an array of problems remarkably similar in some respects to the difficulties in early single-case and typological works. They noted the following.

1. Excessive emphasis on early-childhood socialization practices as a critical, if not the only, determinant of adult behavior.

2. Reliance on unsatisfactory data sources—notably anthropological informants rather than direct observations of representative cross-sections of the relevant populations, whether via interviews and testing or through observations of actual behavior *in situ*.

3. Implicit, uncritical use of the assumption that a culture or society would

in fact *have* a single predominant personality type. (The term *modal* personality was offered by Inkeles and Levinson, 1954, as a substitute for "national character" with a view to leaving empirically open the possibility that a society might not have a single typical personality type but rather might be multimodal or might even have *no* significant personality modalities.)

4. The unspoken assumption that patterns of culture *do* in fact have their roots in personality dynamics—an assumption which in itself is further complicated by the prevailing semantic confusion about what is meant by such terms as "culture," "personality," and "social structure."

5. The tendency to assume, rather than empirically establish, that there are smooth congruences between typical personality patterns in a nation (or, pushing even further back in the causal chain, typical early-childhood socialization practices) and complex historical and sociopolitical phenomena. (It is *de rigeur* in critiques of this aspect of the national-character literature to refer to the inferential flights of the English anthropologist Geoffrey Gorer—for example, his attempt to link the infant-swaddling practices said to have been prevalent in Great Russia during the childhood of the first generation of Soviet leaders with Soviet foreign policy (Gorer and Rickman, 1949) and a passage in his *The American People* [1948; revised edition, 1964, p. 96] in which the alleged irresponsibility of the American House of Representatives vis à vis the Senate is seen as an extension of an alleged tendency for younger brothers in the United States to be irresponsible.)

Another body of literature in which fairly direct and unqualified connections are made between individual psychological motivational patterns, especially the need for achievement, and national economic growth rates is the extended array of studies summarized in McClelland's (1961) work on the presence of achievement motivation in national populations and national economic growth rates. (Also see Hagen, 1962.) Although McClelland's dependent variable is not political,[30] his work and the comments on it by his various critics bear examination by students of personality and politics, since virtually identical issues arise in both literatures.

A final aggregative personality-and-politics literature—also presently out of fashion but, like the national-character literature, always likely to be resurrected in new garb—is on personal psychological needs and the international conflict. Again Freud is a seminal source—notably his *Civilization and Its Discontents* (1930), which argues that the renunciation of instinctual needs required for civilization results in a building up of destructive impulses that fuel aggressiveness and international conflict. Later elaborations of this thesis—many of them under the auspices of UNESCO in the immediate postwar period—tended to operate with similar assumptions but to reach less pessimistic conclusions about the inevitability of war (for example, Klineberg, 1950; Bramson and Goethals, 1964). From time to time there also have been extrapolations from the animal behavior and human physiology literatures with a view to providing biosocial explanations of human conflict (see the summary by J. C. Davies, 1973).

A paradigmatic presentation of the private tensions → international conflict thesis is Talcott Parson's (1947) essay "Certain Primary Sources and Patterns of Aggression in the Social Structure of the Western World." Parsons argues that certain predictable tensions conducive to interpersonal conflict arise from relations in the nuclear family, from the strains of learning to fill occupational roles, and from adult-role requirements. Strong inhibitions exist against expression of these strains in the face-to-face environment. Instead, the well-known ego-defense mechanisms of projection and displacement channel aggressive impulses outward. In the first instance, this channeling contributes to intrasocietal group polarization, but needs to maintain some level of cohesion within the nation lead finally to displacement of aggressive impulses (via nationalist attitudes) into international conflict.

But as Waltz (1959) points out, such human frustrations are more or less constant, but international conflict is variable. Therefore, at a minimum, the individual tensions → war formula would have to be severely qualified and put in the context of a larger, multivariate explanatory model. Further, as Osgood (1955) has pointed out, the entire analysis rests on assumptions about the nature of international conflict and the normal state of international politics, which are ahistorical and unpolitical. There is little appreciation in such analyses of the importance of national-interests determinants of international relations and of the significance of the absence of a central legitimate mechanism for the conduct of politics between nations. The notion of "interest" as a determinant of international relations provides the basis for an account of the motivation of international decision makers that places special emphasis on cognitive orientations about means-ends relationships in the international arena and self-other orientations about the responsibilities of national leaders to reference groups in their own nations, in lieu of Parsons's emphasis on ego-defensive motivational determinants of international conflict. (On the psychology of foreign policy-making, see George, 1972, and de Rivera, 1968.)

Processes of aggregation are not mere summations of the dispositions of the individuals in aggregates for two reasons implicit in the Osgood critique of formulations such as that of Parsons. First, such formulations tend to treat all members of political systems as if they have identical impacts, whereas there is a massively greater impact of leaders than followers on political, including military, outcomes. Second, such formulations tend to assume that behavior is motivated by the ends it serves. Certainly this is sometimes true: Saints and philanthropists may often seek to help others out of a desire to be helpful. But as Adam Smith long ago pointed out, the butcher and the baker purvey their wares for profit rather than to feed society. The aggressiveness-

and-war literature and the animal behavior-human physiology-and-war-literature both tend to assume that aggressive motivations are necessary for aggressive behavior.

Recent research provides instructive illustrations of the shortcomings of such formulations.[31] A quite striking and suggestive research report by Peter Bourne (1971), former chief of the Neuropsychiatry Section of the U.S. Army Medical Team in Vietnam, uses both physiochemical and psychological data in an analysis that is consistent with the monitory themes of this chapter. Using medical and logistical technology that was not available as recently as the Korean war, Bourne measured adrenal function via levels of 17-hydro-oxycorticosteroid in urine, thus obtaining a physical measure of chronic inner stress. He studied members of a helicopter medical aid team and a Special Forces group on hazardous duty in Vietnam. There were regular psychiatric interviews and physiochemical measurements during episodes of relative quiet and during periods of intense combat or imminent threat of combat. Previous research had established normal 17-hydro-oxycorticosteroid levels and normal alterations of level in individuals subjected to stress (race drivers, runners, patients prior to open-heart surgery).

Bourne's findings reveal exactly the sort of complexly interactive pattern that "ought" to be found in careful, theoretically informed analyses of the connections between psychological and physiological variables with behavior. Contrary to the assumption that military activity is likely to have its motivating basis in states of emotional excitation, the helicopter crew members (all of whom were enlisted men) showed abnormally *low* levels of adrenal secretion. These levels did not vary as the intensity of combat exposure increased, although they *did* vary under situations of *personal* stress, such as severe accidental injury. The helicopter crewman appeared able to ward off severe anxiety by concentration on the mechanical tasks at hand and by a series of psychological defenses of a magical-fatalistic sort.

The Special Forces combat team exhibited a somewhat different pattern and certainly one that justifies still another use on my part of the overworked term "complex." Members of this team, which was in enemy territory and "under constant threat of attack by an overwhelmingly superior force," also showed lower mean secretion levels than normal populations. But the secretion levels of officers were significantly higher than those of the enlisted men, and this difference was wholly consistent with the psychiatric evidence that the officers underwent severe stress as a result of the uncertainty and responsibility of leadership, whereas the enlisted men "bound" anxiety via bravado, magical thinking, and a concentration on the routine mechanical aspects of their tasks. Furthermore, at the point of imminent enemy attack on the camp, officers' secretion levels *rose* dramatically and those of enlisted men *declined*. Bourne (1971, p. 287) advances the following speculation at the conclusion of his paper.

At first glance, it might appear that these findings in humans contradict the extensive data on the physiological aspects of aggressive behavior in animals. However, close examination indicates that, for many reasons, warfare among nations cannot be equated either psychologically or physiologically with aggressive behavior in animals. First, it is highly institutionalized, with the individual soldier having virtually no control over and little emotional investment in the decisions made by his leaders. He finds himself compelled to follow their wishes, and his concern becomes one of surviving in a socially acceptable way rather than being in a state of personal aggressive arousal. Second, warfare, particularly for the pilot dropping bombs or even the foot soldier using a gun, has become a mechanistic act which in most instances is quite depersonalized. Much of the time the soldier feels he is merely doing a job and experiences little sense of animosity or aggressivity. Third, human psychic processes enable man to divorce himself emotionally from events that are threatening or aggressive in a way which presumably animals are incapable of doing.

Bourne's conclusion fits remarkably well with the carefully reasoned recent discussion and data presentation by Ray (1972), who argues against the widespread assumption among some political psychologists that "psychopathological" or at least aggressive attitudes are the necessary antecedents of "militarism"; both commentators deny that a single dispositional state can account for military behavior. In this respect, it is also interesting to note Dicks's (1972) conclusion, on the basis of his psychiatric interviews with Nazi S.S. killers, that conformity needs rather than psychiatric disorders of the sort that produce aggressive symptomatology motivated their behavior.

7.2 *Evidence and Inference in the Study of Aggregation*

Here at best it seems possible only to note an array of complementary strategies. In doing so, we will find it helpful to return for a final time to that cornucopia of illustrative points about the problems of studying personality and politics, *The Authoritarian Personality*. There are important aggregative implications to assertions in that work, although they are not so well developed there as they were in one of its intellectual sources, Fromm's *Escape from Freedom* (1941).

Fromm was quite explicit in his belief that authoritarian characterology was a critical link in the submission of a mass population to authoritarian rule in Nazi Germany, as well as a key element contributing to the maintenance of the industrial hierarchies that provide the basis of technologically advanced societies. Adorno and his associates were less prone to make sweeping aggregative inferences, and at various points in *The Authoritarian Personality* or elsewhere (e.g., Frenkel-Brunswik, 1954, p. 228), they have alluded to the complexity of inference from personality structure to political structure. Nevertheless, by describing the character structure they were setting forth as "pre-

Fascist" and by connecting such descriptions with references to the "great . . . Fascist potential" in American society (Adorno *et al.*, 1950, p. 974), they clearly left the implication that the potentiality for authoritarian rule in a society might well be a linear function of the incidence of authoritarian personality types in that society. In such passages, their implicit logic was similar to that of the national-character and international-tensions theorists. (For an important early essay correcting such interpretative practices by an early contributor to the national-character literature, see Leites, 1948.)

One means of avoiding such fallacies of composition is simply to be systematically attentive to the points of linkage between micro- and macrophenomena, since at all the key transitional points it is possible that there will be departures from a simple additivity. We may most usefully do this by drawing on the numbered list of the elements in Figure 3, realizing that each number in that figure constitutes a link in a causal chain that may or may not obtain.

Whereas some of the early culture-and-personality writers tended to make sonality structures to the larger societal structures, there are numerous causal inferences directly from childhood socialization or, at best, adult modal perlinks that need to be explicitly studied before micro → macro inferences can be accepted. Consider this causal chain: physical underpinnings of personality → childhood socialization → contemporary basic personality structures → conscious sociopolitical orientations → immediate environment stimuli → individual and typical political behavior → aggregative effects on immediate and larger environment politics and society. At *each* of these linkage points the causal arrow might better be expressed as an inequality sign, given the considerable likelihood that the connections will be complex and possibly not even necessarily positive.[32] (One more authoritarian guard added to a prison staff may produce an inmate takeover rather than a slightly more rigorous prison authority structure.)

There are no simple rules of aggregative analysis apart from the warning that the aggregator take stock of the complex sequence just summarized in his theory construction and research design. Aggregative analysis is difficult but necessary, for it does in fact seem likely that a great many macrostructures cannot be properly understood without attention to the individuals and types of individuals of whom they are composed. It *is* possible to note a number of promising and potentially complementary strategies that have been used in some of the more rigorous aggregative analyses to date.

1. *"Building up" from direct observation of small-scale political processes.*
The admonition that behavior be analyzed as a joint function of the psychological predispositions of the actors and their environmental setting, if carefully followed, provides a first step toward careful assessment of aggregative relation-

ships in that it establishes empirically rather than assuming *a priori* the links
between predispositions and behavior in the sequence of inequalities just
summarized. For example, if a study is made of the dispositions and role per-
formances of the members of a congressional committee, depending on the way
the committee is organized and the power relationships on it, a different degree
of emphasis might be placed on the chairman's dispositions in seeking to
account for such aspects of the overall performance of the committee as its
success on the floor of Congress.

Specific examples of studies that very carefully articulate personality
analysis, with attention to the "situational texture" of the setting of political
action, are George and George's (1956) analysis of certain of the situations
within which Wilson found himself, such as the Paris Conference that framed
the Versailles Treaty, and the interesting monograph by Hodgson, Levinson,
and Zaleznik (1965), which carefully explores the interconnections of three
top executives of an organization. Also see Zaleznik (1965, 1966) and the
important study of politicians and nonpoliticians in a number of quite disparate political settings by Browning and Jacob (1964) and Browning (1968).[33]

**2. Relating frequencies of psychological characteristics to system charac-
teristics.** Gorer connected the alleged fecklessness of younger brothers in the
United States with an equally undocumented institutional pattern. It is clearly
an advance over this procedure if (a) the distribution of psychological orientations in the population is established empirically, (b) the dependent variable
is also documented, and (c) the dependent variable is one that can reasonably
be assumed to result from the aggregation of individuals falling into the
predicted categories of the independent variables. Several voting surveys have
established convincing relationships of this sort, using psychological data on
conscious political orientations—for example, Angus Campbell's (1960) explanation of the regular decrease of support for the presidential party in the
American midterm congressional elections in terms of the differing psychological characteristics of the presidential and congressional year electorates.[34]

3. Modifying the frequency analysis to take account of "nonadditivity."
As has been several times noted, not all political actors have equal effects on
the political aggregations within which they interact. Therefore, aggregative
analyses of phenomena in which particular role incumbents (whether leaders
or not) are important have to be modified accordingly.

**4. "Working back" from theoretical analyses of systems and their psychologi-
cal requirements.** Political science, like sociology, often raises psychological
issues that differ from those typically of interest to psychologists. The reason
is that the first two disciplines are concerned not with individual functioning
in general but rather with aspects of individual functioning that contribute

to the performance of systems (Inkeles, 1968; Greenstein, 1970a). Thus a further approach to disciplined aggregative analysis involves systematic attention to the roles that constitute whatever institutional pattern interests the political or social analyst. These roles in turn may have distinctive psychological requirements. For an example of such an analysis of role requirements and personality needs, see Lasswell's (1951) essay, "The Democratic Character." (Also see Greenstein, 1966.)

8. THE CONTEXTUAL NATURE OF PERSONALITY-AND-POLITICS CONNECTIONS: AN ILLUSTRATIVE LITERATURE REVIEW

The bewildering profusion of studies and commentaries spawned by the college and university campus conflict in the 1960s and 1970s provides an outstanding opportunity to apply the intellectual strategy of contextual mapping and to search for interactive relationships outlined in this chapter. Colleges and universities have political structures and dynamics. They come conveniently populated with behavior scientists who have a variety of incentives to conduct research on theoretically or practically interesting campus phenomena. And from the mid-1960s through the early 1970s, there were varied manifestations of protest politics that could be studied at the individual, typological, and aggregative levels.

A remarkable number of studies were conducted in various institutions within the extraordinarily variegated American college and university system. The Keniston-Lerner (1971b) bibliographical review lists 211 reports of studies conducted in the United States. (See also Keniston, 1973, and Altbach and Kelly, 1973.) Considerable further research—though most of it not with behavioral-science techniques—has been done on student activism and university politics elsewhere in the world.

Even if only American academia is considered, there is enormous scope for comparison of contexts. The variation is great in both environmental and predispositional variables because of the range of institutional structures—from mega-university to junior college, from rigorous selectivity to open admissions —as well as variation by race, sex, and geographical area. When campus activism and conflict are being studied, the additional variable of *time* is important, since American university conflict of the given period went through the life cycle characteristic of social movements.

All of this would be beside the point for the present purposes were it not also true that much of the popular and specialized discussion of student activism explicitly raises questions about the personal psychological qualities of activists: Were the activists "maladjusted"? Were they intelligent idealists who had the perspicacity to see the unclothed emperor? Were they conforming to a fad? Questions of this sort led to the generation of much personality data on student activists. Many of the interpretative issues in this literature can be rephrased and coordinated in terms of the broad context provided by our map.

The many findings from studies that were done with the typical loose coordination that occurs as different investigators "do their thing" leave the collective impression of a mosaicist's workshop in which there are countless unassembled tiles. It would be optimistic to think that the map will make it possible to put together a single coherent mosaic. Nevertheless, many more of the findings seem to fit together in terms of the distinctions of Figure 3 than might be thought possible. And some seeming conflicts appear reconcilable—for example, the conceptually based disagreement discussed in Part III about whether social or personality characteristics were more important in accounting for student activism.

Space permits reference to only a handful of studies and interpretations that fit into some of the Figure 3 categories, and it should be stressed that this selective literature summary is illustrative and does not purport to reach a "true" conclusion about activism nd campus conflict.

Category 1. *Historical larger-society antecedents* of university conflict, with emphasis on national variation, are reviewed by Shils (1969), who makes it clear that although conflict took distinctive national form in the sixties, there also was an *international contagion* of activism. Thus the entire phenomenon of activism and conflict in the sixties was in part dependent on the historical diffusion of ideologies and behavioral modes. The individual-level concomitants of activism would not have had this consequence at other periods of time.

Category 2. *The immediate environment socialization experiences* of a varied array of types of activists and nonactivists are studied (perforce via retrospective measures) by Block, Haan, and Smith (1969); Flacks (1967); Everson (1970); and Dunlap (1970b). For different periods of time and institutions, different backgrounds and socializing experiences are associated with activism.

Categories 3–6. The *psychological predispositions* of student activists are reported in all the publications cited under the previous heading, plus Keniston (1970) and Kerpelman (1972). Many of the interesting findings and controversies of interpretation revolve around attempts to ascertain whether and to what degree political orientations and behavior of activists served cognitive versus ego-defensive needs. Flacks's (1967) early report of University of Chicago activists rejected the ego-defensive interpretation that student rebels were going through "acting-out" rebellions against parental authority and instead reported data suggesting that the student activists were strong in rational needs and capacities. Flacks failed, however, to theorize or examine his data in ways that might test for student populations Barber's thesis about political system politicians—that they tend to be deviant at both the positive and the negative modes of the distribution of personality strength in the population. Rather, Flacks's implication was that activists were distinguished only by their "healthy" qualities.[35]

Later research came up with intriguing departures from Flacks's findings. Block, Haan, and Smith (1969) reanalyzed the findings from their study of activists in the very first wave of student demonstrations at Berkeley in 1965. Employing a cross-classification typology based on whether the students did or did not participate in social-service and in protest activity, they found that the political behavior of those of the demonstrators who were involved in *both* protest activism *and* social-service activities appeared primarily to be based on their considerable ego-strength and cognitive needs. The behavior of those who were active *only* in protest (the "dissenter" type) showed a more ego-defensive profile. (Also see Smith, Haan, and Block, 1970.)

After these studies of the first wave of activism, research was done at the less prestigious colleges and universities, where activism arrived later and at a time when the physical stigmata of activism (peace symbols, hip regalia) had become fashionable for most young people. Studies of University of Oregon students (Dunlap, 1970b) and students at Southern Illinois University (Everson, 1970) were less likely to find *any* distinctive activist characteristics than the earlier studies of trend-setting student activists at Berkeley and Chicago. Activism for the moment was becoming more of a constant than a variable and therefore was losing its distinctive correlates.[36]

Category 7. Because research has been in such a diverse range of institutional types, varying in such aspects of the student's day-to-day life as class size, faculty-student ratio, academic climate, etc., the literature provides insight into *immediate environment* antecedents of student protest. For a general treatment of universities as political structures, see Parsons (1969). For evidence of the incidence of violent and nonviolent campus by institutional type, see Astin (1970); Bayer and Astin (1969, 1971); Keniston and Lerner (1971a); and Scott and El-Assal (1969). There were year-to-year shifts in the types of institutions that experienced conflict; the protest wave of the 1960s (and those continuing protests of the early 1970s) had distinctive cyclical patterns.

Category 8. One obvious feature of the *contemporary larger society* which in many respects overrode the immediate characteristics of college and universities (cf. Dunlap, 1970a) was the presence of the Vietnam war. Indeed, it was an event in the larger environment, the Nixon Administration's invasion of Cambodia in the spring of 1970 followed by the killing of student protestors at Kent State University, that led to the highest point of college and university protests, including protest activity in institutions that had hitherto never even experienced significant activism (Peterson and Bilorusky, 1971).

I will not continue this analysis through categories 9 and 10 of the listing of variables—the actual incidence of protest behavior (which largely duplicates the types of studies noted under category 7) and the consequences of student political activity for the future states of the students themselves and their immediate and future environments—other than to say that many changes were made in campus governance as a result of the wave of protest activity we have been discussing. Moreover, it is widely believed that the protests were consequential for the larger society even if they were not the sole causes of such celebrated events of the period as the decision of President Johnson not to seek renomination and the removal of United States ground combat forces from South Vietnam during the first four years of the Nixon Administration.

As is evident, the student-activism—campus-conflict literature draws on all three of the basic modes of personality-and-politics inquiry. One senses intuitively that the personal qualities of individual university administrators and student leaders—their values, motivations, political skills, etc.—were an important source of the variance in whether campuswide conflicts occurred and how they manifested themselves, even though the role of individuals in the conflicts of the period has not been carefully examined. The catalytic qualities of leadership undoubtedly account for much of the unexplained variance in comparative analyses of institutional output. Psychological typologies like that of Block, Haan, and Smith noted above abound in the literature. Individuals and types aggregated to produce collective outcomes in the form of conflict and absence of conflict, institutional change, and continuity.

9. SUMMARY AND CONCLUSIONS

The following statements are in part a very generalized summary of themes in the chapter and in part an attempt to make explicit the assumptions and point of view that inform the chapter.

The personal qualities of political actors exercise a ubiquitous and omnipresent influence on political processes. This influence, portions of which are readily evident to anyone who closely observes the "inside" of political events and outcomes, is directly and significantly consequential for the capacity of politics and government to meet the needs of mankind. "Human factors" are involved both in conspicuously "successful" politics and government and in the chronic inability of the human species to manage its own affairs with anything like its capacity to manipulate physical phenomena—including the technology of destruction. If better understanding of the human wellsprings of political behavior is at all likely to contribute to more satisfactory solutions to the problems of governance, systematic efforts to acquire such knowledge seems to be in order. But there are serious obstacles to such efforts.

One such obstacle is the evident complexity of human psychological functioning and of the ways that psychological dispositions link with individual and collective behavior.

A parallel and perhaps more onerous obstacle is the state of discourse about psychology and about the connections between psychology and politics. Not only is there the controversy about personality-and-politics literature noted above, but there also is an abundance of disagreement and controversy within psychology on virtually any and all issues about the nature and proper study of human psychological functioning in general. These obstacles can be mitigated if not eliminated by strategies such as the following.

Conceptual and theoretical clarification seems necessary, even at the risk of generating more words about words, both because existing controversies stand in the way of inquiry and because there is a general need for overall perspective in dealing with such complex phenomena.

Methodological pluralism is in order. The subject matter of personality and politics admits of highly diverse analytic approaches: psychopolitical case studies of single actors, actuarial psychometric studies, historical or participant-observation studies of decision-making processes, experiments, simulations, etc. It is unlikely that any one approach will ever offer "all the answers," and even if such intellectual units were to be established in the long run, the units would occur only through the short-run play of diversity.

Theoretical ecumenicism is in order. There clearly are aspects of political psychology that can be illuminated by the diverse theoretical emphases within personality psychology—for example, the dynamic psychologies, cognitive psychology, learning theory, the functional approach recommended in this chapter, and various social psychological approaches, as well as theories designed to connect personal dispositions with social and political structures. Conceptualizations are needed that are sufficiently wide-ranging and agnostic about ultimate empirical connections not to preclude unraveling the multivariate connections that seem to obtain.

Finally, complex realities call for theories that prepare investigators to identify complex relationships. This is not a counsel of vagueness or an assertion that personality-and-politics connections are too obscure or irregular to be detected and identified. Rather, it is an admonition to search for the contingent, interactive relationships that actually exist. The effects of any psychological variable on political behavior may be moderated or enhanced by structural factors that cause psychological dispositions to have different behavioral consequences in one setting than another and by other individual psychological dispositions that may interact with the variable of interest. Moreover, complexity marks the way that the individual and typical behavior patterns aggregate into larger sociopolitical structures and processes.

* * *

Most of the foregoing summary and conclusion points cannot be "proven," in some cases because knowledge at the present stage of political studies is limited and in others because their heuristic nature makes testability beside the point. Among the presently untested assumptions is the one with which these concluding remarks began: that personal influences on political behavior are highly consequential for the human condition. The greater one's suspicion that this assertion is true in significant respects, the more likely one is to be disposed to seek knowledge in this area, in spite of the obvious obstacles.

NOTES

1. See especially the review by Merelman (1970), which succinctly raises a number of the most fundamental problems that face those who seek to place personality-and-politics inquiry on a solidly cumulative basis.

2. The dualistic distinction of inner-outer is a chronically troublesome issue in philosophy. It would not be profitable to pursue here the well-worn disagreements among philosophical idealists, materialists, empiricists, dualists, etc. For the argument that first the inner-outer issue has been falsely imposed by linguistic and conceptual assumptions deeply embedded in Western thought, and then the "problem," once falsely generated, has become a major source of philosophical make-work, see Geiger (1958) and Dewey and Bentley (1949).

3. For an ideal-typical illustration of such rationalization, see the passage in Lasswell (1930, p. 20) describing the circumstances in which a subject under posthypnotic suggestion follows the instruction to open an umbrella. When asked why he did so, he gives as his "reason" that he wanted to see if it was his, rather than his real motivation, which is out of conscious awareness. Needless to say, it is by no means simple to distinguish a rationalization from a conscious reason for behavior, although psychophysical-measurements technology permitting the measurement of skin conductivity, eyeball contractions, and other somatic concomitants of underlying states offer interesting possibilities.

4. Obviously, Smith's "mediation of self-other relations" and Freud's "superego" have substantially different connotations. Bear in mind, however, that Freud thought of the superego as an internalization by the child of parental values and as a vehicle for identification with them and with ideal examplars (the ego-ideal).

5. Note that in this formulation of the question about how personality and situational factors relate to each other, personality is used in the broad psychologist's sense of referring to predispositions in general. Obviously this formulation can and must be further narrowed in actual contexts of inquiry to refer to particular aspects and levels of personality. Unquestionably the major dividing point between those who do and those who do not consider "personality" to be politically consequential is whether and to what degree the personality levels labeled "functional bases" in Figures 2 and 3 affect politics.

6. The supporting discussion of this proposition and those that follow is presented more fully—with indications of sources—in Greenstein (1969, Chapter 2).

7. Propositions 9 and 11 are slightly rephrased from the comparable propositions in Greenstein (1969).

8. Each of these propositions is more fully supported in Greenstein (1969, Chapter 2).

9. Ackerman and Jahoda (1950) in a study of attitudes toward Jews in a population

of emotionally disturbed individuals discovered anti-Semitism only where the psychiatric symptomatology took the form of externalization of blame for one's difficulties and never among depressive neurotics. This finding, like those of Rutherford, suggests that it is not the distribution of ego defensiveness in general in populations that is likely to be politically consequential, but the distribution of particular types of ego defensiveness.

10. In turn, the external reactions may have internal consequences. For a discussion of how two American politicians, Harry S Truman and Chester A. Arthur, changed their political styles—and possibly also underwent more substantial psychological change—on assuming high office, see Rogow and Laswell (1963). See Neustadt (1960, Chapter 4) for a penetrating analysis of how the President's significant others in the Washington community orient themselves by observing the President's day-to-day activities, emphases, levels of commitment to issues and individuals, etc. On *public* expectations about the President, see Greenstein (1965).

11. For a sensitive discussion of how culturally prevalent patterns—in this case the whipping of children—may produce ego-defensive personality needs in some individuals and not in others, see Erikson (1958, pp. 64–80). A further illustration of the false juxtaposition of cultural and personality determinants of behavior is the argument that Woodrow Wilson's famous refusal to compromise with the Senate of the United States to achieve ratification of the Versailles Treaty resulted from his "Calvinist upbringing" rather than his "personality rigidities." For a penetrating treatment of this assertion about Wilson with broader implications for the present discussion, see George (1971).

12. "When conflicting hypotheses concerning complex processes survive from decade to decade, the explanation may lie in the treachery of words, rather than the structure of the phenomena" (Lasswell, 1951, p. 487). A valuable recent attempt to set the out-of-fashion culture-and-personality literature on firm footing is LeVine (1973).

13. As with my other propositional lists, the rationale of the one that follows is more fully discussed in Greenstein (1969, Chapter 2).

14. For an account of Lenin's role in the October Revolution that is not informed by Hook's concerns but reaches partially similar conclusions, see Daniels, 1967.

15. In which case firm decisions inevitably have to be made at the individual level about such matters as commitment, treatment, and discharge. In this respect the psychotherapist's task is strikingly parallel to that of the psychobiographer seeking to establish the personal contribution of a political actor to some larger event. Psychodiagnoses of single political actors have been conducted for some years by the United States Central Intelligence Agency. These efforts to use psychiatric principles to predict —or at any rate better anticipate—the behavior of individual political actors are said to have been used exclusively on leaders and other figures in nations other than the United States, with the exception of the controversial analysis of Daniel Ellsberg in connection with his release of the Pentagon Papers. The Ellsberg profile was published in the August 3, 1973, *New York Times*.

16. Studies based on very large samples sometimes *do* make it possible to measure highly "specialized" relationships. For example, Morris Rosenberg (1965) found strikingly higher self-esteem among younger brothers whose older siblings "are chiefly and exclusively girls," a finding that was possible only because Rosenberg's original sample was quite large.

17. Unfortunately, there has been no replication of these interesting findings.

18. In terms, for example, of clarity of terminology and the degree to which even potentially falsifiable propositions are enunciated.

19. Also see Wolfenstein's later psychoanalytic interpretation of Churchill, Malcolm X, and Nietzsche (1969).

20. Compare Barber's cautiously inductive psychodiagnosis of President Nixon with Mazlish's (1972) explicit use of psychoanalytic categories.

21. These disagreements have been evident in the flourishing debate over the past decade on the relative merits of behavioristic psychological therapy (behavior therapy) and the more orthodox insight therapies that seek to make patients aware of inner disturbances that are at the root of their symptomatic behavior. See the summary of the literature by Mikulas (1972, especially pp. 90–92).

22. Nothing said here is meant to gainsay the importance of clinical imagination and empathy in single-case analysis. These are aspects of the logic of discovery; my concern here is with demonstration.

23. Lasswell's three terms parallel my phenomenology-dynamics-genesis distinction.

24. It is impossible to name a single discoverer of the construct "authoritarian personality"; this notion was very much "in the air" in the 1930s. It appears in an essay entitled "The Authoritarian Character Structure" by Maslow (1943), in Edwards's (1941) psychometric research on "Fascist attitudes," and above all in the work of a number of emigré German scholars reported in *Studien über Autorität und Familie* (Horkheimer, 1936). One of the latter, Erich Fromm, then went on to popularize the construct in his Freudian-Marxist analysis of the rise of totalitarianism in Germany and the psychological roots of modern industrial societies—*Escape from Freedom* (1941).

25. A belief that later resurrected itself in writings on the psychology of student activities. See especially Bay (1958, 1967) and Berns (1961); also Hampden-Turner (1970).

26. Also note Carr's application of reverse-worded "anomie" scales to samples of poor Southern blacks who agreed with either version of the scale (Carr, 1971; Proctor, 1971). For a convenient bibliographical source of different versions of the F, anomie, and other scales, see Bonjean, Hill, and McLemore (1967). For a study that seeks to use both positive ("agree") and negative ("disagree") response set as measures of personality, see Couch and Keniston (1960). On the study of anomie and alienation, see Yinger (1973).

27. For an attempt to apply his classification to the 1972 presidential candidates, see Barber (1972b). Payne has both expanded on and contracted Barber's approach, devising a series of indexes for classifying politicians in terms of motivational (or, as he puts it, incentive) type but explicitly avoiding characterological issues. For a summary of his and related work, see Payne and Woshinsky (1972) and Payne (1972).

28. I shall not here discuss such matters as measurement of reliability and validity of personality scales. Of the many available works on the topic, the student could appropriately start with the textbooks of Edwards (1970) and Michael (1968).

29. Schulberg (1962) and, especially, Kogan (1956) are among the few investigators who explicitly designed research addressed to the dynamic hypotheses about ego-defensive authoritarianism.

30. However, some political research has been done using McClelland's projective-test indicators of psychological states. See Browning and Jacob (1964); Donley and Winter (1970); Greene and Winter (1971); and Winter and Wiecking (1971).

31. The rest of this paragraph and the following three paragraphs are reprinted with slight changes from Greenstein (1973, pp. 465–466).

32. LeVine (1960) suggests that in simple societies child-rearing practices and modal personality distributions are likely to be directly consistent with overall societal

political structures; in complex modern societies they are not. Also see Greenstein (1968a) and Eckstein (1966).

33. For expanded discussions of these propositions see Greenstein (1969, Chapter 5).

34. For an application of Campbell's argument to British by-elections, see King (1968). Also see the Converse and Dupeux (1962) effort to explain the rise of new parties in France (as compared with the United States) in terms of the low incidence of party identifiers in France.

35. Kerpelman (1972) has since suggested that Flack's original data on the intellectual capacity of the University of Chicago activists he studied in the mid-1960s are suspect in that Flacks relied on students' own reports of their grades. Kerpelman notes that subsequent research shows that student activists *report* but do not actually *receive* higher grades than nonactivists.

36. The more universally popular activism became, the more likely activist ranks were to recruit individuals whose style of mediating self-other relationships takes the form of peer-group conformity. As noted earlier, to the degree that conformity needs determine political behavior, the effects of other predispositions are lessened. A minor but highly publicized subtheme in the later years of 1960s activism was the formation of small, highly violent activist groups such as the Weatherpeople. These groups have not been the subjects of personality tests; the members undoubtedly *did* have distinctive personality qualities.

REFERENCES

Abelson, Robert P., *et al.*, eds. (1968). *Theories of Cognitive Consistency: A Source Book*. Chicago: Rand McNally.

Ackerman, Nathan W., and Marie Jahoda (1950). *Anti-Semitism and Emotional Disorder*. New York: Harper.

Adorno, T. W., Else Frenkel-Brunswik, Daniel J. Levinson, and R. Nevitt Sanford (1950). *The Authoritarian Personality*. New York: Harper.

Alker, Henry A. (1971). "A quasi-paranoid feature of students' extreme attitudes against colonialism." *Behavioral Science* 16:218–27.

_____ (1972). "Is personality situationally specific or intrapsychically consistent?" *Journal of Personality* 40:1–16.

Allison, Graham T. (1969). "Conceptual models and the Cuban missile crisis." *American Political Science Review* (September) 63:689–718.

Allport, Gordon (1937). *Personality: A Psychological Interpretation*. New York: Holt.

_____ (1942). *The Use of Personal Documents in Psychological Science*. New York: Social Science Research Council Bulletin 49.

_____ (1962). "The general and the unique in psychological science." *Journal of Personality* 30:405–22.

Altbach, Philip G. and David H. Kelly (1973). *A Selected Bibliography of Student Activism and Related Topics*. Lexington, Mass.: Lexington Books.

American Psychiatric Association, Committee on Nomenclature and Statistics (1968), *Diagnostic and Statistical Manual of Mental Disorders* 2d edition. Washington, D.C.: American Psychiatric Association.

Argyris, Chris (1973). "Some limits of rational man organizational theory." *Public Administration Review* 33:253–67.

Asch, S. E. (1952). "Effects of group pressure upon the modification and distortion of judgments." In Guy E. Swanson, Theodore M. Newcomb, and Eugene L. Hartley (eds.), *Readings in Social Psychology*. New York: Holt, pp. 2–11.

Astin, Alexander W. (1970). "Determinants of student activism." In Julian Foster and Durward Long (eds.), *Protest! Student Activism in America*. New York: Morrow, pp. 89–101.

Bandura, Albert, and Richard H. Walters (1963). *Social Learning and Personality Development*. New York: Holt, Rinehart and Winston.

Barber, James David (1965). *The Lawmakers: Recruitment and Adaptation to Legislative Life*. New Haven: Yale University Press.

_____ (1968a). "Adult identity and presidential style: the rhetorical emphasis." *Daedalus*, 97:938–68.

_____ (1968b). "Classifying and predicting presidential styles: two weak presidents." *Journal of Social Issues* 24:51–80.

_____ (1971). "The interplay of presidential character and style: a paradigm and five illustrations." In Fred I. Greenstein and Michael Lerner (eds.), *A Source Book for the Study of Personality and Politics*. Chicago: Markham (now distributed by Humanities Press, Atlantic Highlands, N.J.), pp. 384–408.

_____ (1972a). *The Presidential Character: Predicting Performance in the White House*. Englewood Cliffs, N.J.: Prentice-Hall.

_____ (1972b). "The question of presidential character." *Saturday Review* (September 23), pp. 62–6.

_____ (1974). "Strategies for understanding politicians," *American Journal of Political Science* 18:443–67.

Barlow, David H. and Michael Hersen (1973). "Single-case experimental designs: uses in clinical research." *Archives of General Psychiatry* 29:319–25.

Bass, Bernard M. (1965). "Authoritarianism or acquiescence?" *Journal of Abnormal and Social Psychology* 51:616–23.

Bay, Christian (1958). *The Structure of Freedom*. Stanford: Stanford University Press. Paperback with new preface, 1970.

_____ (1967). "Political and apolitical students: facts in search of theory." *Journal of Social Issues* 23:76–91.

Bayer, Alan E., and Alexander W. Astin (1969). "Violence and disruption on the U.S. campus, 1968–69." *Educational Record* (Fall), pp. 337–50.

_____ (1971). "Campus unrest, 1970–71: was it really all that quiet?" *Educational Record* (Fall), pp. 301–13.

Beier, Helen, and Eugenia Hanfmann (1956). "Emotional attitudes of former Soviet citizens, as studied by the technique of projective questions." *Journal of Abnormal and Social Psychology* 53:143–53.

Bendix, Reinhard (1952). "Compliant behavior and individual personality." *American Journal of Sociology* 58:292–303.

Benedict, Ruth F. (1934). *Patterns of Culture*. Boston: Houghton Mifflin.

_____ (1946) . *The Chrysanthemum and the Sword*. Boston: Houghton Mifflin.

Bentler, P. M., Douglas N. Jackson, and Samuel Messick (1971) . "Identification of content and style: a two-dimensional interpretation of acquiescence." *Psychological Bulletin* 76:186–204.

Berns, Walter (1961) . "The behavioral sciences and the study of political things: the case of Christian Bay's 'The Structure of Freedom.'" *American Political Science Review* 55:550–1.

Blalock, Hubert M. (1963) . "Correlated independent variables: the problem of multi-colinearity." *Social Forces* 42:233–7.

_____ (1964). "Controlling for background factors: spuriousness versus developmental sequences." *Social Inquiry* 34:28–39.

Block, Jack (1965) . *The Challenge of Response Sets: Unconfounding Meaning, Acquiescence, and Social Desirability in the MMPI*. New York: Appleton-Century-Crofts.

_____ (1965) . *Lives through Time*. Berkeley, Cal.: Bancroft.

_____ (1972) . "The shifting definitions of acquiescence." *Psychological Bulletin* 78:10–12.

Block, Jeanne H., Norma Haan, and M. Brewster Smith (1969) . "Socialization correlates of student activism." *Journal of Social Issues* 25:143–77.

Bonjean, Charles M., Richard J. Hill, and S. Dale McLemore (1967) . *Sociological Measurement: An Inventory of Scales and Indices*. San Francisco: Chandler.

Bourne, Peter G. (1971). "Altered adrenal function in two combat situations in Viet Nam." In Basil E. Eleftheriou and John Paul Scott (eds.), *The Physiology of Aggression and Defeat*. New York: Plenum, pp. 265–305. Excerpt reprinted by permission.

Bramson, Leon, and George W. Goethals (1964). *War: Studies from Psychology, Sociology, Anthropology*. New York: Basic Books.

Breger, Louis, ed. (1969). *Clinical Cognitive Psychology*. Englewood Cliffs, N.J.: Prentice-Hall.

Brodie, Fawn M. (1959). *Thaddeus Stevens: Scourge of the South*. New York: Norton.

Bronfenbrenner, Urie (1960) . "Personality and participation: the case of the vanishing variables." *Journal of Social Issues* 16:54–63.

Brown, Norman O. (1959) . *Life Against Death*. Middletown: Wesleyan University Press.

Brown, Roger (1965). *Social Psychology*. New York: Free Press.

Brown, Steven R. (1974) . "Intensive analysis in political research." *Political Methodology* 1:1–25.

Browning, Rufus P. (1968) . "The interaction of personality and political system in decisions to run for office: some data and a simulation technique." *Journal of Social Issues* 24:93–109.

Browning, Rufus P., and Herbert Jacob (1964) . "Power motivation and the political personality." *Public Opinion Quarterly* 28:75–90.

Burke, Kenneth (1945) . *A Grammar of Motives*. Englewood Cliffs, N.J.: Prentice-Hall.

_____ (1950) . *A Rhetoric of Motives*. Englewood Cliffs, N.J.: Prentice-Hall.

_____ (1961) . *Attitudes Toward History*. Boston: Beacon.

Burwen, Leroy S., and Donald T. Campbell (1957). "The generality of attitudes toward authority and nonauthority figures." *Journal of Abnormal and Social Psychology* 54:24–31.

Campbell, Angus (1960). "Surge and decline: a study of electoral change." *Public Opinion Quarterly* 24:397–418.

Campbell, Angus, Philip E. Converse, Warren E. Miller, and Donald E. Stokes (1960). *The American Voter.* New York: Wiley.

Campbell, Donald T. (1963). "Social attitudes and other acquired behavioral dispositions." In Sigmund Koch (ed.), *Psychology: A Study of a Science*, Vol. 6. New York: McGraw-Hill.

_____ (1965). "Ethnocentric and other altruistic motives." In David Levine (ed.), *Nebraska Symposium on Motivation.* Lincoln: University of Nebraska Press, pp. 283–311.

Cantor, Norman F. (1967). *The English: A History of Politics and Society to 1970.* New York: Simon and Schuster.

Carlson, Rae (1971). "Where is the person in personality research?" *Psychological Bulletin* 75:203–19.

Carr, Leslie G. (1971). "The Srole items and acquiescence." *American Sociological Review* 36:287–93.

Chomsky, Noam (1959). Review of *Verbal Behavior* by B. F. Skinner. *Language* 35:26–58.

Christie, Richard, and Peggy Cook (1958). "A guide to published literature relating to the authoritarian personality through 1956." *Journal of Psychology* (April) 45:171–99.

Christie, Richard, and Florence L. Geis (1970). *Studies in Machiavellianism.* New York: Academic Press.

_____ (1933) *Lincoln: A Psycho-Biography.* New York: Scribner.

Christie, Richard, John Havel, and Bernard Seidenberg (1958). "Is the F scale irreversible?" *Journal of Abnormal and Social Psychology* 56.

Christie, Richard, and Marie Jahoda, eds. (1954). *Studies in the Scope and Method of "The Authoritarian Personality."* Glencoe, Ill.: Free Press.

Clark, Leon Pierce (1921). "Unconcious motives underlying the personalities of great statesmen and their relation to epoch-making events: a psychologic study of Abraham Lincoln." *Psychoanalytic Review* 8:1–21.

Cole, Michael, and Jerome S. Bruner (1971). "Cultural differences and inferences about psychological processes." *American Psychologist* 26:867–76.

Coleman, James S. (1958). "Relational analysis: the study of social organization with survey methods." *Human Organization* 17:28–36.

_____ (1964). "Group and individual variables." In his *Introduction to Mathematical Sociology.* New York: Free Press of Glencoe, pp. 84–90.

Converse, Philip E. (1970). "Attitudes and non-attitudes: continuation of a dialogue." In Edward R. Tufte (ed.), *The Quantitative Analysis of Social Problems.* Reading, Mass.: Addison-Wesley, pp. 168–69.

Converse, Philip E., and Georges Dupeux (1962). "Politicization of the electorate in France and the United States." *Public Opinion Quarterly* 26:1–23.

Couch, Arthur, and Kenneth R. Keniston (1960). "Yeasayers and naysayers: agreeing response set as a personality variable." *Journal of Abnormal and Social Psychology* 60:151–74.

Crozier, Michael (1964). *The Bureaucratic Phenomena*. Chicago: University of Chicago Press.

Dahlstrom, W. Grant (1972). "Personality systematics and the problem of types." Pamphlet. Morristown, N.J.: General Learning Press.

Daniels, Robert B. (1967). *Red October: The Bolshevik Revolution of 1917*. New York: Scribner.

Davidson, P. O., and C. G. Costello (1969). *N = 1: Experimental Studies of Single Cases*. New York: Van Nostrand Reinhold.

Davies, A. F. (1966). *Private Politics: A Study of Five Political Outlooks*. Melbourne: Melbourne University Press.

_____ (1973). *Politics as Work*. Melbourne Politics Monographs. Parkeville, Australia: Dept. of Politics, Melbourne University.

_____ (1967). "Criteria for the political life history." *Historical Studies of Australia and New Zealand* 13:49, 76–85.

Davies, James C. (1963). *Human Nature in Politics*. New York: Wiley.

_____ (1973). "Aggression, violence, revolution, and war." In Jeanne N. Knutson (ed.), *The Handbook of Political Psychology*. San Francisco: Jossey-Bass. Pp. 234–60.

Denzin, Norman K. (1969). "Symbolic interactionism and ethnomethodology: a proposed synthesis." *American Sociological Review* 34:922–34.

de Rivera, Joseph H. (1968). *The Psychological Dimension of Foreign Policy*. Columbus, O.: Merrill.

Dewey, John, and Arthur F. Bentley (1949). *Knowing and the Known*. Boston: Beacon.

Dicks, Henry V. (1950). "Personality traits and national socialist ideology." *Human Relations* 3:111–54.

_____ (1952). "Observations on contemporary Russian behavior." *Human Relations* 5:111–75.

_____ (1972). *Licensed Mass Murder: A Socio-Psychological Study of Some S. S. Killers*. New York: Basic Books.

Di Palma, Giuseppe, and Herbert McClosky (1970). "Personality and conformity: the learning of political attitudes." *American Political Science Review* 64:1054–73.

Di Renzo, Gordon J. (1967). *Personality, Power and Politics*. Notre Dame, Ind.: University of Notre Dame Press.

Dollard, John (1935). *Criteria for the Life History*. New Haven: Yale University Press.

Donald, David (1960). *Charles Sumner and the Coming of the Civil War*. New York: Knopf.

_____ (1970). *Charles Sumner and the Rights of Man*. New York: Knopf.

Donley, Richard E., and David G. Winter (1970). "Measuring the motives of public officials at a distance: an exploratory study of American presidents." *Behavioral Science* 15:227–36.

Duncan, Otis (1966). "Path analysis: sociological examples." *American Journal of Sociology* 72:17–31.

Dunlap, Riley (1970a). "A comment on 'multiversity, university size, university quality, and student protest: an empirical study'." *American Sociological Review* 35:525–8.

_____ (1970b). "Radical and conservative student activists: a comparison of family backgrounds." *Pacific Sociological Review* 13:171–81.

Durkheim, Emile (1895). *Les Règles de la Méthode Sociologique.* Paris: Alcan. Eng. trans. (1938), *The Rules of Sociological Method.* Chicago: University of Chicago Press. Reprinted (1950), Glencoe, Ill.: Free Press.

_____ (1897). *Le Suicide.* Paris: Alcan. Eng. trans. (1951), *Suicide: A Study in Sociology.* Glencoe, Ill.: Free Press.

Eckstein, Harry (1966). "A theory of stable democracy." In his *Division and Cohesion in Democracy: A Study of Norway.* Princeton: Princeton University Press, pp. 225–88.

Edinger, Lewis J. (1964). "Political science and political biography." *Journal of Politics* 26:423–39, 648–76.

_____ (1965). *Kurt Schumacher: A Study in Personality and Political Behavior.* Stanford: Stanford University Press.

Edwards, Allen L. (1941). "Unlabeled Fascist Attitudes." *Journal of Abnormal and Social Psychology* 36:575–82.

_____ (1970). *The Measurement of Personality Traits by Scales and Inventories.* New York: Holt, Rinehart and Winston.

Eisenstadt, S. N. (1963). "The need for achievement." *Economic Development and Cultural Change* 11:420–31.

Elder, Glen H., Jr. (1973). "On linking social structure and personality." *American Behavioral Scientist* 16:785–800.

Erikson, Erik H. (1958). *Young Man Luther: A Study in Psychoanalysis and History.* New York: Norton.

_____ (1968). "On the nature of psycho-historical evidence: in search of Gandhi." *Daedalus* 97:695–730.

_____ (1969). *Gandhi's Truth: On the Origins of Militant Nonviolence.* New York: Norton.

Everson, David H. (1970). "The background of student support for student protest activities in the university." *Public Affairs Bulletin* (March-April). Carbondale: Southern Illinois University.

Eysenck, Hans J. (1968). "Emil Kraepelin." In D. L. Sills (ed.), *International Encyclopedia of the Social Sciences,* Vol. 8. New York: Macmillan, pp. 599–650.

Eysenck, Hans J., and Sybil Eysenck (1969). *Personality Structure and Measurement.* San Diego: Knapp.

Farrar, Donald E., and Robert R. Glauber (1967). "Multicolinearity in regression analysis: the problem revisited." *Review of Economics and Statistics* 49:92–107.

Farrell, Brian A. (1963). "Introduction." In Sigmund Freud, *Leonardo da Vinci and a Memory of His Childhood.* Harmondsworth, Eng.: Penguin.

Fearing, Franklin (1927). "Psychological studies of historical personalities." *Psychological Bulletin* 24:521–39.

Fiedler, Fred E. (1971). "Leadership." Pamphlet. New York: General Learning Press.

Fiske, Donald W. (1971). *Measuring the Concepts of Personality*. Chicago: Aldine.

_____ (1973). "Can a personality construct be validated empirically?" *Psychological Bulletin* 80:89–92.

Flacks, Richard (1967). "The liberated generation: an exploration of the roots of student protest." *Journal of Social Issues* 23:52–75.

Fodor, Jerry A. (1968). *Psychological Explanation: An Introduction to the Philosophy of Psychology*. New York: Random House.

Freedman, Jonathan L., and David O. Sears (1965). "Selective exposure." In Leonard Berkowitz (ed.), *Advances in Experimental Social Psychology*, Vol. 2. New York: Academic Press, pp. 58–97.

Frenkel-Brunswik, Else (1954). "Further explorations by a contributor to 'The Authoritarian Personality'." In Richard Christie and Marie Jahoda (eds.), *Studies in the Scope and Methodology of "The Authoritarian Personality."* Glencoe, Ill.: Free Press, pp. 226–75.

Freud, Anna (1946). *The Ego and the Mechanisms of Defense*. New York: International Universities Press.

Freud, Sigmund. *The Standard Edition of the Complete Psychological Works of Sigmund Freud*, 24 volumes. J. Strachey (ed.). London: Hogarth, 1953–.

_____ (1900). "The interpretation of dreams." In Standard edition, Vols. 4 and 5.

_____ (1901). "The psychopathology of everyday life." In Standard edition, Vol. 6.

_____ (1905). "Fragment of an analysis of a case of hysteria." In Standard edition, Vol. 7, pp. 3–122.

_____ (1909a). "Analysis of a phobia in a five-year-old boy." In Standard edition, Vol. 10, pp. 3–149.

_____ (1909b). "Notes upon a case of obsessional neurosis." In Standard edition, Vol. 10, pp. 153–318.

_____ (1910). "Leonardo da Vinci and a memory of his childhood." In Standard edition, Vol. 11, pp. 59–137.

_____ (1918). "From the history of an infantile neurosis." In Standard edition, Vol. 17, pp. 3–122.

_____ (1930). "Civilization and its discontents." In Standard edition, Vol. 21, pp. 59–145.

_____ (1938). "Moses and monotheism: three essays." In Standard edition, Vol. 23, p. 223.

Freud, Sigmund, and William C. Bullitt (1967). *Thomas Woodrow Wilson: A Psychological Study*. Boston: Houghton Mifflin.

Fromm, Erich (1941). *Escape from Freedom*. New York: Rinehart.

_____ (1947). *Man for Himself*. New York: Rinehart.

Geiger, George Raymond (1958). *John Dewey in Perspective: A Reassessment.* Oxford: Oxford University Press.

George, Alexander L. (1968). "Power as a compensatory value for political leaders." *Journal of Social Issues* 24:29–49.

————— (1969). "The 'operational code': a neglected approach to the study of political leaders and decision-making." *International Studies Quarterly* 13:190–222.

————— (1971). "Some uses of dynamic psychology in political biography: case materials on Woodrow Wilson." In Fred I. Greenstein and Michael Lerner, *A Source Book for the Study of Personality and Politics.* Chicago: Markham. Now distributed by Humanities Press, Atlantic Highlands, N.J., pp. 78–98.

————— (1972). "The case for multiple advocacy in making foreign policy." *American Political Science Review* 46:751–85.

————— (1974). "Assessing presidential character." *World Politics* 26:234–82.

George, Alexander L., and Juliette L. George (1956). *Woodrow Wilson and Colonel House: A Personality Study.* New York: John Day. Paperback edition with new preface (1964), New York: Dover.

Glad, Betty (1966). *Charles Evans Hughes and the Illusions of Innocence: A Study in American Diplomacy.* Urbana: University of Illinois Press.

Goldhamer, Herbert (1950). "Public opinion and personality." *American Journal of Sociology* 55:346–54.

Gorer, Geoffrey (1948; revised edition, 1964). *The American People.* New York: Norton.

Gorer, Geoffrey, and John Rickman (1949). *The People of Great Russia: A Psychological Study.* London: Cresset.

Greene, Dwight L., and David G. Winter (1971). "Motives, involvements, and leadership among black college students." *Journal of Personality* 39:319–32.

Greenstein, Fred I. (1965). "Public images of the president." *American Journal of Psychiatry* 122:523–9.

————— (1966). "Harold D. Lasswell's concept of democratic character." *Journal of Politics* 30:696–709.

————— (1967a). "Art and science in the political life history: a review of A. F. Davies's *Private Politics*." *Politics* 2:176–80.

————— (1967b). "The impact of personality on politics: an attempt to clear away underbrush." *American Political Science Review* 61:629–41.

————— (1968a). "Political socialization." *International Encyclopedia of the Social Sciences.* New York: Macmillan.

————— (1968b). "Private disorder and the public order." *Psychoanalytic Quarterly* 37:261–81.

————— (1969). *Personality and Politics: Problems of Evidence, Inference, and Conceptualization.* Chicago: Markham. Paperback edition with a new preface, New York: Norton, 1975.

————— (1970a). "A note on the ambiguity of 'political socialization': definitions, criticisms, and strategies of inquiry." *Journal of Politics* 32:969–78.

————— (1970b). Review of Gordon J. di Renzo, *Personality, Power and Politics:*

A Social Psychological Analysis of the Italian Deputy and His Parliamentary System. Political Science Quarterly 85:365–8.

_____ (1970c). "The standing of social and psychological variables: an addendum to Jackman's critique." *Journal of Politics* 32:989–92.

_____ (1971). "The study of personality and politics: overall considerations." In Fred I. Greenstein and Michael Lerner (eds.), *A Source Book for the Study of Personality and Politics.* Chicago: Markham, pp. 4–32. Now distributed by Humanities Press, Atlantic Highlands, N.J.

_____ (1973). "Political psychology: a pluralistic universe." In Jeanne N. Knutson (ed.), *The Handbook of Political Psychology.* San Francisco: Jossey-Bass, pp. 438–70.

Greenstein, Fred I., and Michael Lerner, eds. (1971). *A Source Book for the Study of Personality and Politics.* Chicago: Markham. Now distributed by Humanities Press, Atlantic Highlands, N.J.

Greenstein, Fred I., and Sidney Tarrow (1970). "Political orientations of children: the use of a semi-projective technique in three nations." *Comparative Politics Series No. 01–009* 1. Beverly Hills: Sage, pp. 479–558.

Guterman, Stanley S. (1970). *The Machiavellians: A Social Psychological Study of Moral Character and Organizational Milieu.* Lincoln: University of Nebraska Press.

Gynther, Malcolm (1972). "White norms and black MMPIs: a prescription for discrimination." *Psychological Bulletin* 78:386–402.

Hagen, Everett Einar (1962). *On the Theory of Social Change: How Economic Growth Begins.* Homewood, Ill.: Dorsey.

Hall, Calvin S., and Gardner Lindzey (1957). *Theories of Personality.* New York: Wiley.

_____ (1970). *Theories of Personality,* 2nd edition. New York: Wiley.

Hampden-Turner, Charles (1970). *Radical Man.* Cambridge, Mass.: Schenkman.

Hanfmann, Eugenia, and Jacob W. Getzels (1955). "Interpersonal attitudes of former Soviet citizens, as studied by a semi-projective method." *Psychological Monographs* 69:1–37.

Hastings, Donald W. (1965a). "The psychiatry of presidential assassination: part I: Jackson and Lincoln." *Journal-Lancet* 85:93–100.

_____ (1965b). "The psychiatry of presidential assassination: part II: Garfield and McKinley." *Journal-Lancet* 85:157–62.

_____ (1965c). "The psychiatry of presidential assassination: part III: the Roosevelts." *Journal-Lancet* 85:189–92.

_____ (1965d). "The psychiatry of presidential assassination: part IV: Truman and Kennedy." *Journal-Lancet* 85:294–301.

Hempel, Carl G. (1965). "The theoretician's dilemma: a study in the logic of theory construction." In his *Aspects of Scientific Explanation.* New York: Free Press of Glencoe, pp. 173–226.

Hennessy, Bernard (1959). "Politicals and apoliticals: some measurements of personality traits." *Midwest Journal of Political Science* 3:336–55.

Hodgson, Richard C., Daniel J. Levinson, and Abraham Zaleznik (1965). *The Executive Role Constellation.* Boston: Division of Research, Harvard University Graduate School of Business Administration.

Holland, Norman H. (1968). *The Dynamics of Literary Response.* New York: Oxford University Press.

Holt, Robert R. (1967). "Individuality and generalization in the psychology of personality." In Richard S. Lazarus and Edward M. Opton, Jr. (eds.), *Personality.* Baltimore: Penguin.

Hook, Sidney (1943). *The Hero in History.* New York: John Day.

Horkheimer, Max, ed. (1936). *Studien über Autorität und Familie.* Paris: Alcan.

Hyman, Herbert H. (1955). *Survey Design and Analysis.* Glencoe, Ill.: Free Press.

_____ (1959). *Political Socialization: A Study in the Psychology of Political Behavior.* New York: Free Press.

Hyman, Herbert H., and Paul B. Sheatsley (1954). " 'The authoritarian personality': a methodological critique." In Richard Christie and Marie Jahoda (eds.), *Studies in the Scope and Method of "The Authoritarian Personality."* Glencoe, Ill.: Free Press, pp. 50–122.

Inkeles, Alex (1963). "Sociology and psychology." In Sigmund Koch (ed.), *Psychology: A Study of a Science,* Vol. 6. New York: McGraw-Hill, pp. 354f.

_____ (1968). "Society, social structure and child socialization." In John A. Clausen (ed.), *Socialization and Society.* Boston: Little, Brown, pp. 73–129.

Inkeles, Alex, and Raymond A. Bauer (1959). *The Soviet Citizen: Daily Life in a Totalitarian Society.* Cambridge: Harvard University Press.

Inkeles, Alex, Eugenia Hanfmann, and Helen Beier (1958). "Modal personality and adjustment to the Soviet socio-political system." *Human Relations* 11:3–22.

Inkeles, Alex, and Daniel J. Levinson (1954). "National character: the study of modal personality and sociocultural systems." In Gardner Lindzey (ed.), *Handbook of Social Psychology,* Vol. 2. Cambridge, Mass.: Addison-Wesley, pp. 977-1020. Revised and expanded in Gardner Lindzey and Elliot Aronson (eds.), *The Handbook of Social Psychology,* 2nd edition, 1969, Vol. 4. Reading, Mass.: Addison-Wesley, pp. 418–506.

_____ (1963). "The personal system and the sociocultural system in large-scale organizations." *Sociometry* 26:217–29.

Jackman, Robert W. (1970). "A note on intelligence, social class, and political efficacy in children." *Journal of Politics* 32:984–9.

Jessor, Richard and Shirley L. Jessor (1973). "The perceived environment in political science: some conceptual issues and some illustrative data." *American Behavioral Scientist* 16:801–28.

Kagan, Jerome, Howard A. Moss, and Irving Sigel (1970). "Psychological significance of styles of conceptualization." In Society for Research in Child Development (ed.), *Cognitive Development in Children.* Chicago: University of Chicago Press, pp. 203–42.

Katz, Daniel (1960). "The functional approach to the study of attitudes." *Public Opinion Quarterly* 24:163–204.

_____ (1973). "Patterns of leadership." In Jeanne N. Knutson (ed.), *The Handbook of Political Psychology.* San Francisco: Jossey-Bass, pp. 203–33.

Katz, Irwin, and Lawrence Benjamin (1960). "Effects of white authoritarianism on biracial work groups." *Journal of Abnormal and Social Psychology* 61:448–56.

Kecskemeti, Paul, and Nathan Leites (1947). "Some psychological hypotheses on Nazi Germany: I." *Journal of Social Psychology* 26:141–83.

_____ (1948a). "Some psychological hypotheses on Nazi Germany: II." *Journal of Social Psychology* 27:91–117.

_____ (1948b). "Some psychological hypotheses on Nazi Germany: III." *Journal of Social Psychology* 27:241–70.

_____ (1948c). "Some psychological hypotheses on Nazi Germany: IV." *Journal of Social Psychology* 28:141–64.

Keniston, Kenneth (1970). "Student activism, moral development, and morality." *American Journal of Orthopsychiatry* 40: 577–92.

_____ (1973). *Radicals and Militants: An Annotated Bibliography of Empirical Research.* Lexington, Mass.: Lexington Books.

Keniston, Kenneth, and Michael Lerner (1971a). "Campus characteristics and campus unrest." *Annals of the American Academy of Political and Social Science* 395:39–53.

_____ (1917b). "Selected references on student protest." *Annals of the American Academy of Political and Social Science* 395:184–94.

Kerpelman, Larry C. (1972). *Activists and Nonactivists: A Psychological Study of American College Students.* New York: Behavioral Publications.

King, Anthony (1968). "Why all governments lose by-elections." *New Society* 11:413–5.

Kirscht, John P., and Ronald C. Dillehay (1967). *Dimensions of Authoritarianism.* Lexington: University of Kentucky Press.

Kline, Paul (1972). *Fact and Fantasy in Freudian Theory.* London: Methuen.

Klineberg, Otto (1950). *Tensions Affecting International Understanding.* New York: Social Science Research Council Bulletin 62.

Kluckhohn, Clyde, and Henry A. Murray with the collaboration of David M. Schneider (1953). "Personality formation: the determinants." In Clyde Kluckhohn and Henry A. Murray (eds.), *Personality in Nature, Society, and Culture,* 2nd edition. New York: Knopf, pp. 53–67.

Knutson, Jeanne N., ed. (1973). *The Handbook of Political Psychology.* San Francisco: Jossey-Bass.

Kogan, Nathan (1956). "Authoritarianism and repression." *Journal of Abnormal and Social Psychology* 53:34–7.

Kroeber, Alfred Louis, and Clyde Kluckhohn (1952). "Culture: a critical review of concepts and definitions." *Papers of the Peabody Museum of American Archaeology and Ethnology* 47:1. Cambridge: Harvard University.

Lane, Robert E. (1959a). "Fathers and sons: foundations of political belief." *American Sociological Review* 24:501–11.

_____ (1959b). "The fear of equality." *American Political Science Review* (March), pp. 35–51.

_____ (1959c). *Political Life.* Glencoe, Ill.: Free Press.

_____ (1962). *Political Ideology: Why the American Common Man Believes What He Does.* New York: Free Press of Glencoe.

Lane, Robert E., and David O. Sears (1964). *Public Opinion*. Englewood Cliffs, N.J.: Prentice-Hall.

Lasswell, Harold D. (1930). *Psychopathology and Politics*. Chicago: University of Chicago Press. Reprinted in *The Political Writings of Harold D. Lasswell* (1951), Glencoe, Ill.: Free Press. Also reprinted in paperback edition with "Afterthoughts: Thirty Years Later" (1961), New York: Viking.

_____ (1948). *Power and Personality*. New York: Norton. Paperback edition without appendix (1962), New York: Viking.

_____ (1951). "Democratic character." In *The Political Writings of Harold D. Lasswell*. Glencoe, Ill.: Free Press.

_____ (1960). "Political character and constitution." *Psychoanalysis and the Psychoanalytic Review* 46:1–18.

_____ (1968). "A note on 'types' of political personality; nuclear, co-relational, developmental." *Journal of Social Issues* 24:81–91.

Lasswell, Harold D., and Abraham Kaplan (1950). *Power and Society: A Framework for Political Inquiry*. New Haven: Yale University Press.

Lazarsfeld, Paul F., and Allen H. Barton (1951). "Qualitative measurement in the social sciences: classification, typologies, and indices." In Daniel Lerner and Harold D. Lasswell (eds.), *The Policy Sciences*. Stanford: Stanford University Press.

Lazarsfeld, Paul F.; Anna K. Pasanella; and Morris Rosenberg (1972). *Continuities in the Language of Social Research*. New York: The Free Press.

Leighton, Alexander H. (1967). "Some observations on the prevalence of mental illness in contrasting communities." In the Lord Platt and A. S. Parkes (eds.), *Social and Genetic Influences on Life and Death*. New York: Plenum, pp. 97–111.

Leites, Nathan C. (1948). "Psycho-cultural hypotheses about political acts." *World Politics* 1:102–19.

_____ (1951). *The Operational Code of the Politburo*. New York: McGraw-Hill.

_____ (1953). *A Study of Bolshevism*. Glencoe, Ill.: Free Press.

_____ (1959). *On the Game of Politics in France*. Stanford: Stanford University Press.

_____ (1971). *The New Ego*. New York: Science House.

Lerner, Michael (1969). "A bibliographical note." In Fred I. Greenstein, *Personality and Politics: Problems of Evidence, Inference, and Conceptualization*. Chicago: Markham, pp. 154–84. Paperback edition, New York: Norton, 1975.

_____ (1970). "Personal poiltics." Ph.D. dissertation, Yale University.

LeVine, Robert A. (1960). "The internalization of political values in stateless societies." *Human Organization* 19:51–8.

_____ (1973). *Culture, Society and Personality*. Chicago: Aldine.

Levinson, Daniel J. (1958). "The relevance of personality for political participation." *Public Opinion Quarterly* 22:3–10.

_____ (1959). "Role, personality, and social structure in the organizational setting." *Journal of Abnormal and Social Psychology* 58:170–80.

Lewin, Kurt (1936). *Principles of Topological Psychology*. New York: McGraw-Hill.

Lipset, Seymour M. (1968). "The activists: a profile." In Daniel Bell and Irving Kristol (eds.), *Confrontation: The Student Rebellion and the Universities*. New York: Basic Books, pp. 45–57.

Lipset, Seymour M., and Leo Lowenthal, eds. (1961). *Culture and Social Character: The Work of David Riesman Reviewed.* New York: Free Press of Glencoe.

Little, Graham (1973). *Politics and Personal Style.* Melbourne: Nelson.

McClelland, David C. (1961). *The Achieving Society.* Princeton: Van Nostrand.

McClosky, Herbert (1958). "Conservatism and personality." *American Political Science Review* 52:27–45.

_____ (1967). "Personality and attitude correlates of foreign policy orientation." In James N. Rosenau (ed.), *Domestic Sources of Foreign Policy.* New York: Free Press of Glencoe, pp. 51–109.

McClosky, Herbert, and John H. Schaar (1965). "Psychological dimensions of anomy." *American Sociological Review* 30:14–40.

McGuire, William J. (1968). "Personality and susceptibility to social influence." In Edgar F. Borgatta and William W. Lambert (eds.), *Handbook of Personality Theory and Research.* Chicago: Rand McNally, pp. 1130–87.

McKinney, John C. (1966). *Constructive Typology and Social Theory.* New York: Appleton-Century-Crofts.

Mahrer, Alvin R., ed. (1970). *New Approaches to Personality Classification.* New York: Columbia University Press.

Mandelbaum, David G. (1973). "The study of life history: Gandhi." *Current Anthropology* 14:177–206.

Manis, Jerome G., *et al.* (1964). "Estimating the prevalence of mental illness." *American Sociological Review* 29:84–9, and the sources there cited.

Marcuse, Herbert (1966). *Eros and Civilization,* revised edition. Boston: Beacon.

Maslow, Abraham H. (1943). "The authoritarian character structure." *Journal of Social Psychology* 18:401–11.

Mazlish, Bruce (1972). *In Search of Nixon: A Psychohistorical Inquiry.* New York: Basic Books.

Mead, Margaret (1942). *And Keep Your Powder Dry.* New York: Morrow.

Melnik, Constantin, and Nathan Leites (1958). *The House Without Windows: France Selects a President.* Evanston, Ill.: Row, Peterson.

Merelman, Richard M. (1970). Review of Fred I. Greenstein, *Personality and Politics: Problems of Evidence, Inference, and Conceptualization. American Political Science Review* 64:919.

Mikulas, William L. (1972). "Criticisms of behavior therapy." *Canadian Psychologist* 13:83–104.

Milgram, Stanley (1961). "An experimental approach to studying national differences." *Scientific American* 205:45–51.

Mischel, Walter (1968). *Personality and Assessment.* New York: Wiley.

_____ (1969). "Continuity and change in personality." *American Psychologist* 24:1012–18.

Mitscherlich, Alexander (1969). *Society Without the Father.* London: Tavistock.

Money-Kyrle, Roger E. (1951). *Psychoanalysis and Politics.* New York: Norton.

Murray, Henry A. (1968). "Personality: contemporary viewpoints: components of an evolving personalogical system." *International Encyclopedia of the Social Sciences.* New York: Macmillan.

Neisser, Ulric (1967). *Cognitive Psychology.* New York: Appleton-Century-Crofts.

Neustadt, Richard E. (1960). *Presidential Power: The Politics of Leadership.* New York: Wiley.

Osgood, Robert E. (1955). "Observations on the clinical approach to international tensions." *Social Problems* 2:176–80.

Parenti, Michael (1962). "Ethnic and political attitudes: a depth study of Italian-Americans." Ph.D. dissertation, Yale University.

Parsons, Talcott (1947). "Certain primary sources and patterns of aggression in the social structure of the Western world." *Psychiatry* 10:167–81.

——————— (1969). "The academic system: a sociologist's view." In Daniel Bell and Irving Kristol (eds.), *Confrontation: The Student Rebellion and the Universities.* New York: Basic Books, pp. 159–84.

Payne, James L. (1972). *Incentive Theory and Political Process.* Lexington, Mass.: Lexington Books.

Payne, James L., and Oliver H. Woshinsky (1972). "Incentives for political participation." *World Politics* 24:518–46.

Peterson, Richard E., and John A. Bilorusky (1971). *May 1970: The Campus Aftermath of Cambodia and Kent State.* The Carnegie Foundation for the Advancement of Teaching.

Pettigrew, Thomas F. (1958). "Personality and socio-cultural factors in intergroup attitudes: a cross-national comparison." *Journal of Conflict Resolution* 2:29–42.

Proctor, Charles H. (1971). "Comment on Carr's Srole items." *American Sociological Review* 36:1107–8.

Putnam, Robert D. (1971). "Studying elite political culture: the case of 'ideology'." *American Political Science Review* 55:651–81.

Ray, John J. (1972). "Militarism, authoritarianism, neuroticism, and anti-social behavior." *Journal of Conflict Resolution* 16:319–40.

Riesman, David (1953). "Psychological types and national character: an informal commentary." *American Quarterly* 5:325–43.

Riesman, David, and Nathan Glazer (1952). *Faces in the Crowd: Individual Studies in Character and Politics.* New Haven: Yale University Press. Abridged paperback with new preface (1965).

Riesman, David, Nathan Glazer, and Reuel Denney (1950). *The Lonely Crowd.* New Haven: Yale University Press. Abridged paperback edition with new preface (1961).

Rogow, Arnold A. (1963). *James Forrestal: A Study of Personality, Politics, and Policy.* New York: Macmillan.

Rogow, Arnold A., and Harold D. Lasswell (1963). *Power, Corruption, and Rectitude.* Englewood Cliffs, N.J.: Prentice-Hall.

Rokeach, Milton (1960). *The Open and Closed Mind: Investigations into the Nature of Belief Systems and Personality Systems.* New York: Basic Books.

Rorer, Leonard G. (1965). "The great response-style myth." *Psychological Bulletin* 63:129–56.

Rosenberg, Morris (1965). *Society and the Adolescent Self-Image.* Princeton: Princeton University Press.

_____ (1968). *The Logic of Survey Analysis.* New York: Basic Books.

Rothstein, David A. (1964). "Presidential assassination syndrome." *Archives of General Psychiatry* 11:245–54.

_____ (1966). "Presidential assassination syndrome: II. Application to Lee Harvey Oswald." *Archives of General Psychiatry* 15:260–6.

Rutherford, Brent M. (1966). "Psychopathology, decision-making, and political involvement." *Journal of Conflict Resolution* 10:387–407.

Ryle, Gilbert (1949). *The Concept of Mind.* London: Hutchinson.

Samelson, Franz (1964). "Agreement set and anticontent attitudes in the F scale: a re-interpretation." *Journal of Abnormal and Social Psychology* 68:338–42.

Samelson, Franz, and Jacques F. Yates (1967). "Acquiescence and the F scale: old assumptions and new data." *Psychological Bulletin* 68:91–103.

Sanford, Nevitt (1959). "The approach of 'The Authoritarian Personality'." In James Leslie McCary (ed.), *Psychology of Personality.* New York: Grove. Originally published by Logas Press (1956), pp. 255–319.

_____ (1973). "Authoritarian personality in contemporary perspective." In Jeanne N. Knutson (ed.), *Handbook of Political Psychology.* San Francisco: Jossey-Bass, pp. 139–170.

Schapiro, Meyer (1956). "Leonardo and Freud: an art-historical study." *Journal of Historical Ideas* 17:147–78.

Schulberg, Herbert C. (1962). "Insight, authoritarianism and tendency to agree." *Journal of Nervous and Mental Disorders* 135:481–8.

Schwartz, David C. (1969). "Toward a theory of political recruitment." *Western Political Quarterly* 22:552–71.

Scott, Joseph W., and Mohamed El-Assal (1969). "Multiversity, university size, university quality and student protest: an empirical study." *American Sociological Review* 34:702–9.

Scriven, Michael (1956). "A study of radical behaviorism." In Herbert Feigl and Michael Scriven (eds.), *The Foundations of Science and the Concepts of Psychology and Psychoanalysis; Minnesota Studies in the Philosophy of Science,* 1. Minneapolis: University of Minnesota Press, pp. 88–130.

Shils, Edward Alpert (1954). "Authoritarianism: 'right' and 'left'." In Richard Christie and Marie Jahoda (eds.), *Studies in the Scope and Method of "The Authoritarian Personality."* Glencoe, Ill.: Free Press, pp. 24–49.

_____ (1969). "Plenitude and scarcity: the anatomy of an international cultural crisis." *Encounter* (May), pp. 1–18.

Singer, Milton (1961). "A survey of culture and personality theory and research." In Bert Kaplan (ed.), *Studying Personality Cross-Culturally.* Evanston, Ill.: Row, Peterson, pp. 9–90.

Skinner, Burrhus F. (1953). *Science and Human Behavior.* New York: Macmillan.

_____ (1971). *Beyond Freedom and Dignity.* New York: Knopf.

Smelser, Neil J. (1968). "Personality and the explanation of political phenomena at the social-system level: a methodological statement." *Journal of Social Issues* 24: 111–25.

Smelser, Neil J., and William T. Smelser, eds. (1970). *Personality and Social Systems,* 2nd edition. New York: Wiley.

Smith, M. Brewster (1965). "An analysis of two measures of 'authoritarianism' among Peace Corps teachers." *Journal of Personality* 33:513–35.

_____ (1968a). "A map for the analysis of personality and politics." *Journal of Social Issues* 24:3, 15–28.

_____ (1968b). "Personality in politics: a conceptual map, with application to the problem of political rationality." In Oliver Garceau (ed.), *Political Research and Political Theory.* Cambridge: Harvard University Press, pp. 77–101.

Smith, M. Brewster, Jerome S. Bruner, and Robert W. White (1956). *Opinions and Personality.* New York: Wiley.

Smith, M. Brewster, Norma Haan, and Jeanne Block (1970). "Social psychological aspects of student activism." *Youth and Society* 1:261–88.

Sniderman, Paul M. (1974). *Personality and Democratic Politics.* Berkeley: University of California Press.

Sniderman, Paul M., and Jack Citrin (1971). "Psychological sources of political belief: self-esteem and isolationist attitudes." *American Political Science Review* 65:401–17.

Sofer, Elaine G. (1961). "Inner-direction, other-direction, and autonomy." In Seymour M. Lipset and Leo Lowenthal (eds.), *Culture and Social Character: The Work of David Riesman Reviewed.* New York: Free Press of Glencoe, pp. 295–315.

Solomon, Richard H. (1971). *Mao's Revolution and the Chinese Political Culture,* Berkeley: University of California Press.

Somit, Albert (1972). "Review article: biopolitics." *British Journal of Political Science* 2:209–38.

Sonquist, John A. (1970). *Multivariate Model Building.* Ann Arbor: Survey Research Center, University of Michigan.

Spiro, Melford E. (1951). "Culture and personality: the natural history of a false dichotomy." *Psychiatry* 14:19–46.

Srole, Leo, *et al.* (1962). *Mental Health in the Metropolis.* New York: McGraw-Hill.

Stagner, Ross (1936). "Fascist attitudes: their determining conditions." *Journal of Social Psychology* 7:438–54.

Tannenbaum, Arnold S., and Jerald G. Bachman (1964). "Structural versus individual effects." *American Journal of Sociology* 69:585–95.

Tiryakian, Edward A. (1968). "Typologies." *International Encyclopedia of the Social Sciences,* Vol. 16. New York: Macmillan.

Titus, H. Edwin, and E. P. Hollander (1957). "The California F scale in psychological research: 1950–1955." *Psychological Bulletin* 54:47–64.

Tucker, Robert C. (1965). "The dictator and totalitarianism." *World Politics* 17: 555–83.

_____ (1973). *Stalin as Revolutionary, 1879–1929: A Study in History and Personality.* New York: Norton.

Tyler, Stephan A., ed. (1969). *Cognitive Anthropology.* New York: Holt, Rinehart and Winston.

Verba, Sidney (1961). "Assumptions of rationality and non-rationality in models of the international system." *World Politics* 14:93–117.

_____ (1965). "Conclusion: comparative political culture." In Lucian W. Pye and Sidney Verba (eds.), *Political Culture and Political Development.* Princeton: Princeton University Press, pp. 512–60.

Wallace, Anthony F. C. (1961). *Culture and Personality.* New York: Random House.

Wallas, Graham (1921). *Human Nature in Politics,* 3rd edition. New York: Crofts. Originally published 1908.

Waltz, Kenneth Neal (1959). *Man, the State, and War.* New York: Columbia University Press.

Webster, Murray, Jr. (1973). "Psychological reductionism, methodological individualism, and large-scale problems." *American Sociological Review* 38:258–73.

Weinstein, Fred, and Gerald M. Platt (1969). *The Wish to be Free: Society, Psyche, and Value Change.* Berkeley: University of California Press.

_____ (1973). *Psychoanalytic Sociology: An Essay on the Interpretation of Historical Data and the Phenomena of Collective Behavior.* Baltimore: The Johns Hopkins Press.

Weisz, Alfred E., and Robert L. Taylor (1969). "American presidential assassinations." *Diseases of the Nervous System* 30:658–9.

West, Ranyard (1945). *Conscience and Society: A Study of the Psychological Prerequisites of Law and Order.* New York: Emerson.

White, Elliott S. (1968). "Intelligence and sense of political efficacy in children." *Journal of Politics* 30:50–68.

Wilkinson, Rupert (1972). *The Broken Rebel: A Study in Culture, Politics, and Authoritarian Character.* London: Harper and Row.

Willcox, William B. (1964). *Portrait of a General.* New York: Knopf.

Winter, David G., and Frederick A. Wiecking (1971). "The new Puritans: achievement and power motives of New Left radicals." *Behavioral Science* 16:523–30.

Wolfenstein, E. Victor (1967). *The Revolutionary Personality: Lenin, Trotsky, Gandhi.* Princeton: Princeton University Press.

_____ (1969). *Personality and Politics.* Belmont, Cal.: Dickenson.

Wood, Oscar P., and George Pitcher, eds. (1970). *Ryle: A Collection of Essays.* Garden City, N.Y.: Anchor-Doubleday.

Yinger, Milton (1973). "Anomie, alienation and political behavior." In Jeanne N. Knutson (ed.), *The Handbook of Political Psychology.* San Francisco: Jossey-Bass.

Zaleznik, Abraham (1965). "Interpersonal relations in organizations." In James G. March (ed.), *Handbook of Organizations.* Chicago: Rand McNally, pp. 574–613.

_____ (1966). *Human Dilemmas of Leadership: A Pioneering Study of the Tensions and Conflict Inherent in Assuming Responsibility and in the Development of Individual Strength.* New York: Harper and Row.

2

POLITICAL SOCIALIZATION

DAVID O. SEARS

An individual's behavior is normally analyzed as a joint function of historical and contemporaneous influences. Research on political socialization is intended to deal with historical influences on adult political attitudes and behavior—at least that part of history that has fallen within the individual's life span and bears some proximal relation to his life space. The main purpose of this chapter is to summarize the current state of knowledge about political socialization. My intention is to bring the professional reader or student up to date on this sprawling area of research, as well as to provide a reference entree to the literature. It must be frankly said at the outset that "the current state of knowledge" does not always allow for very definite conclusions. Thus, in many cases I have devoted as much attention to making explicit the various relevant theoretical assumptions as to presenting whatever (often skimpy) data are available. My hope is that this approach may help to pinpoint the key empirical problems that remain. In this sense the chapter is both a status-of-the-field report and, I hope, a prolegomenon to further research.

I am grateful for the facilities and resources offered by the Department of Political Science and its chairman, Carl Rosburg, and the Institute for Personality Assessment and Research and its director, Richard Crutchfield, during my sabbatical year at the University of California, Berkeley. Completion of the manuscript was facilitated by a grant from the National Science Foundation and by the assistance of Janet DePree, Claire Price, Fern Weatherwax, and Natalie Kohon. I am particularly grateful for detailed critical comments by Robert Abelson and Donald R. Kinder and for helpful criticism from Paul Abramson, Joseph Adelson, Jack Citrin, Norval Glenn, Fred I. Greenstein, Jean Knutson, Richard Niemi, K. Warner Schaie, Roberta S. Sigel, Robert R. Sears, Pauline S. Sears, and June Tapp; for the original stimulus to much of my thinking, to Robert E. Lane; and to Joan E. Laurence, John B. McConahay, Helene Smookler, and Gail L. Zellman for dialogue and collaboration while this essay was germinating.

The primary emphasis in the chapter will thus be on the status of substantive theory and research in the several areas covered by the field of "political socialization," rather than on some critical overview of the field as a whole. Nevertheless, for the purpose of orientation, I will begin by saying a little about what the field involves—its history, the political content it is concerned with, the relevant theories, and what general problems it has run into (though detailed evaluation of the last point will be deferred to the end of the chapter, so that it may be dealt with in terms of the field's actual progress).

The field of political socialization has been anticipated, of course, in the political theory of almost every era, from Plato through Rousseau to Mao. Its current incarnation dates mainly from American studies of civic education in the 1920s and 1930s (see Merriam, 1931; Wilson, 1938). However, it had a somewhat delayed entry into the empirically oriented political behavior literature, being rather little noted, for example, in the 1954 major summary of the voting literature in the *Handbook of Social Psychology* (Lipset *et al.*, 1954, pp. 1143–1150). However, research in the area suddenly began to spurt in the late 1950s and early 1960s, inspired principally by Hyman's review essay (1959), by the path-breaking empirical studies of children's attitudes conducted by Fred Greenstein (1960, 1965), and by David Easton and Robert Hess (Hess and Easton, 1960; Hess and Torney, 1967; Easton and Dennis, 1969). By the mid-1960s, the research momentum was such that the review essay on political behavior in the 1969 edition of the *Handbook of Social Psychology* devoted more than a third of its space to political socialization (Sears, 1969a, pp. 370–399, 414–419, 438–443). And since then, research output has increased at a geometric rate, resulting recently in the publication of several texts and readers (Adler and Harrington, 1970; Bullock and Rodgers, 1972; Dawson and Prewitt, 1969; Dennis, 1973; Greenberg, 1970a; Jaros, 1973; Riccards, 1973; Sigel, 1970; Weissberg, 1974). The bibliography for the present essay can also be offered, wanly, as testimony to the rabbitlike promiscuity of researchers in this area (useful histories and bibliographies have also been published by Koeppen, 1970, and Dennis, 1973).

The contents of political socialization most often investigated fall into three rough categories: (1) attachment to the political system, (2) partisan attitudes, and (3) political participation. Attachment normally is defined as focusing on the institutions, structures, and norms of the political system or "regime," and partisanship focuses on the current incumbent "authorities" and other persons, groups, policy stances, and ideologies competing for power and influence (Easton, 1965). The distinction between attachment and partisanship, though intuitively pleasing at first glance, turns out to be a displeasingly fuzzy one empirically, as will be apparent later. Nonetheless, research on each has developed so autonomously from the other that they will be discussed in what are quite naturally two separate sections here.

The third content, political participation, will not be considered here for a variety of reasons. Attachment and partisanship mainly involve attitudes, whereas participation involves overt behavioral acts to a greater extent, so it is hard to fit any very unified theoretical organization to both sets of phenomena. In particular, their development may be related in very different ways to the life cycle (cf. J. D. Barber, 1968; Jennings and Niemi, 1968b). However, those more interested in participation should consult the Verba and Nie chapter in Volume 4 of this *Handbook*.

"Political socialization" has been defined in a wide variety of ways, though the variety boils down to two main alternatives. The most conventional definition implies *society's molding of the child* to some a priori model, usually one perpetuating the status quo. Such terms as "indoctrination," "acculturation," "civilizing," "cultural transmission," and "adopting cultural norms" are common synonyms for this usage. Langton (1969, p. 4) puts it this way: "Political socialization, in the broadest sense, refers to the way society transmits its political culture from generation to generation." More often overlooked is an alternative definition emphasizing *the child's idiosyncratic personal growth,* in which the developing human being gradually attains his own personal identity, which allows him to express himself and to seek to meet his own idiosyncratic needs and values in his own way. Neither is a necessary prerequisite to or consequence of an effort to look at children's political dispositions, or at how they change through life. The study of political socialization is not necessarily the study of conformity and the maintenance of the status quo, despite what some critics have written.

Theories of political socialization also generally take either of two forms, as Easton and Dennis (1969) have noted: "psychological" or "political." "Psychological" theories treat individual dispositions (e.g., the child's political attitudes, level of political involvement, etc.) as the primary output variables of interest, whereas "political" theories treat them as mere way stations to the key output variables which involve some aspect of the political system (e.g., its persistence) or political policy.

Stated another way, to political scientists the most fundamental justification for studying political socialization is that early attitude acquisition ultimately has some consequence in the political system. Psychologists, of course, have a more intrinsic interest in the process of development itself, and this can lead to some pretty puzzling dialogues. The political contents that preoccupy political scientists (e.g., party identification) can seem psychologically peripheral and thus boring to developmental psychologists, whereas esoteric psychological theories without any very obvious relevance to adult political behavior (e.g., those of Piaget) may seem irrelevant to political scientists (cf. Greenstein, 1970). In this essay, psychological theories will not be considered in any very great detail.

The age range during which political development is presumed to occur has undergone wild swings over the years. Today there is a tendency to identify "political socialization" with the study of preadult, or even of preadolescent, political behavior. This, of course, is a reaction against the earlier conviction that the citizen blossomed full-blown upon entry into the electorate, since children had no political thoughts. Much of the most interesting research on political attachment has focused on preadolescents, to be sure, though recently adolescents and young adults have been of great concern. With partisanship, however, it is apparent that development can potentially take quite different forms at a number of crucial points scattered across the entire life span. Space prevents dealing here in much detail with developments later in the life span, though the persistence of early socialization residues is an important issue, addressed at the end of the essay.[1] I think both these issues will be in the forefront of research attention in the future, so I have looked at them quite extensively in another work (Sears, 1975).

Any field that attracts so much research activity soon also attracts those who think some or all of the effort is misguided. Some of the commentators are of course constructive critics, others merely detractors and snipers. For some of the more thoughtful evaluations of the field as a whole, see Dennis (1968, 1973), Greenstein (1970), Kavanagh (1972), Koeppen (1970), Marsh (1971, 1972), Searing, Schwartz, and Lind (1973), and Weissberg (1974). The broader criticisms that have been made mainly concern the possibilities of generally inadequate methodology, political irrelevance, a conservative bias in the research, and lack of persistence of early socialization residues. As indicated above, the emphasis in this essay will be on the substantive findings in the area, rather than on some critical overview of it as an area of research. I will return to these questions at the end of the chapter, since they are most properly dealt with in the context of the research that has been done. To anticipate, though without going into detail here, the first three criticisms generally seem to me not to hold up: important and interesting problems clearly are being investigated, present methodologies seem more imperfect than wholly misguided and misleading, and in recent years system-challenging as well as system-sustaining dispositions have been investigated. The latter criticism, concerning the persistence of early socialization residues, does raise some interesting and thus far unresolved empirical questions, however, which I will take up toward the end.

With that, let us turn to attachment.

ATTACHMENT TO THE POLITICAL SYSTEM

Much attention has been accorded to the child's early attachment to symbols of the political system, partly because it has been thought politically crucial (for the development of an adult sense of political legitimacy) and partly because it is one of the earliest affective responses children seem to make to the political arena. Exactly how one defines attachment or distinguishes it from more partisan attitudes is not so simple a matter as it might seem at first. We will discuss this problem in some detail after reviewing empirical studies on attachment. Briefly, though, the principal contents normally categorized under attachment include affects toward symbols of the regime (flag, public buildings, historical documents, slogans, glorious national heroes and events), generalized political trust, support for institutions, support for public policy (especially foreign policy) and behavioral compliance with it, and endorsement of the reigning rules of the political game.

Childhood Socialization: A Preliminary Point of View

Early data collected in the late 1950s and early 1960s by Fred Greenstein, David Easton, and Robert Hess and their colleagues provided a set of benchmarks against which all subsequent work must be assessed. Their conclusions emphasized the young child's personalized and idealized view of government and thus his positive affective attachment to the political system. However, the data had serious potential limitations in generality, since they had been collected primarily from white, middle-class, urban and suburban American children at only one historical point in time. First, let us briefly review the point of view outlined in that early research (for more detail, see Easton and Dennis, 1969; Greenstein, 1965; Hess and Torney, 1967; or the summary in Sears, 1969a), then consider the qualifications placed on it by later work done in a broader range of historical, national, and cultural circumstances.

Simple chauvinism. The earliest concepts of nation or of the political system seemed to consist of the child's concept of his own nationality. Six-year-olds (in a variety of countries investigated) thought of other nationality groups as dissimilar from themselves and their countrymen as similar (Lambert and Klineberg, 1967). As the child got older, he acquired a strong positive feeling toward various symbols of his nation, though with relatively vague conceptual content. American children of grade school age had strong positive affect attached to the American flag, America as a country, and the American people (Hess and Torney, 1967; Lawson, 1963). The customary rationalizations for this early attachment (e.g., America is great because of its freedom or democracy) appeared only later as the child moved into adolescence.

Personalizing and idealizing. The child initially came into contact with government through familiarity with its most salient leaders. For example, Greenstein (1960, 1965) found that 96 percent of a fourth grade sample could name the president; familiarity with other aspects of government was much skimpier. The child therefore *personalized* government, thinking it consists simply of its great leaders rather than of institutions, roles, laws, or buildings. For example, Easton and Dennis (1965) found that second graders, asked to pick the "two best pictures of government," tended to select George Washington and President Kennedy (86 percent). Similarly, they picked the president as "running the country" (also 86 percent) and as making the laws (76 percent). Easton and Dennis (1969) also concluded that young children viewed government as personified by the policeman, as well, yielding a pattern of early contact with what the investigators called the "head and tail" of government.

Young children also tended to *idealize* the "president." Second graders rated him, along with "father," as close to "my favorite of all"; the president "cares a lot what you think if you write to him," according to 75 percent, and he was rated as highly on "would always help me if I needed it" (Hess and Torney, 1967). Evaluations of President Eisenhower among fourth to eighth graders were so positive in the late 1950s that Greenstein (1960) described him as seeming to be "the benevolent leader" in their eyes.

Young children did not idealize other authority figures to the same degree, although they had generally favorable attitudes toward the various authorities and institutions with which they were familiar. For example, 72 percent of the fourth graders said that "the government" makes mistakes "almost never" or "rarely," as opposed to "sometimes," "often," "usually," or "almost always" (Easton and Dennis, 1965). They similarly approved of the Supreme Court, politicians in general, political candidates, and the policeman. And adults, too, at that time had positive but not extravagent attitudes toward the president (Greenstein, 1965). But the most idealized of all, according to these early studies, was the image of the president in young children's eyes, the very personification of the government.

As children got older, their idealization of the president declined, and they increasingly perceived government not simply in personalized terms, but more broadly in terms of institutions, laws, roles, and other authorities. In the Easton and Hess study, eighth graders personalized government much less often; only 25 percent picked Presidents Washington and Kennedy as symbolizing government, only 58 percent thought the president ran the country, and only 5 percent thought he made the laws (Hess and Torney, 1967). Older children increasingly viewed institutions, such as Congress, as central in the system. And their information about other political roles and bodies markedly increased (Greenstein, 1965). Moreover, approval of other authorities in the system also increased.

So the early studies found that preadolescent children were much more familiar with the president than with any other public figure (or institution), tended to personalize government in the figure of the president, and to idealize him. As children passed into adolescence, they became more aware of other elements of government, began increasingly to perceive government in terms of groups and institutions rather than simply emphasizing individual persons, and tended to idealize the president less, though generally approving the other institutions with which they were familiar.

This pattern bore two general implications. One was psychological: the child's personalizing and idealizing grew out of his cognitive limitations and psychodynamic needs (Greenstein, 1965; Hess and Torney, 1967). The other was political: this early personalizing and idealizing was interpreted as a necessary precondition for the child's allegiance to the political system and later for his adulthood sense of the legitimacy of political authority, which ultimately was seen as a critical precondition for the persistence of the political system (Easton and Dennis, 1969).

Later Critiques

Scores of studies have been conducted since this early research, and they have considered a much wider range of children and of political systems. Investigators have discovered quite a different picture of children's attitudes. They have found that children do not invariably personalize and idealize authority, and they have raised doubts about just how crucial such early socialization is for a later sense of system support. Let us consider each of these issues in turn.

The unknown mover. The notion that children personalize "government" in the form of the president (or other chief of state) implies some special visibility of this role-occupant. The president in this view is thought to tower over a child's life space, much as God must have done in earlier times. Yet the evidence is that the premier political leaders of democratic states do not invariably have this salience.

In the United States, the president is ordinarily the best-known public figure, to be sure, among children and adults alike (Greenstein, 1965; Sears, 1969a). In one 1969–1970 survey of 13-year-olds, 94 percent could identify the president, 60 percent the vice-president, but only 16 percent or fewer their senator, congressman, cabinet officers, or congressional leaders (Greenstein, 1973). So it was with de Gaulle in France, as well (Roig & Billon-Grand, 1968), and the Queen of England (Greenstein, 1973).

But in other nations the political leader is not so well known. In both Australia (Connell, 1971) and Canada (Pammett, 1971), children's familiarity with the American president well outstripped their knowledge of their own prime minister.

Nor is knowledge invariably personalized, either. True enough, in France, England, and the United States children have had more differentiated images of their leaders' (prime minister, president) roles than of their national legislatures' (Greenstein, 1973). But in Canada, children knew more about Parliament than about the prime minister (Pammett, 1971), and in Colombia the youngest children ascribed more centrality in government to Congress and more power to the Supreme Court than to the president (Reading, 1968).

Does the chief of state occupy the central, dominating place in the child's galaxy of heroes? Evidently not very often. Children's "exemplars" ("Who would you most like to be like?") have been investigated in several studies. Greenstein, in 1958, found only 3 percent mentioned the president, with another 7 percent citing Washington or Lincoln (1965). In England, in 1969,

17 percent of the girls cited the queen or someone in the royal family, and only 2 percent cited some current political figure; for boys, it was 8 percent and 7 percent, respectively (Stradling, 1971). Both studies also reviewed surveys made, surprisingly enough, around the turn of the century, to the same effect. And French children in 1964 ignored President de Gaulle almost completely in citing those who had done most for France, whereas 48 percent named Pasteur (Roig and Billon-Grand, 1968). These are certainly not cases of overwhelming centrality of the chief of state. And of German high school students tested in 1967, few cited current leaders as the thing they were most proud of about their country, and 22 percent cited Hitler as the thing they were *least* proud of (Baker, 1970). So even when central, a national leader may not be a hero.

We are left, then, without any very strong evidence that children impose any special need for a strong leader on their perceptions of their own political system. Rather, his centrality seems to be a sometime thing, dependent more on his actual role in the system and on his particular reputation than on children's needs. And in any case, he does not usually occupy a very central spot in the child's galaxy of heroes.

The malevolent and/or fallible leader. Nor do children in general turn out to have an overwhelmingly idealized view of the chief of state. The original "benevolent leader" was discovered among mainly white, middle-class children at the end of Eisenhower's reign and at the beginning of John F. Kennedy's (Greenstein, 1960, 1965; Hess and Easton, 1960; Easton and Dennis, 1965). Now we have available data from a broader historical period (including other, less popular presidents), from a broader range of the population, and from other political systems, and they yield quite a different picture.

Later presidents simply have not elicited such idealized views, even in essentially the same age group (roughly ages 9 to 14 or so). Jaros, Hirsch, and Fleron (1968) found that white children in a strongly Republican area of Appalachia did not evaluate President Johnson very positively at all in 1967, and these investigators introduced the term "the malevolent leader" to describe this youthful cynicism. Samples of children we tested in California in 1968 and 1971 evaluated both Presidents Johnson and Nixon at best lukewarmly, as shown in Table 1. Similarly, Vaillancourt (1972) found San Francisco Bay Area children evaluated Presidents Johnson and Nixon more negatively than positively in 1968–1969. Tolley (1973) tested a wide variety of preadolescent children in 1971 and found predominantly negative attitudes toward President Nixon's handling of Vietnam (p. 65); even among supposedly idealizing third graders, positive evaluations did not vastly outnumber those that were negative (p. 69). He used the term "the fallible leader" here.[2]

No overwhelming idealization has emerged in studies of children in other nations. Roig and Billon-Grand (1968) found that French children were more likely to evaluate then-President de Gaulle negatively than positively, and

TABLE 1   Preadolescent children's evaluations of prominent public figures, 1968 and 1971, in percentages

	Sample	Like (1)	Dislike (2)	Not sure, no feeling (3)	Don't know person (4)	Net affect (1—2)
Martyred leaders and family						
President John F. Kennedy* (post-assassination)	1968 S1	95	1	2	1	+94
Senator Robert F. Kennedy (pre-assassination)	1968 S1	72	6	16	4	+66
Senator Ted Kennedy	1971 F	60	7	12	21	+53
Martin Luther King (post-assassination)	1968 S2	78	5	14	2	+73
Incumbent presidents						
President Lyndon B. Johnson*	1968 S1	46	23	25	5	+23
President Richard M. Nixon	1971 F	31	39	6	24	−8
Other political leaders						
Governor Ronald Reagan*	1968 S1	26	49	21	4	−23
Governor Ronald Reagan	1971 F	24	38	14	24	−14
Richard Nixon	1968 S1	22	20	30	29	+2
Vice-President Hubert Humphrey	1968 S1	37	8	35	21	+29
Senator Edmund Muskie	1971 F	14	9	49	28	+5
Minority leaders						
Cesar Chavez	1971 F	19	14	47	20	+5
Angela Davis	1971 F	18	20	39	23	−2
Martin Luther King (pre-assassination)	1968 S1	21	19	22	38	+2

Note: Children were tested in the Sacramento, California, public schools in April (S_1) and then again in June (S_2) 1968 (n = 1284); and in Fresno, California, public schools (F) in February 1971 (n = 946). The age range was 9 to 14; in Sacramento the racial distribution was 67 percent Anglo, 14 percent black, and 11 percent chicano; in Fresno it was 41 percent, 28 percent, and 25 percent, respectively. The remaining children came from a variety of ethnic groups.
* Only in these cases was the individual's title provided; in all other cases, only his name was given.

among British school children, Stradling and Zurick (1971) found little idealizing and many negative evaluations of British party leaders. Similar findings were obtained by Greenstein and Tarrow (1970) in a study using projective techniques: positive evaluations of the head of state somewhat outnumbered negative ones in the United States, but failed to do so in France or England. Abramsom and Inglehart (1970) report early idealizing of the monarch in England and the Netherlands, but little of the French president or of premiers in the three nations.

Even more telling is the finding that children in some social groups have had sharply negative attitudes toward the president, rather than early idealization. Preadolescent black and Mexican-American children were highly negative toward President Nixon in our California samples, as shown in Table 2. Similar findings are reported by Garcia (1973), Sica (1972), and Tolley (1973, p. 72). On the other hand, data collected during the Kennedy and Johnson administrations, during periods of almost unparalleled presidential support for blacks, reveal strongly positive attitudes toward the president among young black children, frequently more favorable than those of white children (Jaros, 1967; Abramson, 1972a, p. 1264; Sigel, 1965, 1968), though diminishing somewhat by 1968 (Greenberg, 1970d). In Tolley's study of attitudes about Vietnam, middle-income white children (p. 82) and children from military families (p. 77) expressed vastly more positive attitudes toward President Nixon than did those from upper-income and/or civilian families.

Parenthetically, some versions of the earlier work saw children's early attachment to the political system as promoted by their personalizing and idealizing government in the form of the policeman, as well (Easton and Dennis, 1969). But in recent years it has become clear that not all children idealize the police, any more than they idealize unpopular presidents. A 1969 survey in Rochester found that children of both races, but especially black children, less often felt "all laws are fair" than was true in the early 1960s (Liebschutz and Niemi, 1974). And black children have expressed much more antagonism toward the police than have whites in every recent study comparing the two races' attitudes toward the police (Elder, 1970; Laurence, 1970; Greenberg, 1970b, 1970d; Engstrom, 1970; Rodgers and Taylor, 1971). This would seem to reflect the difference in climate of adult opinion. Adult studies conducted during the 1960s repeatedly found the same antipolice antagonisms among blacks (cf. Campbell and Schuman, 1968; Sears and McConahay, 1973).

TABLE 2   Ethnic differences in evaluations of political parties and leaders, net affect in percentages

	Blacks	Chicanos	Anglos
Ted Kennedy	+66	+60	+40
Democrats	+20	+13	+14
Republicans	−10	−5	+13
Richard Nixon	−37	−28	+20
Ronald Reagan	−48	−24	+12
Angela Davis	+34	−4	−23
Cesar Chavez	+10	+34	−11
	N = 261	234	390

Source: 1971 Fresno data (see Table 1 for details). Entry is percentage saying "like" minus percent saying "dislike" in the ethnic group indicated, in response to the question, "How do you feel about (this person) / (the job the ――――――― have been doing)?"

The special appeals of Ike and the Kennedys. How can the idealization of early studies be reconciled with the mixed attitudes characteristic of so many that have appeared subsequently? Let us argue here that to some extent the earlier findings were merely a historical accident. The Easton and Hess and the Greenstein projects were conducted during the Eisenhower and Kennedy administrations—the first, a time of relatively little partisan controversy around an extremely popular president, and the second, we will argue, a president unusually appealing to children.

President Eisenhower was highly esteemed among children, but then he was also vastly esteemed among adults. Even before he became president, he ranked as the most admired man in the country. Throughout his eight years in office, his popularity consistently remained at a level higher than that of any president since FDR. Even his forays into partisan politics did not damage his popularity very much. During his own candidacies (Campbell *et al.*, 1960; Converse and Dupeux, 1966), during his term in office (Mueller, 1973), and during his vice-president's unsuccessful attempt at immediate succession (Key, 1966, p. 140), Eisenhower succeeded in retaining mass approval from the voters, even from Democrats, Stevenson supporters and Kennedy supporters. Indeed, by comparison with the staggering losses in popularity suffered over their terms in office by President Truman, Johnson, and Nixon (and even, in lesser extent, of course, by John Kennedy in his aborted presidency), Eisenhower's retention of mass popularity seems in retrospect quite amazing. It may still be, as Greenstein (1965) argues, that children liked Ike even more than adults did, but even among adults relatively few disliked him.

John F. Kennedy is a different story. He came into office without this transcendent trust and popularity, as an inexperienced and youthful man who barely won the 1960 election after a campaign with bitter overtones of religious bigotry. Although he soon accumulated considerable popularity among the adult public, his evaluations in his last year were not out of line with those of subsequent presidents at comparable stages. Nevertheless, since presidential popularity seems simply to drop with time in office, generally, this meant that JFK's abbreviated presidency had been more popular, on the average, than others were (Mueller, 1973). So there is evidence that JFK, like Ike, was an unusually popular president among adults.

But in addition to that, Kennedy (and later his brothers) seems to have been unusually attractive to children. Perhaps the most compelling demonstration here is simply to compare the Kennedys with other political leaders. Such a comparison is made in Table 1, for our samples of California children in 1968 and 1971. It is plain to see that evaluations of the martyred President Kennedy, and of the living Robert Kennedy and Ted Kennedy, far exceeded those of any other leader. The only near rival was the recently martyred Martin Luther King. But the two incumbent presidents at the time of testing, the incumbent governor on both occasions, and a host of other highly esteemed public officials, all fell far short of the popularity of the Kennedys. Even among minority children, the only rival for the Kennedys was Martin Luther King; as shown in Table 2, Angela Davis was less popular among blacks, and Cesar Chavez less popular among chicanos, than was Ted Kennedy.[3]

It might be thought that all these pro-Kennedy sentiments were simply due to mourning for the martyred President. Indeed, children were very upset by the first Kennedy assassination, especially those in late childhood. Emotional reactions mostly exceeded those of either adults or adolescents, according to Sigel's post-assassination survey (1965). Children worried more about what would happen to the country, and their images of President Kennedy became even more idealized after his death. According to Wolfenstein's excellent clinical study (Wolfenstein and Kliman, 1965), adolescents were especially deeply disturbed, displacing onto him their feelings about more personal pending object losses, anticipating the renunciation of their own parents necessitated by their forthcoming transition to adulthood.

Adults, too, idealized Kennedy after his death. Half the population called him "one of the two or three best Presidents the country ever had" (Sheatsley and Feldman, 1965), though only 59 percent had even approved of the way he was handling the job immediately before (Mueller, 1973). And adults all over the world apparently felt the same way, even behind the Iron Curtain; for example, surveys conducted in Warsaw, Poland, immediately before and after the assassination, found that Kennedy was suddenly perceived as the statesman who had made far and away the greatest contributions to maintaining world peace (Sicinski, 1969). And in the years immediately thereafter, adults did create and perpetuate the Camelot myth of Kennedy's greatness—much like the myths created after Lincoln's death (see Donald, 1956), as Fred Greenstein has pointed out.

However, as the emotional impact of the first assassination receded into memory, adults did not maintain this high level of idealization for the surviving brothers. Robert Kennedy barely won the 1968 Democratic primary in California, and post-Chappaquidick evaluations of Ted Kennedy have been much more restrained among adults than among the children described in Table 1.

Nor has death or assassination in other cases left children with this same highly positive feeling toward the deceased, much less their surviving relatives. Connell (1971, pp. 126–128) reports that Australian children were more upset by the shooting of Robert F. Kennedy than by the drowning of their own prime minister. And Martin Luther King rose sharply in approval after his assassination, but even after his death he was not revered like the Kennedys, as shown in Table 1. White children (and adults) were not in general terribly upset by the King assassination (Clarke and Soule, 1971), and much less so by the assassinations of Malcolm X, Medgar Evers, George Lincoln Rockwell (Kirkham, Levy, and Crotty, 1969; Hofstetter, 1969), or the near-successful attempt on George Wallace.

So it seems likely that the vast popularity of President Kennedy among preadolescent children before his assassination, as revealed in earlier studies, and afterwards, shared also by his brothers, is not due simply to his being president or to his having been assassinated. So why have the Kennedys had this special appeal to children? No one really knows. One can speculate that John Kennedy's loving and highly publicized fatherhood, his self-mocking sense of humor, his personal attractiveness, his vitality, his seeming calm and strength—all added up to everyone's favorite daddy (or movie hero). His seemingly protective role in the nuclear confrontations of the 1960s could have made him especially important to children. Or he could have seemed the youthful David in battle against aging Goliaths. For our purposes, it does not really matter; the point is that any estimate of children's attitudes toward the president will necessarily be favorably biased when relying only on attitudes toward Ike or JFK, as much of the early work did.

These findings therefore suggest important qualifications to earlier work that found children entering the political system by personalizing the government in the form of an idealized chief of state, and/or policeman. The personalizing and idealizing alike seem to have been most common in one historical period (the late 1950s and early 1960s) and one political system (the United States). Later presidents, the police, and chiefs of state in other nations have not consistently drawn such responses from young children. And within the United States itself, certain groups of children have shown very definite disapproval of both president and police, especially when adults' evaluations of them have been antagonistic or conflicted.

Solid Findings

If the picture yielded by the early pathbreaking studies needs to be corrected by later work, what solid empirical findings remain about early acquisition of contents relating to political attachment? As we have seen, the marginal frequencies of various attitudes do vary considerably, but there are some seemingly reliable regularities by age, race, nationality, and sex role. So let us turn our attention to these apparently replicable findings before considering the theoretical implications of the more recent data.

Early positivity, later partisanship. Young children of age 8–10 or so, just becoming aware of the world of politics, are almost invariably much more positive toward its various symbols than are comparable older children as they move into adolescence (i.e., of age 12–15 or so). Such age differences show up almost universally, across administrations, time, nations, ethnic groups, and wherever political socialization research has been done.

Young children's early positive affect has been shown to diminish within this preadolescent age range with respect to the Queen and Premier of the Netherlands, and the President and Prime Minister of France (Abramson and

Inglehart, 1970) ; the President of Colombia (Reading, 1968) ; the government, nation, and party leaders in England (Dennis, Lindberg, and McCrone, 1971; Stradling and Zurick, 1971) ; the President of the United States (Easton and Dennis, 1969, Chapter 8; Greenstein, 1965; Tolley, 1973; Greenberg, 1970d) ; police (Greenberg, 1970b; Easton and Dennis, 1969, Chapter 10) ; law (Hess and Torney, 1967; Rodgers and Taylor, 1970) ; government in general (Greenberg, 1970b, 1970c) ; and generalized political trust (Jennings and Niemi, 1974, Chapter 5).

What exceptions are there to this general decline in positive affect as the child approaches adolescence? Evidently only areas of little or no controversy, such as affect toward the American flag (Lawson, 1963) or the English monarchy (Abramson and Inglehart, 1970), neither of which shows any marked changes with age. Also, details of the political systems' norms, such as the duty to vote or the right of dissent, seem actually to become somewhat *more* positively evaluated with age, but presumably because of increasing information rather than of increasing attachment (Dennis, Lindberg, and McCrone, 1971; Gallatin and Adelson, 1970; Pammett, 1971; Zellman and Sears, 1971). However, the overwhelming finding is that early positive affect diminishes with age.

The growing number of negative evaluations occurs principally as children move toward more partisan evaluations of standard political symbols. Black children showed the greatest drop in respect for the police (Greenberg, 1970b), and Republican children the greatest drop in admiration for President Kennedy (Easton and Dennis, 1969). It is not yet clear whether there is also a drop in positive affect among children who, when grown, would normally be expected to like the political symbol in question, e.g., Democratic children regarding a Democratic president. Available analyses do not permit a definite answer. It appears that some such drop does occur, however (cf. Easton and Dennis, 1969, p. 196). That is, the drop in positive affect is not solely due to growing partisanship.

And there is a good bit of evidence that the drop occurs later with less politically sophisticated children. Low-IQ children, girls, Amish, Mexican-Americans, blacks with naive racial attitudes, and children of low socioeconomic status have all been shown to retain positive attitudes about authority longer than their counterparts (cf. Hess and Torney, 1967; Greenberg, 1970b; Garcia, 1973; Sears, 1973; Jaros and Kolson, 1974).

Black political socialization. Another set of consistent findings concerns racial differences in early political attitudes. The political socialization of black children has very naturally become an important practical question in recent years, and some very different ideas have been expressed about it. On the one hand, there is Myrdal's (1944) well-known observation that blacks are "exaggerated Americans who believe in the American creed more passionately than whites." On the other hand, many observers have written that blacks grow up with more cynical, disaffected, distrustful attitudes than do whites because of the ill treatment they have been subjected to in the United States (cf. Greenberg, 1970a; Laurence, 1970; Bullock and Rodgers, 1972; Lyons, 1970; and many others).

Another question is whether—and how—these racial differences (if they exist) have been changing in recent years. Here the principal issue is whether or not blacks' early political socialization has been changing from mainstream system support to political disaffection. The precipitating historical changes considered crucial in this connection range from the broad population changes of nearly the entire twentieth century (moving blacks from the nineteenth century, semi-illiterate, rural South to the vast contemporary northern urban ghettoes) to more limited historical events, such as the general postwar desegregation of American institutions, the civil rights protest movement of the late 1950s and early 1960s, and the urban riots of the mid-1960s (Abramson, 1972a; Paige, 1970; Sears and McConahay, 1973).

These concerns reduce to two basic questions. Do black children now differ from otherwise comparable white children in political attachment? And has there been a change over historical time in this difference?

First of all, relative to white children, black children have indeed been clearly more negative toward blacks' partisan adversaries, as they have come to be defined in the last decade. They have been dramatically more negative to the *police* and "law and order" than white children (Greenberg, 1970b, 1970d; Laurence, 1970; Rodgers and Taylor, 1971); more negative toward the *Vietnam War* (Laurence, 1970; Tolley, 1973; Smookler, 1971); more negative toward *President Nixon* and other *conservative Republicans,* as shown in Table 2 (also Jaros and Kolson, 1974; Liebschutz and Niemi, 1974; Orum and Cohen, 1973); and they have felt less *efficacious* and powerful in political life (Abramson, 1972a; Laurence, 1970; Lyons, 1970).

On the other hand, they have consistently been more favorable than white children to their political allies, such as the *Kennedys* (Sigel, 1965; see Table 2), and not discernibly less favorable to *President Johnson* (Greenberg, 1970b, 1970d; Jaros, 1967; Sigel, 1968). They have consistently rejected *racial stereotypes* and favored *racial protest* more than have white children. Black children in 1968 and 1971 were highly favorable to black people, knowledgeable about racial issues, and high in black consciousness, in pro-Democratic partisanship, and in political knowledge (Laurence, 1970; Orum and Cohen, 1973).[4] So there is broad evidence of highly partisan socialization of black children since the late 1960s.

But how about attachment to the system? This is a more complex issue, because the line between partisanship and attachment is a fuzzy one. The most unequivocal measures of attachment seem to be those focusing on compliance to the law and generalized political trust. These measures have not generally shown much difference between black and white children. No racial differences were found in support for compliance to the law in three separate studies (Rodgers and Taylor, 1970, 1971; Engstrom, 1970). Much more evidence is available in the general area of political trust and cynicism, and it similarly reveals only minor and inconsistent racial differences. Abramson's (1972a) careful review (as well as the work of Jennings and Niemi, 1974) indicates no racial differences prior to 1967, but he does conclude that black children have been less politically trusting than white children since then. Even this apparent latter-day, post-riot cynicism is open to question, however, as Abramson acknowledges. The racial differences in political trust tend to be rather small, varying between 2 percent and 14 percent, most being of doubtful statistical significance. A study conducted by Greenberg in Philadelphia and Pittsburgh in 1968 is often cited as an example of post-1967 black disattachment, but close examination of the data shows no racial difference in perceived government goodwill, positive role performance, or support for the president (though black children were lower in perceived government benevolence). So of the dozen or so published studies in this area, only those of Lyons (1970) in Toledo and of Orum and Cohen (1973) in Illinois show any major and reliable racial differences in political trust and cynicism.

Where black children seem to be more disattached is on measures whose manifest content concerns attachment, but to which they are clearly responding mostly with racial or political partisanship. Their greater antagonism toward the president and police in recent years probably reflects blacks' partisan reactions against "the authorities" rather than against "the regime" (or the system itself). Table 2 shows clearly that blacks felt positive toward the Democrats, Ted Kennedy, and the black leader Angela Davis, but negative toward the Republicans and Republican leaders Nixon and Reagan.

Black children's basic support for American institutions, but partisan antagonism toward police and Nixon, is shown in another way in Table 3. They were indeed much more negative than whites toward Nixon and the police, but only slightly more negative toward "the president" and "our government" when considering them in a more institutional and less partisan context. Finally, they were even *more* supportive than white children with respect to criticism of government and United States relations with other countries.[5] The major exception is an item on fighting in bad wars, which is probably interpretable in terms of blacks' greater opposition to the Vietnam War.

Or compare our 1971 Fresno data, in which 14 percent of the black children said they "liked" President Nixon and 51 percent said they "disliked" him, with Greenstein's more positive 1970 data, in which 28 percent were coded as expressing favorable attitudes and only 3 percent were unfavorable to the president (Greenstein, 1973). But the former asked the partisan question, whereas the latter asked the child to explain the American presidency (with no mention of Nixon) to a foreign child. So black children clearly are more

TABLE 3　Racial differences: Drawing the line between partisanship and attachment

	(% unfavorable)		Racial
	Whites	Blacks	differences, %
The police and political partisanship			
Do you think *policemen* can be trusted? (% no)	24	60	−36
How do you feel about *Richard Nixon?* (% dislike)	29	51	−22
Do you think that *the President* wants to help rich people more than poor people? (% yes)	16	39	−23
Institutions: President and government			
How do you feel about the *American government?* (% don't like it)	10	17	−7
What do you think about *our government?* It _____ makes mistakes. (% often, usually)	24	35	−11
How often do you think *the President* makes mistakes? (% often)	20	25	−5
If you or your parents wrote *the President* a letter, he would _____. (% care a little, wouldn't care at all)	21	27	−6
Criticism of government and governors			
You should not *say bad things* about the laws of our country. (% disagree)	41	42	−1
Is it all right for a man to say on television that he *disagrees* with what the President is doing in Vietnam? (% yes)	62	58	+4
Once a man has been elected President, you should not *say bad things* about the things he does. (% disagree)	54	40	+14
We should not *say bad things* about the people we have voted for. (% disagree)	38	21	+17
Do you think people would be better off if they just let the government do what it wants, without *complaining* about it? (% no)	70	53	+17
The United States and foreign policy			
If you were a boy and the right age to go into the *army*, would you be willing to fight in a war you thought was a bad war? (% no)	31	51	−20
Other countries should try to make their governments exactly like *our government*. (% disagree)	39	26	+13
Our government knows what is best for other countries. (% disagree)	42	24	+18
All the wars *the United States* has fought were good wars. (% disagree)	73	54	+19
I would like to see *the United States* rule the whole world. (% disagree)	64	40	+24

Source: 1971 Fresno data (see Table 1 for details). Emphasis added by author.

mistrustful of their partisan opponents. Whether in addition they have been less attached to the political system is much more doubtful; indeed, there is little positive evidence of such black disattachment in the published literature.

Nevertheless, there is perceptible evidence of change toward greater racial differences in political cynicism. Historically, adult blacks appear to have been largely as supportive as whites of the political system, excepting, of course, those aspects of it that worked directly, concretely, and explicitly to their disadvantage. We have elsewhere discussed this pattern (Sears and McConahay, 1973, Chapter 12), and other evidence of it is easy to come by (see Hero's 1969 analysis of blacks' support for American foreign policy). Yet it is equally easy to document currently growing political distrust in a variety of manifestations (Aberbach and Walker, 1970; Miller, Brown, and Raine, 1973; Sears, 1969b). What role might political socialization be playing in this change?

Elsewhere we have argued that it has been operating in two general ways (Sears and McConahay, 1973). First, the new pattern of early political socialization characteristic of contemporary northern urban ghettoes, as contrasted with the old rural South, has influenced young black children's earliest political attitudes. Specifically, growing up in the contemporary urban North was hypothesized to have produced important changes in black children's political socialization, increasing their political disaffection, black pride, and sophistication and political activism. Second, adolescents and young adults are hypothesized to have been resocialized to more cynical and militant views by the recent era of civil rights protest and riots. These changes in socializing condition, early socialization, and resocialization have resulted in a generation dubbed "the New Urban Blacks." These changes have presumably increased blacks' opposition to policies and incumbents opposing blacks' interests and promoted political violence, but they have not lessened attachment to the system.

It is hard now to prove conclusively that blacks' postwar northern urban socialization has been consistently different from their southern rural socialization before World War II. Yet many informed observers have speculated that it has been. And adult data are consistent with it. Sears and McConahay (1973) and Paige (1970) have shown that younger, northern- or western-reared, urban, and better-educated blacks (whom the former call "the New Urban Blacks" and Caplan, 1970, calls "the New Ghetto Man") have more positive black identity, more antiwhite antagonism, more generalized political distrust, and more political sophistication (relative to older, southern and/or rural-reared, less-educated blacks). They interpret these differences as reflecting historical changes in blacks' early political socialization, but of course, the evidence is indirect.

The resocializing effects of ghetto riots are explored by Sears and McConahay (1973). They show generational differences among adult blacks in post-"Watts" Los Angeles regarding interpretations of the riot and the desirability of further violence—but no effects of the other variables used to index changed early political socialization. They thus infer that the "New Urban Blacks," numerically dominant in the younger generation, effectively resocialized their agemates of quite different social backgrounds, regarding those novel events for which earlier socialization probably provided no clear norms. And indeed, such resocialization might have been occurring for a longer period prior to the riots, as the civil rights movement had adopted one novel and unprecedented tactic after another.

The era of mass ghetto riots also seems to have increased the cynicism and disaffection of black children's earliest political socialization. Abramson's (1972a) review shows that, if anything, black children were more politically trusting than whites prior to 1967, whereas the reverse, if anything, has been true since then. And the decline in black children's affection for presidents from Kennedy to Nixon has already been documented above. So it seems likely that the riot era both affected children's early socialization and resocialized late adolescents and young adults, both effects building on some longer-term changes in blacks' early political socialization associated with major population movements.

Other subcultures and nations. The limitations of the research with respect to samples and political systems have become more glaring with time (and exposure), so research has increasingly been done on samples other than white middle-class Americans. Jaros and Kolson (1974) have investigated Amish children, for example, whose parents' formal ideology is expressively antipolitical. Indeed, they are quite unsophisticated politically, and appropriately enough most do not plan to vote or fight for their country when they grow up.

With growing militancy among Mexican-Americans, research has started to appear on their early political socialization. We will not go into detail, but they do not seem to differ very greatly from Anglo children in various measures of attachment, such as pride in being an American or perceived benevolence of the government. Their level of political information has generally been much lower, however. And their evaluations of conservative Republican incumbents such as President Nixon and Governor Ronald Reagan have been more negative, as well. They also have been considerably more hostile than Anglo children toward the police and judges (Garcia, 1973; Sica, 1972).

Potentially some of the most interesting research of all ought to emerge from comparison of political socialization across different types of political systems. Attachment to the regime has now been studied in a wide variety of different countries, though so far only in democratic nations. Only rarely, however, have explicit cross-national comparisons been made, unfortunately. Of these, the best examples are Abramson and Inglehart (1970), Adelson and Beall (1970), Greenstein (1973), and the ongoing I.E.A. cross-national study by Torney (1974) and others. From other studies it is difficult to assess national differences because the procedures differ too much. Nevertheless, the volume of work is impressive. It has been done in England (Dennis, Lindberg, and McCrone, 1971; Stradling, 1971; Stradling and Zurick, 1971; Greenstein, 1973; Dennis *et al.,* 1968; Blumler *et al.,* 1971; Adelson and Beall, 1970); in Colombia (Reading, 1968); in Italy (Hennessey, 1969; Dennis *et al.,* 1968; Barnes, 1972); Canada (Pammett, 1971); in France (Greenstein, 1973; Roig and Billon-Grand, 1968; Abramson and Inglehart, 1970); in Australia (Connell, 1971); in West Germany (Baker, 1970; Adelson and Beall, 1970; Dennis *et al.,* 1968; Weiler, 1971); in the Phillipines (Tilman, 1970); in Japan (Langdon, 1967; Okamura, 1968); in the Netherlands (Abramson and Inglehart, 1970); in Tanzania (Prewitt, Von Der Muhll, and Court, 1970); and in Scotland (Jahoda, 1963, 1964). Of course, most research (and researchers) still has stemmed from the United States.

A Political Theory of System Persistence

Easton and Dennis (1969) have made the most concerted effort to design a specifically *political* theory to relate childhood political socialization to variations in the persistence of political systems. Their theory is certainly the most comprehensive, systematic, and specific available, so it is well worth evaluating insofar as possible.

To maximize system persistence, in their theory, early political socialization should proceed as follows: The child first becomes aware of the political system (politicization), chiefly through the proximal figure with whom he has personal contact (the policeman) and the remote personal symbol of government (the president). He thus views government as symbolized by these two persons (personalization), whom he views as powerful and benevolent (idealization). As the child matures, this early idealized and personalized view of government gradually evolves into a view in which government is symbolized by institutions, which the child generally approves and likes (diffuse system support). Diffuse system support among the citizenry is seen as critical to system persistence, at least in the long run.

The basic proposition in this theory is that early idealization and personalization are necessary conditions for later diffuse system support. One implication is that such contingencies should hold within individual children. Easton and Dennis do not test for that, showing instead that age cohorts, in the aggregate, follow such a sequence (or at least they did among their white American children of the late 1950s and early 1960s). So from their data alone we have no way of knowing whether or not an early personalized and idealized view of government is a necessary prerequisite for later diffuse system support. Other data are somewhat more directly relevant to the theory, so let us review them briefly.

We have earlier reviewed data indicating that American children subsequently have not been so prone to idealize the president and policeman, and that children in other democratic countries do not invariably personalize or idealize government. By itself this proves nothing, of course, because these deficiencies could be fatal to diffuse system support in such children. However, several studies do show that patently nonidealizing groups wind up strongly supportive of the system. Hennessey (1969) found in Italy that Communist adolescents were more supportive of democratic norms than non-Communists. Similarly, the evidence given in Table 3 was that black children are at the same time (1) much more derogatory toward the president and the police than are white children, yet (2) fully as supportive of the government and the nation. In this case their nonidealizing early attitudes seem not to have hampered their attachment to the system.

Even so, the most nonidealizing of these Communist and black children could well be the least attached to their political systems, in support of the theory. More relevant than these group comparisons, then, are direct correlations between children's early idealization and their diffuse system support. Two such studies have been done indexing diffuse system support by general political trust and compliance to the law. Engstrom (1970) reports that compliance with the law is related to perceived benevolence of the police among white children (gamma = .30) but not black (gamma = −.07). Conducting a regression analysis, Rodgers and Taylor (1971) similarly found that favorable attitudes toward the police were significant contributors both to compliance with the law and to political trust for white children, but to neither for black children. Since in neither study the races differed in political trust or compliance with law, it seems that idealization of the police was not a necessary prerequisite for system support. Other similar data have been collected overseas. Kavanagh (1972) observes that Dennis, Lindberg, and McCrone's (1971) data indicate British children were not highly jingoistic about their particular form of government, yet wound up highly allegiant nevertheless. Stradling and Zurick (1971) found no tendency at all for idealization of the British monarchy to be related to diffuse system support among British school children (and Blumler *et al.,* 1971, reported the same for British adults). And Roig and Billon-Grand (1968) found no tendency for idealization of the French Revolution to be related to any attitudes toward the present French political system among French children.

So children do not always personalize and idealize, and even when they do not, they frequently wind up highly allegiant. Thus the evidence does not so far indicate that early personalizing and idealizing are critical elements in the formation of children's diffuse system support.

But none of these data on children or on adults deal directly with the key developmental proposition of the theory, that early idealization should anticipate later, adulthood attachment to the political regime. This connection is difficult to document, so it has simply been assumed to exist by most researchers. We will return to it at the end of this chapter, when we consider the persistence of all kinds of early socialization residues into and through adulthood. And then there is the additional question whether there is any such unitary construct as "diffuse system support" in childhood or adulthood. In the next section we consider this question in both forms: the assumption of close relationships in childhood between these positive affects toward political symbols and attachment to the political system, and in adulthood between attachment and some consequential sense of political legitimacy.

As a final note, to test the Easton-Dennis notions as a "political theory" would require a range of values of the key outcome variable: persistence of the political system. However, Easton and Dennis's own data deal with only one value of it: the state of the American political system of the mid-1960s. Thus they fall back to an attempt to account for the diffuse system support (or individual differences in it) of American children as of that era. This then comes down to a more "psychological" effort to account for the attitudes of individual children, though informed by unusual sensitivity to the possibility of broader, systemic consequences of these attitudes.

Intrusion of Partisanship in Measures of Attachment to the System

We began by distinguishing between "attachment to the system" and "partisanship" because they have been investigated quite separately. All the research discussed above was intended to illuminate the former and, indeed, is manifestly concerned with it. We noted at the start that the distinction has its problems; yet we deferred their consideration until the main outlines of the research findings themselves were clear. But now is the time to take a more systematic look at the concept of "attachment."

The most influential taxonomies here are those proposed by Easton (1965). He begins by distinguishing three possible objects of attachment: (1) the political community—the group of persons bound together politically; (2) the regime—the constitutional order, including political roles and institutions and the rules or norms for handling matters politically, especially with respect to who wields power, how they are permitted to wield it, who is to comply, and conditions of their obligation; (3) the authorities—occupants of authority roles. The individual's responses to the latter two objects are those most investigated in the area of political socialization.

Legitimating ideologies are principally focused at the regime level. They concern support for or challenges to the ongoing regime and the right of the authorities to rule, i.e., beliefs in the legitimacy of authority roles and other regime structures. Much of the research we have been discussing was intended to investigate *diffuse system support*, i.e., a generalized belief in the legitimacy of the regime and the authorities: "the conviction on the part of the member that it is right and proper for him to accept and obey the authorities and to abide by the requirements of the regime" (Easton, 1965, p. 278).

On the other hand, *partisan ideologies* are concerned with day-to-day policy preferences and partisan preferences among specific incumbents or candidates (*ibid.*, pp. 286–287, 336–338). They are principally focused at "the authorities" level, though not exclusively concerned with evaluations of incumbent political officials.

Thus we have the familiar and obvious distinction between "attachment to the system" and "partisan predispositions." It is clearly sensible enough in theory. Its problems in practice derive more from difficulty in identifying indicators of system support than from difficulty in identifying indicators of partisanship. These problems are both conceptual and empirical.

The manifest content of measures of system support do not seem at first glance to present major conceptual problems; most seem clearly to focus on the "regime" rather than the "authorities" levels. Let us simply review those we have covered above: (1) *generalized measures of political trust, cynicism, and disaffection* (Abramson, 1972a; Lyons, 1970; Sears and McConahay, 1973; Orum and Cohen, 1973; Rodgers and Taylor, 1971); (2) *support for institutions,* such as legislative (Boynton, Patterson, and Hedlund, 1968), judicial (Weissberg, 1972), the political parties (Dennis, 1966), "the government" (Easton and Dennis, 1965; Greenberg, 1970c, 1970d; Dennis, Lindberg, and McCrone, 1971), the police (Easton and Dennis, 1969; Rodgers and Taylor, 1971; and the president or monarchy (Easton and Dennis, 1969; Abramson and Inglehart, 1970; Greenberg, 1970b, 1970d); (3) *support for regime symbols,* such as "democracy" (Dennis *et al.,* 1968; Tilman, 1970), the flag (Lawson, 1963), glorious past revolutions (Roig and Billon-Grand, 1968), infamous past national misdeeds (Baker, 1970), the monarchy (Blumler *et al.,* 1971), and glorious or infamous past national leaders (Baker, 1970; Greenstein, 1965; Roig and Billon-Grand, 1968; Stradling, 1971); (4) *support for regime norms,* such as freedom of dissent or other specific democratic norms (Dennis *et al.,* 1968; Hennessey, 1969; Pammett, 1971; Prothro and Grigg, 1960; Stouffer, 1955; Zellman and Sears, 1971), and compliance with law (Engstrom, 1970; Hess and Torney, 1967; Rodgers and Taylor, 1971); (5) *behavior consistent with regime norms* or in support of the regime in time of crisis, such as voting and partisanship (Pammett, 1971), lack of interest in emigration (Roig and Billon-Grand, 1968; Tilman, 1970), support of national foreign policy (Hero, 1969; Rogers, Stuhler, and Koenig, 1967), especially in time of crisis (Katz and Piret, 1964; Sears and McConahay, 1973, Chapter 12), support of the president after assassination or election (Mueller, 1973; Sheatsley and Feldman, 1965), and refusal to become involved in protest demonstrations, acts of civil disobedience, or riots (Easton and Dennis, 1969; Sears and McConahay, 1973).

However, not everyone would agree on the face validity of these items. The problem is that regime norms tend to be fuzzy and at times conflicting. Is it normative to feel one's own government is the best of all (Dennis, Lindberg, and McCrone, 1971), or is that just jingoism inconsistent with a higher norm of tolerance (Kavanagh, 1972)? Is it system-supportive for children to model themselves on past national heroes, such as Churchill, Washington, and Louis Pasteur (Greenstein, 1965; Roig and Billon-Grand, 1968; Stradling, 1971), or to reject past leaders like Hitler (Baker, 1970)? Should a child oppose national enemies, such as Communists, or grant them freedom of speech (Zellman and Sears, 1971)? Is civil disobedience an expression of opposition to the system or playing by the system's rules of the game? Should a child rush to the president's support in time of war or oppose the nation's demeaning itself in immoral war crimes (Tolley, 1973)?

These are analytic and conceptual quandaries, not empirical matters. Philosophers as well as politicians will always debate the content and application of regime norms—especially how far the norm of obedience of authorities should take the citizen in violation of other regime norms. No amount of industry or ingenuity will solve these problems for the empirical researcher. Nevertheless, they render research on system support inherently ambiguous; it is never crystal clear just what constitutes support.

But the second major problem is empirical in nature: how to distinguish empirically "legitimacy" of the regime from "partisanship" about incumbent authorities and their policies. In practice, they turn out to be really difficult to untangle. Virtually all the measures that were manifestly focused on system support, as just listed above, turn out empirically to be contaminated by "partisanship." This can be seen in the partisan, racial, or class cleavages that exist in support for the British monarchy (Abramson and Inglehart, 1970; Blumler *et al.*, 1971); presidents, American and otherwise (Converse and Dupeux, 1966; Table 2 above; Mueller, 1973; Tolley, 1973); the Supreme Court (Dolbeare and Hammond, 1968; Murphy and Tanenhaus, 1968) and other aspects of the judicial process (Weissberg, 1972); Congress and other legislative institutions (Boynton, Patterson, and Hedlund, 1968); the police (Laurence, 1970); free elections (Dennis, 1970); freedom of speech (Stouffer, 1955; Zellman and Sears, 1971); American foreign policy (Hero, 1969); going to war (Mueller, 1973; Tolley, 1973); and even reactions to presidential assassinations (Sheatsley and Feldman, 1965; Sigel, 1965). There seems to be no governmental role, incumbent, institution, or norm that does not elicit some partisan cleavage. That is, items ostensibly measuring "legitimacy" invariably also draw "partisan" reactions originating in agreement with specific policies or association with affect-laden partisan symbols. As policies change or new incumbents take over, the locus and often the degree of public support change, as well.

Two points need to be made about this intrusion of partisanship into measures of system support. The methodological point is that none of the ostensible measures of system support cited above are in fact "pure." More sophisticated statistical methods must be employed to distinguish the two sources of variance (diffuse system support and partisanship) in each measure; it cannot be assumed that any one item is a pure measure of either.

The second point is a more interesting substantive question. Although

Easton's regime-versus-authorities distinction may seem intuitively plausible at first glance, it may not correspond to the way people actually think. Possibly system support is constantly varying with various groups' changing and differential satisfaction with outcomes. Hence "legitimacy" may be in question and in flux at all times. That is, the search for two distinct sources of variance may prove largely fruitless.

Indeed, on closer inspection an even more surprising complexity emerges: the reverse intrusion happens as well. The clearest general case of this is what we have termed "the positivity bias," i.e., the tendency to skew evaluations of public figures and institutions in a generally positive direction (Sears, 1969a; Sears and Whitney, 1973a, 1973b). Consequently, even partisan foes rarely get evaluated very negatively, incumbents get returned to office surprisingly often, incoming officeholders are awarded a temporary honeymoon, presidents are generally (though not invariably) supported through thick and thin, and so on. Whatever partisan component exists in mass evaluations of political stimuli appears to be overlaid with another generally positive component, which most likely derives from some fundamental attachment at the regime (or possibly even community) level.

Finally, it might seem appealing to fall back on "behavioral" measures of system support as more valid and unambiguous than these attitudinal measures. But they themselves turn out to be even more impure measures of any underlying legitimacy. The level of coercive restraint or simple opportunity has much to do with such disparate behaviors as registration and voting, engaging in demonstrations or riots, and obeying traffic laws. And even when they do not, the "meaning" of the act is open to much debate. For example, participation in ghetto riots has been interpreted variously as a harmless and meaningless spree, as a justifiable protest against injustice, or as a dangerous revolutionary act against the regime and its system of "law and order."

The distinction between legitimacy and partisanship is certainly an important one to research, not least because it is so great a part of normal political debate. But at present it is difficult to determine that regime attitudes are in fact independent of partisan attitudes, and to separate the two sources of variance in the measures we have discussed. This is an important priority for further research, and fortunately, some have already taken it up (see Citrin, 1972; 1974).

PREADULT DEVELOPMENT OF PARTISAN PREDISPOSITIONS

Partisan predispositions are much simpler to identify, since they are generally less blurred by mixture with other attitudes. They exist in wide variety, focusing on individual political leaders, on various political, social, nationality, and religious groups, on various issue positions, and toward historical events.

It is now well established that partisan predispositions have their origins in childhood. Just how early, how strong, and how persistent these childhood predispositions are and what role the family plays in forming them are questions demanding more attention.

Childhood Beginnings

Primitive partisan affects show up in relation to a number of political and social objects in the early and middle grade school years. This is a complex field of investigation itself, of which here we need only sketch the broadest outlines.

Nationalities. Children soon feel good about their own nationality, and indeed, they can readily express simple affects toward various countries in the earliest grade school years. Tajfel (1969, p. 87) says, "at the age of six and seven children in Britain agree more about which countries they like and dislike than about practically anything else concerning these countries." Usually only by age 10 or so do sizable numbers develop comparable levels of dislike for rival or enemy nationalities—e.g., Israeli children for Arabs, American and West German children for Russians, etc. (cf. Lambert and Klineberg, 1967; Lawson, 1963; Middleton, Tajfel, and Johnson, 1970).

Along with this simple "friends and enemies" partisanship, White (1969) has noted a more sophisticated pattern among adults, which he calls the "pro-us" and "black-top" illusions: adults assume that "the people" in their adversary's country are more friendly than they actually are, and "the government" less friendly than it actually is. This too apparently has childhood roots: in 1971, 37 percent of our sample of preadolescents in Fresno disliked the Chinese government and 43 percent the Russian government, but only 10 percent and 14 percent respectively disliked the Chinese and Russian people.

Races. Systematic racial attitudes also originate in the preschool and early grade school years. Harding *et al.* (1969) suggest that American children normally pass through three distinctive stages: "racial awareness" by ages 3 to 4, "racial orientation" with primitive categories and affects by ages 4 to 8, and clear "racial attitudes" by the early grade school years. Among the classic demonstrations of these early preferences is the Clarks' (1939) black doll–white doll study, in which they observed racial self-derogation by black nursery school children. In more recent years, black children appear to be showing a preference for black dolls, presumably reflecting more positive evaluations of their racial group (Hraba and Grant, 1970). But both studies contribute to the overwhelming evidence for preadolescent acquisition of such racial prides and prejudices (Ashmore, 1970; Proshansky, 1966; Katz, Chabasinski, and Connolly, 1975).

With race, especially, conventional norms are reinforced by the obvious differences in skin color and other anatomical characteristics. These colors themselves also become associated with good and bad affects early in childhood. White children even before kindergarten evaluate white stimuli positively and black negatively, and they associate white with good human qualities and black with bad ones. In one study white children even smashed black Bobo dolls more readily than white ones (Williams and Stabler, 1973).

Social classes and other groups. Differential evaluations of social classes already appear to be present in the beginning grades (Tudor, 1971), as does clear awareness of occupational prestige differences (Simmons and Rosenberg, 1971). Affective preferences for people of certain body builds can be observed in third graders, as can preferences for certain names (Johnson and Staffieri, 1971). And the political consequences of sex role differentiation can also be observed in pre-adolescents. For example, girls or children with more feminine sex-role identification are more opposed to war than are boys or children with more masculine identification (Zellman, 1973). Thus children at ages 6 to 10 adopt partisan affective preferences with respect to a wide variety of social differentiations that are not expressly political.

Party identification: United States. Party identification, too, generally originates prior to adolescence. Early studies in the United States, done in the 1958–1962 period, found a rapid increase in the proportion of children with a party preference to about the fifth grade (age 11 or so), then a more gradual increase during the rest of life. In the Easton-Hess study, 55 percent of the fifth graders had a preference (Hess and Torney, 1967, p. 90), and Greenstein (1965, p. 73) found that 61 percent did (though he offered the children no explicit "independent" alternative). Subsequent studies have verified that the proportion of children with a party identification increases much more slowly after this age. By the twelfth grade, 64 percent had a party preference, as indicated in the excellent 1965 study by Jennings and Niemi (1968b) utilizing a near-representative nationwide sample (though omitting the approximately 26 percent of that group that had dropped out of school; see Niemi, 1973a).

However, young American children nowadays do not seem to acquire a party identification as often as in times past, according to three more recent studies in California. In our 1968 Sacramento sample, 36 percent of the combined fifth and eighth graders had a party identification, and in the 1971 Fresno sample, 38 percent did (without any major age differences). In a 1968–1969 study in the San Francisco Bay Area, Vaillancourt found that 36 percent had a stable preference over a six-month period (1973). All these studies used essentially the same item, so the data are roughly comparable. At the same time, the proportion claiming to be "independent" at this preadolescent level seems not to be increasing; 26 percent in the 1961–1962 period did, against 24 percent and 28 percent in the Fresno and Sacramento samples. Rather, in-

creasing numbers of preadolescents seem in recent years simply to be un-
familiar with the dimension of party preference, and they are unable to place
themselves on the traditional Democrat-Independent-Republican continuum.

Apparently a great many of the latter children have been designating themselves as "Independents" when they reached adolescence and voting age. The
proportion of self-designated "Independents" increases with age markedly up
to mid-adolescence (Jennings and Niemi, 1974). And Glenn's (1972) cohort
analysis documents the sharp increase over the historical period 1957–1971 in
the proportion of new voters who call themselves "Independents." These findings seem to arise from some decrease in recent years in the proportion of
American children acquiring a firm partisan preference, rather than anything
intrinsically related to age (i.e., they are "generational" rather than "life
cycle" effects; see Abramson, 1974; Glenn and Hefner, 1972).

Party identification: Europe. Major differences seem to exist among the Western democracies in this early acquisition of party identification, as indicated
in two cross-national studies by Dennis and McCrone (1970) and Abramson
and Inglehart (1970). British children are most likely to acquire an identification: at 8 to 10 years of age, 80 percent had a preference, and this proportion
held constant or even increased through adolescence. West German, Dutch, and
Belgian children also were quick to acquire a preference, going from 50 percent
to more than 80 percent in the same age range (about 10 to 17 or so). American children appear somewhat laggard by comparison, going from less than
40 percent (in the California data cited above) to 64 percent (Jennings and
Niemi, 1968b). French children are the slowest of all; indeed, they have become
notorious for lack of party preference. Roig and Billon-Grand (1968) found
that only 13 percent (ages 10 to 14) and Abramson and Inglehart (1970) that
26 percent (secondary school) had any party identification at all.[6] Italian children also were markedly less likely than most other European children to adopt
an early party preference.

Important historical changes seem to be discernible in Europe as well as in
the United States, however. Surveys taken at different points in time suggest
that West German, Italian, and French children became *increasingly* partisan
in the late 1950s and 1960s, the period during which American children evidently decreased in partisanship. As with the Americans, Cameron (1972) and
Dennis and McCrone (1970) interpret the European changes as a generaliza-
tional shift, rather than as an effect of age or life stage. Current socialization
is more partisan, they assume, than it was in the politically disrupted days of
previous generations, whether in the interwar, wartime, or immediate postwar
periods. In France, both the partisanship of the Gaullists, and the rather late
enfranchisement of women (1944) have finally begun to raise the general level
of partisanship, as shown by Cameron's (1972) comparison of surveys done in

1958 and 1968. The proportion of adult women with a party preference increased from 43 percent to 78 percent in those ten years, for example.

The strength of early party identification. Since much is made of the later importance of this youthful party identification, it is reasonable to ask whether at this age it generally is very strong. Partisan attitudes rather readily distribute themselves along such a genotypical dimension of psychological strength, varying in commitment, ego-involvement, or whatever term is preferred. Earlier we tried to formalize the notion of such an underlying dimension, anchored at the strong end by attitudes we have called "longstanding partisan predispositions" (Sears, 1969a) or "enduring commitments" (Sears and Whitney, 1973a, 1973b). At the weak end the continuum is anchored by what Converse (1970) has felicitously tagged "non-attitudes," because such expressed opinions appear not to be based on any stable underlying dispositions.[7]

We have proposed using three kinds of empirical indicators to distinguish enduring commitments from non-attitudes: (1) *stability over time,* e.g., high test-retest correlations in panel studies; (2) *affective consistency* over manifestly similar or related cognitive contents, e.g., across variations in item wording, manifestly related policy issues, or different attributes of a candidate; and (3) *power in determining attitudes* on newly arising cognitive contents, e.g., new candidates or new policy issues, when paired with them. Cognitive complexity and extensive differentiation are not necessarily distinguishing factors, however, since the critical genotypical dimension here is the strength of the individual's *affective commitment,* not its cognitive representations.

So, does this early party identification meet the criteria posed above for enduring commitments? First, how *stable* are these early loyalties? The obvious statistic seems to be a test-retest correlation; with adults the best data yield .84 (Pearson r) or .70 (tau-beta) over a two-year period (Converse, 1964, 1974). The results are somewhat but not drastically lower in the several studies of children aged roughly 9 to 15. In the Hess and Torney study, partisan reactions to John F. Kennedy's electoral victory remained highly stable ($r = .83$) over the short two-week period intervening between their tests (1965, p. 423). Vaillancourt (1973) found test-retest tau-beta correlations of .62 over two months, .57 over four months, and .47 over six months, with children from Oakland and Berkeley.

These correlations may be misleading with children, though, because they assume an ordinal scale, and many children (unlike adults) give off-scale responses (e.g., "don't know"). More telling, then, may be the proportion of initially partisan children who later express the same preference. Vaillancourt (1973) found that 70 percent of initial Republicans and Democrats repeated their preferences two months later; in our Sacramento data, 65 percent remained loyal over two months. In these two studies, only 8 percent and 9 percent defected to the opposite party over this interval (the remainder shifting to "Independent" or "don't know").

Children's early party identifications are therefore surprisingly stable, but they do not really begin to approximate the stability of adults' attitudes until midadolescence. Among children aged 9 to 10, Vaillancourt (1972) found a six-month tau-beta of only .30, whereas it was .59 among those aged 13 to 15, not far short of the adult .70 cited by Converse (1964).

Children's early partisan dispositions seem rather *affectively consistent*. Fifth and sixth graders polarized along party lines in reaction to Kennedy's election as much as their teachers did, and they ascribed greater virtue to their own party on a variety of other dimensions (Hess and Torney, 1967). Our data indicate strong partisan polarization over such political figures as Richard Nixon and Ronald Reagan, and somewhat less marked tendencies to claim one's own party's superior ability to solve national problems. These findings, too, appear to resemble adults' preferences (though with a more rarified subsample, to be sure, since only a minority of children have partisan identifications).

There is so far little evidence available on the *power* of children's early party identification over new opinion formation, i.e., on how consistently partisan a reaction they have to new candidates and issues. Further experimental and/or panel studies are required to deal with this question.

These early commitments are cognitively more barren than adults', as has been noted by numerous writers (Greenstein, 1965; Hess and Torney, 1967). Children are quite vague about what the parties are or about the issue or group-interest differences that large numbers of adults are likely to distinguish them on (see Sears, 1969a, for a summary of the adult data). On the other hand, many children do have some feeling for the party membership of the most important political leaders: in our Fresno data, for example, the correct party was often given for Reagan (46 percent), Nixon (48 percent), Kennedy, (37 percent), Humphrey (40 percent), and Agnew (36 percent), with an average of 14 percent giving the wrong party.

Thus the current evidence is that by midadolescence, American children's party identifications are approaching the affective stability and consistency of adults'. However, there is a more gradual development than is usually assumed, both in the *number* of children with commitments and in their *strength*. And the evidence is still somewhat ambiguous on the actual strength of these early attitudes. Their apparent stability over time could arise not from strong commitment but from lack of effective challenge in the attitudinally homogeneous, rather unpolitical environments in which much early political socialization takes place. So it is quite possible that these adolescent attitudes are potentially highly vulnerable to change. More evidence is badly needed on adolescents' level of commitment to these early attitudes. But the main point is that the "early political socialization" of partisan predispositions is a gradual matter, cresting in midadolescence, rather than something finished and done by the end of childhood.

Parental Transmission

Early in the empirical study of political socialization, many scholars reached the general conclusion that children's partisan attitudes were largely copies of parental attitudes, and this rapidly became the conventional wisdom. It was typified by West's (1945) observation, from a study of a small midwestern town, that "a man is born into his political party just as he is born into probable future membership in the church of his parents." Several findings seemed to point to this conclusion. Children did seem widely to adopt a party preference, and they clearly did so without much knowledge about the parties of their leaders (Greenstein, 1965). Hyman's excellent early review of the literature (1959) found a generally high correlation between parents' and offsprings' political attitudes: "Over a great many such correlations from the different studies the median value approximates .5" (p. 72). Such a conclusion also helped to explain the extraordinary continuity of voting patterns in certain geographical areas over many decades; party identification guided the individual's vote and was simply passed from father to son across many generations. It helped to explain the persistence of demographic correlates of various social and political attitudes, e.g., social class differences in party identification or various areas of noneconomic liberalism, regional and class differences in racial prejudice, etc. And when children (Greenstein, 1965), college students (Middleton and Putney, 1964), or mature adults (Kornberg, Smith and Bromley, 1969) were asked about the origins of their early preferences, the most common response was that they got them from their parents.

More recently, though, a much more critical look has been taken at the supposed preeminence of the family in early partisan socialization (Connell, 1972; Jennings and Niemi, 1968a; Niemi, 1973a; Sears, 1969a). In fact, one recent review concluded that "it appears from a substantial body of evidence that processes within the family have been largely irrelevant to the formation of specific opinions" (Connell, 1972, p. 330), with party preference proving the sole major exception rather than a representative instance.

In this section we will evaluate these conflicting points of view. The appropriate starting point is simply to assess the level of agreement between parents and offspring, since that sets a clear ceiling on the maximum possible level of parental influence.

Level of parent-child agreement. The best estimate of parent-offspring agreement in political attitudes comes from the study by Jennings and Niemi (1968a), in which a near-representative national sample of 1992 high school seniors and at least one parent (in 430 cases both parents) were interviewed in 1965. In this study, 59 percent agreed on a party identification (parent and offspring of same party, or both Independents), 7 percent had opposite party identifications, and in the remaining 34 percent of the pairs, one was Independent and the other had a party preference (tau-beta = .59). This finding corresponds to Connell's (1972) estimate of a median correlation over several studies of about .6. And it is not far distant from data on the adult electorate. SRC's 1952 election survey indicated that 52 percent of adult Americans agreed with both parents' party identification, and only 10 percent had the opposite party preference (Campbell, Gurin and Miller, 1954; see Sears, 1969a, p. 376, for the tabulation). Such estimates from later points in the life cycle are of course less reliable, because they invariably depend on the offspring's unvalidated recall of his parents' preference, which most likely exaggerates intrafamilial agreement (Niemi, 1973b).

Yet on most political issues, the rate of agreement is far lower. In his review essay, Connell (1972) estimates a median correlation of about .2 for parent-offspring agreement on issues other than party identification. Of the 20 different political orientations used in the most definitive study (Niemi, 1974), only one (presidential preference) showed higher agreement than party preference (Jennings and Niemi, 1974; Niemi, 1974). A variety of other studies have presented the same pattern (cf. Butler and Stokes, 1969; Dennis, 1969; Dennis and McCrone, 1970; Kubota and Ward, 1970; Friedman, Gold, and Christie, 1972).

These results, then, add up to a picture of only moderate political agreement between parents and their offspring in democratic societies. Even then the agreement seems limited to only a few issues, albeit seemingly the most controversial ones. Elsewhere I have reviewed these findings in detail (Sears, 1975); but to make a long story short, they seem to me to fall into four groups: (1) The greatest agreement between parents and preadults concerns *highly visible events,* such as a presidential candidate, a foreign war, or the threat of nuclear war in a crisis-ridden era. A possible exception must be the failure of parents to communicate their suspicions about a conspiracy to assassinate President Kennedy though certainly the conspiracy was not highly visible even if the assassination was (Orren and Peterson, 1967). (2) *Party identification* yields consistently greater agreement than other political issues ($r \simeq .6$), though the agreement comes slowly, perhaps peaking around 60 percent in late adolescence and drifting off thereafter. It seems in general to be higher in the United States than in other countries. (3) *Social groups and moral clichés* show less though still significant agreement, ranging from the very high level achieved on personal religious denomination to lower levels ($r \simeq .3$) regarding minority groups, racial policies, the details of religious dogma, liberalism-conservatism, and beliefs about morality. (4) *Policy issues, regime norms, and generalized political dispositions* show virtually no agreement. Political efficacy, sense of voting duty, support for government, political trust, support for the party system, concrete applications of civil liberties, political interest, and a wide variety of other issues

(Jennings and Niemi, 1968a, 1974; Connell, 1972; Dennis, 1969) show negligible agreement.

Dynamics of parental influence. The other major question here concerns what determines the degree of parental influence over offspring attitudes. The simplest and most helpful sociopsychological theories in trying to account for family influence (or the lack of it) seem to come broadly from the *reference group* approach. This would be concerned primarily with the communication of group norms (their clarity, strength, and frequency), and with identification with the group (Campbell *et al.,* 1960; Festinger, 1950; McClosky and Dahlgren, 1959; Sears, 1969a). Translated into the terms of the family, such an approach would converge particularly on *the communication of parental political attitudes, affective ties to the parents, and extrafamilial influences.*[8] Of course, this approach disregards the possible contribution of siblings and members of the extended family, but we must start with the simplest of hypotheses, which deals with parental influence alone.

How do these generalized variables plug into the specifics of the family's impact on a child's partisan socialization? Frequent and consistent communication of a parental position should depend on several contingencies. First, there must be a "real" parental attitude to communicate, and presumably this depends on (1) a simple and stable attitude object, (2) stability of parental attitudes over time, and (3) agreement between parents on political issues. Then probability of its communication should vary with (4) the normal level of political involvement of family members, and (5) the occurrence of public events that provoke communication. Simply the fact of parental communication is of course insufficient without (6) full and unbiased reception by the child, which may well be a sometime thing. All these factors ought to affect accurate reception of stable parental attitudes by the child.

Whether such received parental attitudes then positively influence the child, leading to conformity, have no effect on him, or negatively influence him, leading to rebellious counterconformity, ought theoretically to depend on (7) the child's affective ties to the parent(s). Finally, the impact of the entire family group ought to depend as well on (8) the extent to which the attitudes predominant in the child's climate of opinion outside the family tend to reinforce or conflict with family norms.

The most careful and comprehensive empirical work in this area is again that conducted by Jennings and Niemi based on their 1965 survey (Jennings and Niemi, 1974; Niemi, 1973b, 1974). It seems quite evident that the greatest parent-child agreement occurs with respect to simple and stable attitude objects such as the two American political parties), and in areas of maximum stability of parental attitudes (such as party identification or presidential preference) and parental agreement (see Jennings and Niemi, 1974, chapters

2 and 3). By and large, though, parent-offspring communication about political issues must be regarded as very partial and mightily flawed.

Therefore, as a consequence of the numerous obstacles to successful communication of parental attitudes, the child's perceptions are not outstandingly accurate. For example, in the Jennings-Niemi nationwide study of high school seniors, 71 percent were able to classify their parents correctly as Democrats, Independents, or Republicans (see Sears, 1969a). The tau-beta correlations of student's *perception* by parent's reported *characteristic* were. 82 for presidential vote, .68 for voting turnout, .59 for party identification, and .25 for political interest (Niemi, 1973a). This is probably the peak of offspring accuracy since high school seniors are the oldest age cohort to be almost universally inhabiting parental households.

Much of the inaccuracy is no doubt due to the failures in communication suggested above. Yet where ignorance leaves a void, children seem to fill it with certain predictable biases. Most important, they consistently overestimate agreement within the family, inflating parent-offspring correlations, over a variety of attributes, by about .10 (Niemi, 1973a). Interestingly, parents even more mistakenly assume their children follow in their own footsteps, their biases inflating such correlations by .19 (see Niemi, 1974). Children also generously overattribute socially desirable qualities to the parent; e.g., voting parents were mistakenly perceived as not voting by only 2 percent, whereas nonvoting parents were erroneously seen as voting by 39 percent. Similarly, children's distortions overattributed votes for the winning presidential candidate (Niemi, 1973a).

By all the several sociopsychological theories presented above, adoption of family political norms ought to be closely related to the offspring's affective ties to his parents. If he feels strongly positive toward them, he should adopt their attitudes (insofar as he knows them), whereas if he is strongly hostile toward them, he should reject their views, possibly even rebelling or "boomeranging" to an opposite political stance.

Surprisingly enough, there seems to be no such general effect. In the two studies including direct interviews with parents and offspring, closeness to parents (or other indicators of the affective ties between parents and children) was not related to the degree of political agreement (Jennings and Niemi, 1974; Thomas, 1971). However, in the former, parent-child closeness was related to agreement on policy issues. In two other studies, relying exclusively on offspring reports, closeness or dependency was related to conformity (Kubota and Ward, 1970; Middleton and Putney, 1963), and in another, relative closeness to mother or father was related to relative conformity to one or the other (Jennings and Langton, 1969). In earlier studies that relied on offspring reports, extremes of parental discipline seemed to be related to partisan rebellion (Maccoby, Matthews, and Morton, 1954; Middleton and Putney, 1963). With independent reports from parents, this finding did not hold, but it did hold up on certain emotionally laden policy issues (Jennings and Niemi, 1974, p. 80).

Thus, variations in simple informational communication appear to be the most critical determinants of parental influence over offspring political attitudes. The quality of the parent-child relationship, both in the mass public and in more highly politicized families, seems to have less consistent effects.[9]

Surprisingly, there has been relatively little direct research on the politically socializing effects of adolescents' peer groups or broader climates of opinion. Some studies have shown greater defection from parental attitudes in the direction of community norms (Berelson *et al.*, 1954; Maccoby *et al.*, 1954; Hyman, 1959), or the resocializing effects of adolescents' peer group norms (Langton, 1967; Newcomb *et al.*, 1967). A most careful recent study employed sociometric measures within the peer group as well as parent interviews and found that both peers and parents had significant influence over adolescents' partisanship, though the former was less powerful (Jennings and Niemi, 1974, Chapter 9).

THE PERSISTENCE OF RESIDUES FROM PREADULT POLITICAL SOCIALIZATION

The importance of preadult political socialization lies primarily in the impact its residues have on adult attitudes and behavior. To have such an impact they must of course persist into and through adulthood in some form or another. But do they in fact persist? This question has been of anxious concern to virtually all who have written in the area. Some regard persistence as at least partially demonstrated by available data, such as adults' retrospective accounts of their own attitudes (Campbell *et al.*, 1960, pp. 161–164; Butler and Stokes, 1969, Chapter 3; Converse, 1966), or by longitudinal studies (Feldman and Newcomb, 1969, pp. 320–322; Bloom, 1964, p. 173). Others simply assume it (Davies, 1965; Dawson and Prewitt, 1969) or are willing to accept it provisionally even in the absence of hard research (Easton and Dennis, 1969), or raise it as a researchable question (Jennings and Niemi, 1968b; Langton, 1969). Still others view children's attitudes as so unstable that they could not have a major impact on adult orientations (Vaillancourt, 1973) or see major changes as occurring throughout the life span (Jennings and Niemi, 1974, Chapter 10).

Yet all these observations have simply been made in passing or with reference to the findings of a particular study. So far no one has tried to pull together what is now known on the subject and take a hard look at this most important question. The remainder of this chapter is devoted to the question of persistence into later life of the residues of preadult political socialization. However, here it can be considered only briefly and rather superficially; for a more comprehensive analysis see Sears (1975).

In discussing persistence, we must reiterate that we are concerned with only a subset of any individual's attitudes. With respect to content, again we are concerned with *attachment to the system* and *partisan predispositions,* but not with *participatory orientations.* Earlier, we presented the many guises of attachment, and it seems appropriate to consider at least as a working hypothesis, that all are acquired early in life and maintained thereafter. With respect to partisan orientations, some are generally agreed to be involved in early socialization, but many are not. And some partisan attitudes are strong and stable, whereas others are rather weak and transitory. We are here really interested only in the stronger and more stable partisan predispositions, because only through them may political socialization be presumed to leave residues affecting adults' attitudes and behavior. Thus it is critical that we limit our attention according to such a distinction.

If we limit our discussion to "enduring commitments," what attitudes will we be dealing with? The attitudes of American adults, considered as a whole public, do not meet even minimum standards of affective stability, consistency, and power regarding very many attitude objects. The clearest examples are (1) party identification and (2) racial attitudes, at least among those issues regularly measured in contemporary survey research. One can make a good case also (though on the basis of much less definitive data) for widespread commitments to some versions of (3) ethnic and class attitudes, (4) chauvinism and nationalism, (5) sloganized versions of democratic ideology, (6) moral values, and (7) attitudes toward a few public figures (such as FDR, JFK, or Hitler). The data assessing the stability, consistency, and power of mass attitudes in these content areas have been reviewed elsewhere (Sears, 1969a), so we will not consider them here.[10] So what is the evidence on persistence?

Empirical Evidence on Persistence

In general, there have been three kinds of empirical evidence on persistence. The best, of course, is longitudinal evidence, in which the child is tested and then later retested as an adult. A second is to compare people who have been pressured to change with roughly comparable people who have not. A third kind of evidence is cross-sectional, in which the aggregated responses of some age group are compared with those of older people interviewed at the same time point, with the presumption that the differences are due to the latter's attitude changes. A variant is the cohort analysis that compares the aggregated responses of the people born in a particular period and tested at one time with those of a different sample from the same birth cohort, tested at another historical point in time.

Longitudinal studies. Longitudinal evidence is hard to come by. The best data on political attitudes come from some relatively recent studies, especially Jennings and Niemi's (1973) eight-year followup of the high school students cum parents initially interviewed in 1965, and the Newcomb *et al.* (1967) twenty-year followup of Bennington graduates. The SRC three-wave panel, from 1956 through 1958 to 1960 (Converse, 1964, 1970) has been mentioned already, and Greeley and Spaeth (1970) have done a four-year panel study

(1964–68) of a nationwide sample of college graduates. Some other panel studies have been done over a period of several years (Butler and Stokes, 1969; Bachman, 1970; Himmelweit and Swift, 1971) though so far not exploited as fully. Earlier we mentioned some efforts to test the stability of children's attitudes over time (Hess & Torney, 1965; Vaillancourt, 1973; Vaillancourt & Niemi, 1974; Zellman, 1973). There is also an older literature studying the stability of values, mainly following up on college graduates, which has been admirably reviewed by Bloom (1964). Finally, some inventive use is now being made of the limited samples that have been recurrently tested for other, more psychological reasons over the years, e.g., the Terman gifted-child sample, the Berkeley Guidance study, the Fels Institute's longitudinal sample, etc. (Hoge and Bender, 1974; Knutson, 1973; Riley, 1973; Nesselroade and Reese, 1973; Schaie and Parham, 1974).

Yet the harsh truth is that so far such data can only be suggestive, because so few studies have attempted to assess attitude stability over the span we are interested in: from adolescence to or through adulthood. And it is difficult to compare statistics on studies conducted over widely differing spans of time. The test-retest correlation across twice some given time interval ought roughly to be the square of the same correlation across the original time interval. So when comparing four-year panels of the Converse or Greeley and Spaeth variety with twenty-year followups like Newcomb's, one must apply quite different standards.[11]

About all we can do here, then, is to assess the approximate orders of magnitude of stability coefficients in these various studies. First, results from studies of persistence *within* childhood might be noted again, though they are not really relevant here. Tau-beta correlations on party identification of .62 over two months and .47 over six months were reported from children aged 9 to 15 (Vaillancourt, 1973), as was $r = .83$ in partisan reactions to Kennedy's 1960 presidential win (Hess and Torney, 1965). Another way of looking at the former data is to note that about 50 percent of the white children (and 35 percent of the black) were perfectly stable over six months (Vaillancourt and Niemi, 1974). In the area of attachment, comparable correlations hold. Vaillancourt (1973) found over a four-month span that an index of attachment to the president (based on individual items of the Easton-Hess variety) showed a test-retest tau-beta correlation of +.49, and an index of affection for President Nixon showed +.43. The sample spanned an age range of 9 to 15, but among the older (13–15) children, the correlations were higher: +.55 and +.50, respectively. Zellman (1973), using the same age group but a two-month time span, found that the average tau-beta over twelve more complex attachment items (dealing with war, civil liberties, police, and the desirability of partisan conflict) was +.32.

A number of studies have tracked adolescents into early adulthood. The most impressive is Jennings's (1973) followup on 17-year-olds interviewed originally in 1965. For party identification the tau-beta was .40. Greater levels of stability have been reported in studies following people during their adult years. Jennings's (1973) study also tracked the adolescents' parents across the same eight-year period, finding the tau-beta for party identification to be .69. This is comparable to Converse's earlier (1964) report that over a two-year period its test-retest correlation among adults was more than .70. Greeley and Spaeth (1971) interviewed 1961 college alumni during 1964 and 1968, and found switching was not very common on party identification: 75 percent of the initial partisans held firm, with only 8 percent defecting to the opposition (of initial Independents, though, 44 percent moved to one or the other party). The Newcomb *et al.* (1967) twenty-year followup of Bennington alumnae found quite a remarkable degree of stability: their senior year conservatism during the 1930s correlated +.47 with their 1960 conservatism and +.48 with the number of Republican presidential candidates supported in the interim. There also have been some longitudinal studies of basic values, which have shown them to have impressive stability (Bloom, 1964; Kelly, 1955).

Stabilities are markedly lower for policy attitudes or more diffuse and abstract attitudes, as might be expected. Converse (1964), of course, reports two- or four-year stabilities in policy attitudes among adults of around .30. Greeley and Spaeth (1970) found that about one-third of the 1964 "liberals" switched to "conservative" by 1968, with about the same amount of movement in reverse. Finally Himmelweit and Swift's (1971) eleven-year followup of British adolescents obtained relatively few correlations (eight of 32) that were even statistically significant ($r \geqslant .14$) on individual items from a scale of authoritarianism.

Clearly, these data are fragmentary and scarcely support any very final conclusions about the persistence of early socialization. In addition to the problems noted earlier, the reliabilities of most of these measures are not known and may place an artificially low ceiling on the possible test-retest correlations. Yet it is likely that these correlations are good ballpark estimates, and they indicate fairly high levels of persistence of "enduring commitments" in adulthood—but much lower levels in childhood or from adolescence through early adulthood, as well as much lower levels for policy attitudes or for more diffuse and global dimensions of attitude. There might be some dispute about how to interpret test-retest correlations in the .40 to .60 range, but considering the many potential sources of error, they seem rather impressive to me.

Resistance to influence.   Another method of assessing persistence is to compare people who have been exposed to some estimable potential influence with people who have not. There is no general answer as yet to the question of whether people are more susceptible to influence in their youth than in their maturity, because the requisite research has not yet been done (see McGuire,

1969). But some systematic pressures to change have been assessed. Since we have discussed this research in much greater detail elsewhere (Sears, 1975), it will only be synopsized here.

Social mobility exposes adults to the norms of a new social class and hence presses them to abandon their original attitudes. The best evidence so far is that it produces some resocialization (J. A. Barber, 1970; Jackman, 1972a, 1972b; Lopreato and Hazelrigg, 1970), but that most of such resocialization occurs at the time the individual first enters the work force (Abramson, 1972b; Abramson and Books, 1971). Status discrepancies supposedly press some adults to move to a more radical or more ultraconservative position (depending on one's theory), but the best evidence is that they have little political effect above and beyond the reinforcement of early socialization (Knoke, 1972; Treiman, 1970). Mass communications ought to spur attitude change, but the conventional wisdom remains that adults' attitudes are mainly reinforced rather than changed (Hyman and Sheatsley, 1947; Klapper, 1960; Sears and Whitney, 1973a, 1973b).

Some vivid personal experiences do resocialize the individual. The Bennington alumnae studied by Newcomb (1943; Newcomb *et al.*, 1967) are the classic respondents. The socially mobile appear also to be resocialized, if only in early adulthood. Seemingly the great ghetto riots resocialized young blacks (Sears and McConahay, 1973). But very careful, controlled, protracted, and seemingly powerful efforts to resocialize young adults frequently have only marginal effects (Cook, 1970). For a more detailed analysis of resocialization, see Sears (1975).

Therefore the inference we have drawn is that such factors are generally not sufficiently powerful to deflect the adult from the residues of his earlier political socialization (or late-adolescent resocialization). Because of the self-selection of those undergoing such experiences and the heterogeneous character of the experiences, we cannot be firmly confident of this inference; these are clearly not interventions of perfectly known dimensions made on the lives of randomly selected experimental groups. Nevertheless, the pattern of no or minimal effect is impressively uniform.

Possible misinterpretations of aggregate data or age correlates. Two other kinds of data are often mistakenly used to argue either for or against persistence. For one, sometimes the constancy (or change) of aggregated individuals' responses, as measured at different points in time, is used to assert the persistence (or change) of individuals' attitudes. For example, the constancy of the distribution of party identification among American adults though the 1950s and early 1960s was often taken to mean that it was stable within individuals as well. On the other hand, the increase in Independents and declining levels of political trust in the adult population in recent years have been interpreted as reflecting mass individual attitude change. But Miller (1967) and Converse

(1964) have persuasively shown that much individual attitude change can be taking place even when the marginal frequencies of various attitudes are constant over time within the population as a whole.

The other problem is misinterpreting age differences in attitude within a given sample interviewed at one point in time as indicating that individuals' attitudes change as they get older. Hence differences in political trust (Easton and Dennis, 1969), cynicism (Jennings and Niemi, 1968b), and presidential preferences (Lipset and Ladd, 1971) between older and younger people at any given point in time have sometimes wrongly been taken to indicate its change over the life span. Of course, without some control on the historical period of early socialization, it is inappropriate to take this as evidence of attitude change with aging. They may just reflect generational difference.

An analytic strategy that deals with both these problems, at least in part satisfactorily, is the cohort analysis. This involves the comparison of a given birth cohorts' attitudes across two different measurement points—e.g., persons born in the 1924–1931 period are sampled in 1956 and then again in 1960. If the attitudes of these two samples, taken from a common birth cohort, are roughly comparable at the two measurement points, the best guess is that individuals' attitudes have not changed very much (at least they have not changed in any uniform direction).

A number of such studies have been conducted in recent years, and persistence rather than change of attitudes has been by far the most common outcome. Jennings and Niemi (1974) have thoroughly documented the greater partisanship of older people, tested at any given point in time. But using cohort analyses, Glenn (1972) has found no diminution with age in the number of self-professed Independents, and Crittenden (1962), Glenn and Hefner (1972), and Klecka (1971) have found no mad rush to the Republicans or conservatism more generally with age. Abramson (1971, 1974) has found no marked change in the rate of class-based voting as any given birth cohort has aged to (and through) the mature years. And aging, if anything, has moved mature voters slightly in a liberal direction, in line with the overall movement of the electorate (Glenn, 1974). So data from these investigations of age and aging generally support a persistence viewpoint. While in any given case other explanations are possible, of course, the overall burden of evidence is surprisingly uniform.

The specificity of early socialization. One problem that commonly arises with the assessment of persistence is that attitude objects (and the associated attitude items) change rather markedly over the years. The question of persistence then comes down to whether or not a constant affect is expressed to changing stimuli. One next must ask, therefore, whether early political socialization generally involves the conditioning of specific affects to rather specific attitude objects, e.g., the feeling "good" to the object "white"? Or does it also involve the acquisition of more global and generalized cognitive structures, which can be applied much more generally to a wide variety of past, present, and future political objects, such as general dispositions of "diffuse system support," "con-servatism," "alienation," etc.?

This is a matter of considerable debate. Various points of view have been espoused quite vigorously, mostly deriving from some a priori theoretical pre-conceptions. Those approaching the problem from the standpoint of gen-eralized cognitive stages (e.g., Adelson, 1972; Tapp and Kohlberg, 1971) or global personality needs (e.g., Knutson, 1974) tend to view the residues of early socialization in terms of generalized belief systems. They are viewed as not tied closely to specific contents, and presumably easily generalizable to new and emerging attitude objects. Similarly, those like Easton (1965) who ap-proach the problem out of interest in the fate of the political system look for relevant generalized political dispositions, such as political efficacy, benevo-lence of the authorities, trust in government, compliance with the law, etc. These generic dispositions also presumably generalize readily to a wide variety of situations and objects throughout life.

On the other hand, a model of attitude acquisition growing out of a learn-ing approach would see affects as tied much more closely to the original stimu-lus to which they were conditioned (e.g., Anderson, 1971; McMurty and Wil-liams, 1972). Only limited generalization would be expected, largely on the basis of rather simple-minded and superficial similarities between attitude objects.

At the present time the burden of the evidence, in our view, is toward specificity of most original socialization. A number of reasons can be given for this conclusion. First of all, it is clear that children's affective preferences develop more quickly than their store of information (Greenstein, 1965; Sears, 1969a). Second, the same conclusion is slowly emerging from research on social attitudes that are nonpolitical but psychologically analogous. It in-creasingly appears that most people do not have broadly generalized attitudes toward authority, broadly generalized moral codes, tolerance for ambiguity, etc. (Mischel, 1968, pp. 20–28; at least people within a given culture do not differ systematically along such dimensions, however much they may have internalized the common cultural norms). Rather, their attitudes and behavior in these areas tend to be specific to particular attitude objects or situations. Third, little research has been done that positively demonstrates generality (i.e., consistency across various contents) in children's political attitudes. Since this question has not been addressed directly, any conclusion about it must be largely a matter of hunch. But most studies of children's political attitudes rely on individual items rather than scales incorporating several closely related items, and this is so partly for the reason that children's attitudes generally are not closely related across different items. Where such consistency can be found, it usually occurs when the key words in the items are almost identical, e.g., "quite a few of the people running the government are dishonest" and "quite a few politicians are dishonest" (Dennis, 1969, p. 24). When items theoretically measuring the same attitude are worded quite differently, the consistency of response drops off quite noticeably, often to the vanishing point (for examples, see Dennis, 1969; Vaillancourt, 1972; Table 2 above; Zellman and Sears, 1971). And we have earlier presented some evidence against the widespread existence of a unitary dimension of "diffuse system support."

As well as being relatively uncommon among children, such generalized structures seem surprisingly rare in the mass adult public, as well. That scales of generalized political dispositions (e.g. domestic liberalism, political efficacy, political trust, etc.) can often be formed on data from representative samples of adults suggests some underlying attitude structures (e.g., Campbell *et al.*, 1960, Chapter 9; Hensler, 1971; Searing, Schwartz, and Lind, 1973; Sears and McConahay, 1973). But the correlations between items still tend to be rather small (Converse, 1964), and the relationships of such dispositions to specific policy items in other domains tend to be very weak (Searing, Schwartz, and Lind, 1973). The constraints among various attitudes are not very powerful, and the most common organization is closer to the atomized than the centralized.

Most scholars also are skeptical about the existence of widespread over-arching abstract ideological structures among adults. Not very many American adults express or possess any very abstract liberal-conservative ideology (Campbell *et al.*, 1960; Converse, 1964), even when the rhetoric of a heated presidential campaign emphasizes such terms (Field and Anderson, 1969). Abstract procedural principles, such as those of free speech, seem only inconsistently applied to concrete situations (McClosky, 1964; Stouffer, 1955; Zellman and Sears, 1971). Such supposedly global system attitudes as alienation, involvement, efficacy, and political trust turn out, on empirical inspection, to be much more heterogeneous and specific than is often imagined (see Citrin, 1972; Finifter, 1970; Hensler, 1971). Racial and ethnic prejudices also tend to be specific to a particular outgroup rather than to reflect some general factor of tolerance or intolerance (Harding *et al.*, 1969, p. 14; Stember, 1961; D. T. Campbell, 1947).

For these reasons, it seems currently most appropriate to think of early political socialization as mainly providing affective dispositions toward rather specific attitude objects, with rather limited cognitive implications and associations. This view would help to interpret many of what seem to be confusing findings in the literature today. Children seem able to generalize somewhat to a concrete situation of tolerance for dissent from either their attitudes toward the dissenter or a simple slogan of free speech, but the generalization is so limited that it does not appear across concrete situations involving different dissenters (Zellman and Sears, 1971). In adulthood, generalized political dispositions tend to be only indifferently related to policy choices that do not invoke such dispositions explicitly; e.g., generalized political trust was only weakly related to preference among various policy options in Vietnam (Searing, Schwartz, and Lind, 1973). In Key's (1966) analysis of presidential elections from 1936 to 1960, policy preferences were highly consistent with presidential choice only when the candidate or his party was explicitly invoked (see Sears, 1969a, pp. 361–363). And Californians have in recent years voted consistent with their self-designations as "liberal" or "conservative" and held policy attitudes appropriate to these positions in times when the state's major political figures have been explicitly defining themselves and policy issues in these terms (Bicker, 1972; Sears and Kinder, 1971).

If the residues of early political socialization tend most often to be narrow and specific affects, rather than global and generalized dispositions, then the continuity of attitude objects becomes even more critical in determining the persistence of early socialization residues. Clearly, they could persist but *appear* not to if in adulthood (a) the attitude object itself had changed markedly from that present in early socialization, or (b) the appropriate attitude object was not always present as a viable choice. In other words, for persistence to manifest itself in overt behavior, as well as to exist in latent dispositions, it must match up with some option in the range of available response alternatives, whether in an interview schedule or the ballot box or wherever.[12]

Summary: The Persistence of Early Socialization

The persistence view has a strong and a weak form. The strongest is that socialization is largely complete by early adolescence or so, and little attitude change takes place thereafter. The weaker is that socialization proceeds gradually from middle childhood through adolescence and is complete only when young adults either have or have not been resocialized.

At a simple descriptive level, four main findings represent the burden of the evidence on persistence: (1) adults steadily resist any systematic pressure to change their partisan attitudes; nevertheless (2) longitudinal studies indicate some change back and forth with time, and apparently political trust generally erodes with age; (3) any resocialization, even in early adulthood, apparently demands an exacting and unusually powerful social situation; but (4) the major systematic defections from initial childhood socialization appear to be limited to the age period during and immediately following adolescence. In its simplest form, then, the persistence view overstates the case. More plausible is a revisionist version taking account of continuing socialization and occasional resocialization through adolescence and into early adulthood.

There are some reasons to suspect bias in the available evidence, however. The political stability in postwar America probably has led to some overestimate of persistence into early adulthood, though perhaps not through the later years. On the other hand, it is most likely that persistence is generally underestimated in most empirical studies because of (1) changes in attitude items across time in longitudinal studies, (2) changes in the connotations of attitude objects over time. If indeed socialization residues tend to be rather specific and do not generalize readily to other contents, they may be highly persistent in their original form, which is of continuing political relevance as long as the same political and social conflicts persist.

CONCLUDING COMMENT

Finally, it is easy to complain about the quality of research on political socialization, and many have done so (though in this the area has much in common with other areas of social science dealing with natural ongoing processes). It is perhaps worthwhile now to look back in order to note and address the major criticisms that have been made of the field as a whole.

Simply put, the major critiques have been that (1) early political attitudes are whimsical and unreal; (2) they have been only superficially and improperly measured, principally with the questionnaire method; (3) sampling has been so inadequate as to invalidate the research results; (4) early political attitudes do not persist beyond childhood or adolescence; (5) they have little or no influence over adult attitudes and behavior; (6) they have little or no importance within the political system; and (7) research on political socialization has a conservative bias, because it investigates pattern maintenance rather than attitude change (see Kavanagh, 1972; Marsh, 1971, 1972; Searing, Schwartz, and Lind, 1973; Vaillancourt, 1973).

My reaction on surveying this imposing volume of work is rather to be impressed by the marked increase in its quality over the few short years since the excellent pioneering Hyman (1959), Greenstein (1960), and Hess-Easton (1960) efforts first appeared. These critiques do not seem to me as powerful as some others that could be made. Let me take them in turn. The "reality" of early political attitudes can be assessed directly by applying tests of stability, consistency, and power (Sears, 1969a). This seems to be a critical precondition for taking seriously the residues of early socialization, and we have attempted it explicitly in this essay. Many studies have not applied such tests, to be sure, and perhaps they should have.

Methodological problems, such as response measures or peer sampling, I suspect are not now terribly significant difficulties. Whereas detailed interviews (Adelson, 1972) or projective techniques (Greenstein and Tarrow, 1970; Knutson, 1973) certainly deserve a trial, so far they have not produced substantive findings very much different from the standard questionnaire method. And sampling biases have been shown to make a big difference, especially when markedly different political climates are involved (e.g., among blacks, hillbillies, Quakers, army kids, etc.). But as indicated earlier, recent research has moved toward greater attention to minority groups and to other cultures, even if truly comparative research is still in its infancy.

The assumption that the residues of preadult political socialization persist into adulthood is of course an issue that can be settled better with data than with argument, so I have tried to deal with it explicitly in this essay (as well as more extensively elsewhere, see Sears, 1975). Most researchers have simply assumed that early socialization does persist, and this assumption has dictated their research. However, as the foregoing demonstrates, it is my view that this assumption turn outs to have been relatively well founded—but with some important qualifications.

The importance of early political socialization lies not only in the persistence of its residues into adulthood. They must also be powerful in structuring or determining adulthood political orientations. From a social psychologist's point of view, such impact must be considered separately for adult *attitudes* and adult *behavior*. The question of the impact of such residues on adult attitudes is of course beyond the scope of this chapter, since it is a problem of the dynamics of adult public opinion. However, one might have thought it by now obvious that political trust, party identification, racial prejudice, and other such presumed residues of early socialization are central in determining the average citizen's reactions to political events and choices. This has certainly been the burden of most of the major research on mass political behavior in the postwar period, which has been presented in a wide variety of contexts (e.g., Campbell *et al.*, 1966; Citrin, 1972; Key, 1961). This is not the place to review all this evidence (which is considered in some detail elsewhere; see Sears, 1969a, pp. 324–369, 399–443). In my view, the consistency of basic attitudinal dispositions with such outcome measures of adult attitude as direction of vote, policy preference, and candidate evaluations is quite amply documented and should be beyond serious dispute.[13]

But the influence of early socialization residues on adults' political *behavior* is a much trickier issue. For social psychologists it has proven a thorny thicket (cf. Collins, 1970; Freedman, Carlsmith, and Sears, 1974; Mischel, 1968; Wicker, 1969), and political scientists have quite reasonably questioned the power of early-socialized attitudes to control later behaviors such as are involved in active political participation (Greenstein, 1970; Marsh, 1971; Searing *et al.*, 1973; Kavanagh, 1972). The burden of the current evidence is that situational variables play a large role in determining overt behavioral acts, though certainly not to the exclusion of attitudes. The determinants of political participation per se are taken up by Verba and Nie in Volume 4 of this *Handbook,* but the burden of the evidence does not seem to deprive preadult socialization of a role in promoting the partisan commitments and activity levels of future candidates, or of radical activism, etc. (also see Milbrath, 1965).

Even if preadult socialization can be shown to affect the mass adult public's attitudes and behavior, do these attitudes and behavior in turn have any important impact in the political system (Marsh, 1971)? The determinants of government policy are certainly far afield from our limited focus, but the political importance of the public and of public opinion (whether expressed in the vote or otherwise) is surely an assumption lying behind the lion's share of research on mass political behavior and public opinion.

Finally, it has been asserted that political socialization research generally has a conservative political bias, largely because it deals with system-sustaining political dispositions (such as attachment to the system), those that channel discontent into dispositions that perturb the status quo hardly at all (such as party identification), and because to many the concept of "socialization" connotes the enforced conformity of children's attitudes and behavior to conventional adult norms.

It is easy enough to document such a charge. Yet it is a mistake to think that any effort to study the development of political attitudes requires such biases. Much of the research that has been done on black and chicano children in recent years (see Greenberg, 1970a; Laurence, 1970; Garcia, 1973; Button, 1974; Liebschutz and Niemi, 1974) has focused on system-challenging dispositions, often with a sympathetic rather than critical eye. The role of identification with black culture as a factor in promoting sophisticated awareness of social problems and inspiring militancy and social action has similarly been given more play (see Sears and McConahay, 1973; Sears, 1973). And I have suggested that defining successful socialization in terms of an individual's effective maximizing of his own interests rather than in terms of his conformity to conventional norms might lead to some provocative changes in the outcome variables investigated (Sears, 1968). Here though it still appears the dominant tendency is to look at consistency of socialization residues across rather than within individuals.

These critiques are important to raise and evaluate, but to me they are not of dominant importance. I think the real deficiencies in this literature stem rather from two other sources. One is analytic superficiality. Too often, theories are not posed sharply enough nor are the data pushed hard enough to test these theories. The work of Abramson (1974), Glenn and Hefner (1972), and Inglehart (1971) on generational effects, or Citrin (1972), Engstrom (1970), and Rodgers and Taylor (1971) on trust and legitimacy are good counterexamples—models of effective pinpointing of theoretical issues combined with powerful analysis of empirical data.

The other general problem is weak measurement of independent variables. As mentioned, I am less uncomfortable than some of my colleagues with questionnaire-based dependent variables, but the measurement of independent variables, by and large, has been woefully inadequate. Unfortunately, it is easy to give attitude questionnaires to children in school, but it is difficult to get attitude data directly from parents, accurate demographic data on families, solid information on what actually goes on in the classroom, or on the politically relevant contacts the child has with siblings, peers, extrafamilial adults, the media, and political campaigns. Nor is it easy to get good personality or cognitive-stage data on children. The result is that much more is known about the content and structure of children's political attitudes than about their causes.

Finally, it seems likely that the early rush of enthusiasm for studying pre-adolescents will gradually be replaced with attention to the entire life span. Developmental psychology itself is also finally turning in this direction, away from its usual obsessive preoccupation with infants and preschoolers. There is perhaps an initial temptation to regard adulthood, or postadolescence, as more or less undifferentiated spans of life (at least until senescence sets in). But there is much reason to think it is not at all undifferentiated politically, socio-logically, or psychologically. So perhaps the study of "adulthood political social-ization," like the study of "life span developmental psychology," will be able to capitalize on differences between particular stages in later development.

NOTES

1. Political socialization through the entire life span seems to me an area of inquiry of increasing importance in the future. Parallel swings of attention have occurred completely independently (as far as I can tell) in the field of developmental psy-chology as well. In a sense, Freud rediscovered the child, but only recently have de-velopmental psychologists looked again at people older than infants and preschoolers (see Baltes and Schaie, 1973; Kagan and Coles, 1972).

2. Interestingly enough, methodological differences can make quite a difference in these responses. Greenstein, interviewing 10–14-year-olds, asked, "A new child comes to your school. He comes from another country. He says to you, 'There are some things about the United States that I don't understand. Tell me what the President of the United States is.'" Both in 1969, at the beginning of the Nixon Administration, and in 1973, as Watergate was breaking, about half the responses were positive and almost none negative. In this procedure, unlike those cited in the text, (1) Nixon himself was not mentioned, (2) the child is talking directly to an adult, and (3) he quite possibly "underplays (his) nation's warts," being a "cheerful guide to Washing-ton" for the foreign child. All may work toward more positive evaluation. See Green-stein (1973) and Greenstein and Tarrow (1970).

3. These particular data, summarized in Table 1, are not simply artifacts of a sample strongly biased toward Democrats. The Sacramento children were 22 percent Demo-cratic and 14 percent Republican; in Fresno they were 24 percent Democratic and 14 percent Republican. The remainder of the children had no stable party identi-fication. Evidence on the partisan climate of opinion around these children, from an independent mail-back survey of parents in Sacramento and from children's per-ceptions of their parents' and classmates' party preferences in both cities, indicate in both a population generally reflecting the mild advantage Democrats have throughout the state of California. But in neither was the advantage sufficiently great to account for the Kennedys' great popularity.

4. These findings follow the pattern observed earlier for black adults; even following the Watts riot, black adults in the riot area were most favorable to King and white liberals and, on balance, unfavorable to black militants and white conservatives (Sears, 1969b; Sears and McConahay, 1973).

5. One should not take too seriously the latter as reversals. These black children were

generally of lower social class than the white children, and class normally is, if anything, inversely related to attachment in children (Greenberg, 1970d; Hess and Torney, 1967; Greenstein, 1965; Tolley, 1973) and in black adults (Miller, Brown, and Raine, 1973; Sears, 1969b), although the opposite holds in Sica's (1972) study of Mexican-American children. The point argued here about black children, that they are vigorously partisan but not disattached, relative to whites, has been made elsewhere about black adults (Sears and McConahay, 1973, Chapter 12). Citrin (1972, 1974) has most carefully documented the more general point, that measures of political trust in fact draw much partisan feeling about incumbents.

6. One exception is Dennis and McCrone's (1970) report that 61 percent of their sample of French children had a party preference at ages 15 to 16, though with only 54 respondents. One must be cautious about most existing cross-national studies because they normally rely on small samples from just one or two locales, which may or may not be representative of the nation as a whole.

7. Indeed, it will be obvious to most readers that this approach builds very heavily on Converse's most important contributions (1964, 1970, 1974).

8. Averaging and cognitive consistency theories would similarly predict from the value and frequency of communicated messages and the target's evaluation of the source of information (as well as the target's prior attitude, which, with young children, would tend not to be a major factor; Anderson, 1971; Osgood and Tannenbaum, 1955). All three of these theories come from social rather than developmental psychology. They were originated to deal specifically with influence situations, and despite terminological differences, all make approximately the same predictions.

9. Parenthetically, we note that these findings fit into what is known about political persuasion more generally. Elsewhere we have suggested that the critical obstacles to successful change of adult political opinion are (1) the generally low level of reception of political information, (2) rejection of received information due to high levels of prior commitment on the most controversial issues, and (3) partisan evaluation of political communicators, resulting in low credibility for the opposition (Sears and Whitney, 1973a, 1973b). The evidence on parental influence fits exactly what would be expected from that analysis. Children have relatively weak prior attitudes and generally favorable ties to their parents, so rejection of received information is not a major obstacle in intergenerational transmission. Rather, the major problem seems to be with low levels of parent-child political communication, resulting in the child's ignorance and/or distortion of his parents' views.

10. Elsewhere we have presented, rather extensively, the data supporting both the choice of these criteria and their application to these content areas of Americans' political attitudes (Sears, 1969a). This general theoretical framework has also been applied to the analysis of mass political opinion in several different areas: the origins of ghetto violence (Sears and McConahay, 1973), suburban white racism and its impact on voting behavior (Sears and Kinder, 1971), mass political persuasion (Sears and Whitney, 1973a, 1973b), and in the area of political socialization, to the origins of children's tolerance for political dissent (Zellman and Sears, 1971) and the impact of sex-role socialization on the development of political attitudes (Zellman, 1973).

11. I am indebted to Robert P. Abelson for this point.

12. This view appears to accord with that of others who have investigated the life span stability of individual differences in other psychological dispositions. One of the sharpest critics of the assumption of continuity has been Walter Mischel (1968). The core of his critique is that different tests ostensibly measuring the same personality trait across multiple situations generally fail to correlate very highly. From this he argues that personality dispositions are much more situation-specific than is normally recognized. But with respect to attitudes, Mischel's critique is somewhat different, and more consistent with our analysis.

A person's past behavior often can serve to predict his future behavior in similar situations, and many syndromes show considerable stability over long periods of time, especially when relevant stimulus conditions remain stable. . . . Cognitive consistencies tend to be especially strong . . . and the subjective impressions of constancy in oneself and in the personality of others is not an illusion. . . . Consistency over time does seem to be high for the descriptive categories, personality labels, and attitudes and values which individuals attribute to themselves. (Mischel, 1969, pp. 24, 26)

13. Briefly, some recent critical essays in this line have approached the problem in a somewhat mindlessly inductive, shotgun fashion and thus, not surprisingly, have found very little. More theoretically guided examinatons do in fact turn up much more positive results; e.g., compare any of the numerous SRC voting analyses or Citrin's work (1972, 1974) with Searing, Schwartz, and Lind (1973) or the theoretically guided riot participation analysis of Sears and McConahay (1973, especially Chapters 2, 5, 6, 7, and 11) with McPhail (1971).

REFERENCES

Aberbach, Joel D., and Jack L. Walker (1970). "The meanings of black power: a comparison of white and black interpretations of a political slogan." *American Political Science Review* 64:367–88.

Abramson, Paul R. (1971). "Social and political change in Western Europe: a cross-national longitudinal analysis." *Comparative Political Studies* 4:131–55.

——————— (1972a). "Political efficacy and political trust among black school children: two explanations." *Journal of Politics* 34:1243–69.

——————— (1972b). "Intergenerational social mobility and partisan choice." *American Political Science Review* 66:1291–4.

——————— (1974). "Generational change in American electoral behavior." *American Political Science Review* 68:93–105.

Abramson, Paul R., and John W. Books (1971). "Social mobility and political attitudes." *Comparative Politics* 3:403–28.

Abramson, Paul R., and Ronald E. Inglehart (1970). "The development of systemic support in four Western democracies." *Comparative Political Studies* 2:419–42.

Adelson, Joseph (1972). "The political imagination of the young adolescent." In Jerome Kagan and Robert Coles (eds.), *Twelve to Sixteen: Early Adolescence*. New York: Norton, 106–43.

Adelson, Joseph, and Lynette Beall (1970). "Adolescent perspectives on law and government." *Law and Society Review* 4:495–504.

Adler, Norman, and Charles Harrington (1970). *The Learning of Political Behavior*. Glenview, Ill.: Scott, Foresman.

Anderson, Norman H. (1971). "Integration theory and attitude change." *Psychological Review* 78:171–206.

Asch, Solomon E. (1956). "Studies of independence and conformity: I. A minority of one against a unanimous majority." *Psychological Monographs* 70: No. 9.

Ashmore, Richard D. (1970). "Prejudice." In Barry E. Collins, *Social Psychology*. Reading, Mass.: Addison-Wesley.

Bachman, Jerald G. (1970). *Youth in Transition, II: The Impact of Family Background and Intelligence on Tenth Grade Boys.* Ann Arbor, Mich.: Institute for Social Research.

Baker, Kendall L. (1970). "Political alienation and the German youth." *Comparative Political Studies* 3:117–130.

Baltes, Paul B., and K. Warner Schaie, eds. (1973). *Life-Span Developmental Psychology: Personality and Socialization.* New York: Academic Press.

Barber, James Alden, Jr. (1970). *Social Mobility and Voting Behavior.* Chicago: Rand McNally.

Barber, James D. (1968). "Classifying and predicting presidential styles: two weak presidents." *Journal of Social Issues* 24:51-80.

Barnes, Samuel H. (1972). "The legacy of fascism: generational differences in Italian attitudes and behavior." *Comparative Political Studies* 5:41–58.

Bicker, William E. (1972). "Ideology is alive and well in California: party identification, issue positions and voting behavior." Prepared for American Political Science Association Annual Meeting, Washington, D. C.

Bloom, Benjamin S. (1964). *Stability and Change in Human Characteristics.* New York: Wiley.

Blumler, J. G., James R. Brown, A. J. Ewbank, and T. S. Nossiter (1971). "Attitudes to the monarchy: their structure and development during a ceremonial occasion." *Political Studies* 19:149–71.

Boynton, G. R., Samuel Patterson, and Ronald D. Hedlund (1968). "The structure of public support for legislative institutions." *Midwest Journal of Political Science.* 12:163–80.

Bullock, Charles S. III, and Harrell R. Rodgers, Jr. (eds.) (1972). *Black Political Attitudes.* Chicago: Markham.

Butler, David, and Donald Stokes (1969). *Political Change in Britain,* College edition. New York: St. Martin's Press.

Button, Christine Bennett (1974). "Political education for minority groups." In Richard G. Niemi (ed.), *The Politics of Future Citizens.* San Francisco: Jossey-Bass.

Cameron, David R. (1972). "Stability and change in patterns of French partisanship." *Public Opinion Quarterly* 36:19–30.

Campbell, Angus, Philip E. Converse, Warren E. Miller, and Donald E. Stokes (1960). *The American Voter.* New York: Wiley.

———————— (1966). *Elections and the Political Order.* New York: Wiley.

Campbell, Angus, Gerald Gurin, and Warren E. Miller (1954). *The Voter Decides.* Evanston, Ill.: Row, Peterson.

Campbell, Angus, and Howard Schuman (1968). "Racial attitudes in fifteen American cities." In *Supplemental Studies for the National Advisory Commission on Civil Disorders.* Washington: U. S. Government Printing Office.

Campbell, Donald T. (1947). "The generality of a social attitude." Unpublished doctoral dissertation, University of California, Berkeley.

Caplan, Nathan (1970). "The new ghetto man: a review of recent empirical studies." *Journal of Social Issues* 26:59–73.

Chaffee, Steven H., L. Scott Ward, and Leonard P. Tipton (1970). "Mass communication and political socialization." *Journalism Quarterly* 47:647–59.

Citrin, Jack (1972). "Political disaffection in America: 1958–68." Unpublished doctoral dissertation, University of California, Berkeley.

_____ (1974). "Comment: the political relevance of trust in government." *American Political Science Review* 68:973–88.

Clark, Kenneth B., and Mamie Clark (1939). "The development of consciousness of self in the emergence of racial identification in Negro pre-school children." *Journal of Social Psychology* 10:591–97.

Clarke, James W., and John W. Soule (1971). "Political socialization, racial tension, and the acceptance of violence: reactions of Southern school children to the King assassination." In William J. Crotty (ed.), *Assassinations and the Political Order.* New York: Harper and Row.

Collins, Barry E. (1970). *Social Psychology.* Reading, Mass.: Addison-Wesley.

Connell, R. W. (1971). *The Child's Construction of Politics.* Melbourne, Australia: Melbourne University Press.

_____ (1972). "Political socialization in the American family: the evidence re-examined." *Public Opinion Quarterly* 36:323–33.

Converse, Philip E. (1964). "The nature of belief systems in mass publics." In D. E. Apter (ed.), *Ideology and Discontent.* New York: Free Press of Glencoe.

_____ (1966). "The concept of a normal vote." In Angus Campbell, Philip E. Converse, Warren E. Miller, and Donald E. Stokes, *Elections and the Political Order.* New York: Wiley.

_____ (1970). "Attitudes and non-attitudes: continuation of a dialogue." In E. R. Tufte (ed.), *The Quantitative Analysis of Social Problems.* Reading, Mass.: Addison-Wesley.

_____ (1974). "Public opinion and voting behavior." In Fred I. Greenstein and Nelson W. Polsby (eds.), *Handbook of Political Science,* Vol. 4. Reading, Mass.: Addison-Wesley.

Converse, Philip E., and G. Dupeux (1966). "De Gaulle and Eisenhower: the public image of the victorious general." In Angus Campbell, Philip E. Converse, Warren E. Miller, and Donald E. Stokes, *Elections and the Political Order.* New York: Wiley.

Cook, Stuart W. (1970). "Motives in a conceptual analysis of attitude-related behavior." In W. J. Arnold and D. Levine (eds.), *Nebraska Symposium on Motivation, 1969.* Lincoln: University of Nebraska Press.

Crittenden, John (1962). "Aging and party affiliation." *Public Opinion Quarterly* 26:648–57.

Davies, James C. (1965). "The family's role in political socialization." *Annals of the American Academy of Political and Social Science* 361:10–19.

Dawson, Richard E., and Kenneth Prewitt (1969). *Political Socialization.* Boston: Little, Brown.

Dennis, Jack (1966). "Support for the party system by the mass public." *American Political Science Review* 60:600–15.

_____ (1968). "Major problems of political socialization research." *Midwest Journal of Political Science* 12:85–114.

_____ (1969). "Political learning in childhood and adolescence: a study of fifth, eighth, and eleventh graders in Milwaukee, Wisconsin." Madison: Center for Cognitive Learning, Technical Report, No. 98.

_____ (1970). "Support for the institution of elections by the mass public." *American Political Science Review* 64:819–35.

_____ (1973). "Future work on political socialization." In Jack Dennis (ed.), *Socialization to Politics: A Reader*. New York: Wiley.

Dennis, Jack, Leon Lindberg, Donald J. McCrone, and Rodney Stiefbold (1968). "Political socialization to democratic orientations in four Western systems." *Comparative Political Studies* 1:71–100.

Dennis, Jack, Leon Lindberg, and Donald J. McCrone (1971). "Support for nation and government among English children." *British Journal of Political Science* 1:25–48.

Dennis, Jack, and Donald J. McCrone (1970). "Preadult development of political party identification in Western democracies." *Comparative Political Studies* 4:243–63.

Dolbeare, Kenneth M., and Phillip E. Hammond (1968). "The political party basis of attitudes toward the Supreme Court." *Public Opinion Quarterly* 32:16–30.

Donald, David (1956). *Lincoln Reconsidered*, 2nd edition. New York: Vintage.

Easton, David (1965). *A Systems Analysis of Political Life*. New York: Wiley.

Easton, David, and Jack Dennis (1965). "The child's image of government." *Annals of the American Academy of Political and Social Science* 361:40–57.

_____ (1969). *Children in the Political System: Origins of Political Legitimacy*. New York: McGraw-Hill.

Elder, Glen H. (1970). "Socialization and ascent in a racial minority." *Youth and Society* 2:74–110.

Engstrom, Richard L. (1970). "Race and compliance: differential political socialization." *Polity* 3:101–11.

Feldman, Kenneth A., and Theodore M. Newcomb (1969). *The Impact of College on Students: Vol. I. An Analysis of Four Decades of Research*. San Francisco: Jossey-Bass.

Festinger, Leon (1950). "Informal social communication." *Psychological Review* 57:271–82.

Field, John O., and Ronald E. Anderson (1969). "Ideology in the public's conceptualization of the 1964 election." *Public Opinion Quarterly* 33:380–98.

Finifter, Ada W. (1970). "Dimensions of political alienation." *American Political Science Review* 64:389–410.

Freedman, Jonathan L., J. Merrill Carlsmith, and David O. Sears (1974). *Social Psychology*, 2nd edition. Englewood Cliffs, N. J.: Prentice-Hall.

Friedman, Lucy N., Alice R. Gold, and Richard Christie (1972). "Dissecting the generation gap: intergenerational and intrafamilial similarities and differences." *Public Opinion Quarterly* 36:334–46.

Gallatin, Judith, and Joseph Adelson (1970). "Individual rights and the public good: a cross-national study of adolescents." *Comparative Political Studies* 3:226–12.

Garcia, F. Chris (1973). *Political Socialization of Chicano Children: A Comparative Study with Anglos in California Schools*. New York: Praeger.

Gergen, Kenneth J., and Kurt W. Back (1965), "Aging, time perspective, and preferred solutions to international conflicts." *Journal of Conflict Resolution* 9:177–86.

Glenn, Norval D. (1972). "Sources of the shift to political independence: some evidence from a cohort analysis." *Social Science Quarterly* 52:494–519.

—————— (1974). "Aging and conservatism." *Annals of the American Academy of Political and Social Science:* 176–86.

Glenn, Norval D., and Michael Grimes (1968). "Aging, voting, and political interest." *American Sociological Review* 33:563–75.

Glenn, Norval D., and Ted Hefner (1972). "Further evidence on aging and party identification." *Public Opinion Quarterly* 36:31–47.

Greeley, Andrew M. and Joe L. Spaeth (1970). "Political change among college alumni." *Sociology of Education* 43:106–13.

Greenberg, Edward S., ed. (1970a). *Political Socialization.* New York: Atherton.

—————— (1970b). "Orientations of black and white children to political authority figures." *Social Science Quarterly* 51:561–71.

—————— (1970c). "Children and government: a comparison across racial lines." *Midwest Journal of Political Science* 14:249–75.

—————— (1970d). "Black children and the political system." *Public Opinion Quarterly* 34:333–45.

Greenstein, Fred I. (1960). "The benevolent leader: children's images of political authority." *American Political Science Review* 54:934–43.

—————— (1965). *Children and Politics.* New Haven: Yale University Press.

—————— (1969). *Personality and Politics.* Chicago: Markham.

—————— (1970). "A note on the ambiguity of 'political socialization': definitions, criticisms, and strategies of inquiry." *Journal of Politics* 32:969–78.

—————— (1973). "Children's images of political leaders in three democracies: the benevolent leader revisited." Prepared for delivery at the annual meeting of the American Political Science Association, New Orleans.

—————— (1974). "Personality and politics." In Fred I. Greenstein and Nelson W. Polsby (eds.), *Handbook of Political Science, Vol. 2.* Reading, Mass.: Addison-Wesley.

Greenstein, Fred I., and Sidney G. Tarrow (1970). "Political orientations of children: the use of a semi-projective technique in three nations." *Sage Professional Papers in Comparative Politics* 1:479–558.

Harding, John, Harold Proshansky, Bernard Kutner, and Isador Chein (1969). "Prejudice and ethnic relations." In Gardner Lindzey and Elliot Aronson (eds.), *The Handbook of Social Psychology,* 2nd edition, Vol. 5. Reading, Mass.: Addison-Wesley.

Hennessey, Timothy M. (1969). "Democratic attitudinal configurations among Italian youth." *Midwest Journal of Political Science* 13:167–93.

Hensler, Carl P. (1971). "The structure of orientations toward government: involvement, efficacy and evaluation." Prepared for delivery at the Annual Meeting of the American Political Science Association, Chicago.

Hero, Alfred O., Jr. (1969). "American Negroes and U. S. foreign policy: 1937–1967." *Journal of Conflict Resolution* 13:220–51.

Hess, Robert D., and David Easton (1960). "The child's changing image of the president." *Public Opinion Quarterly* 24:632–44.

Hess, Robert D., and Judith V. Torney (1965). *The Development of Basic Attitudes and Values Toward Government and Citizenship During the Elementary School Years, Part I.* Chicago: University of Chicago Press.

_____ (1967). *The Development of Political Attitudes in Children.* Chicago: Aldine.

Himmelweit, Hilde T., and Betty Swift (1971). "Adolescent and adult authoritarianism re-examined: its organization and stability over time." *European Journal of Social Psychology* 1:357–84.

Hofstetter, Richard C. (1969). "Political disengagement and the death of Martin Luther King." *Public Opinion Quarterly* 23:174–79.

Hoge, Dean R., and Irving E. Bender (1974). "Factors influencing value change among college graduates in adult life." *Journal of Personality and Social Psychology* 29:572–85.

Hraba, Joseph (1972). "The doll technique: a measure of racial ethnocentrism?" *Social Forces* 50: 522–27.

Hraba, Joseph, and Geoffrey Grant (1970). "Black is beautiful: a reexamination of racial preference and identification." *Journal of Personality and Social Psychology* 16:398–402.

Hyman, Herbert (1959). *Political Socialization.* Glencoe, Ill.: Free Press.

Hyman, Herbert, and Paul B. Sheatsley (1947). "Some reasons why information campaigns fail." *Public Opinion Quarterly* 11:413–23.

Inglehart, Ronald F. (1971). "The silent revolution in Europe: intergenerational change in post-industrial societies." *American Political Science Review* 65:991–1017.

Jackman, Mary R. (1972a). "Social mobility and attitude toward the political system." *Social Forces* 50:462–72.

_____ (1972b). "The political orientation of the socially mobile in Italy: a re-examination." *American Sociological Review* 37:213–22.

Jahoda, Gustav (1963). "The development of children's ideas about country and nationality. Part II: National symbols and themes." *British Journal of Educational Psychology* 33:143–53.

_____ (1964). "Children's concepts of nationality: a critical study of Piaget's stages." *Child Development* 35:1081–92.

Jaros, Dean (1967). "Children's orientations toward the president: some additional theoretical considerations and data." *Journal of Politics* 29:368–87.

_____ (1973). *Socialization to Politics.* New York: Praeger.

Jaros, Dean, Herbert Hirsch, and F. J. Fleron, Jr. (1968). "The malevolent leader: political socialization in an American subculture." *American Political Science Review* 62:564–75.

Jaros, Dean, and Kenneth L. Kolson (1974). "The multifarious leader: political socialization of Amish, 'Yanks,' Blacks." In Richard G. Niemi (ed.), *The Politics of Future Citizens.* San Francisco: Jossey-Bass.

Jennings, M. Kent (1973). "The variable nature of generational conflict." Prepared for delivery at the International Political Science Association Congress, Montreal.

Jennings, M. Kent, and Kenneth P. Langton (1969). "Mothers vs. fathers: the formation of political orientations among young Americans." *Journal of Politics* 31:329–58.

Jennings, M. Kent, and Richard G. Niemi (1968a). "The transmission of political values from parent to child." *American Political Science Review* 62:169–84.

_____ (1968b). "Patterns of political learning." *Harvard Educational Review* 38:443–67.

_____ (1973). "Continuity and change in political orientations: a longitudinal study of two generations." Prepared for delivery at the annual meeting of the American Political Science Association, New Orleans.

_____ (1974). *The Political Character of Adolescence*. Princeton, N. J.: Princeton University Press.

Johnson, Peter A., and J. Robert Staffieri (1971). "Stereotypic affective properties of personal names and somato-types in children." *Developmental Psychology* 5:176.

Kagan, Jerome, and Robert Coles, eds. (1972). *Twelve to Sixteen: Early Adolescence*. New York: Norton.

Katz, F. E. and F. V. Piret (1964). "Circuitous participation in politics." *American Journal of Sociology* 69:367–373.

Katz, Phyllis A., T. Chabasinski, and H. Connolly (1975). "Anti-Negro prejudice: a review of research." In Phyllis A. Katz (ed.), *Toward the Elimination of Racism*. New York: Pergamon Press.

Kavanagh, Dennis (1972). "Allegiance among English children: a dissent." *British Journal of Political Science* 2:127–31.

Kelly, E. Lowell (1955). "Consistency of the adult personality." *American Psychologist* 10:659–81.

Key, V. O., Jr. (1961). *Public Opinion and American Democracy*. New York: Knopf.

_____ (1966). *The Responsible Electorate*. Cambridge, Mass.: Harvard University Press.

Kirkham, James F., Sheldon Levy and William J. Crotty, eds. (1969). *Assassination and Political Violence*. Washington: U. S. Government Printing Office.

Klapper, Joseph T. (1960). *The Effects of Mass Communications*. Glencoe, Ill.: Free Press.

Klecka, William R. (1971). "Applying political generations to the study of political behavior: a cohort analysis." *Public Opinion Quarterly* 35:358–373.

Knoke, David (1972). "Community and consistency: the ethnic factor in status inconsistency." *Social Forces* 51:23–33.

Knutson, Jeanne Nickell (1973). *The Human Basis of the Polity: A Psychological Study of Political Man*. Chicago: Aldine.

_____ (1974) "Prepolitical ideologies: the basis of political learning." In Richard G. Niemi (ed.), *The Politics of Future Citizens*. San Francisco: Jossey-Bass.

Koeppen, Sheilah R. (1970). "Children and compliance: a comparative analysis of socialization studies." *Law and Society Review* 4:545–64.

Kornberg, Allan, Joel Smith, and David Bromley (1969). "Some differences in the political socialization patterns of Canadian and American party officials: a preliminary report." *Canadian Journal of Political Science* 2:63–88.

Kubota, Akira, and Robert E. Ward (1970). "Family influence and political socialization in Japan: some preliminary findings from a comparative perspective." *Comparative Political Studies* 3:140–75.

Lambert, W. E., and O. Klineberg (1967). *Children's Views of Foreign Peoples*. New York: Appleton-Century-Crofts.

Langdon, Frank (1967). *Politics in Japan*. Boston: Little, Brown.

Langton, Kenneth P. (1967). "Peer group and school and the political socialization process." *American Political Science Review* 61:751–58.

_____ (1969). *Political Socialization*. Boston: Little, Brown.

Laurence, Joan (1970). "White socialization: black reality." *Psychiatry* 33:174–94.

Lawson, Edwin D. (1963). "Development of patriotism in children—a second look." *Journal of Psychology* 55:279–86.

Liebschutz, Sarah F. and Richard G. Niemi (1974). "Political attitudes among black children." In Richard G. Niemi (ed.), *The Politics of Future Citizens*. San Francisco: Jossey-Bass.

Lipset, Seymour Martin, and Everett Carll Ladd, Jr. (1971). "College generations from the 1930's to the 1960's." *The Public Interest* 25:99–113.

Lipset, Seymour Martin, Paul F. Lazarsfeld, A. H. Barton, and J. Linz (1954). "The psychology of voting: an analysis of political behavior." In Gardner Lindzey (ed.), *Handbook of Social Psychology*, Vol. 2. Reading, Mass.: Addison-Wesley.

Lopreato, Joseph, and Lawrence E. Hazelrigg (1970). "Intragenerational versus intergenerational mobility in relation to socio-political attitudes." *Social Forces* 49:200–10.

Lyons, Schley R. (1970). "The political socialization of ghetto children." *Journal of Politics* 32:288–304.

Maccoby, E., R. E. Matthews, and A. S. Morton (1954). "Youth and political change." *Public Opinion Quarterly* 18:23–29.

Marsh, David (1971). "Political socialization: the implicit assumptions questioned." *British Journal of Political Science* 1:453–65.

_____ (1972). "Beliefs about democracy among English adolescents: what significance have they?" *British Journal of Political Science* 2:255–59.

McClosky, Herbert (1964). "Consensus and ideology in American politics." *American Political Science Review* 58:361–82.

McClosky, Herbert, and H. E. Dahlgren (1959). "Primary group influence on party loyalty." *American Political Science Review* 53:757–76.

McGuire, W. J. (1969). "The nature of attitudes and attitude change." In Gardner Lindzey and Elliot Aronson (eds.), *Handbook of Social Psychology*, 2nd edition, Vol. 3. Reading, Mass.: Addison-Wesley.

McMurty, C. Allen, and John E. Williams (1972). "Evaluation dimension of the affective meaning system of the preschool child." *Developmental Psychology* 6:238–246.

McPhail, C. (1971). "Civil disorder participation: a critical examination of recent research." *American Sociological Review* 36:1058–73.

Merelman, Richard M. (1971). "The development of policy thinking in adolescence." *American Political Science Review* 65:1033–47.

Merriam, Charles E. (1931). *The Making of Citizens.* Chicago: University of Chicago Press.

Middleton, Margaret R., Henri Tajfel, and N. B. Johnson (1970). "Cognitive and affective aspects of children's national attitudes." *British Journal of Social and Clinical Psychology* 9:122–34.

Middleton, R., and S. Putney (1963). "Student rebellion against parental political beliefs." *Social Forces* 41:377–83.

_____ (1964). "Influences on the political beliefs of American college students: a study of self-appraisals." *Il Politico* 29:484–92.

Milbrath, Lester W. (1965). *Political Participation.* Chicago: Rand McNally.

Miller, Arthur H., Thad A. Brown, and Alden S. Raine. (1973) "Social conflict and political estrangement, 1958–1972." Prepared for delivery at the Midwest Political Science Association Convention, Chicago.

Miller, Warren E. (1967). "Voting and foreign policy." In James N. Rosenau (ed.), *Domestic Sources of Foreign Policy.* New York: Free Press, 213–30.

Mischel, Walter (1968). *Personality and Assessment.* New York: Wiley.

_____ (1970). "Continuity and change in personality." *American Psychologist* 24:1012–18.

Mueller, John E. (1973). *War, Presidents, and Public Opinion.* New York: Wiley.

Murphy, Walter F., and Joseph Tanenhaus (1968). "Public opinion and the United States Supreme Court: The Goldwater Campaign." *Public Opinion Quarterly* 32:31–50.

Myrdal, Gunnar (1944). *An American Dilemma.* New York: Harper & Row.

Nesselroade, John R., and Hayne W. Reese, eds. (1973). *Life-span Developmental Psychology: Methodological Issues.* New York: Academic Press.

Newcomb, Theodore M. (1943). *Personality and Social Change.* New York: Holt.

Newcomb, Theodore M., K. E. Koenig, R. Flacks, and D. P. Warwick (1967). *Persistence and Change: Bennington College and Its Students after 25 Years.* New York: Wiley.

Niemi, Richard G. (1973a). "Political socialization." In Jeanne Knutson (ed.), *Handbook of Political Psychology.* San Francisco: Jossey-Bass.

_____ (1973b). "Collecting information about the family: a problem in survey methodology." In Jack Dennis (ed.), *Socialization to Politics: A Reader.* New York: Wiley.

_____ (1974). *How Family Members Perceive Each Other.* New Haven: Yale University Press.

Okamura, Tadao (1968). "The child's changing image of the prime minister: a preface to the study of political socialization in contemporary Japan." *The Developing Economies* 6:566–86.

Orren, Karen K., and Paul Peterson (1967). "Presidential assassination: a case study in the dynamics of political socialization." *Journal of Politics* 29:388–404.

Orum, Anthony M., and Roberta S. Cohen (1973). "The development of political orientations among black and white children." *American Sociological Review* 38:62–74.

Osgood, Charles E., and Percy H. Tannenbaum (1955). "The principle of congruity and the prediction of attitude change." *Psychological Review* 62:42–55.

Paige, Jeffrey M. (1970). "Changing patterns of anti-white attitudes among blacks." *Journal of Social Issues* 26:69–86.

Pammett, Jon H. (1971). "The development of political orientations in Canadian schoolchildren." *Canadian Journal of Political Science* 4:132–41.

Prewitt, Kenneth, George Von Der Muhll, and David Court (1970). "School experiences and political socialization: a study of Tanzanian secondary school students." *Comparative Political Studies* 3:203–25.

Proshansky, H. M. (1966). "The development of intergroup attitudes." In Lois W. Hoffman and M. L. Hoffman (eds.), *Review of Child Development Research*, Vol. 2. New York: Russell Sage Foundation.

Prothro, J. W., and C. W. Grigg (1960). "Fundamental principles of democracy: bases of agreement and disagreement." *Journal of Politics* 22:276–294.

Reading, Reid R. (1968). "Political socialization in Colombia and the United States: an exploratory study." *Midwest Journal of Political Science* 12:352–381.

Riccards, Michael P. (1973). *The Making of the American Citizenry: An Introduction to Political Socialization*. New York: Chandler.

Riley, Matilda White (1973). "Aging and cohort succession: interpretations and misinterpretations." *Public Opinion Quarterly* 37:35–49.

Rodgers, Harrell R., and George Taylor (1970). "Pre-adult attitudes toward legal compliance: notes toward a theory." *Social Science Quarterly* 51:539–51.

_____ (1971). "The policeman as an agent of regime legitimation." *Midwest Journal of Political Science* 15:72–86.

Rogers, W. C., Barbara Stuhler, and D. Koenig (1967). "A comparison of informed and general public opinion on U. S. foreign policy." *Public Opinion Quarterly* 31: 242–52.

Roig, Charles, and Francoise Billon-Grand (1968). "La socialisation politique des enfants." *Cahiers de la Fondation Nationale des Sciences Politique,* No. 163. Paris.

Schaie, K. Warner (1970). "A reinterpretation of age related changes in cognitive structure and functioning." In L. R. Goulet, and Paul B. Baltes (eds.), *Life-span Developmental Psychology: Research and Theory.* New York: Academic Press.

Schaie, K. Warner, and Iris A. Parham (1974). "Social responsibility in adulthood: ontogenetic and socio-cultural change." *Journal of Personality and Social Psychology* 30:483–92.

Searing, Donald D., Joel J. Schwartz, and Alden E. Lind (1973). "The structuring principle: political socialization and belief systems." *American Political Science Review* 67:415–32.

Sears, David O. (1968). "Review of the R. Hess and J. Torney, *The Development of Political Attitudes in Children.*" *Harvard Educational Review* 38:571–78.

_____ (1969a). "Political behavior." In G. Lindzey and E. Aronson (eds.) *Handbook of Social Psychology,* 2nd edition, Vol. 5. Reading, Mass.: Addison-Wesley.

———— (1969b). "Black attitudes toward the political system in the aftermath of the Watts insurrection." *Midwest Journal of Political Science* 13:515–44.

———— (1973). "Protest and the residues of preadult political socialization." Paper presented at annual meeting of American Psychological Association, Montreal.

———— (1975). *Political Attitudes Through the Life Cycle*. San Francisco: W. H. Freeman.

Sears, David O., and Donald R. Kinder (1971). "Racial tensions and voting in Los Angeles." In Werner Z. Hirsch (ed.), *Los Angeles: Viability and Prospects for Metropolitan Leadership*. New York: Praeger.

Sears, David O., and John B. McConahay (1973). *The Politics of Violence: The New Urban Blacks and the Watts Riot*. Boston: Houghton-Mifflin.

Sears, David O., and Richard E. Whitney (1973a). *Political Persuasion*. Morristown, N.J. General Learning Press.

———— (1973b). "Political persuasion." In I. deS. Pool and Wilbur Schramm (eds.), *Handbook of Communication*. Chicago: Rand McNally.

Segal, David R. (1970). "Status inconsistency and party choice in Canada: an attempt to replicate." *Canadian Journal of Political Science* 3:471–4.

Sheatsley, Paul B., and Jacob J. Feldman (1965). "A national survey of public reactions and behavior." In B. S. Greenberg and E. B. Parker (eds.), *The Kennedy Assassination and the American Public*. Stanford, Cal.: Stanford University Press.

Sica, Morris G. (1972). "An analysis of the political orientations of Mexican-American and Anglo-American children." Report prepared for the U. S. Department of Health, Education, and Welfare.

Sicinski, Andrzej (1969). "Dallas and Warsaw: the impact of a major national political event on public opinion abroad." *Public Opinion Quarterly* 23:190–96.

Sigel, Roberta S. (1965). "An exploration into some aspects of political socialization: school children's reactions to the death of a president." In Martha Wolfenstein and G. Kliman (eds.), *Children and the Death of a President*. Garden City, N. Y.: Doubleday.

———— (1968). "Image of a president: some insights into the political views of schoolchildren." *American Political Science Review* 62:216–26.

————, ed. (1970). *Learning about politics*. New York: Random House.

———— (1968). "Image of a president: some insights into the political views of school children." *American Political Science Review* 62:216–26.

Simmons, Roberta G., and Morris Rosenberg (1971). "Functions of children's perceptions of the stratification system." *American Sociological Review* 36:235–249.

Smookler, Helene V. (1971). "War, police, and democracy: how children view the issues and the nation." Unpublished manuscript, University of California, Los Angeles.

Stember, C. H. (1961). *Education and Attitude Change*. New York: Institute of Human Relations Press.

Stouffer, Samuel A. (1955). *Communism, Conformity, and Civil Liberties*. New York: Doubleday.

Stradling, Robert (1971). "Socialization of support for political authority in Britain: a long-term view." *British Journal of Political Science* 1:121–22.

Stradling, Robert, and Elia Zurick (1971). "Political and non-political ideals of English primary and secondary school children." *The Sociological Review* 19:203–28.

Tajfel, Henri (1969). "Cognitive aspects of prejudice." *Journal of Social Issues* 25:79–98.

Tapp, June L., and Lawrence Kohlberg (1971). "Developing senses of law and legal justice." *Journal of Social Issues* 27:65–92.

Thomas, L. Eugene (1971). "Family correlates of student political activism." *Developmental Psychology* 4:206–14.

Tilman, R. O. (1970). "Student unrest in the Philippines: the view from the South" *Asian Survey* 10:900–9.

Tolley, Howard, Jr. (1973). *Children and War: Political Socialization to International Conflict.* New York: Teachers College Press.

Torney, Judith V. (1974). "The implications of the IEA cross-national civic education data for understanding the international socialization of American adolescents." Paper presented at American Political Science Association meeting, Chicago.

Treiman, Donald J. (1970). "Status discrepancy and prejudice reconsidered." *American Journal of Sociology* 75:863–5.

Tudor, Jeannette F. (1971). "The development of class awareness in children." *Social Forces* 49:470–6.

Vaillancourt, Pauline Marie (1972). "The political socialization of young people: a panel survey of youngsters in the San Francisco Bay Area." Unpublished doctoral dissertation, University of California, Berkeley.

_____ (1973). "Stability of children's survey responses." *Public Opinion Quarterly* 37:373–87.

Vaillancourt, Pauline Marie, and Richard G. Niemi (1974). "Children's party choices." In Richard G. Niemi (ed.), *The Politics of Future Citizens.* San Francisco: Jossey-Bass.

Verba, Sidney, and Norman Nie (in press). "Citizenship and Civil Milieu." In Fred I. Greenstein, and Nelson W. Polsby (eds.), *Handbook of Political Science,* Vol. 4. Reading: Addison-Wesley.

Weiler, Hans N. (1971). "Schools and the learning of dissent norms: a study of West German youth." Paper delivered at the Annual Meeting of the American Politica¹ Science Association, Chicago.

Weissberg, Robert (1972). "Adolescents' perceptions of political authorities: another look at political virtue and power." *Midwest Journal of Political Science* 16:147–68.

_____ (1974). *Political Learning, Political Choice, and Democratic Citizenship.* Englewood Cliffs, N. J.: Prentice-Hall.

West, J. (1945). *Plainville, U. S. A.* New York: Columbia University Press.

White, Ralph K. (1969). "Three not-so-obvious contributions of psychology to peace." *Journal of Social Issues* 25:23–40.

Wicker, Allan W. (1969). "Attitudes vs. actions: The relationship of verbal and overt behavioral responses to attitude." *Journal of Social Issues* 25:41–78.

Williams, John E., and John R. Stabler (1973). "If white means good, then black ..." *Psychology Today* 7:50–54.

Wilson, Howard E. (1938). *Education for Citizenship*. New York: McGraw-Hill.

Wolfenstein, M., and G. Kliman, eds. (1965). *Children and the Death of a President*. Garden City, N. Y.: Doubleday.

Zellman, Gail L. (1973). "Sex roles and political socialization." Unpublished doctoral dissertation, University of California, Los Angeles.

Zellman, Gail L., and D. O. Sears (1971). "Childhood origins of tolerance for dissent." *Journal of Social Issues* 27:109–36.

3

POLITICAL RECRUITMENT

MOSHE M. CZUDNOWSKI

I. INTRODUCTION: THE RELEVANCE OF RECRUITMENT AND RECRUITMENT STUDIES

The study of political recruitment inquires into the processes through which individuals or groups of individuals are inducted into active political roles. This definition of our subject matter distinguishes it from the study of political elites in two major respects: (1) Whereas political-elite studies refer to the holders of influential positions in politics or to the social strata from which they have been recruited most frequently, recruitment studies are concerned with the social and political processes through which such positions have been attained. (2) Elite studies have traditionally been concerned with ruling elites, whereas the broader concept of "political roles" includes positions held by members of opposition parties, as well as revolutionary leaders and other political counterelites operating outside the institutional framework of a given polity.

Thus defined, the study of recruitment is a relative newcomer to *empirical* political science, although it can be traced back to the emphasis placed on the circulation of elites and on politics as a profession in the writings of the "founding fathers" of modern political sociology, i.e., Mosca, Pareto, and Weber. However, rather than inspecting the "graveyards of aristocracies" (Pareto, 1935), recruitment studies investigate the *development* of political careers.

The theoretical justification for a developmental perspective has been formulated by Marvick (1961a); his argument can be summarized briefly. Nondevelopmental approaches to the study of political actors had attempted to explain the performance of political decision makers by ascribing to their behavior motivations determined by their social origins. However, "the premises of official action derive in large part from considerations only remotely linked

155

to the social background of decision makers." Yet little is known of the differences in skill and ability, in organizational and value commitment, introduced by the selective workings of political recruitment ladders. The purpose of recruitment studies is to explain the processes which result in a differentiation between political elites and masses, and between political and other social elites. The importance of these studies, however, goes beyond their immediate purposes and consists in the expectation that recruitment patterns can explain certain characteristics in the orientations and role performance of office holders and other political elites.

It is possible to assess the degree of centrality of recruitment studies in political science by focusing on three problem areas, in which recruitment research and theory can make significant contributions to the entire discipline. (1) Recruitment is a critical link between polity and society. (2) It is an indicator of the relevance of politics for the achievement of nonpolitical goals. (3) Recruitment studies are capable of reconciling the competing and sometimes mutually exclusive positions in a number of controversies in contemporary political science. Let us consider briefly the role of recruitment studies in each of these areas.

A. Recruitment as a Critical Link between Polity and Society

Defined as the process through which individuals are inducted into active political roles, recruitment is obviously a link between society and the political system. Its importance resides in the function it performs in structuring the relationship between polity and society. This relationship displays three basic dilemmas, resulting from the dual characteristic of the political system as both reflecting and controlling social change.

1. A political order requires institutional continuity, but continuity implies a turnover of personnel.
2. Policy-making aims at relevance, consistency, and effectiveness, but society displays continuous social, economic, and cultural change.
3. Government is predicated on authority, but the maintenance of authority is subject to legitimization through responsiveness or responsibility to society.

The manner in which each of these dilemmas is resolved at any given time depends to a great extent on the prevailing patterns of political recruitment and the changes occuring in these patterns. Thus recruitment is a critical link between polity and society because it can perform the function of "system maintenance" (Almond, 1960) and also serve as a major channel for change.

B. Recruitment as an Indicator of the Relevance of Politics for the Achievement of Nonpolitical Goals

Another area in which the study of recruitment can make a contribution to political science is the analysis of the goal orientations of political activists, candidates, and office holders. The distinction between private (personal) and public (collective) goals in the motivations of politicians provides useful criteria of reference for an assessment of what has been called the "functional quality" or salience of politics and political careers in any given society or subsystem of society (Eulau and Koff, 1962; Czudnowski, 1968).

Many students of elites and elite behavior have assumed that politicians are motivated by either (a) the expectation of personal rewards (material, social, or psychological) or (b) their orientations toward public issues, a leader, or a "cause." Thus private and public goal orientations or incentives were not only distinguished from each other but assumed to operate as separate and nonoverlapping motivations. Others have combined both types of orientation into a single motivational syndrome: Weber's category of "avocational politicians" included those who engage in politics because they *enjoy* the feeling of serving a *cause* (Weber, 1921), and Lasswell described the politician as an individual who displaces a *personal need onto* a *public object* (Lasswell, 1930, 1954). Yet the political process consists of collective actions for the attainment of shared (i.e., public) goals, and candidates for political office neither seek nor receive public support to help them satisfy their personal needs.

This consideration of private and public goals of political behavior points out a basic difference between political and other types of social behavior. Whereas all social behavior has both private and public *observed* consequences, only political (and other community-oriented) behavior can also have both private and public *intended* consequences, i.e., goals. Moreover, the overtly professed and socially accepted goals of nonpolitical behavior are private, whereas in politics the overt and accepted purposes of action are collective or public goals. As a consequence of this characteristic of political behavior, the political scientist has to explain the observed consequences of political action not only in terms of professed public goals but also in terms of more or less covert personal motivations.

Nowhere is this observation more relevant than in the study of recruitment. By espousing a political career, the political actor ranks his personal and public goals as a combined entry on his scale of priorities. Therefore political recruitment is highly indicative of the relative importance of the personal rewards offered by the political system and can serve as the testing ground for the assessment and measurement of the degree of interchangeability between political and nonpolitical means in the pursuit of nonpolitical goals. The degree of this interchangeability is an important variable in every political system, because it is an operational indicator of the system's location on a dimension ranging from totalitarianism, where interchangeability is zero, to liberalism, where interchangeability is high.

C. Recruitment and the Controversies in Contemporary Political Science

From a rather different viewpoint, related to the state of the discipline of political science, recruitment studies can contribute to the clarification of a number of theoretical controversies. There is a parallelism between the linkage position of recruitment in the relationship between polity and society and the consistency, or congruence, of the paradigmatic assumptions of recruitment studies with each of the major competing positions in these controversies.

The first controversy is that between the "institutional tradition" and the "behavioral persuasion" over the claim that political sociology has attempted to "explain away" the politics of the political process by submitting explanations in terms of psychological, social, and economic variables and that, as a consequence, the political process has been reduced from an independent sphere of activity to a mere dependent variable "caused" by nonpolitical factors. The study of recruitment combines elements of both these positions. It focuses on individuals with psychological, social, and economic characteristics who are channeled by institutions and through noninstitutionalized processes, according to politically relevant criteria, into the institutionalized role structure of the political system.

The second controversy is over the claim that empirical political science is inherently oriented toward "what is" and is therefore incapable of dealing with what politics is all about, i.e., conflict about change. Proponents of this view point to the somewhat trivial findings of early empirical studies due to what appears to have been a disproportionate interest in mass political behavior, especially voting, and the relatively slow development of the study of elite behavior. As in the preceding controversy, the study of recruitment is based on assumptions consistent with both positions. The political system reflects and controls social change, and "what is" includes support for system maintenance as well as conflict over change. The normative criteria for change or for the maintenance of the status quo are articulated by political elites, and it is through the process of recruitment that potential elites espousing one or another set of normative criteria are channeled into decision-making roles.

Finally, there is the controversy between holism and methodological individualism. Holism posits that political processes can be understood only with reference to "the whole," i.e., to larger units, whether historical nation-states or analytical systems. Methodological individualism posits that whether we study political behavior in small groups or larger aggregates, the basic unit of analysis is always the individual. Thus micro- and macropolitics were considered as mutually exclusive theoretical frameworks, a distinction which merely concealed the now gradually disappearing inability to conceptualize and interpret behavior at successively more inclusive spatial (ecological) and temporal levels of analysis. The study of recruitment conceptualizes the pathways to political office as consisting of successive interactions between individual-level variables, social screening processes, political organizations and systemic institutions, norms and issues. Recruitment studies are therefore anchored in both micro- and macrotheories of the political process.

If these are the purposes and some of the broader areas of relevance of recruitment and recruitment studies, what is the state of the discipline in this field, what research findings and theoretical insights have emerged from past and current efforts, and what conclusions can be drawn about the direction, scope, and method of future research? It is to these questions that this chapter addresses itself.

The discussion will begin with a clarification of some definitional key concepts and an overview of the perspectives and models adopted in the study of recruitment (Part II). Next is a review of research findings wth emphasis on successive sets of variables on which researchers have focused their investigations (Part III). The order in which these variables are discussed reflects a developmental model of recruitment: social background variables, political socialization, initial political activity, apprenticeship, occupational variables, motivations, and selection. Finally, Part IV combines the available theoretical interpretations of research findings into an outline or model for a recruitment theory, which is also an agenda for future research.

Throughout this chapter, the focus will be microanalytical. A number of excellent macrointerpretations of aggregate data on elite background and careers are available. They include Guttsman (1963) on Britain, Singer (1964) on Ceylon, Frey (1965) on Turkey, Zapf (1966) on Germany, Dogan (1967) on France, and Linz (1973) on Spain. This literature, however, is of greater relevance to the sociological history of elites and political systems than to the study of recruitment processes, and it will not be discussed here. Neither will this chapter deal with the recruitment of elites in Communist and developing Asian and African countries, where the recruitment process has not been very researchable.

II. CONCEPTS, PERSPECTIVES, AND MODELS

After emphasis on the theoretical advantages that can be derived from the conceptualization of recruitment as a developmental process, it is necessary to consider some of the methodological difficulties which the choice of a developmental framework entails. First, there is the problem of an operational definition of the recruitment process. Should it be defined with reference to a point of destination, a state of affairs that indicates the completion of the process? If so, what is the terminal point? Or should it be defined with reference to motivations or behavioral characteristics and the conditions under which they occur? A number of studies, involving different interpretations of some of the key concepts for an operational definition, will be discussed in Section A, which clarifies the concept of "initial recruitment."

Second, recruitment involves potential candidates, recruiting agencies, social and political environments, and a span of time. These dimensions afford different vantage grounds and different perspectives on the recruitment process, involving different strategies of research. Section B covers the relative advantages and shortcomings of these strategies.

Finally, within a given research strategy, the investigator will choose the variables he intends to draw into the analysis. These variables constitute his explanatory framework, his "model." Since the recruitment process is complex and researchers have approached the study of recruitment from different vantage grounds with different areas of emphasis, the literature displays a great variety of models. The most important of these models will be reviewed in Section C.

A. Approaches to an Operational Definition of Recruitment: Some Key Concepts

Few studies have made recruitment the central focus of their inquiry. Recruitment hypotheses and the interpretation of findings are often subsidiary lines of analysis in elite studies that cover a wide range of other issues. Interest in *who* was selected precedes questions on *how* he was selected. Questions pertaining to social and demographic profiles of politicians are also more easily answered than those attempting to reconstruct a process involving past situations, motivations, attitudes, and behavior. Implicit or explicit preoccupations with recruitment can be found in studies of elite behavior in decision-making institutions at different levels of government, in studies focusing primarily on leadership, in analyses of party structure and function and of electoral systems and elections, in political biographies of single actors or descriptions of intergenerational change in the composition of elites, in the study of change or development, and in attempts to discover some regularities in the personality structure of political actors. These different modes of inquiry are evidence of a growing interest and the multiple ramifications of recruitment; they are also indicators of an incipient stage in the development of this field of inquiry, of the search for a paradigm, of competing models, and of methodological agnosticism.

This diversity of perspectives has sometimes blurred the conceptual clarity necessary in the analysis of a complex phenomenon. There has been insufficient clarity even in the denotation ascribed to the concept of political recruitment. In Almond's (1960) functional model of political systems, recruitment is described as the function which "recruits members of the society and of particular subcultures—religious communities, statuses, classes, ethnic communities, and the like—and inducts them into the specialized roles of the political system, trains them in the appropriate skills, provides them with political cognitive maps, values, expectations, and affects." The recruitment function "takes up where the general political socialization function leaves off," but the developmental sequence of the recruitment process displays a greater variety of patterns than political socialization.

The specialized political roles of a political system differ in terms of legal requirements and political avenues of access, in terms of prerequisites of experience or partisan involvement, as much as they differ in the source, scope, incidence, and substantive areas of political authority. It is probably impossible to establish a unidimensional ladder of political offices or roles; political careers reveal, however, that the sequence of roles follows a pattern of an increasingly broader source and incidence of authority, sometimes combined with a decrease in the size of a collegiate body of decision makers or a move from legislative to executive office. Although the "hierarchy" of offices does not necessarily follow the hierarchy of the authority structure, especially in systems in which political authority is separated along both functional and territorial lines, the United States Congressman who seeks a seat in the United States Senate or the French mayor who competes for a seat in the Chamber of Deputies does in fact seek political promotion in a very real sense. Needless to say, the processes of recruitment to a party precinct leadership or to the city council and of recruitment to the national legislature are as different as the offices to which they relate; yet the term "recruitment" is applied in both cases.

In order to differentiate between two types of recruitment in terms of previous experience, it has been suggested that one distinguish between *initial recruitment* and political *promotion* (Jacob, 1962), and many studies do attempt to assess the impact of patterns of initial recruitment on subsequent career development. However, the concept of initial recruitment requires an operational threshold, a cutting point. What are the characteristics of the roles in which initial recruitment can be considered completed? Political systems and cultures may differ in the extent or nature of political activity required to qualify for what is considered, in a given system, the critical threshold of recruitment. A comparison of research findings from different settings therefore requires some theoretically meaningful and operationally applicable common criterion.

This problem can be explored by examining some of the basic differences which have been observed in the behavior, orientations, and commitments to active political involvement among politicians and office holders. One of the distinctions most frequently reported by students of political elites is that between *amateurs* and *professionals*. Essentially it reflects differences in the scope, style, and salience of political involvement, but various observers, referring to different settings and periods, have assigned to these terms more specific meanings, which differ considerably from one another. A closer examination of these interpretations and a review of the evidence adduced to justify the distinction will provide several criteria for an operational definition of "initial recruitment."

Max Weber's 1919 lecture at Munich University "Politics as a Vocation" (Weber, 1921) is still one of the most insightful of all contributions to the empirical theory of political recruitment. For Weber, the *avocational* politician is the *occasional* politician, the notable who engages in politics "on the side." Professionalization consists of a *continuous* dedication to political work. The criterion for this distinction is functional, because "naturally power actually rests in the hands of those who handle the work continuously." Consistent with his functional criterion, Weber refuses to predicate professionalism in politics on the individual's private perspectives or purposes: Vocational politics includes both those who "live for" and those who "live off" politics. Thus, for Weber, the professional is the continuously active or full-time politician, irrespective of the type of reward he expects or receives.

Milbrath (1965) has proposed a "hierarchy" of political involvement in the United States, which ranges from "apathetics" through "spectators" and "transitionals" to "gladiators." The scale can also be thought of as a pyramid, because types of behavior most often engaged in are at the bottom and those least often at the top of the scale. The frequencies with which different types of political behavior are engaged in and thus their rank on the scale, are indicators of involvement and costs of *time* and energy. Yet not all activities included under the gladiatorial category would qualify as professional in the Weberian sense, because they lack the required continuity (e.g. contributing time in a campaign, attending a caucus, soliciting funds). *Some* gladiators, however, make politics their profession, as opposed to leisure-time participation. Milbrath's categories form a continuous dimension and do not distinguish between amateurs and professionals. Note that the only directly measurable variable along the entire range of the cost dimension is *time*.

Continuity of service in party or public office and *full-time* political activity, however, reflect two different kinds of commitment. A party activist who regularly attends one or two weekly committee meetings does not have to give up the commitment to his regular occupation. The full-time office holder will find it extremely difficult, if not impossible, to reconcile his political and nonpolitical duties, even if he is self-employed. Students of elites have sometimes emphasized one or the other of these time dimensions. In his study of U.S. senators, Matthews (1960) combines continuity (length of service) and status of origin in a typology of political careers. The professionals have longer periods of service and appear to be of lower social origin; the amateurs have served for shorter periods of time but were originally recruited from strata with a high social status. Buck's (1963) study of amateurs and professionals in the British House of Commons first defines professional politicians as devoting their full time "to the job" and then distinguishes between amateurs and professionals in terms of length of service. These criteria, of course, are not overlapping, although the 82 M.P.s in Buck's sample who withdrew from politics after initial success (and were thus classified as amateurs) indicated the irreconcilability of two full-time occupations as the most compelling reason for their withdrawal.

For Sartori (1967) professionalization does not involve only full-time activity and living "off politics." The critical distinction is between those who do and those who do not have a potential or actual alternative occupation. In the Socialist and Communist parties in western Europe there are many professionals who *never had* any other occupation. Sartori reports that this category included almost 23 percent of *all* Italian members of parliament in 1958. In other cases, professionalization is a concomitant of the length of a parliamentary career, and it is not easy to determine the point of no return. Sartori therefore considers those who still have at least a potential alternative occupation as semiprofessionals. A similar typology for German parliamentarians has been adopted by Loewenberg (1967) and Fishel (1972), whereas Beyme (1971) takes a more Weberian position.

In the American politics literature of the 1960s the terms "amateur" and "professional" have been applied to motivations and styles of political behavior, as described in Wilson's *The Amateur Democrat* (1962). The amateur finds intrinsic rewards in politics: the determination of public policies on the basis of principles, as opposed to the professional's extrinsic rewards of power, income, status, and the fun of the game. The professional conceives of politics in terms of winning an election or in terms of party interests, conceptions which usually involve making compromises and appeals to specific interests. The amateur conceives of politics in terms of issues—substantive (e.g., Liberalism) or procedural (e.g., Reformism). The professionals operate within the main party organization; the amateurs are based in clubs.

Thus Wilson's amateur lives for politics—in the Weberian sense of the term —but whether or not he is a full-time politician is irrelevant for this categorization. The professional is usually a full-time politician, but he does not necessarily live off politics; he may derive extrinsic rewards of power or status which Weber ascribed to the amateur. In this respect Wilson's construct of the professional comprises both types of political bosses described by Rogow and Lasswell (1963, p. 44): the *game* politician, for whom the game of politics is the principal mode of self-expression and self-realization, and the *gain* politician, who uses his power position to accumulate personal wealth through corrupt practices.

It is the difference between intrinsic and extrinsic rewards which explains the issue-oriented style of the amateur, as opposed to the professional's orientation toward the (local) organization and his willingness to compromise in order to win an election. Differences in the style of political behavior are explained by *different incentives in political recruitment* (Clark and Wilson, 1961), and different incentives tend to be associated with different sociodemographic characteristics. One should note, however, the asymmetry in Wilson's typology: Whereas the professional's political style and goals are congruent with his personal goal orientations, the amateur apparently has no personal goals at all. Even if it were possible to become actively involved in politics without any personal reward, i.e., even without the psychological gratification of fulfilling a moral duty or satisfying a need for self-actualization, the involvement would probably be very brief. This, however, is a highly untenable hypothesis; it is more likely that the expectation of personal gratification is covert and therefore less easy to detect.

Wilson's description of the amateur based in the political clubs in Chicago, Los Angeles, and New York has been confirmed in a number of subsequent studies. Hirschfield, Swanson, and Blank (1962), who studied 409 Democratic, Republican, and Liberal party committeemen in Manhattan, report that the major determinants of political affiliation were ideological rather than socioeconomic, that party organization was considered an instrument for effectuating policy rather than a haven of personal security, and that the committeemen tended to be more interested in social reform than in catering to individual constituents. Members of the dominant Democratic party, however, were more "professional" in their approach to politics than members of the minority parties. The "new style" was also associated with a change in the sociodemographic profile of the urban politician. He is young and well educated (60 percent have college educations), in a middle- or upper-middle-class occupation; almost one-half are women and more than one-third are unmarried. The authors also believe, however, that self-interest remains an important consideration in entering politics, but most activists consciously or unconsciously subordinate it to a concept of "public interest." [1]

Interviews with Goldwater delegates to the Republican Convention of 1964 and with McCarthy delegates to the Democratic Convention of 1968 (Polsby and Wildavsky, 1971) and a survey of 180 delegates to the 1968 Democratic Convention (Soule and Clark, 1970) indicate that the emergence of "amateur" counterelites has not been limited to the political scene of large urban centers. The studies show that the amateur delegates were intrinsically interested in substantive goals and intraparty democracy and, unlike the professionals, reluctant to compromise on issues to save party unity. The professionals were locally oriented; the amateurs had a cosmopolitan orientation. Polsby and Wildavsky describe these amateurs as "purists" whose attitudes toward politics have strongly moralistic overtones. The moral integrity of the presidential candidate was more important than his ability to win. The professionals believed in bargaining and incremental policy changes for the maximization of support.

Hofstetter (1971) has subjected Wilson's constructs of "amateurs" and "professionals" to a rigorous analysis. Using measurements of dispositions toward amateur and professional perceptions of the roles of political organizations (with data collected from regular party ward leaders, members of auxiliary party clubs, and members of an insurgent organization in the Columbus, Ohio, area), he demonstrated that perceived norms of party *procedure* and norms concerning commitment to *issues* could not be organized along a single dimension. Each of these two sets of norms displayed high factor loadings on a different factor in an orthogonal-rotated factor analysis. Hofstetter then used

50 independent criterion variables to validate the two constructs. The variables included sociodemographic characteristics, community integration, criteria used in the evaluation of candidates, campaign techniques, and involvement in politics. Although for most of these variables the correlations were congruent with Wilson's theoretically generated predictions, the procedural dimension displayed considerably higher correlations than the issue dimension. Some of the substantively most important items on which the evidence contradicted the theoretical predictions were (a) "Politicians should play delegate roles"; (b) "Others are active for purposive reasons"; and (c) "View politics as a consensual process." Hofstetter points out that it is unclear in Wilson's work what characteristics are attributed to amateurs and professionals by definition and what properties are hypothesized to be related to the amateur phenomenon and hence are amenable to empirical testing. The factor analysis "clearly suggests that reformulation of the concept of amateurism is necessary."

In Hofstetter's data set and analysis, both the procedural and the issue-participation dimension refer to attitudes toward principles of organization rather than substantive issues. The issue-participation attitudes of the amateurs aim primarily at increasing the responsiveness and responsibility of the leadership to the lower-level activists and the rank-and-file membership. The amateurs propose to achieve this goal by eliminating or drastically reducing the patronage-based sources of support from which the "professional" leaders have been able to build their positions of power, because the need to maintain this support induces the professionals to remain neutral (or become flexible) on issue stands. The amateurs therefore place the emphasis on responsibility in terms of uncompromising issue stands, but no substantive policy goals are attached to these demands. Wherever these attitudes prevail, the amateurs of the 1960s do not seem to differ considerably from proponents of earlier reform movements. If the amateurs are the idealistic campaign workers of Barry Goldwater and Eugene McCarthy (and the volunteers for McGovern in 1972), it is likely that the "new politics" is "one of those recurring features of American politics that political writers are always rediscovering" (Wolfinger, 1972, p. 394). However, Greenstein (1970a, p. 58) points out that at least the amateur Democrats are committed to a specific policy, i.e., civil rights.

The idealistic orientation of the "amateurs" thus combines an opposition to organized power and the espousal of what have been termed "non-acquisitive" or "post bourgeois" values (Inglehart, 1971). Unlike the revolutionary student leaders who have translated these orientations into a utopian anarchism (for example, see Cohn Bendit, 1968), the amateur reformer seeks support through persuasian and works through party institutions. However, he can draw support only from those segments of society which are economically capable of espousing "post bourgeois" values and culturally disposed to do so. As Wolfinger (1972) has forcefully argued, the demographic movements from and into the large urban centers in the United States, where the amateurs have opposed the established party organizations, have caused an increase rather than a decrease in the proportion of the poor and the uneducated. Furthermore, business—small or large—is as natural a clientele for political machines as recent immigrants, if not more so. The reformer who can win an election for public office faces a pluralistic environment. In a legislative assembly (e.g., a city council) he can choose to remain in opposition; in executive office he will have to adapt to the structure of the environment. Essentially, it is his commitment to a continuous political career that will determine whether and the extent to which he will abandon the uncompromising position of the "amateur."

A study of city councillors in the San Francisco Bay area (Black, 1970) indicates that the tendency toward congruence between personal and public goal orientations also prevails in such collegiate bodies as city councils. Black assesses the role perception of political actors in terms of a general definition of professionalization as assimilation to the standards and values prevalent in a given profession. In a pluralistic political system, the standard prevailing in the political profession is brokerage and bargaining. Black's finding, among city councillors in the San Francisco Bay area, indicates that those who perceive the political process as consisting of bargaining and who are themselves committed to bargaining are also more committed to a political career, and that such commitments are a function of city size and competition for office. One may infer that the basic criterion for the professional standard is effectiveness or functionality, since in larger and more heterogeneous cities a bargaining posture is a necessary condition for winning an election. This inference is consistent with the observation that most amateurs who remain in politics are socialized into the ethos of professionalism.

The relationship between the structure of the environment and differences in incentives for political activity has been examined in a comparative study of Democratic and Republican precinct chairmen in a prosperous suburban and a less prosperous rural county (Conway and Feigert, 1968). Distinguishing between "purposive" incentives (corresponding to amateur politics) and "solidary" and "material" incentives (corresponding to professionalism), Conway and Feigert found that in all four organizations two-thirds or more of those who entered politics for purposive reasons reported that what they would miss most—if they had to leave politics—would be nonpurposive satisfactions, but leaders in the affluent suburban county displayed a greater change in their initial purposive motivations than those in the less prosperous rural county. It thus appears that programmatic appeals are a major basis for inducing initial entry, but they are less effective in sustaining activists in their precinct leadership roles. Furthermore, there is some evidence that nonpurposive, self-oriented incentives in initial recruitment do not gradually change into public-oriented, purposive motivations as a result of continuous party activity. Eldersveld (1964, p. 287) reports that 75–97 percent of the Democratic party district chairmen, board members, and precinct leaders in Detroit who began with "personalized motivations" did not change to or toward "impersonal orientations"; among Republicans, the range was 57–92 percent. Among precinct leaders who began with "impersonal motivations," only 12 percent of the Democrats and 22 percent of the Republicans did not adopt a "personalized orientation."

What do these attempts to establish a typology of political role perceptions contribute to the formulation of criteria for a definition of initial recruitment? Any study of recruitment that goes beyond a single-case biography requires a criterion by which initial recruitment can be identified across cases. Generalizing across cases causes problems of comparability and equivalence. For the investigator initial recruitment is always a past event, a stage in the career *history* of the political actors under consideration; and career histories vary considerably. Unless initial recruitment is defined as the first involvement in *any* kind of community-oriented behavior—a definition that would make the concept useless—some critical threshold that can be observed across a large variety of career patterns and settings must be identified.

The preceding discussion of the distinction between amateurs and professionals has shown that the basic criteria of differentiation referred either to *motivational syndromes* or to characteristics of *behavioral involvement* (continuous activity or full-time office). Only Sartori's definition of professionalization as an occupational "point of no return" was anchored in both motivational and behavioral variables. Its applicability, however, is limited to the well-organized and centralized parties of the working classes and other political subcultures in systems with fragmented political cultures. The "point of no return," however, is only a specific case in the range of possible relationships between motivations and behavioral involvement. An examination of these relationships will provide some useful guidelines for the choice of criteria for an operational definition of initial recruitment.

Such concepts as purposive or nonpurposive motivations are broad categorizations of a number of different and discrete goal orientations which may vary considerably in their intensities. Furthermore, the *intensities of public and private orientations are independent of each other;* an individual may have very strong "feelings" about a particular issue but only a weak motivation to participate in a collective effort "to do something about it," because participation involves a cost. When the cost is low, a less intensive personal orientation will suffice to motivate participation in community or political affairs, and many individuals with a variety of nonintensive motivations will be able to "pay" the cost of participation. As cost increases, not only will there be fewer individuals who can afford to invest the necessary resources (primarily time and energy—and in the American context, the ability to mobilize financial resources for a campaign), but more intensive motivations will be required to elicit participation. However, as the required intensity of personal goal orientations for participation in collective action increases, the variety of such motivations will decrease. *At the highest level of cost* (i.e., full-time political office) *the required intensity of motivations will also reach its highest level.* There will be fewer individuals able to "pay" a very high opportunity cost (i.e., cost measured in terms of alternative uses of the required resources), and the *number of motivations* which can reach the level of intensity necessary to forego all possible alternative uses of resources *will be reduced* to a small number of basic human needs. These needs are survival, security, acceptance, esteem (status, prestige, admiration), and self-actualization (influence, power—in general or in specific areas of life), and according to Maslow (1970) they constitute a hierarchy of motivations in human behavior.[2] Thus, at the highest level of behavioral involvement, *comparability* between individual cases (or between groups or systems) also reaches its highest level, because both *costs and intensities of motivation are held constant* and *variability is at its lowest level.*

On the continuum of increasing involvement, cost and intensity of motivations, and decreasing motivational variability, there are *two thresholds* at which there is a steep increase in the slope of both curves: (1) the passage from occasional to continuous participation and (2) that from part-time to full-time involvement. On methodological grounds, therefore, these thresholds increase comparability and can be used as indicators of initial recruitment. The continuity criterion is further supported by Weber's theoretical argument that continuity facilitates the accumulation of power over the part-time, occasional volunteer, and the argument applies *a fortiori* to full-time involvement. There is also an external validating criterion for the steep increase in costs at the passage from part-time to full-time involvement: the change in the actor's nonpolitical commitments, his life style, and probably also his place of residence.

Since these definitions of initial recruitment would include bureaucratic, administrative appointments which may be guided by political but also by civil service criteria, it is useful to limit the use of the concept to elective party or public offices—legislative, executive, or judiciary. The term "full-time" need not be interpreted too narrowly; the time schedule of a full-time academic appointment and that of a full-time assembly-line worker denote quite different expectations. What is and what is not full-time political office in any given system is determined by rules, norms, and customs. The line of demarcation is that which distinguishes between the sphere of activity to which the individual devotes a large part of his work time and effort—irrespective of source of income—and those other areas of life in which his behavioral involvement is occasional or marginal.

The definition of initial recruitment provides an operationalization of the stages at which the recruitment process can be considered completed. In the study of the process leading to this point of completion, investigators have chosen different perspectives and units of analysis. The following section will address itself to an examination of the major considerations for these choices and their respective consequences.

B. Perspectives

All social behavior involves interaction between two or more actors, and such interactions have intended and actual consequences for the actors themselves and for the relevant environments. Each actor and each member of the environment has his own vantage ground, from which he perceives and interprets the action and its consequences. These perceptual spaces and frameworks of interpretation are here referred to as perspectives. The investigator, in turn, has his own perspective, which is related to the unit of analysis he has chosen to investigate and the perspectives of the actors and those of other components of the environment which he decides to draw into the analysis. Furthermore, he determines the level of generalization at which he wishes to interpret his observations. It is the investigator's choice of a particular perspective that determines, to a great extent, his strategy of research. This section discusses the major perspectives and strategies used in the study of recruitment.

The recruitment process involves: (1) the perspective of the potential candidate or set of candidates; (2) the perspective of the recruiting agents or agencies; (3) the perspective of the environment from which the candidate expects to draw the necessary support; and (4) the time perspective. One can conceive of the environment as consisting of social, economic, or cultural groups, of organizations, and of political or administrative units. These components may overlap—partially or totally. One component may include several units of different kinds (e.g., the constituency of a party which includes various ethnic and economic groups). Finally, organizational components display different degrees of dependence or integration between levels of organization (e.g., the respective inputs of a local party committee, a district committee, and a state committee in determining the support given to various candidates in a primary election).

The investigator's choice of a unit of analysis also includes the choice of the level of office he wishes to study in terms of the recruitment pattern of the personnel currently holding or competing for such offices. Whatever the grounds for this decision, any empirical study involving field research will be subject to the inverse relationship between level of office and research accessibility: The higher the level of office, the lower its research accessibility. Furthermore, the distribution of offices is always such that there are many more local and regional (i.e., lower-level) than central, national (i.e., higher-level) political offices—both in government and in political parties. The combined effect of accessibility and distribution is that there are very few empirical studies of higher-level politicians and a constantly growing number of recruitment-oriented studies of local or regional candidates and officials. Adding the time perspective, we shall find that long-term studies of national elites are based almost exclusively on published records and library research. Published records, including newspapers, provide the investigators with a great number of useful objective indicators; at no time, however, do they afford more than a reconstructed glimpse into the individual subjective perspectives of candidates and officeholders in the recent or distant past. When little or no information is available about the individual's perceptions and motivations in recruitment-relevant situations, it is of little consequence for the understanding of the recruitment *process* if the number of cases studied is increased to include several generations or cohorts of officeholders. What is lost in such studies, in terms of relevance for the study of recruitment processes, is compensated for by the longitudinal analysis of the social, economic, and occupational characteristics of elites, which can be compared with indicators of social change in the nonpolitical subsystems of society.

With regard to the manner in which investigators have dealt with the time perspective, the micropolitical literature displays two major strategies of research: (1) long-term "retrospective prediction," i.e., explanation and generalization based on past patterns, and (2) short-term situational analysis. The study of political socialization as a recruitment factor is an example of the first strategy. The analysis of the nomination of candidates for a specific election is an example of the second.

The "retrospective prediction" strategy refers to two different theoretical positions. The most frequently encountered assumes that seeking, accepting, and pursuing a political career is—at least in part—the result of antecedent factors and, more specifically, the experiences to which the present office seeker or holder has been exposed in childhood, adolescence, and adult life. This position also includes personality-oriented approaches to recruitment, since personality traits or psychological needs are rooted in the early developmental stages of the individual. Most of these studies also incorporate variables used in the "situational strategy," such as relevant components of the opportunity structure (competitiveness of the situation, the power potential of an office—to quote only two examples), but the main focus of the argument is on the interaction between the impact of successive past experiences and components of the recruitment situation. The second "postdictive" position has been proposed by Joseph Schlesinger (1966, 1967) as an "ambition theory of politics." It assumes that ambition for public office motivates politicians and that their activities are directed by what they must do to achieve office. A politician's behavior is a response to his office goals. This approach does not inquire into the antecedent of recruitment; why men want to gain public office is a question this approach does not attempt to answer, and Schlesinger draws an analogy between ambition theory and "some useful economic theories which do not inquire why men want to increase their incomes." The difficulty with this long-term interpretation of the opportunity structure is that at the beginning of a career long-term goals are not very relevant, whereas at an advanced stage of the career the motivations in initial recruitment may not be of great interest. Furthermore, ambition is only an instrumental value and can serve as a vehicle for the satisfaction of different needs and goals.

Short-term situational studies, as opposed to long-term postdiction, have the advantage of drawing a far larger number of variables into the analysis. Furthermore, and perhaps not less important, this perspective does not exclude the impact of past experiences on the recruitment situation. However, instead of reconstructing the socialization biography of the aspiring or incumbent politician, it seeks current indicators of both socialization impact and personality structure in situations, occupations, or actual behavior immediately preceding the act of initial recruitment (Czudnowski, 1970b; Beyme, 1971; Black, 1972). This position does not deny anticipatory socialization, i.e., the shaping of present behavior by future-oriented office seeking; it merely accepts the fact that in most cultures, and certainly in Western political cultures, societal norms do not favor personal ambition in politics, and that ambition is therefore not a very researchable variable. Thus the choice of levels of office and of a time perspective greatly influences the researchability of behavioral variables. Researchers have sometimes concentrated on variables drawn from a single dimension, e.g., the motivations and behavior of candidates. More frequently, however, they have combined variables reflecting the perspectives and behavior of candidates, recruiting agencies, and politically relevant environments into specific models. These models will now be examined in somewhat greater detail.

C. Models

Whatever the units of analysis and the perspectives the investigator decides to adopt, he will be able to deal effectively with only a relatively small number of variables. In selecting these variables, he is guided by the assumption that they are capable of explaining a sizable proportion of the observed variation in the recruitment process and its outcomes. It is the assumed explanatory power of this set of variables under given parametric conditions which combines them into a model. The models reviewed in this section will therefore reflect the principal questions researchers have asked about political recruitment. When a model has been used in one study only, the findings of that study will be reported in this section.

The simplest and earliest model for the study of recruitment, suggested by Seligman (1961), views recruitment as consisting of (1) the screening and political channeling that leads to *eligibility* for candidacy; (2) *candidacy—* which is a two-step process requiring initiative and reinforcement; and (3) *selection,* i.e., the actual choice of candidates. The adequacy of this general model has not been challenged; it has only been expanded to include variables which shed additional light on each of the three stages. Several empirical studies have explicitly adopted this model (Valen, 1966; Prewitt, 1970; Czudnowski, 1970a, 1972) .

Jacob (1962) has expanded Seligman's model by adding personality traits and recruitment-relevant positions: Initial recruitment is a process by which individuals possessing certain personality traits and occupying specified social positions in the community are screened by political institutions for elective office. The major personality traits are a need for prestige and power and "to be in the public eye." The characteristic of recruitment-relevant positions is their brokerage role (rather than their occupational status). They teach the relevant skills, provide contacts, facilitate financial backing, and allow time to seek office. Another community factor is the relative standing of politics as an honorable pursuit. Finally, in the screening process Jacob's model distinguishes between "closed recruitment," associated with strong party organizations, and "open recruitment," in which parties are weak and have little control over the choice of candidates.

Barber (1965) introduces a somewhat different model with three dimensions: motivations, resources, and opportunity. Their impact is cumulative, and they cannot be operationalized independently of one another. A potential candidate needs to be motivated to seek office, but a variety of motivations may lead to a candidacy; his resources may consist of such assets as a flexible occupation and the ability to make the necessary financial sacrifice; finally, opportunity comprises compatibility with the selection criteria of a recruiting agency and the degree of uncertainty about the outcome of an election.

Browning (1968) has specified some of the critical variables in motivation and opportunity in a formal model of the interaction of personality and system variables and of the manner in which this interaction affects behavior. He has also presented a computerized simulation technique for the application of the model. Recruitment behavior is determined by motivational syndromes and expectations. Expectations are acquired in the socialization process, and they channel the motivations into the political arena, but the types of offices sought and the politician's behavior are determined by his dominant motivations. When power motives are high and achievement motives low, behavior is organization-oriented; when the strength of those motives is reversed, behavior is policy-concerned; and when both achievement and power motives are high, behavior is policy-influencing. A high affiliation motive leads to passive behavior, and when only status motives are high, behavior is status-oriented. The systemic opportunity variables in Browning's model include rates of turnover in office, rates of access from office to office, the degree of control by party leaders over nominations, and the probability of winning the election.

Seligman's more recent model (1971) is more complex than the model presented in his 1961 paper. Eligibility is defined here as status in the *structure of opportunity and risk,* and opportunity comprises formal rules, effective opportunity, and motivation. Effective opportunity is determined by social status and resources, and resources include organizational sponsorship, financial support, access to the media, and a political program. This definition of resources points up the critical role of parties. Risk is the cost of losing, and it is a function of the competitiveness in the second stage of recruitment, i.e., selection. Risk is also a determinant of eligibility because (1) it attracts a specific kind of motivation into politics (as opposed to more secure occupations); (2) it attracts those who can either afford risk or have nothing to lose; and (3) when risk is high, incumbents will block younger aspirants. In the selection process in Seligman's model three issues determine the outcome: selection by whom, according to what criteria (ascriptive or achievement), and through what mechanism (cooptation, conscription, agency, bureaucracy, and self-starting). Selection can be assessed on the dimension of openness; the variables determining openness and complexity of selections are competitiveness of the parties, the degree of centralization of power within the party, the social heterogeneity of the electorate, and the number of stages in the election process.

The single most important innovation in Seligman's more recent model is the dimension of *risk* (Seligman, 1967, 1971). It is a critical dimension in political life, and if one could measure the amount of risk involved in political candidates or careers, he could determine the location of a system on a continuum ranging from liberal democracy to totalitarian dictatorship, allowing for specific within-system ranges between parties. So far, however, no operational measure of risk has been developed.

Black (1970) has interpreted risk as the cost of a political candidacy and operationalized it as a function of constituency (city) size and competition for office. The cost of a candidacy, however, is merely an investment, whereas risk measures the cost of losing which—if it is relevant at all—is a function not only of past investment (e.g., a U.S. congressman gives up his seat in order to run for the Senate) but also of future consequences for the public and private life of the loser. The measurement of risk would require an outside variable that would serve as a common measuring scale, i.e., a *numeraire,* on which both political investments and nonpolitical losses could be measured. This raises the issue of the exchangeability and the rate of substitution between political and private action for the achievement of a given goal. Black (1972) rightly points to the fact that only a portion of what an individual invests in politics can be applied to a nonpolitical alternative, and that as an individual continues to invest in a political office, a diminishing proportion of his net investment can be transferred to nonpolitical alternatives.

A contextual model for the study of sources and avenues of access to local political office in a nonpartisan context has been proposed by Prewitt and Eulau (1971). Sources of recruitment are identified as auxiliary local government and leadership of civic groups, and the major avenues of access are sponsorship by incumbents and lateral entry. The contextual variables are rate of voter turnout in city elections and rate of eviction, i.e., replacement of incumbents who seek reelection. Dichotomizing the two contextual variables, four types of electorates emerge: (1) permissive—low on both turnout and eviction; (2) supportive—high on turnout and low on eviction; (3) discriminative—low on turnout and high on eviction; and (4) volatile—high on both turnout and eviction.

This typology of electoral contexts, derived inductively, proved to be useful for distinguishing between different patterns of sources and pathways of recruitment to eighty-seven city councils in the San Francisco Bay area. Permissive contexts showed equal recruitment from auxiliary government and leadership positions in civic groups, but they favored sponsored careers over lateral entry. In volatile contexts there was the lowest proportion of sponsored careers, a two-to-one preference for auxiliary government, and lateral entry in 58 percent of the councils. In supportive contexts lateral entry was present in 65 percent of the councils, but there was no clear preference for sponsored careers or sources of recruitment. Finally, in discriminative contexts, auxiliary government was the preferred source of recruitment in 63 percent of the councils, lateral entrants were identified in only 31 percent of the councils, and sponsored careers were relatively frequent in one-half and relatively infrequent in the other half of the councils.

This model deals successfully with the problem of measuring competitiveness in a nonpartisan context, using voter turnout and rate of eviction from office as indicators. It also introduces a distinction between cities in which the social and economic status of the council is more—and those in which it is less—associated with the status and wealth of the community. The single most interesting variable is the rate of incumbent-sponsored careers, because it corresponds to a system of closed or internal candidate selection, as opposed to open or even external selection, in a partisan context. Voter turnout seems to be an independent variable, because a low turnout occurs both in cities where the association between status council and community wealth is very high (.87, Gamma) and in cities where it is very low (−.20, Gamma). The theoretical conclusions from the findings of this study are admittedly speculative. A high rate of eviction probably reflects issue-oriented elections; but a high rate of eviction with low turnout (the discriminative type) is associated with a small and attentive electorate, without any indication why this electorate should be "discriminating," especially since the predominant sources of recruitment are positions in auxiliary government, and one-half of the cities in this category practice incumbent-sponsored recruitment. The theoretical interest in this model resides in the conceptualization of analytical contexts, which combine indicators of mass and elite behavior, and in the analysis of recruitment in terms of these contextual patterns.

Snowiss' (1966) model of congressional recruitment in Chicago centers on recruitment-relevant aspects of *organization*. In a large city with partisan elections, a recruitment system is essentially a system of organization. There are four variables in the model: (1) *The social base,* which, for the party, is the primary rather than the general electorate. (2) *The resources* the organization can use as incentives to mobilize party workers and attract counterelites; *material or nonmaterial.* (3) *Structure:* hierarchical, centralized leadership, impermeable to outside influences (associated with material incentives), or less structured and more permeable (associated with nonmaterial incentives). (4) *Organizational ethos.* Hierarchical structures of urban party organizations promote a *bargaining political ethos;* less structured parties promote an *issue-oriented, ideological ethos.* To the extent that parties can control the selection of candidates, recruitment will reflect the organizational ethos. When recruitment takes place from within the organization, its ethos will prevail in the choice of the candidate. In highly competitive situations, however, the party may deliberately recruit a candidate who does not share its ethos.

Analyzing Chicago congressmen (1948–1964) from inner-city Democratic, suburban Republican, and outer-city competitive districts, Snowiss demonstrates the adequacy of this organizational-situational model, which relates the perspectives of the recruiting agencies and the social composition of the constituency to the characteristics and the political ethos or style of the recruited candidate. Some of his findings can be summarized briefly for illustrative purposes. Inner-city Democratic recruitment is internal and machine-controlled; the inner-city congressmen have been schooled in bargaining, negotiation, and compromise. They value party cohesion, but the organization has not prepared them for an office of national stature in terms of issues of national policy. Furthermore, the inner-city Democrats do not practice personality politics and resent personal publicity.

In contrast, the suburban Republican congressman tends to be an issue-oriented conservative, his skills are in public advocacy, and he does not value party cohesion (even if he did, he could not enforce it). Without an adequate organization, he must engage in personality politics. Because he cannot hope to win, the suburban Democrat is not likely to be an old-line organization man; here recruitment more often serves the "advertising" purposes—professional or political—of young lawyers. The suburban Democrat resembles his Republican opponent by being more issue-oriented and by practicing personality politics, because the material incentives the Democratic organization can offer do not appeal to the wealthier electorate of suburban districts. In the outer city, population changes have created a competitive party system. Although the Democratic organization successfully uses its material resources to attract counterelites, recruitment has been diverted from old-line machine politicians, because in a competitive situation the selection of candidates tends to be decentralized, i.e., left to the evaluation of the local committeemen.

Party control over eligibility and selection is the major variable in another model, formulated for group-oriented recruitment (Czudnowski, 1970a). Group-oriented recruitment is usually associated with list voting and proportional representation. The model refers to organized groups and a multiparty system. The major variables determining party control over group *eligibility* are (1) the group's location in relation to the party (inner or outer groups); (2) interparty competition for the vote of the group; (3) the party's value-orientation toward the group. Party control over eligibility of inner groups is low; with respect to outer groups, it is high when party ideology is indifferent toward the group, irrespective of interparty competition, and when value orientations are positive and party competition low. Party control over candidate *selection* from an eligible group depends primarily on the degree of effectiveness of the group's organization: The more effective the group's organization, the less control the party can exercise over selection of candidates.

Presenting data on recruitment to Israel's legislature, the Knesset, this study documents the interaction between the variables of the model and the impact of changes in societal norms on the selection process. Party control over candidate selection from nonassociational or weakly organized groups is shown to result in a numerical underrepresentation of such groups and the nomination of "symbolic representatives" of ethnic and other socio-demographic groups, who are chosen from the ranks of the party bureaucracy. Given the low turnover of parties in office, associational groups tended to seek representation through the parties which had always been in office, whereas recruitment in the right- and left-wing opposition parties was limited to ideologically motivated activists. Thus recruitment reinforced the pragmatism of center parties and the ideological dogmatism of the parties which had been all or most of the time in opposition to the government.[3]

Kornberg and Winsborough (1968) have constructed a multivariate inter-election probability model. For any given pair of elections, the outcome of the recruitment process for the second election is represented by (1) the mean status of the candidates in the district; (2) the status difference between candidates in a district; and (3) the number of competing candidates. Status is measured in Duncan's numerical estimate of status scores for all detailed occupations. Based on election data for eight Canadian elections (1945–1965) in more than 60 percent of Canada's federal constituencies, the model predicts the values of (1), (2), and (3) as functions of the values of the mean status, the status difference, the number of candidates, and the competition in the previous election. Changes in the number of candidates in the district or changes in the status of individual candidates in the district are election-relevant data of some theoretical interest. The authors demonstrate that the average status of Canadian candidates varies not along an ideological continuum but according to the success of the parties in national elections. Thus there is a 17 score-point difference between the New Democratic Party and the Liberals and a 12 score-point difference between the Social Credit Party and the Conservatives, but only a 3.5 difference between the Conservatives and the Liberals.

Since not all four parties compete in all districts, the number of candidates per district is shown to have an impact on the average status of the first-place candidates: As the number of candidates increases, the average status of the first-place candidates decreases. Finally, across districts, parties, and elections, the average status of candidates decreases systematically from the first through the fourth-place candidates. There are elements of potential interest in this approach, but one would first like to obtain more insight into the methodological soundness and the theoretical or practical relevance of manipulations of central measures with this type of longitudinal aggregate data.

Despite the variety of approaches and the diversity of interests displayed by students of recruitment, the substantive findings of their studies tend to cluster around five groups of variables. Each group of variables has been assumed to constitute a major determinant in the recruitment process or to reflect the observable consequences of such a determinant. Part III will review selected empirical findings related to each cluster of variables.

III. SELECTED EMPIRICAL FINDINGS: THE MAJOR VARIABLES

The characteristics of the stage at which recruitment can be considered as completed are not very helpful in attempts to establish where and when the process begins and what factors determine the patterns of its development. In short-term processes of selection it is possible to rely on direct observation. Political recruitment, however, is a long-term process; it does not involve a prescribed training and can reach its completion at any time in the life cycle of the potential recruit. In the absence of direct evidence, one must rely on tentative theorizing, on the findings of neighboring subfields of the discipline (such as the study of political socialization or the study of parties), on available data on the careers of politicians, and on their own recollections.

It is useful to conceptualize recruitment as a sequence of screenings, in which each screening eliminates a large proportion of the "contestants" and channels the "survivors" into the next stage of selection. One theoretical approach ascribed the probability of surviving the screenings to initial relative advantages derived from social origin and demographic characteristics: class, status, education, or wealth. Socialization theory emphasized the advantages of early learning about politics in a politically active family or through exposure to political actors and events. Others argued that social origin and socialization merely determined eligibility and that advancement in the recruitment process depended on the successful completion of an apprenticeship in party activities, civic organizations, or appointive government office. Skills acquired in specific occupations and the proximity to governmental processes afforded by such occupations have been perceived as yet another link between eligibility and selection. Psychology and psychoanalysis contributed the argument that in the absence of strong motivations, structural proximity or adequate skills were insufficient conditions for recruitment into politics. Finally, criteria of selection and the political opportunity structure were added as components of the last stages of the recruitment process.

Applying to different stages in the recruitment process and drawing their variables from different dimensions, these hypotheses are not mutually exclusive. The areas in which they have been tested and the extent to which they are supported by empirical events are the subjects that will be discussed in the following five sections.

A. Social Background Characteristics

The earliest and perhaps the most intensively researched questions in the study of recruitment focused on the social origins and demographic characteristics of politicians. Many of these studies were exploratory and descriptive; the type of data collected suggests that they were intended to test Mosca's theory of the ruling class, which attributed the formation of ruling classes to the resources or functions certain groups had been able to monopolize (e.g., military skills, land and other forms of wealth, religious functions) (Mosca, 1939, pp. 50–69). Adapting Mosca's theory to modern Western democracies in which the social stratification system is not—and cannot be—completely rigid, these studies confirmed that the social composition of political elites differs from that of the general population, although it does reflect regional variations in the social structure. This section will review the findings of some of the major studies in this area. After examining interparty and cross-system differences, it will question the assumption that sociodemographic characteristics are indicative of specific social and political attitudes, irrespective of the social and political structure of the environment in which individuals act and interact.

Career histories are the major source of information on political elites used by historians, sociologists, and political scientists alike. In 1952, Lasswell, Lerner, and Rothwell codified 50 items of career histories and explained that "the comparative frequency with which selected characteristics are distributed at different intervals along a specified time-space continuum" can serve as indicators of the "direction, scope and rate of changes in the composition of various elites." From a macropolitical and longitudinal perspective, this is a legitimate starting point for the study of elites, because the composition of elites is an indicator of the relationship between social change and changes in the distribution of social and political power.

Historical studies of elites have accumulated impressive data sets on the social background and career patterns of officeholders. Even recruitment-oriented studies concerned with a specific set of officeholders or with a relatively short-term turnover of politicians in a legislature indicate that social background data are the most readily available type of information "somehow" related to the recruitment process with which they were concerned. How this information is supposed to be related to recruitment most researchers "forget" to tell us; yet there is hardly a study which does not report on the age, sex, ethnic origin, religion, education, occupation, father's occupation, income, size of city of residence, marital status, organizational membership, age at first involvement, and other characteristics of the elite population under consideration.

When Matthews published his first monograph on recruitment in 1954, he considered it, as his title indicates, a report on *The Social Background of Political Decision-Makers*. Thirteen years later UNESCO published a volume entitled *Decisions and Decision-Makers in the Modern State* (UNESCO, 1967), which was little more than a collection of social background and career data on legislative and executive elites in different countries. Studies of "elite formation" in rural India (Robins, 1967) or "political recruitment" in Sarawak (Glick, 1966) fall under the same category, as do such early American studies as the report of county chairmen in Oklahoma (Patterson, 1963) and the more recent report on the background of parliamentarianism in New Zealand (Forster, 1969. Jacob (1962) wonders "about the significance of it all," noting that Matthews describes in great detail the age of senators at their election but gives us no hint as to why this is important. Several years earlier, Janowitz had voiced the same criticism of Lasswell's outline for the comparative study of elites (Lasswell, Lerner, and Rothwell, 1952) and of studies of Nazi, Soviet, and Chinese elites: "analysis of a social profile tends to remain a matter of description . . . the dynamics of elite formation are worthy of explicit and independent analysis. While there are few scholars who would deny this, there are equally few who actually proceed on this premise." (Janowitz, 1954)

For some students of recruitment the gathering of social background data was not merely a matter of research convenience. Matthews, for example, had not been as oblivious of the need for theoretical interpretation as Jacob suggested. In his introduction to the 1954 monograph, he wrote: "Subtle social selection processes may eliminate a far larger number of potential decision-makers than do primaries and elections." Noting the overrepresentation of upper-status people in political elites, Matthews adds that perhaps the socially successful have a better chance because others "look up" to the successful. In ascribing the relative advantage of upper-status people to social selection processes and to deference to success, Matthews not only comments on the American stratification system but explicitly denies the existence of a ruling class i.e., the assertion made in both Marxist theory and Mills's *Power Elite* (1956). Implied in the "deference to success" argument is a recognition of the fact that social and especially economic success is independent of political power and that the political opportunity structure does not prevent the transfer of accumulated achievement from one scale of values to another (Prewitt, 1965, p. 98).

Sociodemographic background data are often used to contrast rival elites or to compare office seekers with broader politically active or attentive strata and with mass publics. Some American studies show only minor social differences between Democratic and Republican leaders. A cross-level comparison of 181 Iowa legislators, 484 "attentive constituents" (i.e., the active stratum), 99 lobbyists, and 90 party county chairmen (Patterson and Boynton, 1969) revealed that there were no significant differences in occupation, education, income, and size of place of residence between elite groups, but there were substantial differences between these elites and the electorate. Committeemen of all three parties (Democrats, Republicans, and Liberals) in *Manhattan* did not display important differences in socioeconomic characteristics, with the exception of the ethnic and religious composition of the Democratic party and a somewhat higher percentage of third-generation Americans, Jews, and professionals in the Liberal party (Hirschfield, Swanson, and Blank, 1962). Neither did Althoff and Patterson (1966) find significant differences in social characteristics between Democratic and Republican precinct committeemen in a *rural Illinois* county.

Other studies display significant differences among activists or party leaders. Marvick and Nixon (1961) compared Democratic and Republican volunteer campaigners in Los Angeles in the 1956 election and found that, although both parties recruited primarily from the middle class, Republicans were older and had higher incomes, more prestigious religious affiliations, more prestigious occupations, fuller education, and deeper roots in the community. They interpreted this finding as evidence that politics in Los Angeles was not a game without relationship to the social struggle. Similarly, the singly most significant relationship in Pomper's (1965) data on New Jersey county chairmen was that between social characteristics and party affiliation. Eldersveld's (1964) study of members of party district executive boards and precinct leaders in a large industrial city (Detroit) —where union committees carry on Democratic precinct work and management sets the tone in the Republican party (Greenstein, 1970a, p. 83) —revealed far greater differences in income, education, and occupational status between the parties than those observed among party activists in Los Angeles and party committeemen in Manhattan. Adding a stratification dimension within local party elites, Eldersveld found that at the lower levels in both parties there was a much greater spread in economic status, but in the Republican party reserve groups displayed a reversal of the ethnic, religious, and occupational composition of the top leaders. Stated otherwise, the upward mobiles in the Democratic party hierarchy were far more integrated with the social structure than the more exclusive Republican elites (Eldersveld, 1964).

Interparty differences in the ethnic composition of ward committees have been observed when successive waves of immigrants from different countries had been integrated by different parties. Cornwell, for example, has shown that after the Democratic party in Providence, Rhode Island, had come under Irish control, the "Yankee" Republican leadership sought the support of the new waves of immigrants from Italy, who gradually became the dominant group in the Republican party (Cornwell, 1960; Greenstein, 1970a, p. 60).

Is the party leadership more representative of the electorate or of its own following? Are top party leaders more representative of the social and demographic characteristics of their major support groups than party officials at the lower levels? One may hypothesize that party officeholders more closely approximate, at the aggregate level, the social composition of their primary constituency, whereas public officeholders or candidates for public office will not necessarily be recruited from the strata most typically associated with the party. Two variables probably determine the background profile of candidates more than any other.

The electoral system. In single-member two-party districts, the candidate must be able to appeal to a majority of voters, whatever the social composition of the electorate; in multimember districts, party lists can reflect the major social groups in the constituency.

The relative strength of the party. The majority party will be less concerned with problems of sociodemographic representation, whereas the minority party is likely to attempt to maintain its strength among those groups from which it draws its main support.

Thus, whether typical or atypical candidates will be nominated is a decision that is likely to vary considerably between parties even within the same setting. Valen (1966), reporting for a southern area in Norway, states that "in the non-Socialist parties the higher we move in the hierarchy, the more distinct is the social character of the respective parties . . . [whereas] the Labor Party deviates [from this pattern]: the proportion of manual workers is much smaller among party leaders than among ordinary voters and party identifiers."

The dimensions on which party elites differ in a given setting need not be those on which the parties differ in another setting. For example, a comparative study of local party officials in Massachusetts and North Carolina revealed no differences in occupational status between parties in North Carolina but significant differences in Massachusetts, where only 50 percent of the Democrats held white-collar occupations, as opposed to 87 percent among the Republicans. This difference can perhaps be explained by the two-party system in Massachusetts, where the parties seek support from distinctly different social groups in a highly urbanized setting, as opposed to the modified one-party system in the less urbanized and economically less developed setting in North Carolina (Bowman and Boynton, 1966).

One of the most persistent findings in the United States, at all levels of government, is the very small proportion of politicians with a working-class background and their almost exclusive affiliation with the Democratic party (for the Senate, see Matthews, 1960; for the membership of a national party committee, Cotter and Hennessey, 1964; Epstein, 1967; for state legislators, Zeller, 1954; Key, 1956; Epstein, 1958; Sorauf, 1963; Dye, 1965), but the extent of this difference between parties changes from context to context.

One may conclude from the various descriptions of party leaders in the United States that there do not seem to be sharp differences in socioeconomic characteristics between Democratic and Republican leaders. Most of the differences that have been observed can be explained by regional variations in the degree of industrialization and in the competitiveness of the party system. The absence of a sharp differentiation is not surprising. The high rate of social mobility, the expansion of industrialization, improvements in trans-portation and communications, rapid shifts in population, and an industry oriented toward mass consumption have all contributed to the diminishing of social differentiation. What differences continue to exist, such as pockets of poverty and the concentration of wealth, or the lagging integration of racial and ethnic minorities, do not seem sufficient to bring about a *social* polariza-tion between party elites. If it is true that similar sociodemographic back-grounds are indicators of similar socialization processes, one does not expect party leaders to differ considerably in their political attitudes. Yet McClosky, Hoffmann, and O'Hara (1960), for example, found that Democratic and Re-publican delegates to the national conventions of their parties disagreed con-siderably on almost every issue in the areas of public ownership, economic regulation, equalitarianism and welfare, tax policy, and foreign relations.

To infer from these findings that sociodemographic factors are of limited significance in shaping political attitudes would involve an ecological fallacy, i.e., the fallacy of inferring individual-level relationships from observations made at the aggregate level. One should rather question why objective indi-cators of status, income, or occupation are expected to be associated with simi-lar attitudes (i.e., subjective evaluative or affective orientations) across a variety of sociocultural settings and personal socialization experiences.

The evidence from other political systems may shed some further light on the issues. In countries with a more rigid stratification system, such as Britain, Germany, France, or Italy, there are sharper interparty differences in the social characteristics of parliamentary elites. For the sixth German Bundestag, the German Federal Bureau of Statistics reports (1970) that the Social Democratic (SPD)/Liberal (FDP) coalition was represented by almost twice as many executives and three times as many "workers" as the Christian Democrats (CDU), but by only 25 percent of the number of farmers and 33 percent of the number of businessmen on the benches of the CDU (Beyme, 1971). In the French Fourth Republic (1945–1958), 70 percent of the parliamentarians with a business background were representing the Catholic Party (MRP) and the Poujadist movement, whereas 61 of the 66 teachers and 110 of the 133 "workers" were Communist and Socialist deputies (Dogan, 1961). In his study of British candidates for the House of Commons, Ranney (1965) has calculated an index of constituency winnability for every occupational category among nonincumbents in the Conservative and Labor parties. The five most favored occupations in the Labor party were political organizer, trade union official, chartered accountant, manual worker, and journalist and publicist. In the Conservative party they were farmer, civil servant, individual with private means, political organizer, and journalist and publicist. Note, however, that the index for the Tory journalist was twice as high as that for his Labor counterpart.

These findings suggest that in countries with a more rigid stratification system, occupational categories are more strongly associated with political attitudes and party affiliation than they are in the United States. Furthermore, whether differences between parties and sociocultural cleavages overlap or cut across one another is a major determinant in the relationship between social background characteristics and political recruitment. Finally, pragmatic parties are likely to diversify the sources from which they recruit their personnel, whereas parties with a dogmatic ideology will tend to take a more rigid position in the selection of their cadres. Thus the socioecological and the political environment can modify the relationship between sets of individual social characteristics and both the incentive and the opportunity structure in political recruitment.

More closely related to the recruitment process but far less researched is the role that can be assigned to social background characteristics in the choice of a political career, rather than some other. How social background affects the choice between different careers cannot be assessed from comparisons between leaders or activists of different parties or from comparisons of politicians and the general population. Only by drawing samples from other social elites and using them as control groups in comparisons with political elites is it possible to determine whether some sociodemographic characteristics are more likely to be conducive to a political career than to a business, professional, military, or other career. Although very limited and inconclusive, the available evidence indicates no major differences in the social background profiles of politicians and members of other social elites.

Hacker's (1961) study of 100 U.S. senators and the presidents of America's 100 largest industrial corporations inquires into these differences and sheds some light on a dimension not dealt with in studies of political recruitment. This dimension—size of hometown and geographical mobility—cuts across the otherwise useful distinction between early and adult socialization and closely follows the contrast between the cosmopolitan orientation of the amateur and the community-oriented and community-based profile of the professional. Hacker demonstrates that in terms of national and regional origin or education and precareer mobility, there are no significant differences between the senators and the corporation presidents. However, the hometown of 52 percent of the presidents was a large metropolitan center, whereas 64 percent of the senators were of small-town or rural origin. Furthermore, 71 percent of the senators' current residences were either in their hometowns or less than 100 miles away, but 36 percent of the presidents lived more than 500 miles away, and another 34 percent lived at a distance ranging from 100 to 500 miles. Finally, the typical senator's constituency has relatively narrow territorial limits, in comparison with the typical president's nationwide "constituency" of suppliers, clients, labor unions, etc. One may interpret these findings as indicating that the senator gains a substantively broad but territorially narrow perspective, whereas the future corporation president is exposed to a diversified metropolitan culture in his early socialization, to which his adult socialization adds a substantively narrower perspective while sustaining a broad territorial span and diversity.

Some studies of state legislators and city councillors in the United States (Patterson and Boynton, 1969; Boynton, Patterson, and Hedlund, 1969; Prewitt, 1970) have shown that public officeholders differ considerably from the general population in terms of education and occupational status, but they do not differ significantly from the "active stratum" or the "attentive constituents." [4]

Thus, in some systems the *social* characteristics of political elites are not very good predictors of recruitment into politics, of party affiliation, and of political attitudes, whereas in other systems they are more closely associated with these *political* characteristics. Neither are cross-systemic differences in the stratification system and in rates of social mobility reliable indicators of the social origins of politicians. Commenting on leadership recruitment in the twentieth century in Britain and the United States, Matthews (1954) observed that "the more equalitarian of the two societies" had "fewer members of the lower social strata among its decision-makers than the more rigid and class-bound [English] society." Summarizing the evidence for class-oriented or class-determined recruitment in Western democracies, Epstein (1967) considers the existence of Socialist labor parties as the single most important difference between European and U.S. party systems, and he adds: "a working-class party may be needed in some societies (but not in others) to provide an outlet for leadership. The opportunity might be largely irrelevant in less stratified societies."

This argument reflects a view shared by many American observers. Campbell *et al.* (1960, p. 347), for example, have concluded from their analysis of American voting behavior that the role of social class in political behavior is fluctuating and depends on the degree of status polarization at any given time. Furthermore, the potential for polarization in the United States is low, because the population is distributed along the entire continuum of status ranks, with many intermediate ranks that promote status misidentification through the proximity and interaction of ranks (Campbell *et al.,* 1960, p. 370). The relevance of Epstein's argument in the present discussion seems to be twofold.

1. The social and demographic characteristics of an elite can be indicators of *opportunity,* provided, of course, that one can demonstrate that a better opportunity is associated with the given social attribute in the recruitment process instead of inferring that opportunity from the social characteristics of recruited elites.

2. *What is a relevant indicator of opportunity in one setting need not be relevant in another.* Not only systems but also subsystems have their own patterns of social or cultural cleavages, and whether such cleavages are translated into political conflict or which of these cleavages are so translated and by what coalition of groups may vary from one context to another.

Thus, for example, social characteristics do not have equivalent meanings across contexts, because it is the *distribution* of categories within a region (whether income, education, ethnic origin, or occupation) which determines the social or political meaning of categories. Social behavior, including political elite behavior, acquires its meaning from the interaction between actor and environment, and political behavior is intended to bring about some change in the environment, including the actor's position therein.

Linz has provided an excellent demonstration that context is a major intervening variable between sociodemographic attributes and beliefs in his study of regional differences in Spain (Linz and Miguel, 1966; Linz, 1969). Analyzing beliefs about modernization among different occupational groups and controlling for the level of economic development of the environment (per capita income in provinces), he found, for example, that in middle- and high-income provinces the same proportion of farmers and white-collar workers believed that rapid success in life was due to "luck," whereas in low-income provinces the proportion of farmers holding the same belief was almost three times higher than that of white-collar workers. Similarly, among farmers the proportion of those believed that success was due to "hard work" or "intelligence" was twice as high in high-income as in low-income provinces, whereas white-collar workers did not display significant differences in this respect. Subjective class identifications also varied sharply between low-income and high-income provinces for some occupational groups, but they did not vary for others (Linz, 1969, p. 116).

Edinger and Searing (1967) have reached the same conclusions after comparing French and German social and political leaders in a study in which they attempted to measure which social background variables would best predict various attitudes of the leaders. After finding that nationality was the single best predictor in terms of the number of attitudes predicted, they subdivided their national samples into two contrasting homogeneous groups. In Germany, social background variables became better predictors of attitudes for the subsamples than for the national sample; in France, however, they were less associated with the attitudes of the subsamples than with those of the entire sample. Thus, not only did the association between social characteristics and attitudes vary when national samples and subsamples were considered—a finding which indicates the need for contextual interpretations within systems—but in the cross-systemic comparisons the strength of the association changed in opposite directions. Replicating this study for five nations (i.e., adding the United States, Venezuela, and Israel), Searing (1969) found additional confirmation for the variation in the relative strengths of relationships between background variables and attitudes across systems.

The studies discussed in this section lead to the conclusion that, beyond the general finding that political elites—at the aggregate level—differ considerably in their sociodemographic characteristics from the general population but do not necessarily differ from other elites or among themselves, *there is little of interest for the study of recruitment that one can hope to find in general and noncontextually interpreted indicators of social background.* The task of conceptualizing contextually interpreted indicators of social position consists in describing individual positions in terms of subjective perspectives on objective environments. Such descriptions can be operationalized in topological language (Scheuch, 1969) and compared across contexts and systems.

B. *Political Socialization and Recruitment*

So far, however, the criticism of the "social background approach" to recruitment has been primarily methodological, and even a sound methodology is no substitute for theory. The very argument that a nondiscriminating collection of background data is not very helpful merely points to the need for some discriminating criteria, i.e., some theoretical hypotheses. The study of political socialization has offered a rationale for the selective use of "background data"; indeed, some authors have considered social background categories as "a taxonomy of socialization experiences related to elite attitudes . . . they are not important in and of themeselves" (Searing, 1969). Thus, even age can be a socialization-relevant indicator: An individual who was in his childhood during the economic depression of the late twenties and early thirties is likely to carry into adult life a perception of the economic, social, and political order which will differ considerably from that of a person who was in his late adolescence or early adulthood during the depression years. We are of course not concerned here with socialization theory and research, which are dealt with in a separate chapter of this volume of the *Handbook*. The relevant question is: Do political candidates and officeholders—the recruited politicians—display a socialization pattern that distinguishes them from the mass citizenry *and from other, nonpolitical elites?* Have they been exposed to socializing experiences which could account for their choice of a political career, i.e., events or influences which the remaining 95–98 percent of the population experience very infrequently or not at all? Or perhaps the socializing experiences they shared with a broader stratum have merely predisposed them to political action, and only those who are exposed to more direct stimuli at a later time and place or find themselves in a recruitment-relevant situation engage in activity leading to candidacy for public or party office.

Although avenues of access to initial continuous or full-time political office vary considerably, only a small minority of candidates have had no previous political or governmental experience (except in revolutionary recruitment). The typical candidate is recruited from what Prewitt (1970) has aptly called "apprenticeship positions," in which he has demonstrated his abilities and value orientations. *Political socialization* is therefore best regarded as consisting of a preapprenticeship stage, which the "apprentice" shares with a much broader stratum of the politically active, and of a later stage resembling the apprenticeship status in the medieval guilds, in which the potential candidate comes much closer to the decision-making centers, learns new skills, and is socialized into the formal and informal structure and into the political culture of a specific area of government and politics. There are considerable differences between these two stages; not only is the latter more advanced, but it is also much more constrained by the institutionalization of role structures and the greater specificity of the criteria by which performance is evaluated. Recruitment-oriented studies of socialization, however, have addressed themselves almost exclusively to the earlier, unstructured stage of socialization. The following discussion of the major research orientations and findings will reveal that the unstructured character of socialization in the preapprenticeship period allows for a diversity of patterns that diminishes the explanatory potential of the preadult stages of socialization.

The Family

Socialization is a continuous process. It includes "all political learning, formal and informal, deliberate and unplanned, at every stage of the life-cycle" (Greenstein, 1968). Cultural anthropologists and psychoanalysts have argued that early political socialization is more basic than later learning experiences and is very resistant to change (LeVine, 1963; Erikson, 1950; Pye, 1961). The distinction between early and adult socialization, which pervades the socialization-oriented studies of recruitment, is predicated on this assumption, as well as on the fact that different agents of socialization and sources of influence operate at various stages in the life cycle.

Of the socializing agents operating during childhood and early adolescence, the family is the most important. In addition to the transmission of partisan identifications (Hyman, 1959; Greenstein, 1969), two types of evidence about the role of the family have been presented: (1) the accumulation of political offices within a small number of "political families" and (2) the socializing impact of politically active parents. In both types the evidence is inferential, except where there are political biographies in which the recruitment role of the family has been documented. The few available biographies, however, deal with outstanding leaders and do not provide sufficient grounds for broad generalizations.

The political families. There is evidence for almost hereditary transmission of political offices in eighteenth- and nineteenth-century Britain (for a reconstruction of the transmission of political offices by the Derbys, Salisburys, and Devonshires, see Guttsman, 1963) based on intermarriages within the nobility and cooptation of nonaristocrats by marriage. Kinship rather than inheritance has been more frequently the criterion for opening avenues of access to public offices, both in Europe and in the United States. Hess (1966) has described 16 American political dynasties from which have come 8 presidents, 3 vice-presidents, 30 senators, 12 governors, 56 U.S. representatives and 9 cabinet officers. Furthermore, 700 families have each had two or more members serve in Congress, and those families account for 17 percent of all congressmen since 1774. Of the 85 Congressmen who responded to a questionnaire by Clubok, Wilensky, and Berghorn (1969), 54 percent had relatives in elected office: 26 percent at the local level only, 6 percent at the state level only, 17.5 percent at both local and state levels, and 6 percent in Congress.

In a chronological and regional analysis of kinship percentages in the United States Congress, Clubok and his associates also showed that the highest kinship percentage, defined as the percentage of congressmen who were the sons, grandsons, nephews, brothers, or first cousins of other congressmen, prevailed in southern states, followed by eastern states; both the Midwest and the West displayed considerably lower percentages. Furthermore, the overall percentage in Congress declined steadily from a high of 20–24 percent in the first five Congresses to 16–20 percent in the 26th through 30th Congresses, 8–10 percent in the 51st through 55th Congresses, and 5–6.8 percent in the 81st through 86th Congresses.

Family recruitment is probably not a undimensional phenomenon. In earlier modern times, the role of the family was more diffuse, political functions were less differentiated, and the political elite was a socially more narrowly defined stratum. Clubok and his associates consider the decline of family recruitment in Congress a concomitant of social mobilization and therefore a correlate of political modernization. They also show that the decrease in kinship recruitment is not a consequence of population growth, that the rate of political change was about the same as the rate of social change (demography and education) but lagged behind technological change and the development of communication systems. In contemporary democracies, the recruitment relevance of the family probably comes much closer to Prewitt's (1965) "overexposure" hypothesis. Frequent and intensive exposure to issues and personalities in the family—through a relative in politics or through early observation of the family's participation in a campaign—may create a favorable image of the political career; and an intimate familiarity with some aspects of politics, as well as acquaintance with locally or regionally prominent public figures, may bring about an interest in a political career and the hope of succeeding in the endeavor.

Politically active parents. The family with one or both parents who have been active in politics tends to provide the type of family socialization in which "overexposure to politics" occurs most frequently, i.e., in which more numerous and more favorable cues about political activity are conveyed. Although many researchers have given evidence or theoretical justifications for emphasizing the role of adult socialization (Edinger and Searing, 1967; Hacker, 1961; Prewitt, Eulau, and Zisk, 1966–67; Kornberg and Thomas, 1965; Patterson and Boynton, 1969), some of these authors, as well as many others, also report that a politically active family is very frequently mentioned by their respondents. Prewitt (1965) rightly questions whether valid conclusions can be drawn from such reports so long as it is not known how many persons in the population received similar "abnormal dosages" of political cues but were not drawn into politics. However, one study has provided an estimate of the political activity of American citizens: In the general adult population, one out of ten citizens is active in a general election campaign (Woodward and Roper, 1950). Marvick and Nixon (1961) found that in both parties almost 40 percent of campaign workers in Los Angeles came from families with at least one parent active in politics and used the above estimate to conclude that campaign workers came from considerably politicized families. They suggest that "the politicized families account for the nucleus that sustains a voluntary party apparatus . . . [and] maintains the continuity of talent and skill, experience and conviction."

Comparing politically active businessmen and a matched group of nonpoliticians, Browning (1968) reports that the fathers of one-half of the politicians but of none of the nonpoliticians had been active in politics. Browning believes that an explicit concern for achievement and power can be associated with efforts to achieve success in many different spheres of life. The fact that the active politicians had initiated their own first political activity and run for offices with relatively high power and achievement opportunities—instead of seeking success in a different arena—is explained by prior socialization through the political activity of their fathers. Although the number of cases observed is too small for tests of statistical significance, a ratio of 50 percent to none is certainly indicative of the impact of parental socialization.

Evidence that politicians are very frequently recruited from politically active families is available for party and public officeholders at different levels in the structure of offices. In their study of party activists in two Canadian and two American cities, Kornberg, Smith, and Bromley (1969) have investigated the effects of parental political activity on a number of recruitment-relevant behavioral indicators. Thus parental activity is associated with a difference of almost two years in the time elapsed between completion of schooling and first party work, with a difference of 2.5 years in the U.S. and 2.9 years in Canada in the age of first party work, and with a difference of almost 1.5 years in continuous work for the party. The differences are all in the expected direction, and they are statistically significant; yet all that can be inferred is that parental activity may have brought about a *somewhat earlier* involvement. The largest impact of parental activity is on age of first party identification, and after all the consequences of parental activity have been explored, one still has to account for the fact that 53 percent of the American and 65 percent of the Canadian party workers did not have politically active parents.

The political activity of the families of local party officials in North Carolina and Massachusetts reported by Bowman and Boynton (1966) was less frequent than that of the Seattle and Minneapolis party workers whom Kornberg and his associates compared with Canadian party officials. It ranged from 28 percent for Republicans in Massachusetts to 49 percent for Democrats in North Carolina. For the Democratic party workers in St. Louis the proportion was one-third (Salisbury, 1965–66).

At the city council level, only 14 percent of the councilmen in the San Francisco Bay area mentioned "political family" as their preadult source of political socialization; yet another 28 percent mentioned the family together with school, events, and political personalities (Prewitt, 1970). Given the non-partisan elections to these councils, the impact of parental socialization appears to be relatively high. Among state legislators in four states, the percentage reporting one or more relatives in politics ranged from 41 percent in New Jersey to 59 percent in Ohio and Tennessee (Eulau *et al.,* 1959).

In European Socialist parties, which partly overlap with trade union movements, politically active families have been the major socializing factor in the lives of most of their present leaders. However, in those labor movements which institutionalized the socialization of youth, youth organizations became the single most important source of leadership recruitment (Beyme, 1971). This also applies to the recruitment of the first and second generations of leaders in the Israeli labor parties (on Israel's youth movement, see Eisenstadt, 1967; on German youth movements, Laquer, 1962; on the functions of age-group organizations across cultures, Eisenstadt, 1956).

Preadult and Adult Socialization

Although it is an important source of political socialization, a politicized home environment need not be the origin of a political career. Some researchers have therefore asked their respondents what they considered their source of initial interest in politics. In reviewing their findings, one ought to bear in mind that it may not always have been clear whether the question referred to interest in politics or to interest in becoming politically active.

Kornberg, Smith, and Bromley (1969) distinguish interest as one of three stages of political socialization: *awareness, interest,* and *identification.* They assume the dependence of interest on prior awareness and of identification on prior interests. Yet this does not seem to be the sequence in all cases. Studying party activists, these authors found that in a substantial number of American cases identification preceded awareness and interest, and that the later the period of going to work for a party, the more interest lagged behind awareness and identification.

The justification for the distinction between a politically active family and the family as a source of initial interest is clearly apparent in the data on American state legislators in four states (Eulau *et al.,* 1959). The frequency of responses pointing to the family as initial source of interest is *consistently lower* than that of legislators who reported that they had "one or more relatives in politics." The ratios are 30:43 in California, 34:41 in New Jersey, 39:59 in Ohio, and 35:59 in Tennessee. The family impact is still considerable but not so strong as one would conclude by simple inference from background data. The frequency of participation in school politics and the study of politics, as sources of initial interest, range from 8 percent in Tennessee to 32 percent in California. Between 43 percent and 70 percent of the state legislators reported participation in political activities as sources of initial interest; some of the responses quoted under this category indicate that the respondents referred to interest in a political career rather than interest in politics.

Only 20 percent of Republican and 15 percent of Democratic precinct leaders in Detroit but 40 percent of the St. Louis urban party organization members explained their initial interest by family influences (Eldersveld, 1964; Salisbury, 1965–66). Interestingly, the proportion of cases citing family influence in the 31 to 45 age group was almost twice as large as that in the 21 to 30 age group in the St. Louis sample, and the activists who cited family influence were equally divided between those whose parents had been active in politics and those whose parents had not. It seems that present age, size of community, urbanization, and type of party organization have an impact on the frequency with which family, i.e., preadult socialization, is mentioned. It is more useful, therefore, to simplify the analysis by distinguishing only between preadult and adult circumstances and sources of political interest, assuming that the family performs a dominant role in preadult socialization. This simplification is further warranted by the finding that the proportion of officeholders who developed their first interest in politics before they reached adulthood is fairly stable across levels of office. For state legislators the ratio of preadult to adult socialization is approximately 60:40; for city councillors it was found to be 55:45. Furthermore, no interparty differences are apparent in this pattern among legislators (Prewitt, Eulau, and Zisk, 1966–67).

Recent research increasingly points to the centrality of adult experiences in molding the attitudinal and behavioral patterns of politicians. In their study of 1257 party activists in two American and two Canadian cities, Kornberg, Smith, and Bromley (1969) have reported that 32 percent of their American and 40 percent of their Canadian respondents had changed their party identification once or more than once. The mean ages for the first and second changes of identification, respectively, were 21.9 and 26.8 in Canada, and 20 and 24.7 in the United States.[5] The most frequently mentioned reasons for the second change were the impact of public figures (41–44 percent) and public events (32–38 percent). For the third change, 48–55 percent of the respondents mentioned public figures. Comparing these activists with a cross-sectional sample of the population, the authors found that only 24 percent of the American but 51 percent of the Canadian electorate report having changed their partisan identification. Thus the American activists had changed their identification more often and the Canadian less often than their respective nonactive co-citizens. Yet, the evidence is clear that young adulthood is a stage of life in which major political orientations have changed for one-third to two-fifths of the studied population of activists. This does not necessarily mean that the changes in partisan identification were associated with initial participation in party work; Kornberg *et al.* only report that 50 percent of the Canadian and 61 percent of the American party activists were "late starters," i.e., began their party activity at the age of 26 or later. This example illustrates the justification for inquiring into adult as well as preadult socialization.

Kornberg and Thomas (1965) have used a trichotomic classification—childhood, adolescence, and adulthood—for a comparison of American state legislators and congressmen with Canadian national legislators, demonstrating that each of these stages in the life cycle was associated not merely with different agents of socialization but with different relationships between the actor and the environment. In childhood, political interest stems from family influences; initial interest in adolescence is associated with self-initiated involvement; and adult socialization is induced by external political events, circumstances, or issues. The comparison across levels of office (for the combined American-Canadian group of national legislators) revealed no difference in the adolescence category and slightly more frequent cases of childhood socialization among national legislators. This difference, however, was mainly the result of the considerably higher frequency of childhood socialization among Canadian as opposed to American national legislators. This group of American national state legislators is not a representative sample (it includes only "the top . . . committee chairmen and ranking minority members") and the number is rather small (37). It is interesting to note, however, that among these top leaders, the frequency of adult socialization is not significantly lower than that among legislators. Late socialization also implies relatively late recruitment, but the pathway to seniority and other leadership positions in Congress is much longer than that leading to the state legislatures. Hence one may perhaps infer that it is as easy—or as difficult—for some "late arrivals" to get elected to the state legislature as it is for another set of "late arrivals" to reach leadership positions in Congress. Stated otherwise, these individuals are likely to constitute two different sets or cohorts of office seekers.

The youth and the adult receive and respond to different political messages, and their perceptions of politics and motivations for political activities should vary accordingly. Personal predispositions and political events are the two most frequently mentioned factors in initial political socialization, other than family influence and politically relevant experiences in school or college. However, there is a clear differentiation in the events and predispositions characteristic of preadult and adult socialization. Both state legislators and city councillors with preadult socialization mention presidential, gubernatorial, and senatorial campaigns as sources of initial interest more frequently than do those who were first subjected to political socialization in adult life, whereas political or economic crises and local issues were mentioned more frequently by the "late arrivals." As for predisposition, admiration for politicians and ambition for political power are more closely associated with preadult socialization, whereas a sense of duty or indignation is characteristic of adult socialization (Prewitt, Eulau, and Zisk, 1966–67).

Early preadult socialization of national legislators has been shown to occur more frequently in families with high occupational status, whereas low status is associated almost exclusively with adult socialization. Farmers, more often than any other group, are self-starters with adolescent socialization (Kornberg and Thomas, 1965). An analysis of the American state legislator data set in terms of prerecruitment occupational mobility has also demonstrated that upward mobiles, i.e., those of lower status *origin,* become involved in politics later in life than status-stables (Eulau and Koff, 1962).

In their study of delegates to the 1968 Democratic Convention, Soule and Clarke (1970) found that preadult family socialization was more characteristic of professionals than of amateurs (using Wilson's indicators for the distinction between the two) and that amateurs were more frequently socialized into politics by adult peer groups and sociopolitical events. Although the statistical significance of these findings is not very high $(p < .20)$, they are supported by the fact that two-thirds of the amateurs, as opposed to only one-half of the professionals, came from politically inactive families. The authors offer the admittedly speculative explanation that the early socialization of the professionals focuses primarily on party identification and loyalty; hence the professionals have confidence in the party, and this orientation leads to a more pragmatic approach to the substantive issues of party politics.

Since the use of philosophical principles for making political judgments increases with age (Adelson and O'Neil, 1966), the amateur's idealism can be explained by the fact that ideological concerns rather than the more direct family socialization led to his entry into partisan politics. The amateur's articulate yet abstract rationalization may be a function of his being politically socialized after reaching intellectual maturity. Some evidence for this hypothesis can be found in a comparative recruitment study of state legislators and lobbyists in Massachusetts, North Carolina, Oregon, and Utah (Zeigler and Baer, 1968). Since lobbyists are issue-oriented and do not display an ideological orientation toward politics, one would expect legislators who have shown an early interest in politics and are therefore more acculturated toward the give-and-take of politics to have higher interaction rates with lobbyists than those who were politicized during adulthood. The data support the hypothesis reasonably well, especially in Oregon and Utah.

Political Socialization and Recruitment in Nonpartisan Settings

One of the questions most studies of political elite socialization have not attempted to answer is the extent to which the observed patterns of socialization are characteristic of political elites only. What is the proportion of children raised in political families who do not seek a political career? One assumes that many people are affected by dramatic political events or social crises, but only a very small proportion find their way into politics and then ascribe their interest in a political career to those events. Socialization creates predispositions and expectations, but is it a recruitment variable? Prewitt's extensive study of the careers of 435 city councillors in 87 cities in the San Francisco Bay area indicates that *in the nonpartisan setting of city government, political socialization is not a recruitment-relevant variable* (Prewitt, 1970).

The "eligibles" in Prewitt's study are the members of the dominant social stratum, from which the politically active stratum "emerges." It is from this latter stratum that the "apprentices" and some of the "recruits" are selected. The social eligibles are the upper two-fifths of their communities in terms of education and income; the politically active are at most 10 percent of the population. Concerned with the pathways leading to the active stratum, Prewitt distinguishes between the *politically socialized,* whose active roles are the continuation of prior political involvements and interests (50 percent of the councilmen), and a stratum of "sudden entrants," consisting of the *politically mobilized,* whose political activity precedes the access to public office (38 percent), and the *lateral entrants,* who are directly recruited into public office (12 percent).

The socializing experiences of the group of "politically socialized" have been reported earlier: political families, school experiences, and dramatic political events. With schools becoming more and more politically conscious, councilmen under 40 years of age more frequently (65 percent) mention a school experience as relevant to their entry into the politically active stratum than do councilmen over 55 (35 percent). About 25 percent of the "politically socialized" also mention an ideological attraction to politics. Yet even after the details of their socialization have been noted, no recruitment pattern can be discerned, and Prewitt draws the cogent conclusion that *the accidents of personal life experiences determine who will join the active stratum*. It is true that these "accidents" are not evenly distributed throughout society; there is a bias in favor of the socially eligible. However, the minority of political actives within the larger minority of eligibles reaches the active stratum as a consequence of fortuitous happenings.

Thus political socialization appears to be a residual category in the "pathway to the active stratum," consisting of a variety of personal experiences which do not fit into any other recruitment patterns. In this particular study, it is a residual category which includes 50 percent of the entire population of councilmen. Furthermore, within the active stratum the "politically socialized" are found in both civic and partisan roles.[6] Finally, the "politically socialized" displayed almost the same distribution of attitudes associated with initial activity as did the "politically mobilized"; only in the "general interest" category were they somewhat more numerous.

Although in a partisan context the cognitive map or the psychological attachment to the objects of political orientations are likely to be more structured, there is no evidence indicating that the diversity of socializing experiences is thereby considerably reduced. After all, nonpartisan city government coexists, for the same population of mass and elite actors, with partisan state and federal government. *The study of preadult political socialization is probably far more relevant for theories of attitude formation and mass behavior than it is for a theory of elite recruitment.* Recruitment is likely to be more critically determined by adult experiences and situational variables than by early-acquired general predispositions toward politics (for a discussion of the criticisms of the use of socialization data as explanatory or predictor variables, see Greenstein, 1970b). One type of adult experience more directly related to recruitment is initial active involvement in politics. It is to these activities and positions of apprenticeship that we turn in the following section.

C. Initial Activity and Apprenticeship

No candidate for public office, whatever the level of government and whatever the electoral system, emerges from the anonymous mass of the socially or politically eligible. Not only must he be able to persuade the party recruiters or the primary electorate that he has successfully completed a relevant apprenticeship, but he also needs a group of initial supporters, a constituency. It is his initial activity—in the party, in appointive government office, in civic organization or interest-group leadership—which may enable him to meet both requirements. Specific criteria of recruitment vary, but these requirements are functional prerequisites of a candidacy. Political parties differ in the degree to which they provide apprenticeship positions and avenues of access to public office. In some party systems they are the major if not the exclusive breeding ground for political personnel; in the American system, where a continuous, well-functioning party organization is the exception rather than the rule, apprenticeship is often sought in appointive public office. Yet parties perform the major role in recruitment, both as initiator and sponsor of candidacies, and as gatekeeper for the continuous influx of politically ambitious apprentices. "The party needs power-aspiring careerists because it is a power-seeking group, but it cannot afford too many power aspirants . . . substitutes for power must be found, such as prestige, status, recognition, social gratification" (Eldersveld, 1964).

However, the very function of providing apprenticeship positions requires an organization with organization-minded personnel, and parties also perform other functions, such as screening candidates for office, nominating them, and mobilizing support. And parties also, of course, take stands on public issues. These functions are interrelated, but they require party workers and officials with a variety of skills and orientations. As a voluntary support-mobilizing organization, the party has as one of its major tasks the reconciling of the personal goals of its adherents and officials with the needs of the organization. A party office may or may not be conducive to a candidacy for public office; yet it is a political office, though perhaps only a semi-career (Kornberg, Smith, and Clarke, 1970).

From the available evidence, party officials do aspire to both higher party positions and public office; the extent to which they do so may vary from one setting to another (Patterson, 1963; Eldersveld, 1964; Althoff and Patterson, 1966). They also hold public offices, appointive or elective, prior to and during their tenure of party office (Mayntz, 1961; Pomper, 1965; Ippolito, 1969). The pattern of these careers does not conform to the popular image of a ladder; "it is more like a game of musical chairs" (Pomper, 1965). In some instances, especially in the higher echelons of the European mass parties of the Left, a party position is a stepping-stone to the national legislature or to the executive. The great majority of the parliamentary leadership of the labor parties in France, Germany, Italy, and Austria are professional party politicians (Beyme, 1971). In the United States, Eldersveld (1964) found that two-thirds of the chairmen of district party boards and 57 percent of the precinct leaders aspired not only to positions on the party's central state committees but also to Congress, the state legislatures, and county offices.

At the lower levels of office, party careers tend to be shorter and turnover is high (Marvick and Nixon, 1961; Eldersveld, 1964; Kornberg *et al.*, 1970). At the district-chairman level, the duration of some careers has been between 15 and 25 years. Even at the precinct level, 15 percent of the leaders of both parties in Detroit in 1956 had served for at least 25 years. Some party careers begin at intermediate and even higher levels of office, but a majority of the officials start without a formal position (Kornberg *et al.*, 1970). Intraparty mobility varies considerably. Kornberg and his associates found at least ten different types of party careers in terms of level of first position, duration, diversity of position, and time invested. In Detroit, the mean number of years required by the most highly mobile members of the district board to achieve that position was 14 years. An early precinct leadership is instrumental to rapid mobility (Eldersveld, 1964; Bochel, 1966), and all officials at the district level had been precinct leaders. Bochel also reports that the position of ward secretary in the British Labour party is a prerequisite for a nomination to the city council. Competitive districts offer more opportunities for the upward-mobile regulars, the younger, the less wealthy, and the less-favored ethnic groups (Eldersveld, 1964; Pomper, 1965). Minority-party precinct chairmen are younger (Conway and Feigert, 1968).

Most studies of party officials have inquired into motivations for initial involvement in party work.[7] Eldersveld's typology of sources of involvement (outside influences, self-generating forces, and accidental involvement) has been used in several studies. Somewhat more than one-half of Detroit's precinct leaders had been originally drafted, 16 percent reported self-generating forces, and 22 percent "accidental involvement." Similar distributions were found in Massachusetts and North Carolina (Bowman and Boynton, 1966). In a rural county in Illinois, 80 percent of the precinct committeemen of both parties had been drafted (Althoff and Patterson, 1966). The organizational mobility of those drafted by political leaders and nonparty groups in Detroit was found to be lower than that of any other type of recruit.

Reported motivations for initial activity have sometimes been dichotomized as being oriented toward either (a) ideological, social, or community interests (impersonal motivations) or (b) social contact or material rewards (personal motivations). Party officials and activists in urban settings report ideological and issue-oriented motivations considerably more often than personal orientations and they do so more often than do activists in rural areas (Hirschfield, Swanson, and Blank, 1962; Salisbury, 1965–66; Althoff and Patterson, 1966; Conway and Feigert, 1968; Ippolito, 1969). Reasons for *accepting leadership positions* were indicated in issue- or community-oriented terms, including candidate orientation, and mention of party factional support was frequently associated with such indications (Conway and Feigert, 1968). One of the most insightful research interpretations in this area is Eldersveld's observation that, since 99 percent of the precinct leaders rated certain impersonal orientations as important and yet 93 percent also gave evidence that personal need fulfillment had been important, *there were, in fact, two motivational components in entering party work.* "Most party leaders saw politics as personally instrumental (power, status, mobility and contacts), at the same time claiming involvement for other reasons" (Eldersveld, 1964).[8]

Students of recruitment have usually assumed that self-oriented and public-oriented motivations are mutually exclusive. The assumption has been further strengthened by the contrasting political styles of amateurs and professionals. The mutual exclusiveness of these categories, however, is only apparent. Organization-oriented professionals seeking *only* extrinsic rewards could not win elections. They disagree with the amateurs only on a value judgment, i.e., whether it is preferable to maintain ideological purity at the risk of losing or to compromise in order to win and be able to implement at least part of a policy program. Neither is the amateur seeking *only* policy goals. Ideological volunteers of all kinds act in the name of a commitment to principles, but they are just as much committed to personally participating in the attempt to implement these principles.

No one is actively engaged in politics against his own will. Furthermore, issue stands, policy orientations, or ideological postures are not sufficient conditions for active involvement. These orientations are shared by larger groups of expected beneficiaries of such policies, as well as politically alert and public-oriented citizens; yet only the activists seek or accept the additional "burden" of participating in political clubs or party organizations. One must conclude that they derive some satisfaction from participation per se. When the activist does not or cannot expect other personal "rewards," participation is ipso facto sufficient evidence of a positive orientation toward participation per se and participation as a goal per se is a personal reward.

Political behavior is collective action, and participation in collective action is best analyzed in terms of a two-level interpretation of dual motivations (Olson, 1965; Czudnowski, 1973). Schlesinger's (1966) theory of "ambition in politics" combines an individual-level variable—ambition—with a system-level variable—the structure of opportunity. As such, it is to be preferred to single-level interpretations of recruitment. However, it does *not* account for two levels of *motivations*; furthermore, it is not a theory of initial recruitment, because in initial recruitment the options between different political career lines are still open.

Whether political apprenticeship positions are located in a party or in a civic, ethnic, or economic organization is a matter of structural differences between systems. There is a relative paucity of systematic research and theorizing in this area. Students of recruitment have generally focused on the characteristics of candidates or on the structure of political support. The concept of an apprenticeship stage was first introduced by Prewitt in his 1970 study of councilmen recruitment. If the concept of apprenticeship is to be theoretically useful, it must be clearly operationalized as preceding initial recruitment. It is true, of course, that an elective local government office provides an apprenticeship—in the general sense of an institutionalized on-the-job learning experience—for a potential congressional candidate; but the elected local official is already a recruited politician, and he must have been exposed to an apprenticeship experience—in the narrower recruitment-relevant sense—at some earlier stage of his career.

In his study of city councillors in the San Francisco Bay area, Prewitt has no difficulty in delineating apprenticeship roles, because he deals with a low-level office. Although he considers noninstitutionalized roles, such as participation in ad-hoc campaigns or drives, as apprenticeship experiences, the evidence points in the majority of cases to official or quasi-official positions in auxiliary government—a city planning commission or some other city board (54 percent of all councilmen) —and to leadership positions in civic organizations (50 percent). In an apprenticeship role the aspirant to office can demonstrate his skills publicly, and from the perspective of the recruiting agency, institutionalized apprenticeship helps locate potential candidates. Commenting on the skills on which selection processes place differential premiums and which a potential candidate can develop or demonstrate in an apprenticeship role, Prewitt cites the argument made by Lasswell (1954) that "as we move up the ladders of modern industrial society . . . the number of links with other human beings that must be maintained is a factor in success that reduces the usefulness of arbitrariness." Thus the screening and sorting processes within the politically active stratum will eliminate persons deficient in interpersonal skills. The face-to-face character of political interaction is as true of selection stages as it is of office-holding itself.

In an attempt to answer the question of what determines the apprenticeship roles in a political system, Czudnowski (1970b) conceptualized these roles as *critical linkage positions in communication networks*. Reporting on the positions held by 102 full-time elective politicians in Israel (44 members of the national legislature and 58 mayors) prior to their initial recruitment to elective office, he distinguished between universalistic and system-specific apprenticeship positions. One-half of both central and local government officials had been recruited from universalistic positions, i.e., social and occupational roles which have been frequent sources of recruitment in many modern and transitional societies and which include civil servants, journalists, writers, officials of professional or economic associations, lawyers, secretaries of municipal councils, etc. The remaining 50 percent of elected politicians had been recruited from system-specific positions. These, in turn, displayed characteristics leading to a further distinction between activities related to relatively short-term national issues and goals and those representing distinctive features of long-term social organizations and services. That this typology is not merely impressionistic is demonstrated by the fact that there is a statistically significant difference in the association of level of office and source of recruitment between national legislators (who were recruited primarily from national issue-related positions) and mayors (who were recruited predominantly from social organization and service-related positions). Judgment on the usefulness of this approach must be suspended until further evidence becomes available from different political and cultural settings.

D. Occupations

Unlike other socioeconomic characteristics, an occupation involves a number
of different variables, such as skills, income, and position, which may independently affect eligibility for political office. Furthermore, occupational careers
reflect achievement, and individuals can move up the ladder of occupational
status. Finally, some occupational categories, such as lawyers, seem to combine
a far greater number of politically relevant characteristics than others and
tend to be considerably "overrepresented" among officeholders, especially in
the United States. There is thus sufficient justification for a more detailed
consideration of the role of occupational variables in recruitment. The lawyer
in American politics deserves particular attention, because his situation affords
an opportunity for examining the relationship between personal characteristics
and the structure of the political environment in elite recruitment.

Occupation as a Cluster of Variables

Occupation is a variable that cuts across most, if not all, of the theoretical
perspectives adopted in the study of elites and elite recruitment. For those
approaching recruitment from the viewpoint of social-stratification theory,
occupation is an indicator of class and status. Others consider occupation in
terms of situs, i.e., location in the functional—as opposed to the hierarchical—
division of labor. Business, agriculture, industry, or communications services
are occupational situses. Combining hierarchical status and situs, one can
determine an individual's distance, or proximity, from the centers of political
decision-making. Another approach to the occupational variable in recruitment
studies is the evaluation of the skills associated with a given occupation and
of their relevance for government and politics in any given society, culture,
stage of development, or political situation. The determination of the relevance
of brokerage skills in recruitment, Lasswell's functional theory of the recruitment of "specialists of violence" in a "garrison state," and some interpretations
of lawyers in politics as "specialists in persuasion" are the best-known examples
of this approach (Lasswell, 1948). Occupation has also been taken as an
indicator of income when no other information on economic status was
available; as such, it was then compared with the income of a given political
office. Furthermore, the prestige of an occupation, as compared with that of a
political career, has been analyzed as a recruitment variable (Rosenzweig, 1957;
Eulau and Sprague, 1964; Barber, 1965). Finally, the distinction between self-
employed and employee and the flexibility of an occupation in terms of the
ability of a person engaged in that occupation to accept part- or full-time
political office or to return to his occupation after a temporary absence are
generally considered important recruitment variables ("availability").

    The preceding enumeration of perspectives in which occupation becomes relevant demonstrates that occupation is really a cluster of variables. Some of the variables are highly intercorrelated, such as education, income, and the societal status of an occupation, although within one occupation there may be a wide range of positions and incomes. For example, the fact that the income of lawyers varies from a few thousand dollars a year to hundreds of thousands makes it meaningless, at least in terms of income, to lump them together in a single category. Proximity to political decision-making centers, availability, and politically functional skills need not be associated with one another or with education and income. An occupational profile of a legislature is therefore not very indicative of the underlying recruitment processes.

Two further difficulties are involved in the indiscriminate use of occupational characteristics in recruitment studies. First, in studies where the information on occupation is based on official or other published records, the indicated occupation may conceal a cultural or political bias. Many parliamentarians of the working-class parties are registered as "workers" although they have spent most of their adult lives as labor union officials; many a "farmer" in the European agrarian parties is really an agent of farmers' marketing associations; a party official in charge of press releases sometimes considers himself a "journalist"; and a German *Beamte* (state employee) who graduated from a law school may prefer to go on record as a lawyer. Published occupational data on politicians must therefore be taken with a grain of salt. Second, and theoretically more important, the occupational background of any category of officeholders is not per se a recruitment variable, because it always refers to a small minority of the members of a given occupation and does not reveal any information on the reasons why this particular set of individuals, rather than any others among the hundreds or thousands who are engaged in the same occupation, sought and achieved political office. This criticism, as Prewitt (1965) rightly points out, is valid for any social background variable and for the entire social-stratification approach to recruitment theory. As aggregate data, occupational indicators are relevant primarily for longitudinal macroanalyses of elites.

Mobility

More important, perhaps, than occupation per se are occupational career histories and occupational mobility (Eulau and Koff, 1962; Bowman and Boynton, 1966) because they are potential indicators of a profile of orientations toward the social and political system, as well as indicators of a person's status —and achievement orientation. Furthermore, a political career may serve as a vehicle for occupational or social upward mobility: young men at the beginning stages of occupational careers—most frequently lawyers—often seek temporary political careers in order to become visible, establish contacts, and create reputations.

A political career is also a vehicle for mobility for those who lack the resources necessary for social advancement in the society in which they wish to be integrated. In this category are the low-status minorities and ethnic immigrant groups who become the beneficiaries of the patronage dispensed by urban political machines in the United States. There is a vast literature on ethnic politics in America, including historical, impressionistic, and systematic empirical studies, which describes the dynamics and parameters of ethnic integration through political mobilization and recruitment. This literature has been aptly summarized and interpreted in terms of the "functional quality of politics" (Eulau and Koff, 1962) by Litt (1970). A similar pattern characterized recruitment by parties and party-controlled local government and social agencies, as a vehicle for social and economic integration and advancement, in the period following the mass influx of unskilled Oriental immigrants with traditional cultural backgrounds to the modern social and political structure of Israel (Czudnowski, 1970a, 1972a).

The struggle for civil rights, educational opportunity, and economic development of the blacks in the United States has followed a more complex pattern. It includes a retarded integration into the prevailing institutional framework, as well as protest and outright rejection of these institutions. Only after a sizable proportion of the rapidly growing black minority had migrated into the large metropolitan centers of the North did the emerging black leadership have a sufficient constituency to carry their demands to the city councils, to the state assemblies, and finally to Congress. Although in some cities, such as Chicago, the recruitment of black leaders proceeded through the Democratic party machine, the black subculture developed its own community leadership roles, which served as apprenticeship positions for those who sought integration through the party system. No empirical studies of the recruitment of black politicians are available, but descriptions of the occupational background of black leaders in the 1950s include a sizable proportion of clergymen, morticians, social workers, activists and officials of the NAACP and of labor unions, physicians, and teachers, as well as lawyers [9] (R. E. Martin, 1953; Barth and Abu-Laban, 1959; Pfautz, 1962; Wilson, 1960; Ladd, 1966). The enactment of the civil rights legislation and the creation of special-welfare and racial-relations agencies provided numerous additional apprenticeship positions for black leaders. Several of the recently elected black congressmen had held such positions. A more militant leadership emerged in the late 1960s; it has since displayed a diversity of orientations toward parties and public office, which has not yet been sufficiently documented.

In some political cultures or stages of modernization, occupation is the single most important social indicator of potential sources of recruitment. Thus, in his detailed study of the Turkish political elite between 1920 and 1957, Frey (1965) describes the role of occupation as the "portal to politics" in a political system in transition from an Islamic military institution to a secular modern state. In the transitional period under consideration, only 9

percent of all deputies to the Assembly were in agricultural occupations, whereas agriculture provided the occupations of 60 to 68 percent of the male population; government and military officials accounted for 33 percent of the
deputies, against a range of 1.6 percent to 11.3 percent in the population; and
the overrepresentation of professionals, 60 percent of whom were lawyers, was
at least twice as great as that of the officials. These examples illustrate the fact
that the relevance of occupation as a social indicator of potential sources of
recruitment is a function not only of the social structure but also of an ideology
or a political regime; i.e., within a given system, occupation may also indicate
an orientation toward politics or toward the regime.

Fluctuations in the absolute size of an occupational group in a community
or society may—but need not—be reflected in the occupational composition of
legislative assemblies. The changing relevance of politics for a given occupational group is more likely to be associated with fluctuations in the proportion
of legislators drawn from that group. Jewell and Patterson (1966) report that
in periods of economic difficulties, the proportion of farmers in the state legislatures increases (in states with a sizable agricultural sector), whereas in times of
prosperity the proportion of farmers decreases and that of lawyers increases. Does
the comparison with lawyers imply that lawyers, too, are an interest group?
It has been shown that the proportion of lawyers in the Connecticut legislature
was associated with changes in the percentage of lawyers in the population;
similarly, the proportion of members listing occupation as "retired" followed
the percentage change in the proportion of the population over the age of
65 (Barber, 1965).

With the increase in the professionalization of political careers it also
becomes increasingly necessary to specify whether one refers to the occupation
from which a politician has been recruited into continuous full-time office or
to the occupation in which he remains more or less active while holding
political office. The occupation from which an officeholder is recruited into
full-time politics may be indicative of some similarity between its roles and
those of political office, whereas the occupation of a part-time politician may
simply indicate the economic interests he represents in politics (e.g., the
farmers). The relationship becomes even more complex when we consider the
full-time political officeholder who either has an independent income or is a
former executive of a corporation who has been released by his superiors to
run for political office. In both cases it is not the occupation but the source of
income which facilitates recruitment into politics. The increasing importance
of management careers of both lawyers and economists as an avenue to political
office has been noted, not only in the United States, but also in Europe. Beyme
(1971) reports on the growing proportion of this career pattern among the top
leadership of the German parties; in Britain, 33 percent of the Conservative
members of the House of Commons in 1955–1959 were "directors of public
companies" (Berrington and Finer, 1967). Kim (1967) found a similar pro-

portion of company executives and employees among Japanese prefectural assemblymen.

It is not likely that a political career very often offers a "second chance" after occupational failure; yet even the successful middle-aged businessman, lawyer, or college professor who abandons his profession for a full-time political career implicitly admits that there was something unsatisfactory, at least psychologically, in the occupation of his first choice.

Lawyers in Politics

One of the most persistent findings is the ubiquity of a relatively large proportion of lawyers in legislative assemblies. They are in many countries the single largest occupational group in parliament, followed by farmers and businessmen or, in western European countries with large Communist and Socialist parties, by farmers and "workers." For the lower houses in American state legislatures, Hyneman (1940) reported a proportion of lawyers of 28 percent in 1925–1935, and although it decreased in the 1940s, it increased considerably in some states in the 1950s (Barber, 1965; Jewell and Patterson, 1966). Systematic information for all states over longer periods of time is not available. In the 85th Congress, lawyers accounted for 65 percent of the Senate and 55 percent of the House of Representatives (Jewell and Patterson, 1966). Schlesinger (1957) reported that 46 percent of 995 elected governors in all American states between 1870 and 1950 had been practicing lawyers. In other countries proportions are much lower. In Italy the proportion of lawyers in the legislature declined from 32.8 percent in 1946 to 20.8 percent in 1958 (Sartori, 1967). In France lawyers accounted for 24 percent of the legislators elected between the two world wars, but for only 13 percent in the Fourth Republic (Dogan, 1961). In Britain there were 22 percent barristers and solicitors among the newly elected Conservative M.P.s in 1950 and 13 percent of all Conservatives in 1955; the total proportion in the House of Commons of 1951 was only 19 percent (Berrington and Finer, 1967; Dogan, 1961). In post–World War II Germany the percentages in the Bundestag were 7 percent in 1949 and 1953, and 9.3 percent in 1965 (Dogan, 1961; Beyme, 1971). Finally, in Norway the number of lawyers in the Storting seems to be "surprisingly low" (Valen, 1966), and Kim (1967) reports that there were very few lawyers in Japanese prefectural assemblies in 1963.

Most students of politics, especially of American politics—historians, sociologists, and jurists—have been puzzled by the large numbers of lawyers in political positions and have tried to offer plausible explanations. This rich literature has been cogently summarized and interpreted from the viewpoint of political science by Eulau and Sprague (1964), who have added a detailed analysis of the lawyer-legislators in four American state legislatures.

Tocqueville believed that the high class position of the legal profession facilitated the access of lawyers to politics. Weber attributed the predominance of the lawyer to his independent position, including his availability, in modern capitalist economies. Bryce (1894) believed that the two-level constitutional structure of American federalism sensitized the student of law to the relationship between law and politics. More recently, Matthews (1954) further developed the Weberian argument by suggesting that lawyers are more easily available for political office because the law changes slowly and even extended absence from legal practice will not impair their ability to return to their profession.

As mentioned earlier, in contemporary American society the argument of the high status and income of the legal profession is not very accurate. Wells (1964) has shown that the legal profession is segmented in terms of size and volume of practice. The large law firm does not resemble the small partnership or the solo practitioner in metropolitan areas, and the lawyers in small cities, in turn, have had to adopt a different style. These three classes of lawyers also differ in terms of ethnic, religious, and other social characteristics. Furthermore, some lawyers may enter politics because they are well-to-do and available, but for others a legislative salary is a substantial supplement to their private income. Finally, the "advertiser" is most often a young lawyer, but the evidence analyzed by Eulau and Sprague does not clearly confirm that the young lawyers retire from the legislature after achieving their goals.

A forceful institutional argument has been presented by Schlesinger (1957), who indicates that about one-third of all lawyer-governors advanced directly from law-enforcement offices. Their monopoly over law-enforcement offices gives lawyers a distinct advantage in the political competition for the governorship: 51–68 percent of governors elected between 1870 and 1950 had been lawyers, and of these, 56–85 percent had held law-enforcement positions. Furthermore, the last public office before election to the U.S. Senate was a law-enforcement position for 12 percent of all senators, but another 13.5 percent had held law-enforcement offices at earlier stages of their careers. Eulau and Sprague have shown that 27–36 percent of lawyer-legislators at the state level had held judicial and other law-enforcement offices. Neither Schlesinger's data nor those of Eulau and Sprague reveal how many of the law-enforcement offices were elective and how many appointive. The distinction is important, because an elective office requires a political following and offers considerable political experience.

Schlesinger has also argued that the compatibility of the professions of law and politics operates to the advantage of lawyers primarily when they are career politicians. The evidence for this statement consists in the fact that the longer a man was in public office before his election to the governorship, the higher the probability that he is a lawyer. The frequency distributions for the lawyers, ranging from 20 percent among governors with no previous experience in public office to 58 percent among governors with 10 to 14 years of experience, are convincing. The argument, however, is not relevant to recruitment unless one is willing to assume that young people with political ambitions prefer a legal training because it facilitates access to a political career. Woodrow Wilson's statement that he "entered" the law because he had "chosen" politics as a profession is often quoted in support of this assumption; Eulau and Sprague have demonstrated that the lawyer-legislator shows an earlier interest in politics and has more relatives in local judicial, state, legislative, and party offices than the legislator who is not a lawyer. He also has worked more frequently for a party in his prelegislative career and conceives of himself as a self-recruited politician more often than his nonlawyer colleague. These findings seem to point toward a more intensive political socialization and a stronger political orientation.

Yet the legal profession also offers other possibilities. Lawyers have made fortunes in business (Miller, 1951), and Fiellin (1967) has presented evidence that for the congressman-lawyer from New York City, congressional office is a stepping-stone to a judicial appointment. Thirteen of the fifteen lawyers in the New York delegation who voluntarily gave up their seats in Congress between 1946 and 1956 received judgeships, and one was appointed District Attorney. The Eulau and Sprague data on state legislators also show that lawyer-legislators more frequently aspire to local or state judicial office and to the state senate than nonlawyer-legislators.

Thus the lawyer can aspire to four different careers. (1) If he meets the selective social criteria of the large law firms, he can embark on a highly successful and lucrative legal practice; if not, he can still establish himself in a less prestigious but lucrative legal practice. (2) He can establish himself in business or in business and finance management. (3) He can establish a reputation in politics for the purpose of furthering his legal practice or of obtaining an elective or appointive judgeship. (4) He can embark on a political career. What remains to be explained is the reason for the frequent occurrence of (3) and (4), i.e., why lawyers have an advantage in politics, irrespective of their aspirations. The most frequently encountered explanation is the functional similarity between the roles of the lawyer and the politician: the *similarity between the lawyer-client relationship and political representation,* the lawyer's role as an *advocate* who pleads in court for his client's side in a legal controversy, his role as a *negotiating, mediating, or arbitrating attorney* (brokerage role), and his role as a *counselor.* Eulau and Sprague have shown that, despite the lawyer's training and experience in politically relevant roles, his behavior in the political arena does not differ from that of the nonlawyer-legislator. More than 50 years ago, Weber observed that the lawyer was prototypical of the modern professional politician. Eulau and Sprague developed this notion and, interpreting their findings, suggested the hypothesis of an *isomorphism* of the legal and political professions, as a consequence of their functional (and historical) *convergence* in response to the requirements of an increasing complexity in the social order.

In an occupational role-profile analysis of political recruitment, Czudnow-ski (1970b) suggests that the isomorphism between the legal and political professions is merely one of several instances of a role similarity conceptualized at a higher level of generalization, a role similarity which lawyers share with several other occupational sources of recruitment. This higher-level conceptualization refers to a *generalist* orientation, associated with the ability to perform *complex* operations, and location in a *critical linkage* position in a formal or informal network of communications. Fifty-two of 979 occupational titles share the characteristics of the political role profile, and a Smallest Space Analysis reveals that some of the most frequent occupational sources of recruitment cluster together in the space determined by the relevant occupational role-profile variables. Beyme (1971) considers the increasing number of political candidacies of publicists and scientists in Germany as evidence confirming the communication-linkage dimension of this role profile, but he believes that as a consequence of the differentiation of political roles, the generalist orientation can be imputed only to some of the top political elites.

A comparative assessment of the "ubiquity" of lawyers in politics would lead to the conclusion that the American situation is an exception. The "overrepresentation" of lawyers displays two components: (1) a cross-nationally valid component reflecting a role similarity that accounts for a 10–20 percent proportion of lawyers in national legislatures; (2) a system-specific component in American politics, accounting for an additional share of 35–45 percent of congressional seats, which needs to be explained in historical and theoretical terms.

Eulau and Sprague indicate that the lawyer's ascendancy in politics coincided with periods of commercial and economic growth, i.e., periods of increasing division of labor. But why did the corresponding period of economic growth and division of labor in Europe fail to create a similar opportunity for the legal profession? Tocqueville, one of the most penetrating observers in Western intellectual history, ascribed the ascendancy of the lawyer in American politics to the absence of a ruling class. He also made the observation, as pertinent today as it was 150 years ago, that "scarcely any question arises in the United States which does not become, sooner or later, a subject of judicial debates." Although these are questions that the social and economic historian or the cultural anthropologist is better equipped to answer than the political scientist, it seems that Tocqueville's observations are not entirely unrelated. Schlesinger's comparative interstate perspective (1957) affords an insight into one part of the answer. In his study of the role of lawyers in politics, he draws attention to the fact that the proportion of lawyers among governors varies considerably. Thus the occupational role profile alone does not account for the "overrepresentation" of lawyers in politics; specific regional economic or ecological contexts are also involved. The expanding economy created political demands for regulation of railroads, insurance, oil interests, and mining industries. One of the frequent demands was for legal litigation of conflicting economic interests, made first by competing owner groups and later by management and labor. These conditions placed judges and public attorneys in conspicuous and strategic positions.

In long-established European societies, economic growth and industrialization created social and economic conflicts between the classes of rigid stratification systems. Jurists were everywhere called on to assist in the management of public affairs, in the adaptation of obsolete systems of government and law to new demands. Yet their task was only to *transform and adapt* an existing order to the interests of the upper class and of the upper bourgeoisie. The task was not particularly difficult, since these classes had monopolized judicial offices and legal careers. In the United States, there was neither a rigid class stratification nor a traditionally entrenched social and political order. A federal structure, the proliferation of law-enforcement offices, and their economic and political roles, as well as an individualistic ethos, facilitated the lawyer's access to politics.

It is true, as Eulau and Sprague indicate, that in more recent times the development of large corporations, trade associations, labor unions, and administrative regulatory agencies and the expansion of the public sector of the economy have brought law and politics even closer to each other. Yet the argument that applied from the middle to the end of the nineteenth century does not apply in the twentieth. One must thus explain the *persistence* of lawyers in politics as a separate phenomenon. The political scientist is inclined to point to the loose structure of political parties in the United States, their relative heterogeneity, and the absence of socially entrenched dogmatic ideologies. In a sociopolitical system, in which party machines and the economic, social, and political purposes they serve are localized and transitory, the individual entrepreneur steps in. For this task, the lawyer was far better equipped than most of his competitors, and the law-enforcement offices provided him with an institutionalized monopoly over a major avenue of access. This explanation is supported by the fact that in European systems the proportion of lawyers in politics varies considerably between different types of parties. There are significantly more lawyers in the less rigidly organized parties in Italy, France, and Germany. There were 25 percent lawyers among the deputies of the French "Independents" between 1945 and 1958 and 22.5 percent among the "Radicals," the least disciplined of the French parties in the Third and Fourth Republics, but there were only 11.6 percent among the Catholic MRP and 14 percent among the Socialists. Similarly, the lowest percentages of lawyers in the Italian parliament were in the Communist, Socialist, and Christian Democratic parties, the highest amongst the deputies of the Liberal, Republican, and Social Democratic parties. In Germany, even after the Social Democratic party had become a respectable alternative and then a winning party, there were somewhat more lawyers in the Christian Democratic Union (computations and rankings based on data in Dogan, 1961; Sartori, 1967; Beyme, 1971).

This analysis further illustrates the need for a contextual interpretation of socio-demographic characteristics. Not only do lawyers differ from those in other occupations in terms of their skills, the client-agent relationship, and their proximity to governmental processes, but their relative advantage in the recruitment process over those in other occupations depends on the structure of the recruiting parties. In seeking recruitment to elective office, many lawyers are private political entrepreneurs, and well-organized parties with somewhat rigid hierarchical structures do not favor the advancement of private political entrepreneurs. With loosely organized and decentralized parties, the lawyer-entrepreneur is in a much better position to make his initial advantage over members of other occupational groups prevail in the recruitment process.

E. Motivations

The interest in the social origins, the occupational background, and the apprenticeship positions of political elites reflects a sociological approach to the study of recruitment. The units of analysis are sets of aggregate recruitment data, and even when one accounts for the interaction between the characteristics of an occupation and the structure of a specific environment, the differences between individual members of that occupational category are relegated to the parameters of the analysis. One thus assumes that at the aggregate level these differences do not affect the relationship between the observed variables.

This parametric assumption of the political sociologist is a limitation imposed on his research model by the fact that he can deal effectively with only a small number of variables, by his insufficient training, if any, in psychology, and perhaps by his reluctance to accept the analytical constructs of psychology and psychoanalysis, which have a great variety of empirical referents and no generally accepted rules of interpretation. Stated otherwise, there is no theoretical justification for the decision to relegate differences in personality to the inoperative parameters of elite research. In fact, there is a critical gap in theorizing about elite recruitment because no researchable hypotheses have been offered to explain why only some members of a social category, group, or occupation with recruitment-relevant characteristics seek a political career while others do not.

Attempts to bridge this gap involve conflicting hypotheses or differences in emphasis concerning (1) the relationship between personality "traits" or psychological motivations which affect political behavior and the total configuration of personality; (2) the relationship between such personality "traits" and areas of nonpolitical behavior in which they may also be revealed; and (3) the interaction between personality and specific political situations or environments, as opposed to a generalized concept of orientation toward politics.

Research in political psychology has focused primarily on the belief systems and behavioral patterns of politicians, rather than on the role of personality variables in recruitment. This literature is reviewed and discussed in Greenstein's chapter in this volume and in the contributions to the *Handbook of Political Psychology* (Knutson, 1973). This section will review only studies of direct interest to recruitment theory. The available evidence is scarce and inconclusive, and it can be best summarized as revolving around the question of whether there is a "political personality," i.e., a motivational syndrome characteristic of politicians only.

In the studies of initial recruitment discussed in the preceding sections of this chapter, the term "motivation" has been applied to orientations toward sociopolitical goals, as well as self-centered orientations toward social, material, and psychological rewards. In the "personality-and-politics" literature, "motivation" denotes a psychological predisposition, a personality "trait," need, or drive. These studies assume that individuals who seek active political roles are "motivated" by a desire or urge to satisfy such needs and that, consequently, political candidates should display greater intensities of the relevant "psychological predispositions" than citizens with similar social, economic, and educational characteristics who do not seek active political roles. As Greenstein's chapter in this volume amply demonstrates, psychology-oriented analyses of political behavior perceive *personality as mediating and being mediated by social, cultural, and situational factors*. Greenstein's "expanded conceptualization" for the analysis of personality and politics offers the additional dimensions of a three-level socioecological space and a three-stage time perspective. Interpreting the intermediate socioecological level, i.e., the microenvironment," as including the actor's own location in the environment, and considering these levels of socioecological organization as involving empirically and analytically distinct perceptual perspectives, one finds it possible to combine in this "expanded conceptual framework," designed for psychological predispositions, *both connotations of the concept of motivations*. Thus personality factors, individual-level goals, and intended public consequences are three facets of the motivational analysis of political behavior.

In an earlier work, Greenstein (1969) systematically summarized the propositions put forward in the literature which refer to the *relative* impact of personality factors in role performance. Of these, the specificity of role expectations and the ambiguity of the situation are of particular relevance for an evaluation of the relative impact of psychological predispositions on recruitment to active political roles. The less specific the role expectations or the more ambiguous the situation, the greater the impact of personality factors on role performance. The argument has been generalized for types or levels of political activity by Knutson (1973): "the influence of personality is directly related to the specificity of the politically relevant behavior"; for broadly popular acts (e.g. voting), social and cultural norms often "carry the action." Recruitment into active political roles involves greater situational ambiguity and less specific expectations than does casting a vote on election day for one of two or three candidates. Predispositions should therefore be a more discriminating criterion in comparing politicians and nonpoliticians than in comparing voters. Commenting on the psychobiographies of American Presidents, Greenstein (1973) has added that the greater the consequences of the actor's behavior, the more necessary it is to study (the psychological properties of) that leader intensively.

The argument applies to the conditions of interaction between psychological and environmental variables in "role-determining," as opposed to "role-determined," behavior. Recruitment is an instance of "role-taking" rather than "role-performance"; however, it is role-taking behavior in an area in which, in most Western societies, there are no specific expectations at all. The citizen is expected to vote, but there is no expectation that he will also become an activist or candidate for office. In some political cultures, political candidacy is considered a form of deviant behavior, drawing exceptional people toward it.

The proposition that personality factors are likely to be a major recruitment-relevant variable is intuitively appealing, but efforts to *demonstrate* the relevance of predispositions in recruitment have been neither numerous nor very successful. Although modern political psychology began with Lasswell's inferences from psychopathology to political involvement (Lasswell, 1930), most political scientists who are oriented toward psychology and psychoanalysis have been preoccupied with the more researchable problems of the relationship between personality traits and political attitudes and behavior. Beyond researchability, however, there are several theoretical and methodological problems. Psychological theory has offered a number of analytical constructs, but the utility of these constructs depends on validating the meaning of the measures employed in assessing the behavior imputed to motivational constructs. This, in turn, involves the problem of cross-situational validation, which is compounded by the fact that there is considerable *selectivity* in the manner in which motivations, such as a politician's drive for power, express themselves even in the relevant context of political interaction (George, 1968). One could argue, against Knutson's (1973) complaint that personality assessment has made a poor demonstration for the "existence" of the constructs which it purports to demonstrate, that such constructs "exist," after all, only in the mind of the analyst. However, the argument would miss the empirically more salient question of the assumed stability and coherence of personality over time, as well as its constant or predictably variable relationship to matters political. Socialization theory and research, as well as Rokeach's work on the structure of belief systems (1968), combine to support the hypothesis of the early establishment of a basic personality structure, but political psychology allows for "important new developments and partial restructurings throughout life" (Levinson, 1958). More recently, Greenstein (1973) has expanded the hypothesis of interaction, as well as potential disjunction, to five sets of variables in a causal chain leading from the characteristics of individuals to collective sociopolitical outcomes: (1) genetic and acquired physiochemical dispositions; (2) childhood environmental influences; (3) adult personality; (4) adult sociopolitical orientations; and (5) individual behavior. The assumption of a personality-determined stability of motivations in political behavior has been most directly challenged by Maslow's theory of *growth* along a hierarchical scale of basic needs: (1) physical needs (food, water, sex) ; (2) safety (e.g., order, predictability) ; (3) love, affection, belongingness; (4) self-esteem; (5) self-actualization (Maslow, 1970; Davies, 1963) . However, the structure implied in Maslow's theory is more easily researchable than the dynamics of change (Knutson, 1972; Inglehart, 1971) .

Less concerned with the psychogenesis of personality, students of recruitment have been engaged in a search for the *modal political personality*. Theorizing about a power-centered personality began with Lasswell's conception of political man in terms of *private motives displaced upon public objects and rationalized in terms of a common good* (Lasswell, 1930, 1954) . He added that the accent on power rather than some other value was a result of the fact that limitations on access to other values had been overcome by the use of power. Thus "power is a defense," and "individuals turn to it in the hope of overcoming low estimates of the self." In the 1954 formulation of his hypotheses, Lasswell also stated that leaders in large-scale modern polities, where comparatively free institutions exist, are oriented toward power as a secondary coordinate or value with other values, such as respect (popularity) , rectitude (reputation as public servant) , or wealth (a livelihood) . Intensely power-centered persons tend to be relegated to comparatively minor roles. Thus, in a democracy, a basically healthy personality is essential to survival amid the perpetual uncertainties of political life, but in totalitarian regimes, egocentric and authoritarian personalities can rise to high positions (Lasswell, 1954; Tucker, 1965) . The view that the political culture of a regime selectively recruits individuals with a personality structure which is functional in terms of the organizational principle of the regime applies probably more accurately to higher-level offices in relatively centralized and monolithic political systems than to lower-level offices in pluralistic regimes. Furthermore, one has to bear in mind that recruitment processes begin in localized settings, at lower levels of organization, which may allow for considerable cultural variability. Finally, what may be true of the relevance of a power orientation in recruitment need not apply to other basic human needs and need fulfillment in the recruitment process.

In an attempt to replicate Lasswell's method of applying insights from psychopathology to the study of political psychology, Rutherford (1966) has examined participation in the ward council of a psychiatric hospital. He found that among leaders of the ward council 46 percent were paranoids, as opposed to only 12 percent in the population from which they had been selected. In Rutherford's study the term "paranoid" does not refer to a type of mental illness (which would be referred to as psychotic paranoia); it refers to a particular psychological pattern of relating to the environment, which shares many characteristics with what this author believes to be *the* political personality. The dynamics of paranoia are projection and aggression, yet with great sensitivity to social norms. The paranoid personality often gives the impression of self-sufficiency and superiority. Ego strength, self-confidence, and a sense of effectiveness—all concomitants of active political participation—are also descriptions of the paranoid personality. The thesis that well-integrated personalities will participate more frequently but anxiety-ridden individuals will avoid leadership roles does not contradict, according to Rutherford, the prevalence of paranoids among participants. The paranoid personality projects and displaces guilt and anxiety and is so well integrated that it does not require perceptual or consensual validation of its beliefs. This author concludes that in the search for the personality type of the political participant one should distinguish between internalizers and externalizers. The political world offers numerous opportunities for externalizers to project and displace their anxiety and intrapsychic conflict.

There are severe limitations to the inferences one can draw from Rutherford's study. The findings are based on a highly distinctive population, and the author assumes that there is just a single type of political personality. Yet elements of extreme paranoid delusion in the behavior of political leaders have been described in psychobiographical studies of Hitler (Langer, 1972) and Stalin (Tucker, 1971). More important, perhaps, is the hypothesis that anxiety, i.e., an unfulfilled need for security, can also lead to externalization in politics.

Another psychiatrically oriented study reports somewhat different findings. Marcus (1969) applied a 22-item screening instrument of psychiatric symptoms indicating impairment to two random samples in a white and a black community, to high-ranking party officials and to staff members of civil-rights organizations. The instrument (Langner, 1962), validated by tests on a group of psychiatric patients and a control group of healthy individuals, included items such as "feel weak all over," "very low spirits," "restlessness," "worrying type," "trouble getting to sleep," "memory not all right," "cold sweats often," "feel somewhat apart even among friends," etc. Marcus found that "traditional" activists did not differ in their test scores from the populations from which they were chosen (mean scores 2.67 and 2.74, respectively), but "innovative" participants (civil-rights activists) scored significantly higher (mean score 4.31). Furthermore, "in the case of innovative participation, the attribute of psychopathology was one to which the community political recruitment system was sensitive," i.e., an attribute for positive selection. Marcus rightly points out that labeling behavior in a given society as abnormal implies making assumptions about the legitimacy of the social institutions in which the behavior occurs. Deviant behavior indicates that this legitimacy is being questioned; and when institutions are being challenged, the prevailing conceptions of self and normality are also challenged. However, there is no indication that the observed psychic characteristics in recruitment into political activity are not shared by members of other social elites.

The preceding observation applies also to the study of party committeemen by Schwartz (1969). He explicitly hypothesized the existence of "a rather unique personality set of needs, values and cognitions which predispose men to political activity." Comparing the scores of his sample on the Edwards Personal Preference Schedule with those of a nationwide sample of household heads and a sample of college students, he found that the mean scores of politicians on *achievement, autonomy, dominance,* and *aggression* were significantly higher than those of the college and general population (but standard deviations were smaller). To conclude, as Schwartz does, that these findings are indicative of a personality structure characteristics *only* of politicians, is to misinterpret the mean scores of the general population as a substitute for the scores of control groups from other social elites.

Earlier researchers have found a different pattern in their search for a modal political personality. McConaughy (1950) applied several personality inventories and attitude tests to 18 South Carolina legislators and two non-random groups. He found that the political leaders were *far less neurotic* than the average male adult, *less introverted, more self-sufficient,* and *slightly more dominant.* They were also much higher than average in *ascendancy* in social situations and in *lack of inferiority feelings;* however, they averaged below the control group in fascist tendencies. Hennessy (1959) compared two groups matched on socioeconomic and educational characteristics, one consisting of 72 partisan activists, officeholders, and candidates, the other of 138 voting-age citizens in Tucson, Arizona. The "politicals" scored considerably higher than the "apoliticals" on a scale of *power orientations,* and male apoliticals scored higher than female politicals. On a *"willingness to compromise"* scale, apoliticals scored uniformly higher, whereas politicals tended to score higher on a *"willingness to risk"* scale. No significant differences were found on "tough-mindedness" and "authoritarianism," although the politicals were all somewhat higher on authoritarianism.

Using a different technique (a projective Thematic Apperception Test of Motivations) in different settings, Browning and Jacob (1964) found *no significant differences in power-, affiliation-, and achievement-motivations between politicians and nonpoliticians.* The test groups were a random sample of politically active or office-holding businessmen, a matched group of nonactive businessmen in an eastern city, and two thirds of all elected local officials in two Louisiana counties. Furthermore, there were wide dispersions around the mean scores, but businessmen-politicians were somewhat more concerned than non-politicians with friendship (affiliation). However, individuals in political positions with high power and achievement potential also had higher power- and achievement-motivation scores; thus offices with a high power potential seem to attract men with relatively strong power motivations. Finally, the motivational characteristics of officeholders in positions with high power potential were similar to those of candidates for such offices. The authors also commented on the differential impact of vigorous partisan or factional politics, as opposed to nonpartisan offices, on the motivational characteristics of candidates and officeholders. In a subsequent paper based on the same data set of businessmen-politicians, Browning (1968) reported that motivational patterns were also associated with initiative in initial recruitment and with types of behavioral orientations in role performance. Those who displayed high achievement and power orientation, combined with low affiliation motives had also been more frequently self-starters (see also Part II, Section C).

Barber's argument, in his study of Connecticut legislators, begins with the observation that the very groups which tend to be most active in voting and voluntary group participation—the high-income, college-educated, professional, and managerial categories—are those least likely to see politics as a desirable occupation. There is a tendency for politics to be relegated to "localists," and the modern organization man is too mobile to establish the necessary local ties. Furthermore, the economics of legislative service prevent most young or middle-aged business or professional men from entering legislative politics. Finally, the turnover among state legislators is high, primarily (in Connecticut) because of the preelection retirement of incumbents. Thus, in the task confronting the recruiter, much depends on the personal motivations of potential office seekers and the satisfaction they expect to derive from holding office. Since continuous political office-holding is not an extension of voluntary part-time activity, one should not expect candidates for the legislature to display even more of the healthy, confident personality attributes characteristic of activists at increasing levels of part-time participation. In fact, three of the four types of legislators in Barber's study—the "spectators," "advertisers," and "reluctants"—appear as people with rather severe deficiencies in self-esteem, who seek out political opportunities to compensate for feelings of personal inadequacy. Only the "lawmakers" have such high self-esteem that they can "manage the threats, strains and anxieties" involved in the change from a nonpolitical to a political career. When self-esteem is "cripplingly low," it is not likely to be conducive to political candidacy; but for "those whose self-doubt is not disabling," politics may satisfy their need for confirmation of a higher self-esteem.

Low self-esteem is an awareness of a disparity between the ideal self and the perceived self. The resulting tension can be reduced by somehow translating the person's problem into political terms. This linkage may be the result of predispositions developed through identification with political figures, or of experience in being deprived by various political forces (e.g., the experience of discrimination against ethnic or religious minorities or low economic status groups). For the "advertisers" it is an opportunity "to join those he cannot lick"; for others, politics may offer a second chance in terms of occupation, or in the search for approval or respect.

Although not sufficiently documented, Barber's thesis is of considerable interest for an explanation of the "deviant" case, especially with reference to the patterns of selection associated with low self-esteem candidacies. However, whether a case is "deviant" or not depends on the opportunity structure of supply, demand, and risk, and it is precisely in these terms that "reluctants" and "spectators" do not fit into the same category as "advertisers." Stated otherwise, low self-esteem becomes recruitment-relevant only through a mediating variable—a specific opportunity structure: It is very unlikely that people with very low self-esteem are oriented toward a political career merely because of their feeling of inadequacy, even if they identify with political figures or are members of minority groups. Similarly, high self-esteem is not a monopoly of political candidates; it can be equally conducive to a business, scientific, or military career. Self-esteem is based, rightly or wrongly, on evaluations of adequacy in roles with a high ego-involvement (Sherif and Cantril, 1947). There seem to be a variety of such roles, but only some of them turn out to be relevant in recruitment to political office. Thus, although the psychological dimension in Barber's motivational analysis is not sufficiently discriminating, it confirms the assumption of his model that motivation, resources, and opportunity are interdependent in their recruitment relevance. Furthermore, Barber's motivational typology explicitly refutes the hypothesis of a unimodal political personality type.

More recently, Barber (1972) has expanded his model in a characterological study of American presidents. Character is discernible in childhood, world view in adolescence, and style in the period of the first independent political success. Character provides the main thrust, but subsequently cultural environment and historical accidents add their impact in shaping world view and political style. The style displayed in the first independent political success is adopted in subsequent behavior. Barber documents the psychogenesis of four types of presidential styles: active-negative, active-positive, passive-positive, and passive-negative. The styles combine a measure of invested energy and a dimension of felt satisfaction. This characterology further demonstrates the motivational diversity of political actors, but it is not intended to provide a motivational explanation of recruitment per se.

A complex pattern of interdependence between personality and structural political variables emerges from DiRenzo's (1967) study of Italian legislators, which combines two major research dimensions in political psychology: level of activity and ideology. DiRenzo found that the mean score on a scale of dogmatism was higher for nonactive supporters of the Communist and Socialist parties than for the leaders of those parties in the Italian Chamber of Deputies, but the relationship was reversed for the Christian Democrats, the Social Democrats, and the right-wing Italian Social Movement (MSI). One possible explanation, offered by DiRenzo, is party-determined differences in patterns of recruitment, associated with differences in the power potential of legislative offices between parties. The study also revealed that differences in the range and mean scores of dogmatism between party leaders were *not* clearly associated with the party's location on the left/right ideological continuum. Di-Renzo draws party structure and factionalism into the analysis in order to explain his findings, but Greenstein (1970c) has questioned the validity of DiRenzo's measurement on the dogmatism scale.

A recent demonstration of the motivational diversity of political leaders can be found in Payne's studies of "incentives for political participation" (Payne, 1972; Payne and Woshinsy, 1972). These studies have resulted in an inductively derived typology of motivations and behavioral ("identifying") characteristics, conceptualized at the operational level of political involvement. Thus, through political activity, leaders can gain satisfaction as shown in the following table.

Activity	*Type of incentive*
Working on specific public policies	Program
Attaining and exhibiting prestige	Status
Personal praise and affection of others	Adulation
Commitment to a transcendental cause which gives meaning to life	Mission
Relieving anxieties of conscience	Obligation
Pleasing others and being accepted	Conviviality
Competing with others in structured interactions	Game

These incentives appear to be lower-level operationalizations of the three highest ranking basic human needs in Maslow's theory of motivations (see p. 212). It is hypothesized that these incentives *sustain* political participation; they are therefore intended to explain style of behavior in office rather than recruitment into a political career.

Incentives are defined as emotional needs, in contradistinction to "formal goals" or "instrumental values"; thus Payne adheres to the position that public orientations alone do not reflect the entire motivational syndrome of active political participants, and he describes the various nonmaterial and noninstrumental personal orientations encountered in three studies of legislators and other political elites in different political cultures.

In a random sample of only 16 Connecticut state legislators, the most frequent incentive was "program" (6), followed by "game" (5). Among elites in the Dominican Republic ($N = 32$), the most frequently observed incentive was "adulation" (50 percent), followed by "program" (19 percent). Among a random sample of 50 French Deputies, "mission" ranked first (38 percent), followed by "program" (28 percent).

"Program" is the only incentive with a relatively high frequency in all three samples; it is also somewhat more ambiguous in its conceptualization. Payne emphasizes (p. 83) that it refers not to any specific policy goal but to the satisfaction derived from working on public policy matters. It is neither a sense of duty nor altruistic sacrifice, but a "selfish" need gratification. Yet gratifying one's need to fulfill an obligation to society through political participation also involves a general orientation toward public issues and policies rather than interest in a specific problem. The difference Payne wishes to establish between the "moderate" problem-solver (program incentive) and the intransigent militant probably reflects different intensities of commitment, as well as general nonpolitical characteristics of personality, rather than different incentives in political participation.

More important is Payne's assertion that "mixed incentives almost never occur. Political leaders have only one incentive, not combinations of two or more." The evidence adduced in support of this assertion consists of excerpts from interviews, but they were admittedly chosen as illustrations from the totality of reconstructed, i.e., not recorded, interviews. Furthermore, no independent validating criteria were applied (for an example of such validating procedures in incentive studies, see Hofstetter's analysis of the construct "amateurs" discussed in Part II, Section A). Such methodological difficulties are less critical in the identification of strongly contrasting styles, such as "adulation," which refers to the behavior of other actors, and "obligation," which refers to the behavior of the respondent and his own orientation toward his role. When only differences in degree are involved, the researcher is on less safe ground.

Since there appear to be only three or four dominant incentive types in every political culture (and they are not identical cultures), it would be useful to pursue this comparative analysis in order to explore the cultural and structural determinants of incentive patterns, their relative stability, and their impact on recruitment, on individual careers (testing Payne's hypotheses concerning the association between incentives and career patterns in the Dominican Republic), and on systemic outputs.

It is hardly surprising that with such a variety of personality constructs, measuring instruments, and types of political office, motivational studies do not yield conclusive evidence. The only possible exception is a refutation of the assumptions about a modal political personality, but even this conclusion is tentative. It is likely that there is a syndrome of personality traits, which in various combinations are functional in various recruitment situations. One of the least explored areas in this field is a comparison of personality types in recruitment to *different levels of office*. However, that syndrome of personality traits need not be characteristic of politicians alone.

In addition to the problems of cross-situational validation of the meanings of measures of personality needs, the student of recruitment has to address himself to the fact that interviewing and testing political elites, in order to collect information on motivations in a past situation, constitute at best a very difficult research technique. Despite unobtrusive measurements, interviews and tests depend on gaining the respondent's confidence and cooperation, but since politicians are always in the public eye, they are capable of impersonating and do impersonate many different roles in different styles. They resemble dramatic actors, often sharing with them an audience-orientation and a need for applause. Furthermore, politicians are more sensitive to opinions about their personality and work than many other occupational groups. Finally, there is "anticipatory socialization," i.e., the adoption of attitudes believed to be characteristic of an anticipated role in an office for which one intends to run in the future. In the absence of theoretical guidelines and more reliable techniques, it seems advisable to concentrate on the reconstruction of motivation in the recruitment situation, thus focusing on a particular behavioral sequence in a specific environment. This procedure enables the researcher to interpret the information received from his respondents in terms of written records and personal testimonies of other actors involved in the process. To a certain extent, it means adding to the methods of modern social science those of the historian or the biographer.

This approach to motivations in recruitment was used in a study of 45 members of the Israeli legislature (Czudnowski, 1972a), which also introduced levels of office at initial recruitment and ethnic status as filter variables. Dominant orientations toward initial political office displayed a fourfold distribution: material rewards (M); status orientations (S); expressive, ideological orientations (E); and power motivations (P). Eighty-six percent of the high-ethnic-status respondents were included in categories E and P, and seventy-seven percent of the low-ethnic-status respondents displayed M and S orientations in initial recruitment. Furthermore, levels of office at initial recruitment were clearly associated with types of motivations: at the lower levels a predominance of categories M and S; at the higher level, a concentration of the quasi-totality of categories E and P. These findings suggest a correspondence between socioeconomic strata and levels of initial recruitment, mediated by a scale of motivations which reflects the type of rewards political office can offer at each level and the salience of the rewards for different status groups.

F. Selection

Apprenticeship and motivation are necessary conditions for a *potential* political candidacy; it is through the selection process that potential candidates become actual candidates for political office. But among the many eligibles, who are the potential candidates and how does one identify them? These questions refer to what is perhaps the most crucial stage in the recruitment process; it is an informal stage, however, in which different actors take different perspectives in ascribing potential candidacy to different individuals. Aspiring politicians, sponsoring groups, and recruiting agencies do not necessarily agree on who is and who is not a potential candidate. Only in the selection process does it become apparent who has been considered for nomination.

Thus the more institutionalized and the more open the selection process, the easier it is to identify and anticipate selection procedures and criteria which determine the potential sources of recruitment. In the selection process, recruitment is channeled into the institutional infrastructure of politics and government. This infrastructure usually follows the pattern of the formal structure of government, its hierarchy of authority, its territorial subdivisions, and its electoral laws. Within this infrastructure, the selection of candidates follows the pattern of all institutions; i.e., important decisions are made informally by groups of influentials, and ratification is more often a procedural formality. American primary elections, as a selection procedure, are the only exception in this widely observed pattern.

Since party unity has to be reestablished after the factional struggle and bargaining have resulted in a choice, selection agencies are reluctant to disseminate information on the objections raised against the unsuccessful potential candidates. Political scientists have therefore been limited in most cases to observing the structure, mechanism, and some environmental parameters of selection processes and to relating the outcome of selection to these observations. Since political parties are the most important recruiting agencies, more or less detailed descriptions of selection structures and processes can be found in the literature on political parties. Seligman (1967, 1971) has combined these observations into a general model of selection, which is also a systematic conceptualization and statement of the research interests of a student of recruitment in this difficult area.

As mentioned in Part II, Section C, Seligman's basic mapping sentence consists of three questions regarding selection: (1) by whom, (2) according to what criteria, and (3) through what mechanisms? One of the central issues of theoretical interest, which also pervades Seligman's discussion of selection and cuts across structural and procedural criteria, is the *degree of control* the party organization has over eligibility and over criteria of selection among the eligibles. Information on this issue reveals the relationship between the internal party structure, the party system, and the relevant aspects of the social, economic, and cultural environment in which the parties operate. This has been exemplified in Snowiss' (1966) study of congressional recruitment in the Chicago area and in studies of group-oriented recruitment (Seligman, 1964; Valen, 1966; Czudnowski, 1970a).

Answering the first question in the mapping sentence involves a distinction between the roles of parties, interest groups, and other sponsoring or endorsing associations. Interest groups do not just sponsor candidates and thereby participate in the policy input inherent in the recruitment process; they also provide organizational resources, financial contributions, and votes. It is their ability to provide resources and support which enables them to gain influence in the selection process. Consequently, the degree of control parties can maintain is a function of the organizational and ideological linkage—ranging from autonomy to complete integration—between interest groups and parties. Thus political independence associated with an effective organization and material resources increase a group's ability to influence the selection process; however, whether a group can exert such influence over more than one party in the system depends on the ideological or social distance between the parties and on their relative electoral strength. In a noncompetitive situation, a party may not require the additional support provided by the sponsoring group and may prefer a minimum winning coalition.

In his study of legislators in Israel, Seligman (1964) suggests a typology of parties, in terms of their group-orientation in recruitment, based on the structure of the support a party seeks or is able to secure. He distinguishes between populist parties which are the least group-oriented, pluralist parties which represent different types of groups, and sectarian parties which represent primarily one single group. The parties which have been in opposition to the government most of the time are identified by Seligman as populist parties, and the party which has been pivotal in all government coalitions is the most pluralist. The two sectarian parties are the conservative and the labor-oriented factions of the orthodox religious movement; the former has almost continuously opposed the government, whereas the latter supported it frequently.

Sectarian parties which represent only one group necessarily recruit their candidates from among the leadership of the group; the "populist" orientation of the remaining opposition parties in Israel requires an explanation, however. Czudnowski (1970a) suggests that under Israel's relatively noncompetitive party system economic or occupational interest groups have gravitated toward the parties more likely to participate in the governing coalition, thus increasing the pluralism of these parties and narrowing the sources of recruitment of opposition parties. "Populist" opposition parties have therefore become even less group-oriented and have increasingly selected their candidates from among those traditionally or ideologically committed to the party. Thus recruitment has reinforced the pluralism and pragmàtism of the center parties, as well as the rigidity of the opposition.

Another structural criterion of selection is centralization versus decentralization. In this respect party selection seems to be closely related to the electoral system. Where a candidate has to be *elected* by a local or regional constituency, he will tend to be *selected* by the local or regional party organization. In large multimember constituencies, with proportional assignment of seats from party lists, including national party lists, central party organizations have a far greater influence, if not a monopoly, on candidate selection. When selection devolves to local or district branches, various patterns of relationships may prevail between central headquarters and the district.

Ranney's *Pathways to Parliament* (1965) is a detailed inquiry into these relationships in selection of candidates for the British House of Commons. This study, based on interviews with both candidates and recruiting agencies, documents the disparity between the formal powers at the disposal of both the

Conservative and Labour central party institutions (which would enable them to "place," endorse, or veto candidates for parliamentary seats), and the actual practice, according to which the selection power of the local party organization is almost never challenged. The Labour party, however, has attempted to intervene in the local selection process more often than the Conservatives. There are informal processes through which consultation between central and local party organizations takes place, in which the regional "agent"—an official of the central office—often plays an important role.

The two major parties in Britain also differ in terms of the mechanisms through which potential candidates are identified. In the local Conservative association, any member can put forward his name, but preselection lobbying is likely to disqualify him; in the Constituency Labour party, only a body directly affiliated with the party—a ward committee, a local socialist society, or a trade union—can sponsor a candidate, and it is not unusual for campaigns to be conducted for the sponsored candidate prior to the selection conference. Thus candidate selection is controlled to some degree by affiliated organizations and ward committees which grant or withhold nominations.

Another aspect of selection related to sponsorship, on which the two major British parties differ, is campaign financing. The Tories, since their 1949 party reform, have dissociated selection from financial contributions in order to prevent the "purchase of seats," and they assign very low limits to the contributions a candidate can make. The Labour party, however, explicitly expects a sponsoring trade union or cooperative society to bear the major financial burden of the campaign and contribute to the local party funds. This difference between the parties may be a result of the fact that until the broadening of the social base of the Labour party under the leadership of Hugh Gaitskell and especially of Harold Wilson, Labour and Tories drew their electoral and financial support from distinct social strata which differed considerably in ability to provide for the financial needs of their party on an individual rather than an organizational basis.

The great heterogeneity and the loose articulation of the American parties, combined with the openness of the primary elections as a selection method, are also reflected in the mechanics of the processes which lead to formal selection. Seligman's (1961) study of candidate selection for the lower house of the state legislature in four districts in Oregon is the first empirical investigation of the relationship between selection patterns and party structure. Hypothesizing that the competitiveness of the district would be the major variable structuring the selection process, Seligman compared a predominantly Democratic district, one that was predominantly Republican, and two competitive districts and found the following pattern of party intervention in instigating and supporting candidates for the 1958 primaries. (1) In areas safe for the majority party, party officials were *least* active in recruiting candidates, and various groups and individuals were free to promote candidacies. However, this inactivity may have resulted from the fact that a great number of safe incumbents were filing again. In safe Democratic districts factionalism played a more important role than in safe Republican districts. (2) The minority party, in districts safe for the majority, had to conscript candidates, and recruitment was completely *central-ized* by the party. (3) In competitive districts, the candidate "market" was wide open, and factions played an important role in initiating and supporting candidacies. The competitiveness of the district did not bring about greater party cohesion or centralization of recruitment. Thus centralization prevailed only in the minority parties in districts dominated by the majority party, al-though there was more frequent reliance on party-instigated recruitment among Democrats, and a greater intervention of interest groups and other associations in the selection of Republican candidates.

Patterson and Boynton (1969) have documented this aspect of the selection process in Iowa by inquiring into interpersonal contacts for recruitment pur-poses between county party chairmen $(N = 90)$, legislators $(N = 181)$, lob-byists $(N = 99)$, and the "attentive constituents," i.e., the politically active stratum in the legislators' constituencies $(N = 484)$. Party leaders reported the highest frequencies of both "being contacted by potential candidates" and "suggesting candidacies," but about one-half of the attentive constituents also reported a considerable share in these contacts. The legislators confirmed that initiating and supporting candidacies for the state legislature constituted a widely diffuse process within the active stratum. They reported that they had been contacted to run by local businessmen (58 percent), county party chair-men (56 percent), former legislators (45 percent), and local public officials (43 percent). Lobbyists ranked very low on this scale. Many more Republi-cans than Democrats had been contacted by businessmen and publishers of local newspapers.

In general, urban party leaders are more involved in recruitment than rural party chairmen, but rural Democratic leaders in Iowa—with the excep-tion of those in safe districts—made greater efforts to recruit candidates than their urban counterparts. Controlling for the competitiveness of the district reveals that more recruitment activity is reported in competitive districts by party leaders, legislators, and attentive constituents alike. However, Demo-cratic party leaders reported the highest recruitment activity in the most Demo-cratic districts, thus contradicting Seligman's findings in Oregon.

No similar information is available for the selection of congressional can-didates. A study of career paths to the U.S. House of Representatives between 1949 and 1967 revealed that about two-thirds of all Congressmen had held at least one major political office at the state or local level, and about 25 percent of all Congressmen had held two positions (Mezey, 1970). This information does not include unsuccessful congressional candidates. Previously held posi-tions at the state or local level probably provide a frequent point of departure for both party-sponsored and self-initiated potential candidacies for Congress.

Thirty-six percent of all congressmen had held no previous public office, but Mezey does not report whether they had held important party positions; they need not have been inexperienced political amateurs, as this study seems to suggest. This is confirmed by Fishel's (1973) recently published study of congressional challengers in 1964. Among these challengers, 62 percent of the Democrats and 70 percent of the Republicans had held party positions at the national, state, or local level. Previous public office experience had been considerably less frequent: 50 percent among Democrats and only 40 percent among Republicans (Fishel, 1973, p. 50).

Criteria of eligibility for potential political candidacy have been studied more frequently than criteria for the selection of candidates. Barber's (1965) discussion of the selection process in several typical examples of "reluctants," "spectators," "advertisers," and "legislators" in the Connecticut state legislature provides some insights into criteria of selection in recruitment situations. The situations are described in terms of environmental characteristics and the probability of winning. "The "reluctant" comes from a small rural town where social roles overlap and social contacts are narrow and continuous. Politics is not serious, the choice is between individuals, not parties or groups, and "there are prizes enough for everyone." Incumbents are often reelected, and when they retire from office, they often pick their successors. The main criterion of selection seems to be avoidance of conflict: The candidate has lived in his town for the greater part of his lifetime, has been involved in many social roles, and is known by practically everybody. The "reluctants" are old or early-retired men, who see in politics "a chance to demonstrate that they are still important."

"Spectators" are recruited more often in middle-sized towns. In the minority party, they are the members of the party committee, who rotate for nomination to the various offices they cannot hope to win unless they happen to benefit from the coattails of a race for a higher office. The majority party seeks a candidate who will "not only run but also serve." The retiring incumbent tends to select a candidate "whom he considers safe, friendly and persuasible." He may be "short on competence for political leadership" but " long on availability and . . . on caution, tact and loyalty." Generally apolitical and unambitious, he is flattered by the honor of becoming an insider.

"Advertisers" are recruited predominantly from middle-sized and large towns. The selection criterion is not to fill the ticket but to strengthen it in an expanding and politically competitive community. Hence the preference for a candidate of relatively high socioeconomic status with special training or achievements.

Finally, the "lawmakers" are also recruited predominantly in middle-sized and larger towns and share many of the socioeconomic characteristics of the "advertisers." The partisan setting is competitive, and when both parties nominate well-qualified candidates, the recruiters need an additional criterion to increase the winnability of a legislative seat. In the case of the "lawmakers" it is an issue orientation: "a candidate who can handle not only the supermarket handshaking tour but also the neighborhood political tea party," a candidate who satisfies the increasing demand of the issue-oriented participants within the party. He is politically motivated and has worked in civic organizations.

This summary of Barber's profiles indicates that *criteria of selection, as a function of the opportunity structure, will vary* from one setting to another. For purposes of comparability and theoretical generalization, the major variable in the analysis of selection is therefore the degree of control the party can exercise over eligibility and over criteria of selection. In fact, the mechanisms of selection—cooptation, conscription, agency (interest-group representation), and self-selection—reflect fairly well, in decreasing order of magnitude, a party's degree of control over the selection process. Patterson and Boynton (1969) have conceptualized the "recruitment culture" as a continuum ranging from party centralization (associated with material rewards) to self-recruitment (associated with status anxiety and ambition); they consider the recruitment of state legislators as characterized by a mixed and diffuse civic culture and by a variety of motivational syndromes.

Outside the United States, where no primary elections are held, parties have complete control over eligibility and selection. Of course, they cannot disregard the constraints of an electoral situation, although some Constituency Labour parties in Britain, not unlike the 1964 supporters of the Goldwater candidacy in the United States, claim that "it is better to lose with a true believer than win with an agnostic" (Ranney, 1965). Ideology is indeed one of the few criteria which distinguish between Labour and Conservatives in terms of *professed* principles of selection. Labour's National Executive Committee has vetoed the candidacies of several left-wingers, but the local party organizations and the sponsoring trade unions do not seem to be very much concerned with the "correctness" of a candidate's views on the issues of the moment if he has given substantial service to the party or the sponsoring organization. Unlike the Conservatives, the Labour party considers service and loyalty to the party as the major criterion of selection, next only, perhaps, to the man's "personal qualities," although precisely what is meant by desirable personal qualities seems to vary from place to place. Ranney believes, contrary to a widely held assumption, that local Labour and Tory activists "choose men they think will make *better* candidates than themselves, better because they have more education, and have the skills and demeanor that better equip them to represent the party before the public. For they . . . know they are choosing the party's leaders." It is likely, given the nature of the British parliamentary and party systems, that these criteria of selection are more typical in British party organizations than in the loosely articulated parties in the United States.

Although the selection process in the British parties assigns the final responsibility to relatively large bodies,[10] not more than a small minority of activists, together with the elected party officials, participate in the selection process.

Liberal estimates of the proportion of Conservative members participating regularly in party activities range between 3 and 7 percent, and the full membership of the Labour Management Committee comprises between 10 and 15 percent of the local party members, but only a minority of delegates appear and vote in the selection of candidates. Their meetings are never like those in the closed and smoke-filled rooms of the city-machine bosses, but the evidence clearly confirms that, irrespective of how the recruiting agents convene and decide, whether according to hierarchically controlled or according to wide-open criteria, only a small minority of party officials and regular activists participate in the final stages of candidate recruitment.

Continuity of service seems to be a requirement of the functional specialization inherent in the political division of labor, but only a few can or care to satisfy this requirement. The social base and the ideological orientation of a party determine whether this minority of activists is a cross-section of most if not all segments of the constituency, or a coalition of specific strata or interest groups.[11] However, even within this minority of activists, the full-time or continuously active party officials are in a far better position to control the selection process than the part-time activists. Since there are fewer full-time professional politicians in the loosely articulated organizations of the middle-class parties than there are in the Socialist or Marxist labor parties, the party chairman of a local British Conservative association or a district chairman of the German Christian Democrat Union has probably greater personal influence on the selection process than his counterpart in the British Labour or the German Social Democratic party. Yet, given the party discipline in both the House of Commons and the Bundestag, this difference in styles of recruitment may be of little consequence. What seems to vary between the parties is the concern for intraparty relationships, as opposed to an interest in gaining or maintaining the support of outer groups (Beyme, 1971).

One of the few studies which inquire systematically into *criteria of selection* is Valen's report on interviews with 149 local party leaders in the Stavanger area in southwestern Norway in 1957 (Valen, 1966). Asked what qualities they would require of the nominees to the party list, the leaders of the various parties expressed different preferences. All Conservative and almost all Center party leaders most frequently mentioned the candidate's *political and professional competence* and visibility, but only about 60 percent of the Liberals and Christian People's party leaders and only 41 percent of the Labor leaders shared this opinion. *Moral qualities,* such as honesty and reliability, were emphasized only by the Liberals, and Labor leaders mentioned *party loyalty and experience* far more frequently than did the leaders of any other party. This seems to be characteristic of all European labor parties. Only the Christian People's party and the Center party emphasized a group-oriented representativeness of the nominee. However, when the leaders were asked to explain why each of the five top candidates on their respective lists had been selected, the second most frequent response in *all* parties was the *representation of group interests.* Even in the Labor party, firmness of conviction and party loyalty were less frequently mentioned than the representation of group interests. This finding, however, should not be interpreted as referring to mutually exclusive criteria. Group representation, especially with reference to trade unions, easily coincides with party loyalty and ideological commitment.

Discussing the findings of selection studies in the German Federal Republic, Beyme (1971) cites two differences in selection criteria for the Bundestag between CDU and SPD: the emphasis on group representation in the CDU and on younger age groups in the SPD. In both parties the potential candidate has strong local ties (whereas in Britain only about one-third of all candidates have local connections). Beyme notes that the subordinate role of personal qualities and adequacy for parliamentary office as selection criteria is a consequence of the increasing power of party machines. Occupational qualifications and prestige are apparently of greater importance, because they can be identified and evaluated more easily by the district selection committee. Group support is a central criterion; in the SPD the groups are intraparty organizations, and in the CDU they are functional interest groups and the youth movement affiliated with the party. There is hardly any intervention from central party headquarters, but regional connections are instrumental for obtaining the nomination. A strong localist orientation prevails, and local connections are both personal and institutional. (One-half of all candidates nominated in districts had held local political offices, and 19 to 25 percent had held seats in the state legislature, the Landtag; one-half had been district party chairmen, and no one who had not been at least a local party chairman was likely to be considered.)

This localist orientation, which is unlikely to promote individuals with a desire or ability to advance within the parliamentary party in Bonn, is counterbalanced only to a certain extent by the fact that one-half of the Bundestag is elected from party lists, which supplement the number of district seats won by each party according to proportional representation. Few candidates who were not also nominated in their districts have been allotted reasonably safe rankings on the list. The list is a safety device for the state or national leadership of the party, as well as a means for "balancing" a ticket by adding interest-group representatives or by increasing the number of women, who have less chances of winning local nomination. It should be of great interest for students of recruitment to observe more closely the workings of the dual selection system in the German Federal Republic.

It has already been pointed out that where the list system is not combined with direct personal candidacies, there is an even stronger group orientation in the selection of candidates. Under the list system, the occupational, ethnic, or other relevant socioeconomic characteristics of candidates are criteria of group eligibility rather than personal selection. When a group becomes eligible for representation, additional criteria have to be applied in the selection of candidates; these may be ascriptive or achievement-oriented, but achievement can refer either to party service or to nonpolitical community action and other highly valued activities. That sociocultural variables have different meanings for group eligibility and personal selection has been demonstrated in a study of low-status immigrant recruitment in Israel (Czudnowski, 1970a).

In a recent study of the impact of electoral systems on the representativeness of selection outcomes, Goodman, Swanson, and Cornwell (1970) concluded that, given provisions for popular election of some sort, outcomes are similar, regardless of structural differences. From a macroperspective on aggregate outcomes, this evaluation appears to be fairly accurate; from the perspective of the candidate, the structure of the selection process, the number of stages, and the degree of control available to the actors or factors involved at each stage are central variables determining sources and chances of selection. One should add, however, that considering selection systems as independent variables leads to descriptive analyses of little theoretical relevance. Selection systems serve political purposes; they are adopted for political purposes and can be changed for political purposes. The rigidity of selection systems is itself a politically relevant cultural variable, which should focus attention on recruitment systems as indicators of rewards—or of access to the distribution of rewards—in the context of those values which are the object of collective action in any given political system.

Nonpartisan politics at the local government level have been examined primarily in terms of the representativeness of the electoral system. Nonpartisan elections were intended to force voters to concentrate on the personal qualifications and credentials of individual candidates, rather than on party cues. As a consequence, nonpartisan elections gave an advantage to the higher socioeconomic strata. Prewitt's (1970) recruitment study of city councilmen in the San Francisco Bay area and the Prewitt and Eulau (1969, 1971) studies of the effect of sponsorship and of the electoral context on leadership selection are the only systematic attempts to identify the major modalities of selection in a nonpartisan setting. The main findings of these studies have been reported in Part II, Section C, and Part III, Sections B and C. What remain to be added are some of the findings more closely related to candidate selection. Thus 25 percent of the councilmen had originally been appointed to their offices, almost 60 percent of the elected and 72 percent of those initially appointed had known incumbents well before becoming themselves members of the council, and for more than 20 percent of the total, an incumbent councilman had been instrumental in initiating the future candidate's activity in politics. One-half of the originally appointed and 40 percent of the elected councilmen had served as members of auxiliary government commissions. Thus *cooptation* appears to be one of the major modalities of selection in this nonpartisan setting. Furthermore, incumbents are not often challenged; 80 percent of both originally appointed and originally elected incumbents are reelected, and vacancies occur frequently through voluntary retirement.

Appointment and cooptation are selection methods that can serve three different purposes: (1) ensuring like-minded successors; (2) coopting spokesmen of dissident groups; and (3) building coalitions. Some of these purposes may overlap. One of the few black councilmen in the San Francisco Bay area was appointed to forestall the election of a more militant black. By limiting the sources of recruitment to like-minded members of the politically active stratum from which the incumbents themselves have been recruited, appointment and cooptation ensure continuity in city politics.

In partisan settings political parties provide opportunities for apprenticeship and perform the function of recruiting agents. In the nonpartisan city politics in the San Francisco Bay area, the first of these functions devolves to civic organizations and auxiliary government, the second—in most cases—to the incumbent officeholders. How appointment and cooptation affect the responsiveness of city government cannot be inferred from Prewitt's study, but it is likely that the electorate supports these selection strategies only so long as the issues of city government and politics do not reflect community cleavages along the same lines of differentiation that account for the non-representativeness of the governing elites (Czudnowski, 1972b).

IV. CONCLUSION: A RESEARCHABLE MODEL FOR THE STUDY OF RECRUITMENT

The preceding review and discussion of research findings illustrate the fact that—significant exceptions notwithstanding—empirical research and empirical theorizing have addressed themselevs to different stages of the recruitment process, and that both long-term and short-term perspectives have been predicated on postdictive, i.e., inverted, research designs. A multistage and multivariate model is difficult to handle, especially in a subfield of the discipline which is still in search of a basic theoretical framework. Specific career patterns and differential sources of recruitment between parties are important subjects for research; however, they cannot lead to a theory capable of distinguishing—within the category of political actives—between those who will and those who will not become potential candidates for political office. Using an inverted research design, i.e., a design which begins to investigate recruitment *after* the process has been completed, instead of observing recruitment as an ongoing process, is a consequence of the absence of a guiding theory which would point to critical stages and critical control groups in the recruitment process. A longitudinal research design is necessarily unrealistic. Concentrating on the situation immediately preceding initial recruitment into continuous or full-time politics could increase researchability without any loss of the input of personality factors and previous socialization (Czudnowski, 1970b; Beyme, 1971).

Political candidates are not recruited from an undifferentiated mass of politically involved citizens. The concept of "apprenticeship positions" combines two sets of variables: a personality structure compatible with occupations or positions that share the role profile of political office, and a location in the social structure that is characterized by both proximity to political decision-making centers and a control over recruitment-relevant resources. The major task of a theory of recruitment, therefore, seems to be the identification of the recruitment-relevant apprenticeship positions. These positions could of course vary from system to system or culture to culture; furthermore, there probably are "lateral entrants" in most recruitment systems. However, the role of this theory would be to posit and demonstrate the common dimensions of apprenticeship positions across systems, and to explain the conditions under which lateral entrance is possible.

Political recruitment is more likely to occur (a) when *personality* structure is politically functional; (b) when *social position* is recruitment-relevant; (c) when *politics* is personally and socially salient. This mapping sentence for a theory of recruitment reflects the distinction between three perspectives, but no assumption is made about their interdependence or independence of each other. The empirically oriented theorist who seeks a point of departure for recruitment research and theory would then ask himself: in which of these three frames of reference has empirical theory made greater advances, and which is more easily researchable? At the time of writing, there can be little doubt that the answer to both questions is social position, given the more rapid development of social psychology as an empirical science, which was itself a consequence of research accessibility. The political recruitment-relevance of social positions has not been investigated empirically; only aggregate data on the previous occupations of politicians are available, and theory has been concentrated on social stratification systems or on skills. In the mapping sentence above, "social position" refers to a *sociopsychological profile,* not to rank on one of the conventional scales of education, income, or status. Occupational sociology has shown that certain role-profile characteristics are indeed associated with higher ranks in the hierarchy of status or income, but for recruitment theory the role profile itself is more relevant. In a modern pluralistic society the politician is a member of the "talking classes"—his role profile includes *ability to deal with people* and abstract *ideas* or data and to handle complex situations. Politicians are therefore likely to be recruited from social positions with sociopsychological profiles matching these requirements.

There are many occupational roles with a similar sociopsychological profile, but some of them require more specialization than others. Mitscherlich (1967) advances the thesis that "the truly modern form of authority is that of the specialist." Is the role profile of the politician that of a specialist? It is true that with the growing intervention of government in many areas of life, specialists—for example, in the area of economics or managment—are increasingly drawn into political life. The example of management suggests, however, that specialization and complexity are two different dimensions: Management theory and practice apply to almost every area of organization. Complex is the opposite of simple, and special or specific is the opposite of general. The special-general dimension is not Parsons's specific-diffuse variable; a generalist orientation implies a synthesis of several specific attitudes or categories, whereas diffuseness implies the absence of specific categories. It is true that the processes of social and occupational specialization have been the result of an increasing complexity of relationships, of needs, and of problems, and a specialist is assumed to have mastered the complexity of issues or techniques *in a given substantive area.* Thus specialization implies complex activities. However, not all complex operations imply a specialist orientation. Management is associated with *complex operations* and a *generalist orientation.* "Political functions consist in the mobilization and integration of resources for the achievement of goals. The integration of a highly diversified and specialized infrastructure requires a highly complex organization. Political roles are leadership roles in this organization. The integrative aspect of these roles accounts for both their *generalist orientation* and the *complexity of the operations* involved." (Czudnowski, 1970b) The professionalization of politics requires a specialization in terms of skills, but not of goal orientation.

The criteria of dealing with people and data, of handling complex operations, and the ability to subordinate them to a generalist orientation have introduced some specificity into the description of sociopsychological profiles of political roles and have reduced the number and variety of social positions with similar profiles from which politicians are likely to be recruited. Adding two further filter variables: The distinction between thinkers and doers (which would exclude from "recruitment-relevant positions" most professors of political science) and a distinction between business (or self) and social orientation reduce the possible sources of recruitment even further.

However, the similarity of occupational role profiles is not a sufficient condition for the recruitment relevance of a social position. The literature on political recruitment often distinguishes between self-starters and sponsored candidates. It would be more accurate to consider the self-starter as a self-assigned image. Seligman (1961) pointed out some time ago that "candidate entry in the primaries, with rare exceptions, is a *group enterprise.* More commonly, the so-called self-generated entrepreneurial candidate has a network of social relationships. He often activates politically some members of this network, but he relies heavily on their support to bolster his political aspirations." A recruitment theory would posit that candidacies originate in central linkage positions in a communication network (Czudnowski, 1970b, Beyme, 1971). Communication and organization research demonstrated many years ago that a central location in a communication network ipso facto facilitates the performance of leadership roles (Bavelas, 1951; Berkowitz, 1965; Glanzer and

Glaser, 1965). In organization research "attention has traditionally been paid to the communication net involved in the exercise of authority relations within organizations" (Guetzkow, 1965). It seems that the conditions facilitating the emergence of leadership in small groups correspond closely to the structural requisites of political recruitment in larger societies, because the analysis of initial candidacies almost invariably leads back to an identifiable and relatively small group. When initial recruitment occurs at high levels of office, intensive previous exposure to the mass media in nonpolitical roles is frequently a functional equivalent of a core group of supporters (e.g., military commanders, famous actors, or writers).

A "critical linkage position in a communication network" can be defined as one involving a certain degree of *control* over the flow and distribution of information. The control of information is generally a source of influence but does not necessarily imply power, authority, or leadership. However, it is a structural-functional facilitator in the development of social leadership relations.[12] The relevance of such critical linkage positions in political recruitment derives from the fact that claims to political authority or leadership can emerge either from linkage positions or from positions of social leadership, which are usually associated with linkage positions in communication networks. "Social power which cannot put forward a claim to social leadership and is not associated with a critical linkage position, is less likely to be used as a manifest base for a claim to political authority" (Czudnowski, 1970b).

These explorations of the recruitment relevance of social positions suggest that statement (b) in the mapping sentence of recruitment theory offers a fertile ground for research and theory, which could lead to theoretical propositions about statements (a) and (c). A dimension of participation (e.g., in the activities of a political party) would not only relate the personal and social salience of politics—statement (c)—to the structural parameters of statement (b) but also provide an additional filter variable for the operational definition of an *experimental group* in a recruitment research design focusing on the observation of potential political candidates. Similarly, an experimental group of this kind could be compared to a *control group* matched on role profiles and social position but consisting of politically noninvolved individuals, in order to explore difference in personality structure.

The findings and generalizations of such microtheoretically oriented research could then be integrated into a model allowing for environmental or opportunity-structure variables: competitiveness, party structure and party system, and stable versus crisis recruitment. Studies of *crisis recruitment,* such as Dogan's demonstration of the effects of the Resistance in post–World War II recruitment in France and of de Gaulle's charismatic impact on legislative candidacies in 1962 (Dogan, 1961; 1965), Legg's (1969) study of recruitment in Greece, and Ludz's (1968) documentation of the transformations of East German elites are instances of aggregate analyses demonstrating the effects of discontinuities in the prevailing political norms concerning sources of recruitment. How such discontinuities affect the motivations and the structural-functional prerequisites of recruitment is a question which cannot be answered in the absence of a microtheory of recruitment and selection. The development of this microtheory is, therefore, the first item on the agenda of recruitment research, for which a researchable model has been delineated in the concluding section of this chapter.

NOTES

1. A study of 118 members of Democratic ward and township organizations in St. Louis (Salisbury, 1965–66) suggests, however, that in some large cities the party is more impervious to amateur politics than in others. The St. Louis activists and club members do not fit into either the amateur or the professional model. Issue orientations do not seem to be very relevant to political participation, and family influence looms very large as the initial stimulus to participation, which is habitual rather than purposive. Forty percent are women, but educational levels are closer to those of the professionals, and in occupational profiles the St. Louis activists are somewhere between the professionals and the amateurs. Fourteen percent held patronage jobs, but only six percent gave this as a reason for joining the club. Another 30 percent had held temporary patronage jobs at various times. No explanation is offered for the absence of an "amateur" counterelite in the St. Louis setting, and this issue will not be pursued here.

2. For an analysis of political behavior in terms of Maslow's hierarchy of needs, see Davies (1963) and Knutsen (1972). Payne (1972; Payne and Woshinsky, 1972) has operationalized the attitudinal and stylistic components of a similar typology of incentives, which will be discussed in the section on motivations in Part III of this chapter.

3. Factionalism and interest groups have generally been studied from the viewpoint of party power structures, representation, and policy inputs. Zariski (1960) examined factions comparatively and pointed at the difference in the nature and stability of factions between caucus parties and branch parties and at the relationship between changing social structures and factionalism. Nicholson (1972a, 1972b) has recently developed a typology of factional patterns and examined the role of intraparty factions in the career patterns of members of the Council of Ministers in India. He indicates that although factional recruitment reflects a lack of stable and formalized recruitment procedures (i.e., cooptation), it performs the adaptive function of a linkage in the mobilization of support and the distribution of policy outputs between local, state and central government, a function that elites recruited "at large" can not perform very successfully. Given the particularistic nature of functionalism and cooptation and the lack of comparative empirical studies of factional recruitment, the conditions and criteria of factional recruitment have remained largely unexplored.

4. In the Boynton, Patterson, and Hedlund study of Iowa state legislators, the only overrepresented occupational category among officeholders, as opposed to attentive constituents, was farmers, but very few of these legislators actually resided on farms.

5. These figures refer to those who had changed their party identification twice. The mean age for first and only change was 25 in Canada and 23.5 in the United States.

6. In this population of councilmen elected in nonpartisan elections, the "politically socialized" accounted for 85 percent of the 8 percent minority of councilmen who were ushered into the active stratum from partisan roles.

7. Although the techniques used (i.e., direct questions in more or less structured interviews) are not very reliable, this is the only type of available evidence relating to motivations for initial involvement. Personality inventories and thematic apperception tests used in recruitment studies refer to personality variables and are discussed in Part III, Section E.

8. See also the findings reported in the discussion of amateurs and professionals in Part II, Section A.

9. The role of the lawyer in black recruitment probably differs considerably from that of the nonblack lawyer, with the exception of lawyers in law-enforcement positions.

10. A meeting of all members of the local Conservative association, and the General Management Committee of the local Labour party, subject only to the endorsement of the National Executive Committee.

11. Ranney has recently shown that even in the American presidential primaries (between 1948 and 1968), the average turnout of voters was only 27 percent, compared with an average of 62 percent in the ensuing general presidential elections, and that the party-identifying primary participants in the two states he examined in greater detail—New Hampshire and Wisconsin—differed considerably from their nonparticipating fellow partisans on a number of socioeconomic dimensions and other measures of representativeness. See Austin Ranney, "Turnout and representation in a presidential primary elections," *American Political Science Review*, 64 (1972): 21–37.

12. Some evidence of the relative advantage associated with *political* linkage positions has been presented by Marvick (1970). Using a communication model of political parties, Marvick describes the role of key linkage figures in the transmission and interpretation of messages between the "remote" upper echelons and local "outpost" activists in the 1967 general election campaign in India. Marvick also reports that linkage cadres have a consistent edge over the "remote" upper echelons and even more so over the "outpost" activists in terms of college education, professional occupations, public office-holding, and full-time party offices.

REFERENCES

Adelson, Joseph, and Robert P. O'Neil (1966). "Growth of political ideas in adolescence: the sense of community." *Journal of Personality and Social Psychology* 4:295–306.

Almond, Gabriel A. (1960). "A functional approach to comparative politics." In Gabriel A. Almond and James S. Coleman (eds.), *The Politics of the Developing Area*. Princeton: Princeton University Press.

_____ (1965). "A developmental approach to political systems." *World Politics* 17:183–214.

Althoff, Phillip, and Samuel C. Patterson (1966). "Political activism in a rural county." *Midwest Journal of Political Science* 10:37–51.

Barber, James D. (1965). *The Lawmakers*. New Haven: Yale University Press.

_____ (1972). *The Presidential Character*. Englewood Cliffs, N.J.: Prentice-Hall.

Barth, Ernest, and Baha Abu-Laban (1959). "Power structure and the Negro sub-community." *American Sociological Review* 24:69–76.

Bavelas, A. (1951). "Communication patterns in task-oriented groups." In Daniel Lerner and Harold D. Lasswell (eds.), *The Policy Sciences*. Stanford, Cal.: Stanford University Press.

Berkowitz, L. (1965). "Personality and group position." In A. P. Hare, E. F. Borgatta, and R. F. Bales (eds.), *Small Groups*. New York: Knopf.

Berrington, H. B., and S. E. Finer (1967). "United Kingdom: the House of Commons." In *Decisions and Decision-Makers in the Modern State*. Paris: UNESCO.

Beyme, Klaus von (1971). *Die Politische Elite in der Bundesrepublik Deutschland*. Munich: Piper.

Black, Gordon S. (1970). "A theory of professionalization in politics." *American Political Science Review* 64:865–78.

——————— (1972). "A theory of political ambition: career choices and the role of structural incentives." *American Political Science Review* 66:144–59.

Bochel, J. M. (1966). "The recruitment of local councillors: a case study." *Political Studies* 14:360–4.

Bowles, B. Dean (1966). "Local government participation as a route of recruitment to the state legislature in California and Pennsylvania, 1900–1962." *Western Political Quarterly* 19:491–503.

Bowman, Lewis, and G. R. Boynton (1966). "Recruitment patterns among local party officials: a model and some preliminary findings in selected locales." *American Political Science Review* 60:667–76.

Boynton, G. R., Samuel C. Patterson, and Ronald D. Hedlund (1969). "The missing link in legislative politics: attentive constituents." *Journal of Politics* 31:700–21.

Browning, Rufus P. (1968). "The interaction of personality and political system in decisions to run for office: some data and a simulation technique." *Journal of Social Issues* 24:93–109.

Browning, Rufus P., and Herbert Jacob (1964). "Power motivation and the political personality." *Public Opinion Quarterly* 28:75–90.

Bryce, James (1894). *The American Commonwealth*. New York: Macmillan.

Buck, Philip W. (1963). *Amateurs and Professionals in British Politics*. Chicago: University of Chicago Press.

Bullit, Stimson (1959). *To Be a Politician*. Garden City, N.Y.: Doubleday.

Campbell, Angus, Philip E. Converse, Warren E. Miller, and Donald E. Stokes (1960). *The American Voter*. New York: Wiley.

Clark, Peter B., and James Q. Wilson (1961). "Incentive systems. A theory of organizations." *Administrative Science Quarterly* 6:134–7.

Clubok, Alfred B., Norman M. Wilensky, and Forrest J. Berghorn (1969). "Family relationships. Congressional recruitment and political modernization." *Journal of Politics* 31:1035–62.

Cohn-Bendit, Daniel, and Gabriel Cohn-Bendit (1968). *Obsolete Communism: The Left-Wing Alternative*. London: André Deutsch.

Conway, M. Margaret, and Frank B. Feigert (1968). "Motivation, incentive systems, and the political party organization." *American Political Science Review* 62:1159–73.

Cornwell, Elmer E., Jr. (1960). "Party absorption of ethnic groups: the case of Providence, Rhode Island." *Social Forces* 38:205-10.

Cotter, Cornelius P., and Bernard C. Hennessy (1964). *Politics Without Power.* New York: Atherton Press.

Czudnowski, Moshe M. (1968). "A salience dimension of politics for the study of political culture." *American Political Science Review* 62:878–88.

_____ (1970a). "Legislative recruitment under proportional representation in Israel: a model and a case study." *Midwest Journal of Political Science* 14:216–48.

_____ (1970b). "Toward a new research strategy for the comparative study of political recruitment." *International Political Science Association.* Eighth World Congress, Munich.

_____ (1972a). "Sociocultural variables and legislative recruitment." *Comparative Politics* 4:561–87.

_____ (1972b). Review of K. Prewitt, *The Recruitment of Political Leaders: A Study of Citizen Politicians. American Political Science Review* 66.

_____ (1975). *Comparing Political Behavior.* Chicago: Aldine-Atherton.

Davies, James C. (1963). *Human Nature and Politics.* New York: Wiley.

DiRenzo, Gordon (1967). *Personality, Power and Politics.* Notre Dame, Ind.: University of Notre Dame Press.

Dogan, Mattei (1961). "Political ascent in a class society: French deputies 1870–1958." In Dwaine Marvick (ed.), *Political Decision-Makers.* Glencoe, Ill.: Free Press.

_____ (1965). "Le personnel politique et la personalité charismatique." *Revue française de Sociologie* 6:305–24.

_____ (1967). "Les filières de la carrière politique en France." *Revue française de Sociologie* 8:468–92.

Dye, Thomas R. (1965). "State legislative politics." In Herbert Jacob and Kenneth Vines (eds.), *Politics in the American States.* Boston: Little, Brown.

Edinger, Lewis J. (1960). "Post-totalitarian leadership: elites in the German Federal Republic." *American Political Science Review* 54:58–82.

Edinger, Lewis J., and Donald D. Searing (1967). "Social background in elite analysis: a methodological inquiry." *American Political Science Review* 61:428–45.

Eisenstadt, S. N. (1956). *From Generation to Generation.* Glencoe, Ill.: Free Press.

_____ (1967). *Israeli Society.* London: Weidenfeld and Nicolson.

Eldersveld, Samuel J. (1964). *Political Parties. A Behavioral Analysis.* Chicago: Rand McNally.

Epstein, Leon (1958). *Politics in Wisconsin.* Madison: University of Wisconsin Press.

_____ (1967). *Political Parties in Western Democracies.* New York: Praeger.

Erikson, Erik (1950). *Childhood and Society.* New York: Norton.

Eulau, Heinz, William Buchanan, Leroy Ferguson, and John C. Wahlke (1959). "The political socialization of American state legislators." *Midwest Journal of Political Science* 3:188–206.

Eulau, Heinz, and David Koff (1962). "Occupational mobility and political career." *Western Political Quarterly* 15:507–21.

Eulau, Heinz, and John D. Sprague (1964). *Lawyers in Politics.* Indianapolis: Bobbs-Merrill.

Feld, Richard D., and Donald S. Lutz (1972). "Recruitment in the Houston city council." *Journal of Politics* 34:924–33.

Fiellin, Alan (1967). "Recruitment and legislative role conceptions: a conceptual scheme and a case study." *Western Political Quarterly* 20: 271–87.

Fishel, Jeff (1972). "Parliamentary candidates and party professionalism in Western Germany." *Western Political Quarterly* 25:64–80.

_____ (1973). *Party and Opposition.* New York: McKay.

Forster, John (1969). "A note on the background of parliamentarians." *Political Science* 21:42–7.

Frey, Frederick W. (1965). *The Turkish Political Elite.* Cambridge, Mass.: M.I.T. Press.

George, Alexander (1968). "Power as a compensatory value for political leaders." *Journal of Social Issues* 24:29–49.

Gerth, H. H., and C. Wright Mills (1958). *From Max Weber.* New York: Oxford University Press.

Glanzer, M., and R. Glaser (1965). "Techniques for the study of group structure and behavior: empirical studies of the effects of structure in small groups." In A. P. Hare, E. F. Borgatta, and R. F. Bales (eds.), *Small Groups.* New York: Knopf.

Glick, Henry Robert (1966). "Political recruitment in Sarawak: a case study in a new state." *Journal of Politics* 28:81–99.

Goodman, Jay S., Wayne R. Swanson, and Elmer E. Cornwell (1970). "Political recruitment in four selection systems." *Western Political Quarterly* 23:92–103.

Greenstein, Fred I. (1968). "Political socialization." In *International Encyclopedia of the Social Sciences.* New York: Macmillan and Free Press.

_____ (1969). *Personality and Politics.* Chicago: Markham.

_____ (1970a). *The American Party System and the American People,* 2nd edition. Englewood Cliffs, N. J.: Prentice-Hall.

_____ (1970b). "A note on the ambiguity of 'political socialization': definitions, criticisms and strategies of inquiry." *Journal of Politics* 32:969–78.

_____ (1970c). Review of Gordon J. DiRenzo, *Personality, Power and Politics. Political Science Quarterly* 85:365–8.

_____ (1973). "Political psychology: a pluralistic universe." In Jeanne N. Knutson (ed.), *The Handbook of Political Psychology.* San Francisco: Jossey-Bass.

Guetzkow, Harold (1965). "Communication in organizations." In James March (ed.), *Handbook of Organizations.* Chicago: Rand McNally.

Guttsman, W. L. (1963). *The British Political Elite.* New York: Basic Books.

Hacker, Andrew (1961). "The elected and the anointed: two American elites." *American Political Science Review* 55:539–49.

Hennessy, B. (1959). "Politicals and apoliticals: some measurements of personality traits." *Midwest Journal of Political Science* 3:336–55.

Herzog, Dietrich (1970). "The structure of elites in post-war German political parties." In *Transactions of the Sixth World Congress of Sociology.* Geneva: International Sociological Association.

Hess, Stephen (1966). *America's Political Dynasties.* Garden City, N.Y.: Doubleday.

Hirshfield, Robert S., Bert E. Swanson, and Blanche D. Blank (1962). "A profile of political activists in Manhattan." *Western Political Quarterly* 15:489–506.

Hofstetter, Richard C. (1971). "The amateur politician: a problem in construct validation." *Midwest Journal of Political Science* 15:31–56.

Hyman, Herbert (1959). *Political Socialization.* Glencoe, Ill.: Free Press.

Hyneman, Charles S. (1940). "Who makes our laws?" *Political Science Quarterly* 55:556–81

Inglehart, Ronald (1971). "The silent revolution in Europe: integrational change in post-industrial societies." *American Political Science Review* 65:991–1017.

Ippolito, Dennis S. (1969). "Political perspectives of suburban party leaders." *Social Sciences Quarterly* 49:800–15.

Jacob, Herbert (1962). "Initial recruitment of elected officials in the U.S.—a model." *Journal of Politics* 24:703–16.

Janowitz, Morris (1954). "The systematic analysis of political biography." *World Politics* 6:405–12.

Jewell, Malcolm E., and Samuel C. Patterson (1966). *The Legislative Process in the United States.* New York: Random House.

Keller, Suzanne (1963). *Beyond the Ruling Class. Strategic Elites in Modern Society.* New York: Random House.

Key, V. O., Jr. (1956). *American State Politics.* New York: Knopf.

Kim, Young C. (1967). "Political recruitment: the case of Japanese prefectural assemblymen." *American Political Science Review* 61:1036–52.

Kirchheimer, Otto (1950). "The composition of the German Bundestag." *Western Political Quarterly* 3:590–601.

Knutson, Jeanne N. (1972). *The Human Basis of the Polity: A Psychological Study of Political Man.* Chicago: Aldine-Atherton.

——————— (1973). "Personality in the study of politics." In Jeanne N. Knutson (ed.), *The Handbook of Political Psychology.* San Francisco: Jossey-Bass.

Kornberg, Allan, Joel Smith, and David Bromley (1969). "Some differences in the political socialization patterns of Canadian and American party officials: a preliminary report." *Canadian Journal of Political Science* 2:64–88.

Kornberg, Allan, Joel Smith, and Harold D. Clarke (1970). *Semi-Careers In Political Work: The Dilemma of Party Organizations.* Beverly Hills, Cal.: Sage Professional Papers in Comparative Politics.

Kornberg, Allan, and Norman Thomas (1965). "The political socialization of national legislative elites in the United States and Canada." *Journal of Politics* 27:761–75.

Kornberg, Allan, and Hal W. Winsborough (1968). "The recruitment of candidates for the Canadian House of Commons." *American Political Science Review* 62:1242–57.

Ladd, Everett Carli, Jr. (1966). *Negro Political Leadership in the South.* Ithaca, N.Y.: Cornell University Press.

Langer, Walter C. (1972). *The Mind of Adolf Hitler.* New York: Basic Books.

Langner, Thomas S. (1962). "A twenty-two item screening score of psychiatric symptoms indicating impairment." *Journal of Health and Human Behavior* 3:29.

Langton, Kenneth P. (1969). *Political Socialization.* New York: Oxford University Press.

Laqueur, Walter Z. (1962). *Young Germany, a History of the German Youth Movement:* New York: Basic Books.

Lasswell, Harold D. (1930). *Psychopathology and Politics.* Chicago: University of Chicago Press. Reprinted in *The Political Writings of Harold D. Lasswell* (1951). Glencoe, Ill.: Free Press.

——————— (1948). "The garrison state and specialists on violence." In Harold Lasswell, *The Analysis of Political Behavior.* London: Routledge, Kegan Paul.

——————— (1954). "The selective effect of personality on political participation." In

Richard Christie and Marie Jahoda (eds.), *Studies in the Scope and Method of the Authoritarian Personality*. Glencoe, Ill.: Free Press.

Lasswell, Harold D., Daniel Lerner, and C. Easton Rothwell (1952). *The Comparative Study of Elites*. Stanford, Cal.: Stanford University Press.

Legg, Keith R. (1969). "Political recruitment and political crises: the case of Greece." *Comparative Political Studies*. 1:527–55.

LeVine, Robert (1963). "Political socialization and cultural change." In Clifford Geertz (ed.), *Old Societies and New States*. Glencoe, Ill.: Free Press.

Levinson, D. J. (1958). "The relevance of personality for political participation." *Public Opinion Quarterly* 22:3–10.

Linz, Juan J. (1969). "Ecological analysis and survey research." In Mattei Dogan and Stein Rokkan (eds.), *Quantitative Ecological Analysis in the Social Sciences*. Cambridge, Mass.: M.I.T. Press.

_____ (1973). "Continuidad y discontinuidad en la élite politica española." In *Estudios de Ciencia Politica y Sociologia*. Madrid (publisher not given).

Linz, Juan J., and Amando de Miguel (1966). "Within-nation differences and comparisons: the eight Spains." In Richard L. Merritt and Stein Rokkan, *Comparing Nations*. New Haven: Yale University Press.

Litt, Edgar (1970). *Ethnic Politics in America*. Glenview, Ill.: Scott Foresman.

Loewenberg, Gerhard (1967). *Parliament in the German Political System*. Ithaca, N.Y.: Cornell University Press.

Ludz, Peter Christian (1968). *Parteielite im Wandel*. Cologne: Westdeutscher Verlag.

McCloskey, Herbert, Paul J. Hoffmann, and Rosemary O'Hara (1960). "Issue conflict and consensus among party leaders and followers." *American Political Science Review* 54:406–29.

McConaughy, John B. (1950). "Certain personality factors of state legislators in South Carolina." *American Political Science Review* 44:897–903.

Marcus, George E. (1969). "Psychopathology and political recruitment." *Journal of Politics* 31:913–31.

Martin, A. W. (1956). "The legislative assembly of New South Wales, 1856–1900." *Australian Journal of Politics and History* 2:46–67.

Martin, Robert E. (1953). "The relative political status of the Negro in the United States." *Journal of Negro Education* 22:363–79.

Marvick, Dwaine (1961). "Introduction: political decision-makers in contrasting milieus." In Dwaine Marvick (ed.), *Political Decision-Makers*. Glencoe, Ill.: Free Press.

_____ (1968). "Political recruitment and careers." In *International Encyclopedia of the Social Sciences*. New York: Macmillan.

_____ (1970). "Party cadres and receptive partisan voters in the 1967 Indian national elections."*Asian Survey* 10:949–66.

Marvick, Dwaine, and Charles R. Nixon (1961). "Recruitment contrasts in rival campaign groups." In Dwaine Marvick (ed.), *Political Decision-Makers*. Glencoe, Ill.: Free Press.

Maslow, Abraham H. (1970). *Motivation and Personality*, 2nd edition. New York: Harper & Row.

Matthews, Donald R. (1954). *The Social Background of Political Decision-Makers*. New York: Random House.

240 Political Recruitment

_____ (1960) . *U.S. Senators and Their World.* New York: Vintage Books.

Mayntz, Renate (1961) . "Oligarchic problems in a German party district." In Dwaine Marvick (ed.) , *Political Decision-Makers.* Glencoe, Ill.: Free Press.

Mezey, Michael L. (1970) . "Ambition theory and the office of congressman." *Journal of Politics* 32:563–79.

Milbrath, Lester W. (1965) . *Political Participation.* Chicago: Rand McNally.

Miller, William (1951) . "American lawyers in business and in politics." *Yale Law Journal* 60:66–76.

Mills, Charles Wright (1956) . *The Power Elite.* New York: Oxford University Press.

Mitscherlich, Alexander (1967) . "Changing patterns of political authority: a psychiatric interpretation." in Lewis J. Edinger (ed.) , *Political Leadership in Industrialized Societies.* New York: Wiley.

Monsma, Stephen V. (1971) . "Potential leaders and democratic values." *Public Opinion Quarterly* 35:350–7.

Mosca, Gaetano (1939). *The Ruling Class.* New York: McGraw-Hill. (Translation of Elementi di Scienza Politica, 1896.)

Nicholson, Norman K. (1972a) . "The factional model and the study of politics." *Comparative Political Studies* 5:291–314.

_____ (1972b) . "Factionalism and the Indian Council of Ministers." *Journal of Commonwealth Political Studies* 10:179–97.

Olson, Mancur, Jr. (1965) . *The Logic of Collective Action.* Cambridge, Mass.: Harvard University Press.

Pareto, Vilfredo (1935) . *The Mind and Society.* London: Jonathan Cape. (Translation of *Trattato di Sociologia Generale, * Florence, 1923.)

Parsons, Talcott (1959) . *The Social System.* Glencoe, Ill.: Free Press.

Patterson, Samuel C. (1963) . "Characteristics of party leaders." *Western Political Quarterly* 16:332–52.

Patterson, Samuel C., and G. R. Boynton (1969) . "Legislative recruitment in a civic culture." *Social Science Quarterly* 50:243–63.

Payne, James L. (1972) . *Incentive Theory and Political Process.* Lexington, Mass.: D. C. Heath.

Payne, James L., and Oliver H. Woshinsky (1972) . "Incentives for political participation." *World Politics* 24:518–46.

Pfautz, Harold W. (1962) . "The power structure of the Negro sub-community: a case study and a comparative view." *Phylon* 23:156–66.

Polsby, Nelson W., and Aaron B. Wildavsky (1971) . *Presidential Elections,* 3rd edition. New York: Scribner.

Pomper, Gerald (1965) . "New Jersey county chairmen." *Western Political Quarterly* 18:186–197.

Prewitt, Kenneth (1965) . "Political socialization and leadership selection." *The Annals of the American Academy of Political and Social Science* 361:91–111.

_____ (1970) . *The Recruitment of Political Leaders: A Study of Citizen Politicians.* Indianapolis: Bobbs-Merrill.

Prewitt, Kenneth, and Heinz Eulau (1969) . "Political matrix and political representation: prolegomenon to a new departure from an old problem." *American Political Science Review* 63:427–41.

_____ (1971). "Social bias in leadership selection, political recruitment and electoral context." *Journal of Politics* 33:293–315.

Prewitt, Kenneth. Heinz Eulau, and Betty H. Zisk (1966–67). "Political socialization and political roles." *Public Opinion Quarterly* 30:569–82.

Pye, Lucian W. (1961). "Personal identity and political ideology." In Dwaine Marvick (ed.), *Political Decision-Makers. Glencoe, Ill.*: Free Press.

Quandt, William B. (1970). *The Comparative Study of Political Elites.* Beverly Hills, Cal.: Sage Professional Papers in Comparative Politics.

Ranney, Austin (1965). *Pathways to Parliament. Candidate Selection in Britain.* Madison: University of Wisconsin Press.

Robins, Robert S. (1967). "Political elite formation in rural India." *Journal of Politics* 29:838–60.

Rogow, Arnold A., and Harold D. Lasswell (1963). *Power, Corruption and Rectitude.* Englewood Cliffs, N.J.: Prentice-Hall.

Rokeach, Milton (1968). *Beliefs, Attitudes and Values.* San Francisco: Jossey-Bass.

Rosenberg, Morris (1957). *Occupations and Values.* Glencoe, Ill.: Free Press.

Rosenzweig, Robert M. (1957). "The politician and the career in politics." *Midwest Journal of Political Science* 1:163–72.

Rutherford, Brent M. (1966). "Psychopathology, decision-making, and political involvement." *Journal of Conflict Resolution* 10:387–407.

Salisbury, Robert H. (1965–66). "The urban party organization member." *Public Opinion Quarterly* 29:550–64.

Sartori, Giovanni (1967). "Members of Parliament." In *Decisions and Decision-Makers in the Modern State.* Paris: UNESCO.

Scheuch, Erwin K. (1969). "Social context and individual behavior." In Mattei Dogan and Stein Rokkan (eds.), *Quantitative Ecological Analysis in the Social Sciences.* Cambridge, Mass.: M.I.T. Press.

Schlesinger, Joseph A. (1957). "Lawyers and American politics: a clarified view." *Midwest Journal of Political Science* 1:26–39.

_____ (1966). *Ambition and Politics.* Chicago: Rand McNally.

_____ (1967). "Political careers and party leadership." In Lewis J. Edinger (ed.), *Political Leadership in Industrialized Societies.* New York: Wiley.

Schwartz, David C. (1969). "Toward a theory of political recruitment." *Western Political Quarterly* 22:552–71.

Searing, Donald D. (1969). "The comparative study of elite socialization." *Comparative Political Studies* 1:471–500.

Seligman, Lester G. (1961). "Political recruitment and party structure: a case study." *American Political Science Review* 55:77–86.

_____ (1964). *Leadership in a New Nation.* New York: Atherton Press.

_____ (1967). "Political parties and the recruitment of political leadership." In Lewis J. Edinger (ed.), *Political Leadership in Industrialized Societies.* New York: Wiley.

_____ (1971). *Recruiting Political Elites.* New York: General Learning Press.

Sharpe, L. J. (1966). "Leadership and representation in local government." *Political Quarterly* 37:149–58.

Sherif, Muzafer, and Hadley Cantril (1947). *The Psychology of Ego-Involvements.* New York: Wiley.

Singer, Marshall R. (1964). *The Emerging Elite.* Cambridge, Mass.: M.I.T. Press.

Snowiss, Leo M. (1966). "Congressional recruitment and representation. *American Political Science Review* 60:627–39.

Sorauf, Frank J. (1963). *Party and Representation.* New York: Atherton Press.

Soule, John W., and James W. Clarke (1970). "Amateurs and professionals: a study of delegates to the 1968 Democratic National Convention." *American Political Science Review* 64:888–98.

Tucker, Robert C. (1965). "The dictator and totalitarianism." *World Politics* 17:555–83.

_____ (1971). *The Soviet Political Mind.* New York: Norton.

United Nations Educational, Scientific and Cultural Organization (1967). *Decisions and Decision-Makers in the Modern State.* Paris: UNESCO.

Valen, Henry (1966). "The recruitment of parliamentary nominees in Norway." *Scandinavian Political Studies* 1:121–66.

Verba, Sidney (1961). *Small Groups and Political Behavior.* Princeton: Princeton University Press.

Wahlke, John, Heinz Eulau, William Buchanan, and LeRoy Ferguson (1962). *The Legislative System.* New York: Wiley.

Weber, Max (1921). *Gesammelte Politische Schriften.* Munich. (See also Gerth and Mills, 1958.)

Wells, Richard S. (1964). "The legal profession and politics." *Midwest Journal of Political Science* 8:166–90.

Wilson, James Q. (1960). *Negro Politics.* New York: Free Press.

_____ (1962). *The Amateur Democrat.* Chicago: University of Chicago Press.

Wolfinger, Raymond E. (1972). "Why political machines have not withered away and other revisionist thoughts." *Journal of Politics* 34:365–98.

Woodward, Julian L., and Elmo Roper (1950). "Political activity of American citizens." *American Political Science Review* 44:872–85.

Zapf, Wolfgang (1966). *Wandlungen der Deutschen Elite.* Munich: Piper.

Zariski, Raphael (1960). "Party factions and comparative politics." *Midwest Journal of Political Science* 4:27–51.

Zeigler, Harmon, and Michael A. Baer (1968). "The recruitment of lobbyists and legislators." *Midwest Journal of Political Science* 12:493–513.

Zeller, Belle (1954). *American State Legislatures.* New York: Crowell-Collier.

4
GROUP THEORIES

J. DAVID GREENSTONE

INTRODUCTION: ECONOMY, SOCIETY, AND POLITICAL GROUPS

Among American political scientists the group theories tradition has been the most important and sustained attempt to resolve two ancient issues in their discipline. To what extent do social relationships and economic activities shape the norms, institutions, conflicts, and policy decisions of the political system? Conversely, to what extent have economic and social life been affected by these characteristics of the polity? Particularly because a number of excellent studies have already considered this tradition more generally, the present essay concentrates intensively on five of its most influential and representative figures—Arthur F. Bentley, David B. Truman, Robert A. Dahl, Grant McConnell and Theodore J. Lowi.[1] Even with respect to these scholars we will further concentrate on three central issues. First, despite sometimes pointed disagreements among their proponents, American group theories display major elements of continuity; they do indeed form a tradition. Second, in certain respects later group theorists have changed Bentley's initial processual formulation by seeing political reality in terms of stability and constraint. Third, these later writers' continuing adherence to Bentley's basic method, the means of identifying politically relevant groups, together with their divergence from him on the issue of stability, have left the tradition unable to account for some—though far from all—of the connections between politics and social

I am very indebted to a number of colleagues for their penetrating comments and suggestions, including Fred Greenstein, Marshall Langberg, Haskel Levi, Paul Peterson, and Mark Solomon. I should like to mention in particular Nelson Polsby, who I am sure continues unconvinced by an argument which his challenging criticisms have nevertheless considerably improved.

and economic life. Before turning to the work of Bentley and those who followed him, we will outline these arguments in a preliminary fashion.

Elements of Continuity: Political Interest Groups and Specific Policy Goals

On some issues group theorists have differed sharply among themselves. It is sometimes overlooked, for example, that Dahl explicitly places much less stress on organized groups than Truman, McConnell, or Lowi, and that in this respect he most closely resembles Bentley. As is much more commonly recognized, these five authors and many others often disagree with one another over the ethical status of their subject matter. To some, notably Truman and Dahl in his work on New Haven, political interest group activities seem at least compatible with, if not essential to, the health of American politics. To others, such as McConnell and Lowi, interest group behavior often malignly subverts the highest ideals of liberal democracy. This issue, however, has apparently been less empirical than normative; the facts and observations adduced by each side have not ordinarily been challenged.[2]

Considered as a scholarly enterprise, the group theories tradition, of course, does not provide the rigor and fully operationalized terms common in the natural sciences. Nevertheless, it does offer a cu...ulative body of research which has increased both the scope and specificity of its empirical propositions, including descriptive information about group activities and their consequences, and a wide range of conditions which contribute to or limit the influence of particular interests and in some cases interest groups as a whole. These factors include the effects of governmental institutions, leadership strategies and influence, the constraints imposed by political regime norms, and the importance of the group's own bureaucratic organization.

Much of this success must be attributed to a continuity of assumptions about group politics and political activity from Bentley's time to the present—most important the definition of the political interest group itself. For group theorists, economic and social influences are observable in the efforts of *particular sets of individuals seeking specific policy goals related to their social or economic situation.* As Herring puts it in his classic study of early twentieth century lobbying, the interest group "may be defined as a number of individuals bound together in a common cause or united by similar interests into an articulate unit" (1929, p. 6). Or as Bentley said two decades earlier, "to state more and more adequately the raw materials of political life . . . in terms of the groups of men it affects, . . . the groups directly insisting on [a policy], . . . those directly opposing it, and those more indirectly concerned in it—is much more complete than any statement in terms of self interest, theories or ideals" (1967, p. 204).

To Bentley, as to many others, the basic concern for most groups was economic. E. E. Schattschneider takes it "for granted" in his memorable study of tariff politics "that there is a connection between economic interest and political behavior" (1935, 4). This interest, moreover, manifests itself through group activities, which create the issue agendas for political conflict and deliberation and then affect the authoritative allocation of values that follows (Easton, 1965, 1953). For later theorists, as we shall see, the causation involving the political group is reciprocal: the group's activities, demands, and even preferences are themselves influenced by the attributes of the polity itself. But even though these later developments represent important modifications of Bentley's approach, they have not disturbed the tradition's basic definition of a political interest group in terms of its members' attitudes and especially their activities with respect to a specific policy issue.

This policy stress, of course, by no means characterizes every empirical study of American group politics. Yet it extends far beyond the five writers considered here, to include, in addition to Herring and Schattschneider, Odegard's (1928) famous study of the Anti-Saloon League; Zeigler's (1961) concern with small business organizations as pressure groups; Kariel's (1961) comprehensive discussion of the way American political values affect the political activity of organized economic interests; Wildavsky's (1962) study of public versus private electric power; and Selznick's (1953) study of the TVA.[3]

Nor has this influence of the group theory perspective been limited to America. Sensitized by the group theories approach, a number of American scholars interested in western Europe have evidently perceived the sometimes subtle instances of group influence on the political authorities that most European scholars, focusing on such broader social categories as class or religion, have tended to underemphasize.[4]

In some respects, as Hartz (1955, 1964) maintains, these elements of continuity constitute a shared view of political reality which reflects the plural and fluid character of American politics—in particular the lower salience of class alignments and thus the comparative weakness of socialist parties and trade unions. American politics, this argument runs, has seen a bewildering succession of different political demands, issues, and controversies, which can be too readily obscured by a concentration of such stable elements of social life as race, class, corporate capitalism, and the like. Precisely because the group theories approach categorizes individuals according to their activities on behalf of often changing policy preferences, it is therefore well equipped to capture a fluid pattern of maneuver, countermaneuver, and adjustment to changing conditions (see Bauer, Poole, and Dexter, 1963). Given their obvious stability, it is much harder to relate classes and other broad social categories to such changing patterns.

The policy-specific view of interest groups, then, was in part based on their substantive understanding of American political realities. In Polsby's words, "it is a mistake to impute to the apparently inescapable fact of class membership any sort of class consciousness" (1963, p. 118). Indeed, since American society is "fractured into a congeries of hundreds of small special interest groups, . . . it is not only inefficient but usually unnecessary for entire classes to be mobilized when the preferences of class members are pressed and often satisfied . . . piecemeal" (*ibid.*) or, as Bentley remarked, "in practically all cases in modern society . . . the varying sets of interests will not so settle or consolidate themselves upon masses of men as to make one classification adequate for all interests" (1967, p. 206).

This emphasis on groups with specific policy interests does not necessarily mean, as might be assumed, that group theorists are unable to deal with every intense or massive conflict, such as the race, Vietnam, or ecology issues of the 1960s. Rather, the critique offered here will attempt to show that these group theories have encountered certain specific difficulties in connecting such stable social differences as class or race to suddenly emergent political protests, which seek to *transform* rather than marginally alter these basic social patterns. To press a more sweeping indictment, to deny that group theorists can deal with any important, rapidly emerging social conflict would be to misunderstand the developments in this tradition since Bentley.

The Group Theories Tradition: An Overview of Its Development

The crux of Bentley's approach to the governmental process and thus the source of his insistence on defining groups in terms of their policy goals was his paradoxical appearing equation of a group, its activity and its interest. In effect, Bentley *meant* by a political group the shared political activity of its members, which in turn was identified (distinguished from other activity) by the goal it sought to achieve, that is, the group's interest. In somewhat more contemporary language, each group's members were united by their shared preferences on specific policies, and the preferences were revealed by the members' activity or behavior (which sought to secure the policy) .

This equation served two purposes for Bentley. As already indicated, it helped him describe the political *process,* continuous changes in strategies, tactics, and group demands, and thus in the character of the groups themselves. But this equation also reflected Bentley's explicit and careful attention to espistemological considerations, which distinguishes him from most other group theorists, including empirically important work in the immediately following generation by Herring, Odegard, and especially Schattschneider. Only with Truman's *The Governmental Process,* the pivotal work in the entire group theories tradition, does Bentley's epistemological and analytic focus— e.g., an extensive discussion of the appropriate definition of a group and the methods for describing it—reemerge as a central issue in American political science.

For all his becoming modesty, however, Truman's treatise also provided the most comprehensive and systematic shift in the group theories tradition's substantive understanding of American political reality. For where Bentley repeatedly stressed the decisive importance of the processual flow of activity, Truman explicitly considered those stable social and economic groups which do not necessarily have continuing policy goals but can suddenly "intervene" in politics. And he paid still more attention both to the role of political institutions in the government and to the group's own formal organizations as relatively stable elements of repetitive activity which constrained and shaped the group's efforts to influence public policy. In effect, Truman introduced and systematically considered elements of pattern or structure into his analysis of both political and social life.

Although Dahl, McConnell, and Lowi each differs from Truman decisively in certain important respects, the argument which follows tries to show the ways in which each of them develops still further Truman's departure from Bentley's initial processual vision. Dahl, for example, shares somewhat more of Bentley's stress on the fluid character of political life than does Truman. But in his theoretically informed study of New Haven on which we focus here, Dahl goes beyond Truman in examining the ways in which group activities are limited by the activities, goals, and alliances of political activists, and by the norms of the American political regime they regularly espouse. Equally important for our purposes, he spells out in greater detail than Truman the conditions which may lead nonpolitical social group to suddenly become active on behalf of a certain public policy.

For his part, McConnell details much more specifically than Truman exactly how the particular demands that political interest groups themselves make are shaped first by the democratic or undemocratic character of their own organizations (in effect, the narrowness or breadth of participation in their internal governance), and even more by the degree of each group's own social or economic heterogeneity. But this heterogeneity, he argues, is in turn, affected by political factors, particularly the breadth and diversity of the constituency to which public officials and governmental agencies are responsive. By thus focusing on the institutionally prescribed breadth or narrowness of all social and economic group constituencies, McConnell formulated in a single proposition a general approach to variations in group behavior of great theoretical importance.

In certain respects, Lowi takes this analysis a step further. Group behavior and demands are conditioned not just by the way political institutions shape their constituencies but by the pattern of public *policies*. This pattern of previous *governmental* decisions determines in turn whether a policy, its outputs, and the groups' own behavior will conform, in terms of Lowi's (1964b) well-known arenas of power typology, to the broadly redistributive pattern of political activity, to the highly individualistic distributive pattern, or to the regulatory pattern emphasized by most studies of organized groups. Once established, these patterns become so rigid and constraining, Lowi believes, that no well-organized political interest group can be a source of major change (1969,

1971) . From one point of view, Lowi remains consistent with Bentley's identification of politically important groups in terms of their policy demands, since
these social movements do have fairly specific issue attitudes. In another sense,
however, he makes fully explicit the recognition by other post-Bentley group
theorists that a satisfactory group theory must take account of the way that
groups defined in social-economic terms do in fact intervene to alter political
life.

Alternatives to the Group Theories Tradition

Although Bentley made very sweeping claims about the applicability of his
methods, a number of critics (Rothman, 1960; Weinstein, 1962) have asserted
and Truman himself (1960) has readily conceded that group theorists by no
means offer a complete theory of politics. Prevailing cultural and political
norms, the character of both political and economic institutions, traditional
relationships among social classes, regions and religious denominations, party
competition, and problems of aggregating individual and group demands, may
all affect or be affected by the behavior of the political authorities, or indeed
by the broader character of the regime itself—e.g., whether it is democratic
or authoritarian—and all this may happen without the direct and visible involvement of policy-oriented interest groups.

By contrast, the group theories tradition, which followed Bentley, although
it remains concerned with policy-oriented groups, maintains this concern primarily to examine the ways economic and social preferences are expressed
politically and then help shape policy decisions. And it is this set of issues
which concerns us here. For this reason we shall not discuss those studies of
public policy which look at the correlates of particular units (such as American states) but do not directly examine group activities as such (Dye, 1965,
1969; Sharkansky, 1971, 1972; Wolfinger and Field, 1966; Walker, 1969). Indeed, we shall consider such topics as Dahl's major work on democratic
theory in the last decade (1967, 1970, 1971, 1973) , McConnell's stress on organizational maintenance (1953) , and Lowi's concern with administrative juris-
prudence and federal-city relations (1969, chapters 5 and 7) only where they
help illuminate the constrains which shape group activity. Even the seminal
work of economically oriented theorists of collective action (Frolich, Oppenheimer, and Young, 1971; and particularly, Olson, 1965) , which focus on how
like-minded individuals agree to act on their preferences, will be considered
only when we look at an array of reasons for the failure of certain groups to
make demands. Not only is their analysis examined elsewhere in this *Handbook,* but the Bentleyan tradition largely concentrates on a different point:
What happens to various social-economic groups after (in whatever manner)
their members do succeed in acting together collectively in politics.

But as the developments of the group theories tradition itself from Truman
to Lowi make clear, there is one alternative view of politics and social and

economic life which cannot be as readily considered irrelevant to our present purpose: an approach which defines politically important groups in terms of social or economic characteristics rather than policy preferences. Just such collectivities appear as vital elements in the single comprehensive interpretation of political life offered by classical political philosophy. In some cases, a single term—democratic, aristocratic, oligarchic—could simultaneously categorize a political regime, a dominant social stratum, and the typical activity of individual citizens. Where successful, such formulations achieve an elegance and economy of analysis far greater than that of the group theorists, while focusing on the political regime in a way that Bentley surely did not.

This classical approach, nevertheless, has important limitations in heterogeneous contemporary politics, where open conflict between very different social strata and major changes in policy and patterns of political activity can take place without endangering or substantially altering the regime itself. Yet an at least analogously comprehensive approach more suited to modern politics has been adopted by those analysts who interpret political activity in terms of the overt conflict and covert tensions among basic social groups distinguished by their own life styles and subcultures as well as economic positions. Even if entire regimes seem too diverse for convenient classification by a single term, this concern with broad social classes, estates, and the like provides a limited number of categories with which to discuss simultaneously both the macrolevel of institutions and broad social communities and the microlevel of the individual's political behavior. Thus, for any given regime, once we have correctly identified an individual's class, we are likely to know both who his political allies are and what political goals they pursued in concert. This approach has had an obvious attractiveness for European scholars of such very different orientations as Tocqueville, Bagehot, Disraeli, Bryce, and a number of Marxists. Many of their interpretations have had an enduring value in illuminating political life in America as well as Europe. Equally important, since class, at least, is both an economic and social category, class analysis offers an alternative way of accounting for social and economic influences on political life. Indeed, one perceptive English scholar (MacKenzie, 1955) has argued that the best American work on group politics has examined social and economic groups, such as farmers, workers, or businessmen, which are broadly defined in ordinary political discourse rather than designated by particular policy goals.[5]

It seems clear, however, that at least in the American case, individual citizens are too much affected by diverse policies, relevant to their many social statuses and roles in a complex urban industrial society, to be *fully* encompassed by such broad social categories. An individual's social position, in other words, has become a less and less certain predictor of his or her political attitudes and activity. Some group theorists, for example, Truman and McConnell, do indeed consider politically influential groups under such general—economically defined—headings as businessmen, farmers, and workers. Their work, however, typically concentrates on formal organizations to which some of the individuals in these categories belong, but which are united enough to take relatively clear positions on specific policy proposals.

All four post-Bentleyan groups. theorists considered here have also recognized, of course, that at some points, on some issues, groups designated in terms of social and economic categories without reference to their formal organization can in fact influence—indeed, intervene in—political life. But eclectically conceding in this way the partial validity of these alternatives to the group theories approach raises in turn the problem of the appropriate boundary between the two approaches. First, in which types of observable cases is a group theory approach deficient? Where, in other words, must we look beyond policy-interested groups to those broader social categories that also affect policymakers and indeed the activity of the political interest groups themselves? Although these issues are surely too complex to be fully resolved here, it may be useful to conclude this introductory discussion by stating as sharply as possible the issue that divides the group theories' identification of groups in terms of the policy orientation from an approach that begins with classes, estates, races, or other groups identified in terms of social-economic attributes.

Group Theories and the Problem of Social/Economic Groups

The essential issue between the two approaches can be stated somewhat crudely in terms of how to "percentage" political groups, that is, the empirical procedure for assessing social and economic influences on any given policy issue. On one side, the main group theories approach surveys those individuals active on a particular policy and divides them on the basis of their policy preferences. This method then observes the social and economic characteristics of each such set of participants, both winners and losers. For example, if oil companies dominate the winning coalition on a given issue, and oil consumers are most numerous among the losers, the economic position and power of the oil companies can be said to have shaped public policy in this instance. In principle, then, this method compares the fortunes of each policy-oriented faction among the active participants on the issue, each denominator being all observably active individuals and each numerator being the number supporting a particular policy alternative.

As Bentley himself saw very clearly, this procedure does not eliminate the observer's need to *group* the individual participants; on the contrary, all those active on the issue are divided by the observer on the basis of their preferences. As we shall see, however, Bentley insistently favored this method of identifying interest groups because both the numerator of the fraction (those favoring a given policy alternative) and the denominator (the total number of participants) are based on the participants' *observable* behavior. He rejected reliance on the observer's expectations about who *should* be active and the participants' own *verbal claims* about their group allegiance, both of which can be dangerously misleading.

There may be some cases, however, in which this group theories method leads to problematic results. Consider, for example, a proposal for social reform to be paid for by some progressive tax on high incomes. As measured by visible political activity, this reform is successfully opposed by both a majority of some small group, such as large employers, and by a minority of a very large group, such as hourly employees. (The proponents, in this hypothetical case, were self-described middle-class "humanitarians.") Given the much larger number of employees in the whole society, it is possible that they considerably outnumber the employers in the winning coalition. And in that case the group theories method for assessing social economic influences would indicate either that the proposal was defeated by an employ*ee*-dominated group or, at best, that social-economic influences could not be clearly determined.

One way to avoid this intuitively unsatisfying conclusion is to argue that since the policy plainly benefited the workers, while progressively taxing the employers, the employers' economic interests were in fact served by the outcome, and thus they were victorious. This *objective interest* approach has been rejected by many group theorists because it requires the observer to assert that the employees would have benefited from the policy even though most of the employees who happened to be politically active opposed the policy. In fact, however, an approach emphasizing social classes, or even occupational (that is, entirely economically defined) groups, offers another perhaps more straightforward and empirically grounded way to begin to account for situations of this sort. In the hypothesized case just considered, the *proportion* of employers actively opposed to the policy among all employers in the country was much larger than the corresponding *proportion* of like-minded hourly employees. Indeed, it is this quite obvious consideration which helps make the result produced by the group theories method so intuitively unacceptable. But this same consideration also leads to a very different way of identifying politically relevant groups in order to assess social-economic influences on a given policy issue. At least in principle, it produces a fraction whose numerator is made up of the politically active employees favoring this policy (or in some cases the number actively in favor less those actively opposed) and whose denominator is the total number of hourly employees in the society.

One indicator of social economic influence, then, involves assessing which social or economic group was, with respect to its total membership, proportionately most active in successfully favoring or opposing a policy. The observer has again grouped the relevant individuals—in this case active and inactive alike—but in terms of economic or social characteristics regardless of political activity. This approach, as compared with the group theorist method, becomes all the more attractive in those cases where many previously inactive group members—e.g., hourly workers with respect to our social reform proposal—suddenly become very active in supporting it. I shall argue at the end of this essay that there seems to be no fully satisfactory way to discuss this crucial *change* in the pattern of economic and social influences on the fate of the proposal without saying that the politically active proportion of the relevant *social-economic group* did, in fact, increase over time.

But by what warrant does the observer single out hourly employees as the relevant group—to make the number of active workers the numerator and the total number of workers the denominator of the relevant fraction? Certainly, we can observe that these employees all share one or more economic characteristics, e.g., being paid by the hour. But there are other equally observable attributes which might be equally relevant, such as region, religious affiliation, race, sex, or employment by a particular firm or industry.

As we shall emphasize presently, Bentley in fact tentatively proposed a solution to the problem of such changes, which was much more extensively formulated by Truman, still more elaborately worked out by Dahl, and adopted frequently by both McConnell and Lowi. To state this solution all too briefly, the sudden surge in *political* activity is interpreted as a new effort to secure some good, such as a regular income, which had previously been secured by social or economic activity alone, but could subsequently be preserved (or restored) only with governmental help. The great virtue of this formulation is that it preserves Bentley's view of interest; the criterion of the group members' own activity remains the basis for singling out one particular collectivity, e.g., hourly employees. They are the relevant group, not because the observer believes that proposed policy will benefit them, but because the group members themselves in private life have actively sought to secure the same good now sought politically by support for the proposed policy. Thus the group members' *own* activity in seeking one particular goal identifies a social-economic group both before and after its members become politically active. Crucially, the departure from the basic group theories approach is thus minimized.

Although this formulation does indeed account for many important instances of social groups' "intervening" in politics, the later sections of this paper will argue that it fails to account for those cases in which the members of the social groups seek not to protect or restore a given benefit but to reverse or transform, that is, completely change the previously existing situation. And it is at this point, this argument will assert, that satisfactorily identifying the relevant social-economic group returns us to an objective interest analysis, that is, identifying group interest in terms of who benefits from a particular policy, rather than determining the interest in terms of the goals the group members actively pursue. A discussion of the precise situation in which this approach is necessary and the ways it can be defended against Bentley's epistemological criticisms must be postponed until later sections of the paper, where we will briefly consider the key place of ideology and culture.

To sum up, then, Bentley's insistence on identifying interest groups in terms of their specific policy demands resolved the methodological question of reliably assessing the thrust or goal of a group's activity and at the same time faithfully captured his view of American reality as a changing process among a plurality of groups. Later group theorists, however, changed Bentley's view of a processual reality without altering his method of identifying politically relevant groups. In the discussion which follows, my own position will be, first, to agree with Bentley and later group theorists about the plural character of (at least American) political reality, i.e., that conflict takes place along several social-economic and indeed political and cultural dimensions of differentiation; second, to agree with Bentley's followers in insisting on a more patterned or structured—that is, less fluid and processual—view of political and social life, in other words, to argue that governmental institutions and stable social-economic groups do in fact matter; but third, to try to demonstrate in some detail that this change in Bentley's view of reality can be fully successful only if it is accompanied by some change—which later writers have not adopted—in our understanding of what we mean by "group" and "interest."

BENTLEY'S VISION OF POLITICAL PROCESS: GROUP = ACTIVITY = INTEREST

The work of few American political scientists has been subjected to as repeated and often penetrating criticisms as that of Arthur F. Bentley (1967). (See Weinstein, 1962, and sources cited therein; Crick, 1959; Kress, 1970; Hale, 1960; Balbus, 1971; Dowling, 1960.) My goal therefore, is less to add another critique than to review, as sympathetically as I can, what Bentley sought to do and then turn to a major problem in his treatment of process, which has led more recent group theorists to adopt a more structural perspective.

Bentley, after all, resolved the problem of connecting the political system with economic and social life by minimizing the distinctions between them, that is, by considering as politically relevant social and economic aggregates only those groups that were already politically active. It follows that economic and social influences on politics were part—Bentley thought a large part—of what we *mean* by and observe as political activity. As he himself says:

> If I may be pardoned a remark from my own experience, I will say that my interest in politics is not primary, but . . . that I hope from this [political] approach to gain a better understanding of economic life. (1967, p. 200)

It is this highly monistic view, which lacks any clearly separate realms of economic and political activity, that leads Bentley to his celebrated if paradoxical equation of the group, its activity, and its interests.

The Group-Interest-Activity Equation

"The raw material for the study of government," Bentley maintains, "is first, last, and always activity, action, 'something doing,' the shunting by some men of other men's conduct along changed lines, . . . the dispersal of one grouping of forces by another grouping." Moreover, this "raw material . . . the actually performed legislation-administrative-adjudicating activities of the nation" are not individual actions but rather the shared activities of the groups: "group and group activity are equivalent terms." At the same time, "An interest as the term will be used in this work, is the equivalent of a group. . . . The group and the interest are not separate. There exists only one thing, so many men bound together in or along the path of a certain activity" (1967, pp. 175–76, 180, 211). *The Process of Government* thus focuses on collective (i.e., group) goal-seeking activity, where the activity is named and defined by the interest it seeks to secure, and the group is defined by its activity, that is, by what its members do.

This equation of the group, its activity, and its interests may well appear paradoxical because in ordinary discourse groups can be identified either by the members' own verbally expressed allegiance or, as noted earlier, by some attribute of importance to others, such as occupation. In other words, groups are often spoken and thought of as politically "at rest," so that most or all group members might not be engaged in a common political activity. *The Process of Government* makes clear that two considerations led Bentley to deny this broader view of group: first, a perception of political reality as a continually changing process, and second, an epistemological concern with correctly identifying the group and assessing its political impact.

Group Activity as a Political Process

Bentley objected to basing his political analysis on groups such as classes, in part, precisely because they were often so stable. For him "the real question" about contemporary politics was why "the living acting men and women change their forms of action and cease to do now what they did formerly" (1967, p. 18). As David G. Smith (1964) cogently argues, process has for many decades been a pervasive yet problematic term in both the pragmatist and group theory traditions of American political thought. (See also Kress, 1970; Jacobson, 1964.) Although *The Process of Government* does not provide a single explicit definition, the stress on political fluidity and change is clear. "The activity ever goes on. Here actions conflict; at once opinion groups, opinion activities appear; these pass on, transforming themselves, organizing, reflecting various subgroups, combining groups, passing into new stages of activity." Indeed, by the "very nature" of the process, the groups "are freely combining, dissolving, and recombining in accordance with their lines." In traditional societies, classes, races, or ethnic communities may have enjoyed or suffered from relatively permanent positions of advantage or disadvantage. But for the American case, at least, Marx's theory of classes is "too hard and fast" (1967, pp. 242, 359, 467; see also pp. 404, 421–22). Different sets of groups seem important at different times and on different issues, with all policies subject to attack and modification by those dissatisfied.[6] In sum, political life is evidently too fluid, too contingent, too easily characterized as process, to be consistent with explanations or abstractions based on formal authority and political philosophy. Bentley thus belonged to what Morton White (1957) has so aptly termed a "revolt against formalism."[7]

This concern with process is also clearly compatible with Bentley's stress on groups with specific policy interests. Groups which have multiple interests, such as classes or races, if they are politically important, would be likely to persist rather than dissolve, combine and redissolve, or wax and wane in relevance, in part because they will become involved in many situations and on many issues.[8] Bentley believed, however, that the groups with specific policy interests were politically most important. Groups which made sweeping claims to represent large, diffuse sets of individuals, such as the socialists of Bentley's time, could not be considered as "counting in the governing process" when they "pretend to represent human group activity" universally or even "a very large proportion of the human beings." Only "as we move inward toward the specialized socialist theories," he continues, do "we get a chance to state them in terms of groups much more limited in character," that is, socialist "parties close in to action . . . [with] programmes still more specific." For all his criticisms, then, Bentley by no means dismisses Marx as substantively wrong but complains primarily that he deals in "abstractions," with collectivities too general, stable, and vague to be relevant for actual political life. What "counts" for Bentley are not rhetorical postures but "the most immediately practical policies or programmes" (1967, pp. 437, 139).

This same view of reality as continuously changing also accounts for Bentley's often misunderstood rejection of individual mental traits or national characteristics and attitudes as "spooks." Both broad-scale ideologies and abstractly discussed character traits can be seen as imposing a false stability on a highly fluid political life—more appropriately described as an ever-moving process—in which each individual continuously adjusts his behavior to meet changing conditions.

Group Interests and the Study of Politics

The second consideration leading to Bentley's group-activity-interest equation is his concern with validly identifying the groups and determining their political impact. In the study of either a group or a policy process, the first step is to identify the interest, the *direction* of these "changed lines" in which some men are "shunting" the "conduct" of others. But in taking this step, Bentley at least implicitly intends his method to resolve the problem emphasized by the Marxian doctrine of ideology. He recognizes that many of the verbal formulations which describe group activity may very well obscure rather than accurately describe and explain. For one thing, these descriptions, by both observers and participants, were part of the group activity itself: "writing and talking and speech-making are activity just as much as any other" (1967, p. 176). Indeed "there is no idea which is not a reflection of social activity" and like many Marxists Bentley particularly refers to economic activity.

> The economic basis of political life must, of course, be fully recognized though it does not *necessarily* follow that [it] . . . is the exclusive or even *in every detail* the dominant basis. (p. 209, emphasis supplied)

To put this point more generally, if individuals could rather freely select the policies they favored and dissolve old groups or form new ones, they could also verbally misrepresent their goals if it suited their purposes, convenience, or especially their prospects of success. Indeed, since even scholarly analyses might well foster political or economic interests, they can no more be taken at face value than the pronouncements of politicians. For this reason Bentley shuns a group's rhetoric and uses its activity—what it is observably trying to achieve in its dealing with other groups—to determine its interest. Thus in his chapter on "The Gradation of Groups," Bentley dismisses the actor's own speech, the "discussion side" of group activity, as

> a *bewildering* wonderland of theory and *dreaming* of exhortation and tirade, of fact and *fiction*, every bit of it reflecting something of the living world of men when it arises, nearly every bit of it presumptuously asserting itself to be the center of the living universe. (p. 435, emphasis supplied)

For what he calls "a convenient illustration" of such "discussion groups" Bentley turns to the socialism of his time, in a passage already discussed, which also shows his concern with acquiring valid and reliable knowledge. At its most universal and purely theoretical level, "the socialism as put forth would *pretend* to represent human group activity detachable from limitations of time and place." Rather than such unsubstantial claims, Bentley insists on reliable data based on activity: "*evidence* of force of pressure . . . adjustments under way in which we could *see* the group directly involved.

For this reason, among others, Bentley feels most comfortable as an observer with socialist parties that have specific programs. In such cases, "the pressures represented are easily *discoverable* and to some extent capable of *exact estimate.*" For it is only at the level of the active group itself, i.e., where one is "close in" to the action, that we find that "the opposition pressures are very accurately estimated . . . and the representation of actually existing interests is vastly truer." "It is always," Bentley concludes, "a question needing *measurement and proof,* as to just what values, what influence any one of the phases of the discussion has for or upon any of the other phases" (1967, pp. 437, 438, 439; emphasis is supplied in each case).

This attack on the reliability of the *verbally* stated purposes which individuals offer to account for their behavior by no means led Bentley to reject the idea of purposive, goal-directed social action. This idea indeed was vital for his view of group interest, at least in *The Governmental Process*. Like many of the later group theorists, Bentley was in fact far from a crude deterministic behaviorism which ignores human motivation. For example, his objection to focusing on character traits is primarily methodological. Explanations of behavior in terms of bravery or miserliness, he maintains, are mere descriptive tautologies, since evidence showing that the individual is miserly (the cause) turns out to be the miserly character of the behavior to be explained (the effect). "I have not denied," he insisted, "the existence of a real living intelligent . . . feeling, thinking ideal-following material [which] is the stuff we have before us in interpreting society" (1967, p 165). And he observed repeatedly in *The Process of Government* that, when properly used, attitudes and especially goals were important data.

Consistent with this purposive view, Bentley sees no value in attributing interests to individuals who in fact do not recognize them sufficiently to *actively* seek the goals or benefits in question. Although, as Balbus (1971, pp. 226–27) points out, Bentley at one point reflects some uncertainty about this position, he generally insists that by sharing interests, individuals also necessarily shared purposes. He thus dismisses the notion of " 'objective utility' to use the economists' term . . . for no such 'objective utility' appears in politics at all . . . [It] is . . . a social nullity" (1967, p. 213). Even though such utilities might help one predict later events, they have no *empirical* status; they could not be linked to actual—that is, *observable*—activity.

> A man who is wise enough may legitimately predict, if he is addicted to the habit of prediction, that a group activity will *ultimately* form along lines marked out by some objective condition which he *thinks* he detects. But the interests that we can take into account must lie a good deal closer to the *actual* existing masses of men. (p. 213, emphasis supplied; see also pp. 214, 227)

Initially, Bentley's insistence that the observer not accept the participants' own account of their interests (their "verbal formulation") may seem inconsistent with his equally pointed refusal to allow the observer himself to suggest an objective interest which the participants do not recognize. Yet, quite defensibly in my view, Bentley advocates a carefully chosen middle position which stresses neither what the participants *claim* to be seeking, nor the observer's judgment as to what they *should* seek, but rather the goals that the participants in fact *do* seek as *revealed* by their own behavior, to use the more contemporary term of certain economists who have a similar view. To be sure, he recognizes fully the ambiguities and obscurities of meaning that such behavior could have; interpretations by the analyst were necessary, but these could and should be based on empirical observation of "their social consequences," that is, the observable impact that the activity of one group had on other groups. In effect, because he can not rely on the actors to provide adequate meaning, he turns to the relevant social context. "We have," he says, "one great moving process to study and . . . it is impossible to state any part except as valued in terms of other parts." For only "as we get all the group activities together and all valued in terms of each, each value in terms of all," will the "scientific truth" emerge (1967, pp. 184, 178, 243).

The Difficulties with Bentley's Processual Vision

If Bentley's epistemological arguments for interpreting group interests in terms of behaviorally revealed preferences have not been directly challenged by later group theorists, his insistence on a processual substantive interpretation of political life has appeared far more problematic. Even in terms of his own writings, his position appears to create serious difficulties for an understanding of political life, especially with respect to the government institutions which Truman emphasizes. Admittedly the issue is somewhat obscured by Bentley's complex view of government. "In the broadest sense," Bentley could define government in entirely noninstitutional terms as "the process of the adjustment of a set of interest groups . . . without any differentiated activity or organ to center attention on just what is happening." To be sure, from a narrower point of view, Bentley sees government as "a differentiated, representative group or sets of groups (organ or set of organs)," so that he by no means entirely ignores institutions. In the end, though, institutions are themselves part of the flow of activity since organ itself is "merely an inept word to indicate a peculiar kind of representative . . . not a certain number of people but a certain network of activities." Indeed, Bentley at one point equates the phenomena of "the governing body" with "the governing process" (1967, pp. 260, 261, 300).

Institutions, in other words, have significance only in terms of "the deeper-lying interests" which "function through" the institutions in question. But such group interests, Bentley says repeatedly, are themselves continuously in motion. Bentley was too shrewd a political observer to ignore entirely the phenomena of institutional stabilty. Thus he recognizes that of various institutions ". . . with all sorts of values and . . . degrees of permanence . . . these two [courts and legislatures] are the ones which established themselves most solidly. . . . Yet the value of any such institution depends entirely . . . on what the pressures are that were working through it." But this approach leaves Bentley unable to explain how and why a four-year presidential term can be so "fixed," when all the important group interests represented through it are themselves in constant flux (1967, pp. 300, 308, 306).

More generally, Bentley seems to have dismissed as unimportant those repetitive activities whose goals are so regularly achieved that the intergroup struggle, indeed the constant change and flow of the group process, are thus absent or of very limited relevance. He thus has little if anything to say about the effects of institutional arrangements, such as the separation of powers, the congressional committee system, and the practice of judicial review as factors independent of the social and economic groups in the society which support or oppose particular policies.

> The governing body has no value in itself, except as one aspect of the process, and cannot even be adequately described except in terms of the deep-lying interests which function through it. It therefore appears hopeless to attempt to classify governing bodies as abstractedly stated by themselves. (p. 300)

This tension between process assumptions and the observable stability of institutions evidently led to occasionally contorted analysis in which language itself seems on the verge of breaking down.

> Now if a law establishes itself and works along smoothly . . . we find as a matter of fact that it usually maintains itself. . . . This seemingly indifferent activity is a real group activity even though the abstracting of an interest, a value, a meaning in terms of other groups seems difficult . . . the difficulty is only in the use of words to make it seem positively worthwhile in common speech. (p. 293)

Bentley's insistence on the pervasive fluidity of group activity also hampers his discussion of broader if less easily operationalized differences in political regimes, which concern Dahl. In his view, these differences are not questions of shared norms which provide stable limits on political behavior by prohibiting some activities; rather, they are differences in group techniques (differences in types of group activities), so that the process of groups seeking very similar goals encompasses at certain points violence rather than persuasion. Thus in Tsarist Russia,

> there is just no available technique for the most depressed groups but violence or a show of violence. In the United States, with its fixed four year presidency and its Supreme Court . . . we break through into violence at times but we can nevertheless count on running pretty steadily without it. (p. 306)

Differences between despotism and democracy are thus mainly a matter of degree, reflecting the different ways interests are represented.

> Except in the case of a subjected population immediately under the heel of the conqueror . . . the ruling class is to a certain extent the chosen (that is, the accepted) ruler of the ruled class, not merely its master, but also its representative, and the despot . . . is representative of both his own class and to a smaller but not the less real extent of the ruled class as well. (p. 314)

Many of these observations about political attitudes, including the norma-tive rules of oligarchic, democratic, or despotic regimes, seems shrewd enough. But Bentley's insistence on emphasizing the conflict of group against group leaves little room for incorporating into his analysis symbols and implicit un-derstandings relating to regimes and constitutions which are intersubjectively shared by members of different groups and which (1) themselves deserved to be explained and (2) have *independent* effects of their own in shaping politi-cal behavior.[9]

Most striking of all, perhaps, the difficulties created by his extremely fluid processual view even apply to Bentley's own primary unit of analysis, the group itself. Dissent by a group member, he writes, *"may* not take him out of the ranks. Under *some* circumstances, it will, or rather it represents his actual transfer to another group position. But under *other* circumstances dissent may be a *wrong* expression of the group position and the dissenter may be actually arrayed in cooperation with his supposed opponents" (p. 225, emphasis sup-plied). In this passage, Bentley's crucial three-termed equation of interest, group, and activity is at best under extreme stress, since members of the same group may not have the same behaviorally revealed interests. Thus, if the activity which defines the group is itself constantly in flux, it is difficult to make the political group itself the clear unequivocal unit Bentley seeks. And as we shall soon see, it was this basic problem that later group theorists attack and to a significant extent correct.

In effect, Bentley resolves his epistemological problem by identifying groups with their activity and thus commits himself to a processual view of politics that seems inconsistent with a reasonable interpretation of political facts—or at least facts important to the group theorists who followed him. Nevertheless, as the later part of this essay maintains, these same group theorists who mod-ify Bentley's processual view of political reality encounter certain difficulties in their view of political group which Bentley's position carefully avoids.

Bentley's Ethical Optimism: Toward the Stability-Disruption-Protest Model

Tacitly, at least, Bentley recognizes a second difficulty with his processual equa-tion of group, interest, and activity. In certain cases, the nonpolitical groups, those not directly concerned with influencing policies, could become politi-cized, develop an interest, by acquiring policy goals. In *The Process of Govern-ment* Bentley primarily recognizes this possibility as he articulates his remark-ably complex ethical attitude toward the American politics of his time, which itself is closely tied to his processual vision. In some respects, Bentley's ethical position resembles those of many other progressive intellectuals, some of whom, like Bentley, supported LaFollette in 1924. In contrast to Marxism, *The Process of Government,* of course, has no discussion of a global philosophy of his-tory, of the alienation of labor, or of the central political role of the proletariat in a capitalist social order. On the other hand, Bentley's stress on economic factors, his view of ideology in terms of group interest, and his emphasis on social contexts as the source of political meaning parallel certain strands of Marxist thought. It is not surprising, then, that Bentley attacks many entrenched practices and institutions, in part from a processual perspective, since many of these abuses threatened to entrench stable inequalities inconsistent with a fluid society. In his first chapter, for example, he singles out such characteristic features of industrializing capitalism as strike-breaking by the Chicago meat packers, starvation wages, and the use of child labor.

These criticisms of specific abuses, however, do not lead Bentley to denounce all of American society, for reasons suggested by his critical observations about political machines as predators, as "marauders in a fertile—but for time being—seemingly helpless country. The interjection suggests an optimistic belief that the fluidity of American group relations will produce decidedly un-Marxian outcomes in the American group process. In the end, he feels, he can rely on "the adjustment of interest." "Compromise—not merely in the logical sense but in practical life—is the very process itself of the crisscross of groups in action." Such compromises would occur, and the abuses would be limited, in part because the victorious groups are self-limiting. As Bentley puts it, "The very nature of the group process . . . is this . . . the lion when he has satisfied his physical need will lie down quite lamblike, however much louder his roars were than his appetite justified" (1967, pp. 229, 371, 205, 359).

Self-limitation, however, was far from the only source of these adjustments in intergroup relations. The same fluidity which justified Bentley's criticisms of certain developments also meant that, for any extended period of time, the relevant policy decision could neither be wholly dictated nor anticipated by even the most powerful actors. Highly processual politics of this sort guaranteed in the end more nearly equitable outcomes by allowing disadvantaged groups to change the situation. Looking at a ten- or twenty-year period, he concedes,

> one may be easily tempted to say we have a government which tends to favor class dominance. But . . . we have avenues of approach through the government such that the class tendency can only advance to a certain degree before being overwhelmed. (p. 358)

Crucially, those who would overwhelm a too successful class in this way were evidently uninvolved in the initial struggle. As Bentley puts it, "When the struggle proceeds too harshly at any point, there will become insistent in the society a group more powerful than either of those involved which tends to suppress the struggle" (p. 415).

Evidently, Bentley had been considerably impressed by the capacity of politically quiescent groups, whether workers or the general public, to intervene politically if the decisions or behavior of the political authorities became too unacceptable. For example, he observes that "the history of the use of spoils . . .

is well enough known: how the party once organized outside the legislature
. . . pressed itself into the government offices . . . how the evils of the system in
time stirred up a group antagonism to them, which we now know as the civil
service reform movement" (p. 415) .

However much one group achieves a seemingly permanent advantage over
others, this disruption in a previously stable relationship would lead to a
counter movement to restore the relationship through political protest to at
least a somewhat equitable balance—somewhat similar at least to what Truman two generations later would call an "equilibrium" in group relations. In
Bentley's own words, such prepolitical activities are not "manifest, or evident
or palpable . . . to the same extent at the stage of their progress in which we
have to search them out. They are activities which can perhaps be pictured by
the use of the word 'potential'. . . . These tendencies are activities themselves
. . . they are stages of activity just as much as any other activity" (pp. 184–85).
It seems that these observations make sense only if interpreted to mean that a
social or economic group's ongoing nonpolitical activities are also "potential"
from the standpoint of political analysis; that is, *if* such nonpolitical activities
can no longer be pursued effectively, the group will turn to politics, and the
activity *then* becomes palpable. But whether this interpretation of Bentley is
correct or not, it does describe the route that later group theorists followed.

At best, Bentley's position is obscured by his effort to maintain that activities could be simultaneously observable, politically relevant, and merely potential. It was in clarifying this point and thus the substantive argument that
David Truman made one of his major contributions to the group theories tradition and at the same time departed significantly from Bentley's position.

ORGANIZATIONAL AND INSTITUTIONAL CONSTRAINTS IN TRUMAN'S THE GOVERNMENTAL PROCESS

The Governmental Process (1953) is widely recognized as the definitive survey
of both American political interest group behavior through the 1940s and the
relevant literature in other social sciences. David Truman's book, however,
ranks as the pivotal work in the entire group theory tradition for two additional
reasons: Truman explicitly reintroduced and reemphasized Bentley's approach
in the study of American group politics, and he simultaneously modified Bentley's position by emphasizing elements of both political and social constraint
on the flow of the group process.

Nor are the latter changes merely incidental to his enterprise. Some scholars (e.g., MacKenzie, 1955) have treated *The Governmental Process* as essentially two enterprises: a problematic "theoretical" introduction, which defines
concepts and introduces themes, and a longer, more persuasive synthesis of the
relevant data. In fact, however, the introductory concepts, assumptions, and
distinctions inform and shape Truman's later empirical analysis.

Truman's Bentleyan View of Interest and Process

Like Bentley, Truman evidently feels that some policy outcomes in the United States might well be unacceptably inegalitarian or incompatible with meaningful political democracy. On the other hand, although he is not as explicit as Bentley on this point in *The Governmental Process,* he generally seems to accept the pattern of group politics as he found it.

> It seems probable that the widespread unorganized interests are adequately strong within . . . the United States. [Thus] . . . dangers to the continuance of representative government derive less from lack of basic support for these interests than from other features of the political system *per se.* (Truman, 1953, p. 519)

Or as he puts it a few pages before, America has a political system in which "organized interest groups . . . from their very nature bulk large in the political process" and whose very "activities . . . imply controversy and conflict" which is not only desirable but is, indeed, the "essence of politics" (pp. 503–4). In consequence, he concludes, "The great political task now as in the past is to *perpetuate* a viable system by *maintaining* the conditions under which such widespread understanding and appreciation [of the moderate claims of organized interests] can exist" (p. 524, emphasis supplied).

Truman also accepts Bentley's view of political and social life as purposive and goal-directed, defining political interest groups in terms of clear policy concerns that make claims on the government. Accordingly, he joins Bentley in rejecting any objective interest perspective. For example, in dismissing a public interest as a useful concept for political analysis, where public is defined as a whole which cannot be dissolved into its components, he rests his case on the divergence of expressed opinions. As he remarks—quoting Bentley—"there are always some parts of the nation [i.e., public] to be found arrayed against others," that is, some minority which does not endorse the purported public interest (Bentley, 1967, p. 220, quoted by Truman, 1953, p. 50). "Even in war," Truman himself adds, " . . . we always find pacifists, conscientious objectors, spies and subversives, who reflect interests opposed to those of 'the nation as a whole' " (p. 50).[10]

Truman's opposition to the definition of the public as an indivisible whole also seems in part to stem from his rather Bentleyan view of a continuously changing process in which an aggregate as stable as the total public has no plausible place. Thus, although Truman stresses formally organized groups in his empirical analysis, his account of their interactions with one another, as they seek their policy goals, generally stresses change and movement. Even very powerful political interest groups, Truman says, can exercise only unstable control over both public opinion (Chapter 8) and the political parties, given the latter's own "protean character." And he rarely describes a group so powerful that it can fully control its relationships with other groups. Rather, these usually well-organized groups fight, bargain, and compromise, with different groups assuming prominence at different points in time on different issues, under such varying conditions that the groups themselves cannot reliably anticipate the outcomes.

> Government decisons are the resultant of effective access by various interests, of which organized groups may be only a segment. These decisions *may be more or less stable* depending on the strength of the supporting interests and on the *severity of the disturbances which affect that strength.* (p. 507, emphasis supplied) [11]

Heavily influenced by the work of Michels (1958), **Truman** recognizes, as Bentley does not, that the "active minorities" which control the organized groups' internal life introduce a considerable element of intragroup stability (Chapter 5). Yet his analysis suggests that even these minorities make a contribution to the fluid character of group politics. The effective pressure and counterpressure necessary for intergroup conflict and bargaining depends on the groups' internal cohesion, and in his account groups must primarily rely for this cohesion on the efforts of these same active minorities.

The Place of Institutions and Social Groups

Truman's divergence from Bentley appears in his first chapters, where he is much more explicit and systematic in distinguishing political and nonpolitical groups. On the one hand, he excludes entirely from his analysis those "categoric groups" defined only by some characteristic of the members—"farmers, insurance men, blondes, illiterates, mothers, neurotics and so on."[12] On the other hand, he considers a set of individuals to be a socially significant group if, on the basis of the "interactions" or "relationships of the persons involved," the group members have certain "shared attitudes" or "frames of reference." Such groups could very conceivably include classes, races, religious denominations, and occupations, which to clarify later discussions will be referred to throughout this article as *social groups* to distinguish them sharply from what Truman himself calls *interest groups.* He stipulates that members of the latter must share, in addition to frames of references, "attitudes toward what is needed or wanted in a given situation, observable as demands or claims upon other groups in the society." Finally, an interest group becomes a *political interest group* "if and when it makes claims from or upon any of the institutions of government" (Truman, 1953, pp. 23–24, 33–34, 37).

Having included social groups in his typology, Truman goes on to observe that they themselves may shape political life.

> "Perhaps the most basic factor affecting access [to public officials] is the position of the group or its spokesman in the social structure. . . . The deference accorded a high-status group not only facilitates the acceptance of its propaganda, but also eases its approach to government." (p. 265)

Truman gives even more emphasis to stable patterns of political behavior, that is, government institutions and the interest groups' own formal organizations. Although Bentley could not give a satisfactory account of these phenomena and, even more important, fails to assess their independent political impact, Truman, as Leonard Binder first pointed out to me, affirmatively emphasizes first how these institutions overtly constrain the political process which Bentley stresses and second how they shape group influence and access of many key actors (chapters 11 and 15). Thus, early in Chapter 2, quoting George Lundberg (1939, p. 375), he discusses the "stability, uniformity, and generality" of such institutionalized groups, as the "courts, legislatures and executives, and other political institutions" (p. 26). Although these were precisely the sorts of governmental units with which Bentley has such difficulty, Truman's analysis of their importance in shaping group activity—for example, "The Ordeal of the Executive"—is among the most perceptive in *The Governmental Process*. His discussion of "access," particularly in the legislative arena, introduced a new term that seems to have helped focus later empirical research. And Truman applies this same perspective to the groups' own governance. Thus a section on the "structural types" of internal group life discusses the importance of the "federated form" of organization (such as the AFL) on the leaders' control, as well as the importance of functional as opposed to geographic forms of group affiliation (pp. 115–19, 122). To be sure, Truman agrees with Bentley's insistence that an institution is a "pattern of interaction different only in degree from other group patterns in society" (p. 263). But the difference of degree is substantial. The "formal institutions of government in the United States do not prescribe all the meanderings of the stream of politics. They do mark some of its limits, however, and designate certain points through which it must flow" (p. 322). Finally, this explicit concern with stable patterned activity, particularly in social groups, has still another advantage in permitting Truman to account much more systematically than Bentley for the way politically inactive groups sometimes intervene in the policy process.

The Stability-Disruption-Protest Model

Early in *The Governmental Process* Truman discusses the way "institutionalized groups"—those which are well organized, stable, and widely distributed in a society—maintain themselves. Many such groups, he asserts, are characterized by "an equilibrium among the interactions of the participants" involving behavior "along standard lines." This equilibrium tends to be self-perpetuating. Indeed, we mean "by the stability of an institution," a "tendency to maintain or revert to equilibrium." [13] And this tendency to maintain or restore previously existing patterns characterizes much social life outside these institutions. Apart from aberrant or neurotic behavior, individuals and groups faced with such disruption will seek to end the disruption through "the formation of new groups that may function to restore the balance. . . . These new groups are . . . likely to become political groups, although, they need not do so." The crucial point, then, is that the disequalibrating events can produce new political claims which seem to be a "compensation for the disturbances in the equilibrium of existing institutionalized groups" (Truman, 1953, pp. 27, 31, 32) .[41]

Truman believes that these organized group responses to such disturbances are in fact frequent features of American politics. Thus farm groups "came with the spread of commercial farming. . . . [since the] accompanying specialization exposed farmers to unpredictable insecurities stemming from changes in the market." A basic point about business organizations is "that trade associations have emerged in response to changes or disturbances in the habitual relationships (interactions) of groups of individuals, and that these associations have had to resort to the institution of government in order to stabilize relationships within and between groups" (Truman, 1953, pp. 87, 75) .[15]

In his best-known application of this stability-disruption-protest model, Truman attempts to account for the ability of the American and other political systems to "obviate the possibility of irreconcilable conflict," by considering "the unorganized interest, or potential interest group." This widely attacked formulation parallels Bentley's notion of "potential activity." Indeed, Truman refers to these unorganized interests as "systems of belief" or the "general ideological consensus"—much like Bentley's "habit background." The potential groups which Truman discusses most explicitly emerge to protect "the rules of the game." Citing Bentley (1967, p. 397) , he asserts that members of potential groups will become active, will indeed form "newly organized" interest groups, to restrict "marked and prolonged deviation" from the constitutional requirements and "democratic mold" that shape the American regime (Truman, 1953, pp. 510–11, 512, 513–14) .

Truman, however, is careful to extend his analysis beyond regime maintenance to any "disturbance in established relationships and expectations *anywhere* in society." [16]   And this situation may even affect particular organized groups—social groups in the terminology of this essay—such as families, businesses, or churches—that is sets of individuals engaged in common activities but "which do not operate continuously as interest groups or political interest groups" seeking public policy goals. In other words, Truman assumes that a given social group has a set of constant but nonpolitical goals, including, to use his own examples, child-rearing, appropriate religious worship and observance, or the successful operation of a business. The social group is likely to acquire a political interest to the degree that the accustomed ways (patterns) of achieving these goals are disrupted (Truman, 1953, p. 511, emphasis supplied) .

This account seems more satisfactory than Bentley's because it can draw on Truman's discussion of social groups for which Bentley had no clear counterpart. But it is equally important to note the extent to which this approach preserves much of Bentley's three-termed group-activity-interest equation, by restricting it to the realm of political action. For Truman, groups become politically relevant—i.e., become *political* interest groups—only at the point where they engage in *political* activities. The activities in turn are considered political only when they are linked to a political interest, i.e., seeking a policy goal. It is then, when the nonpolitical activity which defines a social group (and its interest) is frustrated, when the group's relations are disrupted, that the social group makes claims on others including the government, acquires a *political* interest, and thus becomes a political interest group.

Many critics have attacked this potential group formulation as illegitimately extending the meaning of group and thus diluting the concept. In my view, however, this formulation makes a good deal of sense if it is understood in conjunction with Truman's social group–interest group–political interest group typology. Although Truman's language is less precise than it might be, potential groups can usefully be considered as social groups that are not yet politicized; they are potential only in this lack of *presently* political goals. This is not to say that Truman's discussion is fully satisfactory but only that any critique must be carefully and rather narrowly drawn—as I shall try to do at the conclusion of this essay.

DAHL'S WHO GOVERNS?: *ACTIVE LEADERSHIP, REGIME NORMS, AND CITIZEN QUIESCENCE IN THE GROUP PROCESS*

Robert Dahl did empirical research on New Haven politics and wrote *Who Governs?* (1961) in conjunction with his theoretical critique of the ruling elite model of American politics (1958). It is in the context of this critique and his related discussion of the social, economic, and political sources of influence and power in the American regime that Dahl's contribution to the group theories acquires its special importance. The concentration in this essay on such relatively early work unfortunately ignores Dahl's later writings on democratic regimes in the United States and elsewhere—writings which have a rather different perspective on the ethical status of American politics than that in *Who Governs?* (See Dahl, 1967, 1970, 1971, 1973.) It is, nevertheless, *Who Governs?* that connects most directly with the other analyses considered here. Specifically, although the book resembles the work of Bentley and Truman on several key points, it makes a distinctive contribution in connecting the restraints imposed on group activity to the regime's own norms, especially as they are accepted and acted on by its most active citizens. Equally important, by distinguishing so sharply between the political participation of these activists and the average citizen, Dahl is able to elaborate the stability-disruption-protest model. In particular, by specifying in detail the apolitical aspects of those social groups before they become politicized, he is able to account more plausibly for the way they intervene in and appreciably alter ongoing group processes.

Dahl's View of Interest and Process

Like other group theorists, Dahl thinks of relevant political groups as having
clear policy commitments, and they could therefore be defined as sets of individuals "with some values, purposes and demands in common." And at least
in two of the policy areas examined in New Haven, Dahl finds a pattern so
fluid that many of the crucial groups were themselves in flux. On the issue of
city redevolepment, new policy proposals were primarily generated not by an
existing interest group at all but by Mayor Lee, an ambitious and able politician. Indeed, rather than groups' exerting pressure for this policy, Lee created
the most important group of highly influential individuals to support his proposals. Although some relatively long-established groups became interested in
the issue, and their general support was very helpful to Lee, Dahl concludes
that, overall, they played a relatively passive role. And even those groups which
were relatively stable (notably several formal organizations in the education
field) at least varied widely in their importance over and across issue areas.
Education "policy making," to be sure, was in fact "far more routinized than
in redevelopment," allowing perhaps for greater interest group influence. But
the Roman Catholic Church had little direct influence. And although the
Teachers' League (but not the PTA) had a more significant impact, it was
the mayor, once again, who created rather than responded to the major interest group seeking educational change, that is, the Citizen Advisory Committee
on Education (Dahl, 1961, pp. 5, 137–38, chapters 10–11, pp. 148, 151, 155–59).

Dahl's position in *Who Governs?* on the limited influence of stable organized interests, which places him closer to Bentley than to such later writers
as Truman, extends beyond his empirical findings in New Haven. In a general
introductory discussion, Dahl considers several stable social elements as possible
answers to the question "Who Governs?" and concludes that all of them—political parties, economic elites, *and* interest groups—were defective insofar as
they stripped politics of its contingent character. "By contrast," he maintains
"an older view . . . stressed the enormous political potential of the cunning,
resourceful, masterful leader . . . a leader who knew how to use his resources
to the maximum is not so much the agent of others, as others are his agent."
Here Dahl identifies for politics in general a source of change which Mayor
Lee of New Haven exemplified. Yet in Dahl's account, even the mayor's position varied with the relevant circumstances, including each mayor's aggressiveness on particular issues. Thus the very pattern of political alliances in the city
shifted considerably from autonomous functional policy spheres in one era to
an executive-centered coalition in another, just as the average citizen, regardless
of group affiliation, reacted very much to specific political developments (Dahl,
1961, p. 6, chapters 10–11, 16–17).

Very clearly, this analysis shares Bentley's and Truman's pluralist view
of American politics. For New Haven at least, Dahl concludes that no one
stable interest group or set of groups controlled the political system, in part

because of "the fluctuations in . . . the use of political resources that occur over time." New Haven was "a system dominated by many different sets of leaders each having access to a different combination of political responses. It was, in short, a pluralist system" (Dahl, 1961, pp. 300, 86) .[17]

Once again Dahl generalizes these remarks to the sphere of American politics. As he sums it up, "most citizens who participate at all are, as we have observed, occasional, specialized participants." The way individuals invest their resources in politics varies with "the different events [that] take place . . . in the political system. Most people employ their resources sporadically if at all" except for elections (1961, pp. 300, 273) .

As this remark suggests, such political activity is also purposive or voluntaristic, and Dahl accordingly rejects the use of objective or unrecognized interests in political research, because they were generally unconnected with any observable goal-seeking activity. Thus, although Dahl recognizes the importance of "the objective situation in which individuals are placed," he insists that such "differences in objective situations take on meaning for the individual only as they are translated into . . . subjective factors . . . such as values, predisposition, information and identification."[18] "The subjective life of the individual," as a result, "has a style and pattern often connected ,only in loose fashion to his 'objective' situation" (1961, p. 275).

These views lead him to argue at length in an imaginary dialogue that a group's influence must be understood as depending not just on the available resources but on its observable disposition to use them for an acknowledged policy goal (Chapter 24). *Who Governs?* discusses New Haven's black population, as well as the Irish, Italian, and German, only in those specific cases, such as elections, where their visibly purposeful activity led them to make important political demands.

Regime Norms and Political Leadership as Constraints on Group Politics

If in these respects Dahl follows Bentley very closely, he is nevertheless no more ready than Truman to accept an extremely processual view of American politics. But where Truman pays most attention to government institutions and group organizations as elements of stable constraint, Dahl stresses, first, the character of the regime in which these institutions are embedded, and second, the initiative of political leaders for whom these regime norms are particularly important. To be sure, his research on New Haven by no means ignores institutions and organized groups. He points out that the mayor's formal status enabled him at least to initiate proposals quite independently of all the most obviously important economic units and indeed to resist any intraparty challenge to his own renomination. At a number of other places Dahl points out the impact of other public officials who sometimes acted in alliance with organized interests—including cases where the Board of Park Commissioners and the Teachers' League were able to frustrate and limit the power of Mayor Lee and his allies (1961, Chapter 10, p. 111, Chapter 17) .

Dahl's own work, however, focuses primarily on the political norms and expectations—the psychological "inner world"—that patterns the regime-maintaining behavior of American citizens and most particularly that of the elites who command key institutions and organizations. These rules, which require counting votes fairly, granting public office to the victors, respecting the freedom to speak and dissent, and the like, constrain the way all groups exercise and seek political authority. Of course, Dahl sees that

> Neither the prevailing consensus, the creed nor even the political system itself are immutable products of democratic ideas . . . they are always open in some measure, to alteration through those complex processes of symbiosis and change.

Yet at least in New Haven, he found that "The essential characteristics of the political system as I described them have remained substantially intact for the past century." Admittedly, most citizens cannot readily articulate a principled belief in "certain democratic norms, rules, or procedures." But Dahl argues at length that the strength of this democratic creed for the United States as a whole does not depend on "the numbers of persons who adhere to it, but [on] . . . the amount of resources they use—or are expected to use—in acting on their beliefs" (1961, pp. 325, 313, 314) .

It is rather in the political stratum and its beliefs that Dahl finds the real source of regime stability, as well as many initiatives on specific public policies which Mayor Lee and his allies so vigorously began and to which various interest groups responded. Specifically, he maintains that "over long periods of time, the great bulk of the citizens possess a fairly stable set of democratic beliefs at a high level of abstraction." By comparison, however, "members of the political stratum" have a "more consistent, more ideological, more detailed and explicit . . . agreement on the norms." And it is the behavior of this *homo politicus,* to use Dahl's term, that is most significantly patterned or structured by these stable liberal democratic regime norms which, in turn, maintain the American regime in the pluralist form he found in New Haven. Since the behavior of political interest groups is in turn shaped by these leaders operating according to these norms, Dahl's departure from Bentley is very clear. In effect he asserts the constraining and stabilizing consequence for political interest group activity of precisely those structured variations in regimes that Bentley considers to be mainly the different "techniques" by which group interests are expressed and satisfied (1961, pp. 316, 319, 321) .

Dahl's Elaboration of the Stability-Disruption-Protest Model

Who Governs? is of course well known among political scientists for its emphasis on the ordinarily nonpolitical proclivities of most American citizens—

an emphasis buttressed by Dahl's empirical analysis of the repetitive, regularized, largely nonconflictual and nonpolitical activities of most social groups.

On the basis of an impressive combination of historical and field research methods, Dahl finds that New Haven's social and economic notables had become politically quiescent in the 1950s, even though they had been dominant during parts of the nineteenth century. Nevertheless, it is clear that Mayor Lee was concerned about the reactions of the New Haven business community, among other social groups, and equally important, that under certain conditions even lower-status social groups could intervene in contemporary politics. And it is in analyzing such interventions that he elaborates even more fully than Truman the stability-disruption-protest model.

Although he assumes that the average citizen (*homo civicus*) is usually apolitical, Dahl observes that "if men are frustrated in their primary activities, and if they may find or think they find in political activity a means to satisfy their primary needs, then politics may become more salient" (1961, p. 279). He vividly illustrated this generalization with a concrete case in point from New Haven politics—the controversy over the metal houses, which was meticulously described by William Muir (1955). Unlike the other issues that Dahl considers, the metal houses issue was initiated by a grass-roots political interest group which emerged very suddenly and without the significant leadership of politically experienced individuals familiar with regime norms. Instead, this group, formally called after a time the Hill Civic Association, was formed by residents of a lower-middle-income neighborhood to protest an attempt to erect 65 metal houses in a heavily Italian working-class area. This neighborhood, "the hasty observer might easily conclude, was a likely spot in which to find the politics of a mass society," that is, a politics without effective group life (Dahl, 1961, p. 196). In fact, however, the area was populated by "youthful, vigorous, hardworking" residents, who "took pride in their homes, their work, their children and their neighborhood" (1961, p. 193). Here in Truman's terms were individuals with collectively shared attitudes based on frequent interaction who had remained a social group without seeing the need to make distinctive claims against others and then seek to secure them politically. In this case, however,

> the proposal to erect the metal houses . . . seemed to nearby residents to constitute a clear threat to the neighborhood . . . [including] an influx of Negroes, a decline in property values, a sharp change in an area in which many of the residents had lived their entire lives." (Dahl, 1961, p. 193)

"And so," Dahl observes, "these essentially apolitical people turned briefly to political action to avert the danger they thought confronted them" (1961, p. 193), collectively protesting the plan to various public officials, organizing a formal interest group, and making alliances with sympathetic influential citizens.

Dahl himself believes this incident rather atypical, given the "apathy, indifference and general agreement" which usually characterizes New Haven politics. Indeed, the residents of the Hill became active politically "not from a sense of duty nor out of a sustained interest in politics but only because *primary* goals at the *focus* of their lives were endangered, and political action was thought to be the *only* way to ward off the danger." Yet however idiosyncratic the metal houses case was in its particular aspects, Dahl also describes a number of citywide issues, such as education and redevelopment, which also conform substantially to the stability-disruption-protest pattern. Mayor Lee, for example, could win strong support for urban redevelopment because the deterioration in the New Haven slums had threatened housing opportunities, made shopping in the downtown area increasingly inconvenient, and economically threatened important businessmen, some of whom saw the danger. Similarly, Dahl indicates that it was the deterioration of the physical plant of both the elementary and high schools which stimulated increased group activity in New Haven school politics after World War II and led to new school policy organization (1961, pp. 198, 197, emphasis supplied; 120, 135, 160–61, 306).

All of these cases, then, conform to the expectation in the group theories literature that new groups are likely to emerge after the disruption of a previous equilibrium which permitted them to obtain certain benefits without resort to politics. Even then, political activity is not certain. As Dahl puts it, "in a political culture where individual achievement and nongovernmental techniques are assigned a high priority in problem-solving, men may be frustrated in their primary activities without ever turning to politics for solutions." Indeed, such movements will appear only after a sharp shift in the cost benefit ratio of what he calls "the psychic economy of the individual" (1961, pp. 279–80).

McCONNELL'S ANTIPLURALIST CRITIQUE: PRIVATE POWER AS A CONSTRAINT ON THE GROUP PROCESS

Grant McConnell's *Private Power and American Democracy* (1966) is the most important and empirically detailed ethical critique of American group politics written since World War II. Although he never intended to write a comprehensive theory of all American politics, McConnell's contributions to empirical analysis of group activities are equally impressive. He goes even further than Truman in demonstrating the degree to which political institutions and the interest groups' own organizations limit group activities. At the same time, he adds to Dahl's discussion of prevailing political norms an analysis of an American "orothodoxy on the central problem of private power" (p. 51). By celebrating localism, decentralization, and grass-roots democracy, this doctrine encourages the further quiescence of the socially deprived and politically uninvolved, and it discriminates against the "general public." For all this added emphasis on the patterned constraints that limit the group process, McConnell is far from entirely pessimistic; *some* relatively open, fluid group activity remains possible, given favorable political conditions. In part perhaps because he so carefully addresses writers like Truman in their own terms, he thus presents a theory of constituency size and diversity, explicitly based on Madison's *Tenth Federalist*, which accounts more comprehensively for the variation in group goals and activities and in policy outcomes than any comparable interpretation in the group theories tradition.[19]

McConnell as a Group Theorist

McConnell agrees with other group theorists' position in his estimate of the impact that policy-oriented (and as in Truman's account, usually well-organized) political interest groups have on American politics. "Since early in the history of the American republic," he writes, "organized interest groups have wielded a strong degree of political power," whereas social classes have had limited relevance. "Where European politics and European political thought have been cast in the mold of classes and class conflict, American politics has been largely free of class divisions." For this reason, "Marxian formulas have fared ill over the long span." [20] Like Dahl in particular, McConnell also rejects C. Wright Mills's power elite interpretation of American politics. Despite some acknowledged overlap between his thesis and Mills's on the way private economic interests limit group conflict, McConnell is impressed by

> the sheer *multiplicity* of organized groups in private life, many with heavy influence sometimes amounting to control of public agencies and many with marked power through ties to particular congressional committees.

The account of the prevailing American political norms in *Private Power* also parallels rather closely Dahl's stress on the dominance of private concerns for most Americans. "Ultimately," according to these widely shared political norms, "the only test seemed to be individual choice—not what was objectively good, but what each individual rightly or wrongly declared to be his own interest." Nor does McConnell ignore the virtues of this privatistic pluralism so important to other group theorists, a "vision by which one interest opposes another and ambition checks ambition." Although the vision is often frustrated, where achieved it is perhaps the American polity's "greatest merit," for in those cases "virtually no definable group has been compelled for long to consider itself hopelessly outside" the group system (McConnell, 1966, pp. 13, 25, 337, emphasis supplied, 364, 164, 26) .

McConnell also agrees with other group theorists in treating group interests as subjectively held preferences rather than as objective benefits identified by observers without regard to the group members' own views. Such, at least, is his view at a number of points in *Private Power*. Thus he writes that "many of the *values* Americans *hold* in the highest esteem can only be realized through large constituencies." Or again, the exclusion of some groups from the existing policy process is largely discussed in terms of already recognized interests. The character of state political institutions, to take one example, "minimizes—or suppresses—the *voices* of significant elements of the state populations." Indeed, he appears to accept, as well, Bentley's epistemologically grounded insistence that such preferences can be reliably known only through overt behavior. As we shall see, the critical element for McConnell in assessing a political group involves identifying its constituency. But we cannot be satisfied with the group's own often self-serving characterizations. Rather, "it is necessary to specify the *actual* constituencies larger than those in whose interest they customarily act . . . . Behavior is a better guide" (McConnell, 1966, pp. 366–67, 181, emphasis supplied; p. 344, McConnell's emphasis) .

Finally, McConnell frequently uses the group theorists' stability-disruption-protest model to account for important new political protest groups. In *The Decline of Agrarian Democracy,* he interprets the rise of populism as a response to an obviously disrupting decline in farm prices and sees rising prices as accounting for the movement's later demise. Similarly, the later development of organized pressure groups was a response to the farmers' perception that they had become *"increasingly* the victims of the . . . blind forces of market fluctuation" (1953, p. 10; p. 44, emphasis supplied) . Again in *Private Power* he interprets progressivism and the more ephemeral working-class protests of the Knights of Labor and the IWW as responses to the fact that "the corporation *assumed* its modern form and . . . *acquired* an unprecedented influence over the affairs of ordinary men" (1966, p. 30, emphasis supplied) .

The Group Theories Tradition and Ethical Criticism of American Group Politics

McConnell's ethical criticisms resemble the negative side of Bentley's ambivalent attitude toward American politics—the side which concentrated on numerous instances or abuses, special privileges, and inequality. Like Dahl and Truman, for example, McConnell identifies constraints on group activity, including the decentralization of parties and the federal system of government and policy administration, but he finds them far more severe than any of the three theorists than we have so far considered. Indeed he condemns these patterns because they violate the group theorists' shared commitment to an open, fluid, processual, liberal democracy. On the one side, narrow interest group politics produces patterns of stable social inequality through "the oppression of the weak." On the other hand, it constricts meaningful freedom, since the dominant units are "so small that they lack formal institutions of government," encouraging "pressures for conformity" that are especially "intense and extreme" (1966, p. 348).

By comparison with Truman, McConnell places much greater emphasis on the degree and consequences of elite control within the organization, i.e.,

Truman's active minorities (McConnell, 1966, Chapter 5), and somewhat greater stress on the tendency of governmental institutions to favor entrenched interests. At the same time, McConnell considers certain regime norms and values in addition to those concerned with elections and civil liberties that are so important to Dahl. In particular, *Private Power* discusses the norms of informal spontaneous grass-roots democracy and decentralization, which he believes frustrate genuine democratic control by remanding policy decisions to group elites (pp. 112, 115, 166, 337, 351–52). Thus McConnell accepts Dahl's point about the lack of widespread political activism but takes it as an indication of the exclusion of ordinary citizens, e.g., poor farmers, from the critical decision-making areas, e.g., agricultural politics (McConnell, 1953).

These normative and institutional sources of constraints, as McConnell interprets them, have particularly unfortunate consequences when they operate together, since they remove the different elements of process or fluidity which Dahl and Truman each retain despite their departures from Bentley's views on process. McConnell's assertions about the extremely oligarchic character of organized groups suggest a barrier to the rapid activation of politically quiescent individuals that Dahl does not include among the many sources of quiescence that he considers. Conversely, the importance of a belief in decentralization grass-roots democracy—which McConnell calls (1966, p. 91) the "American Orthodoxy"—undermines, for McConnell, Truman's assumption that organized groups often compete meaningfully. Rather, he believes that by seizing nearly exclusive control of a particular policy area, groups stabilize the pattern of decision-making, exclude unexpected interventions of other groups, and thus reduce the importance of the open intergroup conflict so important for Truman. In sum, McConnell rejects both Dahl's reliance on groups which emerge rather quickly in response to particular issues and Truman's reliance on the competition among established groups as sources of open unconstrained political life.

Public Interest, Size of Constituency, and Constraints on Group Activity

McConnell also differs from some others in the group theory tradition in that he strongly asserts the importance of the public interest as an analytically or empirically useful concept. Bentley and Truman reject this usage because there are no issues on which one could expect unanimity throughout the country, and McConnell does agree that "it is difficult to have an interest *all* men would agree that they shared" (1966, p. 364, emphasis supplied). Consistent with Bentley's and Truman's epistemological skepticism, he also agrees that the claim to be "in the public interest" can readily be a disguise for "the selfish ends of narrow groups" (1966, p. 368).[21]

The precise disagreement over this concept, then, must therefore be stated carefully. Both Bentley and Truman, after all, refer to a pattern of behavior in which a much broader aggregate may intervene to limit or restrain the parties immediately involved in a particular policy issue when their conflict or activities harm those not immediately involved. This pattern resembles fairly closely McConnell's view of the "public," taken from Bentley's coauthor, John Dewey (1927), i.e., individuals or groups not directly involved in the conflict over a particular issue who may be affected adversely by those more actively involved (for example, the effect on the general population of health and environmental policies shaped by particular groups) (McConnell, 1966, p. 366). It is in this context, he observes, with a holistic emphasis rather different from some other group theorists, that "it is not meaningless to speak of public values. They are public in the sense that they are shared by broad constituencies" (1966, p. 366). To use quite different language, which he himself does not employ, McConnell is concerned with a tendency to supply private, often relatively divisible goods demanded by limited interest groups, e.g., policies aiding oil industry profits, at the expense of public goods, such as unpolluted air and water, the protection of scenic beauty, and the like. The public interest is thus analytically important insofar as it refers to the "mobilization of broad constituencies" on behalf of public goods when and if this occurs (p. 366). But in McConnell's usage broad constituencies clearly need not be identical to the entire population. It follows, therefore, that his expectations about some specific protests by previously uninvolved groups are not in fact diametrically opposed to the usage and expectations of Truman and Bentley.

McConnell's use of the public interest, then, divides him from some other group theorists less for what the concept actually denotes by itself than for its place in his more general interpretation of American group politics. "The public," in effect, is the limiting case, the broadest of those large, diverse constituencies whose interests are in conflict with the demands of much more narrowly limited groups. This contrast between broad and narrow groups is, in turn, central to McConnell's crucial analysis of the way that the size and diversity of a group's constituency shapes its behavior and success. The normative, institutional and social-economic constraints on the flow of group activity which McConnell considers in terms of constituency size and diversity were also important to other group theorists dissatisfied with Bentley's extremely processual views. But McConnell's formulation is so important because it achieves a level of generality (by applying to and differentiating essentially all groups) and economy (by providing a carefully limited set of explanatory variables) new to the group theory tradition. Specifically, McConnell maintains that policies controlled by groups with small homogeneous geographic constituencies (such as local unions) and similar functional constituencies (such as individual commodiy groups in agriculture) favor the privileged and harm the general public. By contrast, where the relevant political interest group is large and diverse, it will favor policies that are relatively egalitarian or responsive to public values or both. McConnell is so ethically critical of American group politics because groups with small homogeneous constituencies have dominated the conflict over public policy, partly as a result of the conservative American orthodoxy, which exalts grass-roots decision-making and partly as a result of the progressive movement, which weakened the formal political institutions and party organizations that favor large constituency politics.

The constituency approach in sum, links the character of organized groups and institutions and the character of the regime norms discussed by other group theorists to the policy outputs affected by group activities. Equally important, to once again depart from McConnell's own language, it specifies a clear, comprehensive cluster of independent variables (size and diversity of constituency) and links them to the crucial dependent variables (the character of group demands and policy outputs secured by the most powerful groups) through a wealth of empirical analysis.

Social Groups, the Presidency, and the Limits of Size of Constituency Analysis

McConnell's theory, of course, provides assertions that, properly specified, are empirically testable. But the turbulent politics of the late 1960s and early 1970s suggest that, in terms of his own values, his expectations in *Private Power* are too optimistic in some respects and too pessimistic in others. On one side, those institutions which McConnell thought would encourage large constituency politics, particularly the presidency and the executive branch of the federal government, do not appear to have done so from the latter half of the Johnson administration through at least the Nixon presidency. Large constituency politics, for McConnell, is inclusive rather than exclusive and thus involves large numbers of participants. McConnell, to be sure, did recognize that the constituencies of some groups which have sought equality and change through widespread participation may gradually narrow over time—especially after they have secured their own organizational position.[22] The difficulty here seems to be that national political institutions with constituencies that remain *formally* very large may also shift from encouraging broad constituency politics; indeed—as Mills and others allege—such institutions may engage in essentially collusive politics that exclude most citizens and restrict diverse groups from participating, as the politics of the Vietnam war attests. The intensity of group conflict and, in turn, the extent to which the group process is indeed fluid and open are thus not so fully determined—though they are assuredly influenced—by the size and diversity of the relevant political constituencies. As I shall presently try to argue, other factors—notably including the degree to which objective group interests are recognized subjectively—are also important.

The question of objective interests is equally relevant in analyzing those developments which make McConnell's expectations appear to be overpessimistic, namely, the emergence of those large constituency interest groups which McConnell favored. In fact, the late 1960s were marked not just by protests over the Vietnam war and presidential power, but by the rise of such issues as consumer protection, conservation, and the environment. Although these broader groups, including the ecology movement and Ralph Nader's consumer and worker-oriented safety movement, were numerically small in terms of active members, they sought indivisible benefits for very large, diffuse groups and aroused at least some diffuse support, thus offering some limited confirmation of Bentley's expectation that ordinarily uninvolved interests will eventually make themselves heard. As it happens, McConnell himself played a significant role in the conservation movement, and he notes in *Private Power* that even "by the early 1960s, then, there were some grounds for believing progress toward the development of a politically effective general constituency" in at least some of these areas "was in sight." Nevertheless, he felt that "the record to this point has been unfortunate" (1966, p. 229). What is left largely unexplained is how the emergence of these several protest groups can be accounted for.

As we have seen, McConnell often relies, like other group theorists, on the stability-disruption-protest model. But as Dahl in particular makes clear, this model holds that such new groups emerge in order to achieve goals that had been satisfactorily secured in the past through nonpolitical means. The groups which emerged in the 1960s often appeared to turn to politics on behalf of goals that were qualitatively new. Such *new* demands we shall maintain shortly are much more easily handled by an objective interest analysis. This question, as well as the question of *collusive* large constituency politics, can be clarified somewhat by turning to the work of Theodore J. Lowi, which most fully illustrates the tension between the group theorists' continued rejection of objective interests (basically on Bentley's epistemological grounds) and their increasingly emphatic belief, *contra* Bentley, that American group politics is by no means fully open and processual.

RIGIDIFIED GROUP POLITICS: PUBLIC POLICY CONSTRAINTS IN THE WORK OF THEODORE J. LOWI

Although much of Theodore J. Lowi's work as a group theorist is still too recent to be readily placed in a proper perspective, four considerations indicate its importance. First, Lowi's discussion of the arenas of power (1964b) is the most influential typology developed by an American group theorist in the 1960s. Second, by pointing out the degree to which group activities vary with the type of public policy at issue, Lowi identifies still another element of political structure, a regular pattern of primarily political behavior, which constrains the flow of group activities. Third, Lowi uses a dramatic vocabulary and a remarkable range of literatures (from economics to public law to party history) in order to both restate and extend McConnell's ethical critique of American group politics. Finally, by directly considering the protest-oriented group activities of the 1960s, his more recent writings (especially 1971) illuminate certain weakness in the group theorists' stability-disruption-protest model.

Policy Constraints On Group Activity: The Arenas Of Power

Lowi's 1964 typology of distributive, regulatory and redistributive arenas in American politics (1964b)[23] systematically distinguishes among the patterns of collective political activities too often lumped together as "group politics." *Redistributive* politics, including nineteenth-century public lands or tariff legislation and contemporary rivers and harbors programs, often benefits individuals or single firms, producing so much variation from case to case that the resulting decisions often cannot be properly called a policy. These highly divisible outputs encourage independent political activity by many very small groups or even individuals, which minimizes overt conflict, because "the indulged and deprived, the loser and the recipient, need never come into direct confrontation" (1964b, p. 689).

Policies in the *regulatory* arena also benefit or deprive specific individuals, but without "the almost infinite amount of disaggregation" in the distributive case. There is, in other words, "a direct choice as to who will be indulged or deprived" between the active organized groups, such as railroads or truckers. These groups, moreover, typically carry their struggles onto the House or Senate floor, using alliances which are "far less stable than in the distributive arena," where issues are resolved quietly in congressional committees (1964b, pp. 690, 695, 697).

In the *redistributive* case, where policy outputs are not readily divisible (disaggregable) at all, the winners and losers "approach" the size and breadth of "social classes . . . crudely speaking haves and have-nots . . . bourgeois and proletariat" (1964b, p. 691).[24] Thus the crucial organizational actors are typically peak associations, such as the AFL-CIO or the Chamber of Commerce, claiming at least to speak for very broad strata, and the basic decisions are often, though not always, it seems, made in their negotiations with key administrative and legislative leaders, rather than in public legislative showdowns.[25]

In this discussion, Lowi strikingly reverses the at least implicit causal ordering which Bentley asserted. He seems to explain which groups are active on a particular policy issue and what kind of actions they take, in terms of past *governmental* decisions about the divisibility of the relevant outputs. Such past policy decisions, Lowi argues, shape the actors' present expectations and thus determine whether in their activity they treat the issue as distributive, redistributive, or regulatory. In sum, it is the stable patterns of past governmental decisions that shape the groups' activities, rather than the group activities that simply determine the governmental decisions.

Although this typology has influenced the very vocabulary of many specialists in American politics, it has also evoked a number of searching criticisms. Lowi's various writings, for example, do not fully operationalize his typology to help us readily and unequivocally locate each policy in a particular category. Part of this problem may be that Lowi identifies at least four elements which characterize and differentiate the several arenas: first, the actual aggregability (indivisibility) of policy outputs; second, the expectations of actors (e.g., group members) about this aggregability; third, the institutional setting in which each issue is resolved; and finally, the intensity of conflict (or coercion) in each arena. He is less clear, however, on the relative importance of these factors.[26]

Despite these deficiencies and despite the problem of objective interest analysis common to all the writers considered here, the extent to which Lowi has worked out a careful rationale should not be ignored. Indeed, it is this rationale which accounts in good part for the typology's impact on other contemporary political scientists. All decisions, Lowi recognizes, may eventually redistribute valued goods from one broadly defined group to another. But Lowi persuasively maintains that the three types can be distinguished on the basis of the group members' expectations about of how *immediately* divisible (disaggregable) the policy outputs in question will be (1964b, pp. 689–90). Indeed, by concentrating on this aggregability dimension, one can in principle locate all specific policies within the 1964 arenas typology. Evidently these patterns of group activity and policy output, as empirically observed in their appropriate institutional settings, form the three distinct types, distributive, regulatory, and redistributive, which fall along the aggregability dimension.

More important than these particular deficiencies and virtues, the arenas typology recasts with a single stroke the often fruitless discussions about the extent to which interest group politics encompasses the entire political process. By maintaining that ordinary *organized* interest group politics occurs only on regulatory issues, Lowi excludes most cases of class or individual influence from the bounds of ordinary group theory, but he thereby leaves a group interpretation of the regulatory arena itself all the more solid and persuasive. At the same time, by making this distinction, Lowi helps focus research on the degree to which organized group politics is the most dominant mode for achieving economic or social goals. The 1964 article itself focused on a shift of tariff policies from the pre-New Deal distributive pattern, where individual firms were often crucial, to the regulatory arena, where organized groups and associations were dominant (e.g., 1964b, pp. 693–94, 699). Many possible factors may explain this change (e.g., the New Deal's extension of economic regulation and an increase in the frequency of overt group conflict which occurred in the 1930s), but whatever the correct explanation, it is Lowi's typology that poses the problem for analysis.

Lowi as a Group Theorist

Lowi makes these contributions from within the framework of the group theories tradition. The arenas typology itself classifies groups by their political goals and thus assumes that politically relevant groups have policy-specific interests. Similarly, *The End of Liberalism* concentrates its attention and polemical attack almost entirely on organized groups with clear policy concerns, such as unions, corporations, and associations of commercial farmers (1969, pp. 33ff).[27] Lowi also evidently agrees with other group theorists on the closely related point that for purposes of empirical analysis, group interests should be considered subjective and thus as presumably revealed by some activity. Accordingly, he criticizes organized groups because they cannot "incorporate all persons who share . . . the interests *being pursued* by the organization. . . . An organization like a labor union cannot possibly represent the interests of all those who *feel* that labor unions are *salient* to their interests" (1971, pp. 18–19, emphasis supplied). Like McConnell, Lowi attacks the exclusion from group politics of those interests which are evidently felt (or recognized) by the individuals concerned, rather than being objective or unrecognized. Since on this view interests must be recognized to be politically significant, knowing an individual's social or economic position is insufficient to predict the extent or effectiveness of his activity. In fact, Lowi agrees with Dahl in rejecting any "simple relationship between status and power" (1964b, p. 679). Political resources matter only when they are used politically on behalf of recognized policy goals, that is, subjective interests.

Consistent with this focus on the subjective interests of groups with specific policy goals, Lowi relies on the stability-disruption-protest model developed by other group theorists. On one side, Lowi agrees with Truman that "normal" intergroup relations can generally be described in equilibrium terms. Such indeed "is the nature of modern life" (1971, p. 34). Much—although, as we shall see, by no means all—significant political protest consequently represents a response to the disruption of these stable patterns of social and economic life. The "intense" rural protests of late nineteenth century were a response to the "commercialization of agriculture" after which "all farmers suddenly found themselves subject to transportation, storage, exchange and bank problems" (1971, p. 6). And this pattern was by no means limited to agricultural politics.[28]

Lowi also agrees with other group theorists that in the United States such policy- and goal-oriented groups are politically more important than broad social classes. Marxists may have been right about the inegalitarian, essentially capitalist control of American government (especially after the Civil War). But with respect to the "basic interests represented by organizations able and willing to use power," he holds that "the pluralist model is overwhelmingly superior" (1969, pp. 41–42, emphasis supplied; see also 1971, p. 4).

Finally, Lowi's ethical criticisms of group political activity more often parallel those of such group theorists as McConnell than those of socialists or radicals. In *The End of Liberalism,* Lowi makes clear his general opposition to what McConnell considers small constituency politics, which parcels "out to private parties the power to make public policy, [and] as a result, sovereignty itself." Like McConnell, Lowi also believes that this pattern heavily weights "access and power in favor of the established interests" and against the general public, such as consumers of farm products (Lowi, 1969, pp. 58, 76, 92) .[29]

In *The Politics of Disorder,* Lowi extensively considers another of McConnell's themes, the undemocratic, often conservative character of the groups' own internal life (1971, pp. 38ff) . If anything, Lowi carries this indictment even further than McConnell. "*All* established groups," he writes, "are conservative" (1969, p. 66, his emphasis) , conforming to an "iron law" of decadence or declining militancy. This fate, increasing external caution and rigidified undemocratic internal life, awaits even the most vigorous social movement once it organizes formally (1971, pp. 40 ff) . Indeed, since "liberals and conservatives, Republicans and Democrats" differ mainly "in terms of the interest groups with which they identify," the issues between them are rather limited; both sides by the late 1960s had become equally uninterested in meaningful change (1969, p. 72) .

Lowi resembles some other group theorists in another respect. Although McConnell opposes small constituency politics because it excludes groups which might challenge established elites and thus reduces the processual flow of activity, he recognizes that appeals to openness and spontaneity can also be justifications for small constituency politics (McConnell, 1966, chapter 3). Similarly, Lowi on the one hand favors a genuinely open, fluid, spontaneous political life, which he sees precluded by specially entrenched groups; he therefore welcomes disorder to break stable complexes of interest group power (Lowi, 1971, pp. xix, 37–38). On the other hand, Lowi maintains that the apparently free clash organized interests may only be spurious; group interactions may in fact keep "the major combatants apart." Indeed, in a political situation which is all too easily justified by the processual rhetoric of interest group liberalism, the government may merely ratify "the agreements and adjustments" among "the more effectively organized." It is for this reason that Lowi attacks "pluralistic government," where "there is . . . not substance. Neither is there procedure. There is only process" (Lowi, 1969, pp. 71, 97; cf. p. x) .

Lowi's Development of the Group Theories Tradition: The Analysis of Pathological Public Policy

Lowi's arenas typology and his critique of American politics reinforce each other. In effect, as Mark Solomon has pointed out to me, Lowi attacks interest group liberalism (1969) because it encourages regulatory politics with its vigorous intergroup competition to degenerate into a distributive politics, that is, minimal conflict and private particularistic arrangements among entrenched small interests. Moreover, in terms of the 1964 arenas analysis, the prevalence of this distributive political pattern constrains groups and individuals so that they will continue to define political issues in distributive terms. For Lowi, American group politics is thus severely constrained by policy "feedback loops"

(Easton, 1965) through which past policy decisions affect all efforts to influence new decisions.[30] It follows that there is an almost inescapable tendency for organized groups with clear policy goals to conform to the pattern of adjustments and compromises that presently prevail and have been ratified and legitimated by the government. The result is an interpretation of American group politics that goes well beyond McConnell in asserting the rigidified character of American group politics and in thus rejecting Bentley's perception of an open, fluid process.

The degree to which Lowi extends the group theories tradition's view of the political constraints on group activity can best be understood, perhaps, by explicitly comparing him with McConnell. For McConnell, much of the unfortunate constraint on group activity can be blamed on the ill-fated institutional reforms of the progressive era, which sought to increase political participation but in fact encouraged small constituency politics and in turn the entrenched hegemony of private interests. There remain, nevertheless, certain conditions, especially certain types of institutions, such as the presidency, which encourage large constituency politics and thus more egalitarian public interest—oriented programs, as illustrated by McConnell's study (1953) of the Farm Security Administration and its temporary success. Lowi's view is appreciably bleaker because for him the New Deal and its successors themselves encouraged the largely distributive politics of interest group liberalism. More generally, McConnell believes that the president rather than Congress, the national government rather than the states, senators rather than congressmen, centralized parties rather than localistic parties, are more likely to produce a genuinely open and conflictual politics. And critically, desirable public policies remain very much the product of group interaction, of *political* (not juridical) action by diverse interests incorporated into sufficiently broad heterogeneous aggregations (led by national parties or presidents as national politicians). *Political* conflict and real compromise, which McConnell sharply distinguishes from the log rolling so common in distributive politics, would thus continue (McConnell, 1966, p. 350; see also pp. 351–52).

For Lowi, by contrast, the solution is not better political outcomes based on group interactions, but better patterns of institutional behavior on the part of the government—a point on which he stresses his differences with other group theorists.[31] Indeed, it is this reliance on government to limit distributive politics that separates Lowi more sharply than any other group theorist from Bentley's view that a process in which some groups freely react to and counter others can be counted on to remedy serious abuses.

Lowi's Development of the Group Theories Tradition: Juridical Democracy as a Cure

Lowi's diagnosis of pathological group politics emphasizes the refusal of interest group liberalism to frame *consistent* principles of government action which protect both deprived social strata and the general public from policies imposed by entrenched private interests. Such desired governmental behavior is feasible only if it often uses coercion often against those already favored, i.e., these entrenched interests. In turn, such coercion is likely only if the administrative authorities have clear and unequivocal goals and need not rely on their own discretion. Lowi confidently relies on *government* coercion as particularly efficacious, because its citizens have "internalized the [government] sanctions which might be applied." Such coercion, in other words, is "well enough accepted to go unnoticed" and is thus "legitimate." Accordingly, Lowi calls for *juridical democracy,* clear unequivocal government action in the form of such legal rules as specific standards for school desegregation. The evils of interest group liberalism can thus be reduced by making rules so precise that administrative discretion in response to group pressures can indeed be avoided. This is particularly true if the decisions are implemented by civil servants in a hierarchical bureaucracy professionally committed to the "self conscious formal adaptation of means to ends" (Lowi, 1969, pp. 52, 276 ff, 310 ff, 30; see also pp. 299, 303–4).

Juridical democracy, then, insists on those forms of regulatory or redistributive politics where structured bipolar interest group conflicts force the authorities to make relatively unequivocal policy choices and then to implement the choices with as much coercion as necessary. Only in this way can government maintain its autonomy from interest group pressures.

Social Movements in a Rigidified Political Order

The very bleakness of Lowi's empirical analysis raises a serious question. How is juridical democracy to be implemented, given the existing constraints on the group process, which seem to favor the perpetuation of interest group liberalism? Not surprisingly, his reliance on juridical democracy has in fact been criticized as entirely impractical, because it ignores political resistance to the imposition of formal rules, as in the case of the Northern white resistance to the sweeping school integration Lowi favors (Lowi, 1969, p. 279).[32]

In order to respond to these doubts, Lowi looks beyond the orbit of organized interest groups—since their very organization suggests constraint, conservatism, and collusive bargaining. Specifically, he turns to social movements, that is, social groups animated by some severe grievance who seek substantial change through conflict, before they become frozen into highly organized groups with collusive alliances and arrangements. In fact, Lowi emphasizes just those social groups which have not figured prominently in the group theory tradition because they are described in social terms and not by their policy goals. Such movements in his view will either directly secure the specific substantive rules of law Lowi favors or create the disorder which leads others to develop such rules, much as the demands of the blacks' civil rights movement in the early 1960s led to federal civil rights legislation (1971, p. xix, Chapter 2, pp. 50–51, 58 ff).

This concern with social movements may seem consistent with the stability-disruption-protest model which other group theorists (and as noted above, Lowi himself) have used to account for the political interventions of various social groups. In fact, however, Lowi seems to recognize that his focus on such groups as the civil rights movement took him beyond this model and thus the main body of the group theory tradition. "Successful criticism," as he puts it, "takes the form of arguing from a larger frame of reference." And Lowi does indeed consider movements which may sometimes attack and disrupt rather than seek to restore previously stable patterns of group relations, which for him otfen exemplified stultifying conservatism (1969, p. 8).

As we shall see when we will return to Lowi's work, the problem with this approach is not that he focuses on such movements which seek to transform rather than restore previously stable relationships. Rather, the problem is that this view of social movements is not entirely consistent with his view of political groups and group interests and especially the issue of objective versus subjective group interests. But before we can examine Lowi's position further, we must first turn more explicitly to the entire question of the strengths and deficiencies of the stability-disruption-protest model itself.

GROUP THEORIES, SOCIAL GROUPS, AND DEMANDS FOR RADICAL CHANGE

The assertion that group theorists from Bentley to Lowi share a set of vital assumptions and perspectives may seem to overlook, if not flagrantly ignore, their pointed and at times apparently irreconcilable disagreements over the ethical character of American politics. Much of this conflict, of course, can be explained as the result of different empirical concerns and sets of data. McConnell, Lowi, and other critics emphasize the weakness of the general public and socially underprivileged groups, and their illustrations often come from administrative politics. Truman and others with more favorable assessments tend to focus on relationships among the *already* politically active, particularly in the legislative arena. At the same time, Dahl and some of his students emphasize the importance of electoral freedom and political rights, at least in New Haven. Nevertheless, the extent to which these authors are in fact studying different situations—as opposed to various aspects of the same policy-making process—remains unclear. And for our purposes the important point is that both sides in the debate share many of the same strengths and weaknesses, in particular on the complex question of social (nonpolitical) groups.

Social Groups and Group Politics

Truman's *The Governmental Process* is the pivotal work in the group theory tradition, in large part because it so systematically introduces structural elements, i.e., regularly patterned activities, into his analysis of American group politics. Yet for Truman, as well as for Dahl, McConnell, and Lowi, most of these patterned elements are political in character: *regime* norms, *political* constituencies, *governmental* institutions, coalitions assembled by *political* leaders, the formal organizations of explicitly *political* interest groups, *public* (governmental) policies. On the other hand, Truman does discuss social groups—religious, economic, regional, etc.—which do not make claims on others and are held together by the behavioral interaction of their members, leading in turn to shared "frames of reference" (1953, pp. 24, 33). It is these frames of reference and patterns of behavior which structure and differentiate the repetitive activities of different social groups.

Some of these groups have obvious political importance—and the group theory literature is replete with references to them. To recapitulate earlier observations, Bentley himself recognizes the dominant political role of classes, estates, and the like in earlier periods—much as Dahl points out the influence of social and then economic notables on New Haven politics, at least up to the Civil War. Truman observes the differential impact of a group's social status on its access to the authorities, and McConnell describes in detail the impact on the rural poor of the battle over the Farm Security Administration. Finally, Lowi focuses much of his attention on the failure of contemporary interest group politics to treat black Americans equally or justly.

In these instances, social groups are not central for contemporary policy making as such. The focus is on the effects that the policies have *on* the groups (McConnell and Lowi) or the influential activity of such groups in an *earlier* period (Bentley and Dahl) or the *indirect* effect of the groups on access (Truman) or elections (Dahl). The four later writers, who add structural factors in these ways, thus remain close to Bentley in not emphasizing large stable social groups as the main units of analysis, the central actors in the present group politics drama.

One obvious rationale for this view is that social group membership is not defined in terms of political goals, so that group members are likely to be divided on controversial political issues. To be sure, social groups in Truman's view do undertake purposive activity, but because they do not have claims against others, such groups do not make continuous choices about ends or means. Rather, when Truman refers to "frames of reference," he correctly designates the fundamental orientations within which such conscious choices about policies can be made. As Dahl suggests in his discussion of the predominantly non-political activities of the *homo civicus,* most families or occupational groups do not consciously choose how to raise children or perform their work. Such social groups ordinarily rely on past experience and routines, which have typically been internalized and thus taken for granted, thus saving the time and energy which continuously choosing among alternatives requires.[33]

There are nevertheless real advantages in developing propositions which more directly connect social group activities with policy decisions. On one side, this step widens the range of data and variables group theories can incorporate; on the other, such propositions specify the conditions under which such social group impacts occur, thus increasing the dynamic character of the entire group theory approach. One virtue of the stability-disruption-protest model is that it does connect social groups with the conflict and deliberation over public policy, while retaining an emphasis on subjectively recognized and acted-on group interests. Accordingly, the crucial question about the place of social groups in the group theories approach is not whether but to what extent its concepts and basic assumptions as embodied in the stability-disruption model permit a satisfactory account of these social groups' policy impact.

Social Groups and the Stability-Disruption-Protest Model

The prominence of the stability-disruption model varies somewhat in the work of different group theorists. Although his discussion of the metal houses case provides a particularly well-developed illustration of the model, Dahl in fact believes this controversy was a "rarity" (1961, p. 198). Although not directly disagreeing with this judgment about the frequency of such activity, Lowi sees such intervention by social movements—in effect, large protest-oriented social groups—as potentially very important. It is also true that in some cases certain elements of the model are somewhat vague, for example, Bentley's and Truman's rather brief discussion of "potential activity" and "potential groups," respectively. On the other hand, we have seen that the model is at least invoked by all group theorists considered here, and it is quite feasible to avoid the vagueness of "potential" as a concept by identifying relevant nonpoliticized groups in conventional ways, relying as Truman does on occupational, neighborhood, religious, and racial categories.

As used in this way, the stability-disruption-protest model is neither a wholly reductionist attempt to interpret political behavior as the simple reflex of social life nor an entirely "political" theory, in which political activity can be explained by the imperatives of the policy itself. On the one hand, most group theorists specifically assume with Dahl that nonpolitical private goals related to "food, sex, love, . . . play, shelter, comfort, friendship, social esteem and the like" (1961, p. 279) are sufficiently primary and dominant for most American citizens that political activity regularly takes a secondary or instrumental position. As a result, the concern of the neighborhood in the metal houses case with continuing its traditional way of life is transferred to politics only when ordinary nonpolitical activities are no longer effective. On the other hand, this social activity and the political activity which follows a disruption are both consistently seen as purposive. Whatever its origins, then, group political activity is seen not as the blind response to social imperatives imposed by the external situation but as an attempt of the group members themselves to achieve the group's long-established objectives. And as already noted, the attempt to achieve these private goals politically is shaped by the array of political conditions—institutional, normative, and the like—which group theorists have themselves detailed.[34]

In sum, this model does enable group theorists to recognize the often dominant position of nonpolitical motives and goals, without treating political activity as the simple reflex of nonpolitical behavior. Accordingly, when the model is stripped of certain conceptual difficulties connoted by such terms as "equilibrium" and "potential" activity, as the group theorists themselves have done in their empirical work, it provides a rather complex and subtle way of discussing and perhaps explaining many of the prominent protest movements in American political history.

"Organization" and "Repression" Costs in the Stability-Disruption-Protest Model

The capacity of this stability-disruption model to account for relevant and important protest activities, notably those that emerged during the conflict-ridden 1960s, has been strengthened during this same period by the development of at least two new areas of related research and analysis: the costs individuals must pay in building new political organizations and the reprisals some protestors can expect from their political foes.

Although organization costs have not been extensively considered by the particular group theorists discussed here, Dahl for one has suggested that members of social groups may well fail to protest their grievances—e.g., when their social activities are disrupted—because such protests would divert time, energy, and money from other ongoing private activities. To use Dahl's own terms, the emergence of political interest groups very much depends on the relevant "economy of incentives." Only where the disruption severely disturbs that economy, as in the metal houses case, will activity result. One reason such activity is relatively limited may be the large costs of developing effective organizations.

The significance of "organization costs" has been elegantly formulated in Mancur Olson's seminal discussion of *The Logic of Collective Action*.[35] Summarized all too briefly, Olson's analysis considers the problem of the "free rider" in situations where the desired benefit is "public" or "collective." A benefit is public in this sense if *all* members of a social group or other collectivity will enjoy the benefit (e.g., cleaner air or better public transportation) once *any* member is supplied the benefit. In other words, the benefit cannot be feasibly divided up and given to one or a few individuals but must be simultaneously supplied to all. Olson maintains that in such cases, if the social group is large, it is usually "rational" (i.e., self-interested) to let other group members work for the benefit—for example, by organizing a political protest—precisely because inactive individuals will profit from it as much as those who pay the costs of organizing the protest. Thus, in the case of strikers seeking the collective good of a factory-wide wage increase, "rational workers" in Olson's sense would ride free, i.e., either continue working or (if social pressures made that unprofitable) at least not spend their time and energy actively participating in the strike.

As Olson points out, however, if all members of the social group acted "rationally" in this way, no one would work for the collective good by striking, and the effort would fail. In the case of the stability-disruption model, unless this free-rider problem is overcome, the disruption of an existing pattern of activity will not lead to significant political protest, and the previous stable pattern may well not be restored. Nevertheless such protests, as in the metal houses case, do take place. At least in some instances, social group members do not ride free. And other analysts of organization costs and incentives (Barnard, 1938; Clark and Wilson, 1961; and especially Salisbury, 1969, and Frolich, Oppenheimer, and Young, 1971) have partially explained such developments in terms of leaders skillfully inducing potential supporters to make individual "donations" to the common effort.[36]

It seems clear, however, that not every failure to organize in order to seek a collective good can be explained by the inability of would-be leaders to overcome the free-rider problem. Other scholars have stressed a very different set of costs: threatened future reprisals against potential protestors and present sanctions against those who previously have tried to protest. These costs are imposed by the group's adversaries, who in terms of the stability-disruption model benefit from the existing pattern of social-economic relations and would suffer if an effective protest were to emerge. This assertion—that various forms of coercion, repression, and suppression keep many interests from intervening in the group process—has appeared to some as a sweeping indictment not just of American group politics itself but of the group politics literature which concentrates only on active, visible groups. Such a restricted perspective, Bachrach and Baratz (1962) have so strikingly argued in their celebrated critique of *Who Governs?*, excludes from empirical discussion one of "The Two Faces of Power." Yet this entire argument fits quite comfortably into the group theory position —at least that position articulated by writers critical of American group politics. As we have seen, McConnell explicitly indicts small constituency politics because it excludes or suppresses many group interests; thus the organization of farm policy by the national government has systematically excluded the interests of poorer farmers, tenants, and share croppers while benefiting more prosperous and politically influential farmers. Even when nonpolitical activity is disrupted, then, the benefits of political activity must be greater than both the costs of organizing a protest and the harm that repression or reprisal may do to the protestors. Although the actual extent of such repression is far from clear on the basis of research done so far, the existence of some repression, in such "indisputable cases" as American race relations, is generally acknowledged (Wolfinger, 1971, p. 1077).

Viewed in this way, a concern with "repression costs" strengthens the stability-disruption-protest model. For example, if we ignore these costs, it may seem puzzling indeed that, as Tocqueville pointed out many years ago, protest by disadvantaged groups often follows a decline in oppression or inequality, for if the grievance is less acute, so is their interest in making the protest (as measured in Olson's terms by the magnitude of the collective good which the protest seeks to secure). Protest may nevertheless result in these conditions because, from the repression-costs perspective, it is clear that a decline in inequality may also mean a decline in current repression or its likely occurrence in the future. In other words, while there is a decline in the size of the collective benefit to be won by the protest, there may also be an even greater decline in the costs imposed by the repression. A concern with "repression costs" also helps account for the fact that some members of a social group suffering from a disrupted pattern of previous nonpolitical activity do not join the protesting political interest group which seeks a collective benefit for all its members. In many cases, such decisions to participate or not to participate can be readily accounted for by the *different* vulnerability of these various group members to repression.[37]

Since there is no reason in principle why a class cannot be considered a social group, it is even possible to include protests by entire political classes in a group theories analysis when—and if—they occur. As noted in our discussion of each author, group theorists do not give class politics the prominence that it has for Marxists and many European scholars with other perspectives. But this empirical judgment does not preclude discussions of class or near-class political activity where the facts justify it—as Dahl indeed suggests they do in the case of the pre–Civil War New Haven, or as McConnell suggests in the end of the nineteenth-century rural protest, or as Lowi evidently believes with respect to certain New Deal or pre–New Deal union movements and, more recently, certain "peak associations." At the same time, the limited scope of class politics can be partly accounted for in terms of the organization and repression costs which so often make collective action difficult, especially for very large groups.

Taken as a whole, then, the group theories tradition can in fact analyze a substantial number of situations where groups defined class, race, or religious terms have been an important element in the political situation—or have been conspicuously quiescent. Having asserted this point, we can now focus in the discussion that follows on the more limited area where the group theories tradition encounters certain difficulties, namely, those cases in which a particular social group seeks to transform its previously stable economic or social relationships. This point can be conveniently illustrated by turning to the most important source of domestic political conflict during the generation that followed World War II, black demands for social, economic, and political equality.

The Stability-Disruption-Protest Model and the Montgomery Bus Boycott

In the years that followed World War II, black Americans continued to be members of a social group. They interacted frequently with one another and shared a common life style—indeed, a recognizable subculture. At the same time, however, their massive protests demanding equal civil rights profoundly reshaped American politics. The importance of these protests for a group theories approach is conveniently illustrated by the first important case of such black demands, the boycott of the Montgomery, Alabama, city bus system in late 1955 led by Dr. Martin Luther King, Jr.

To summarize the complicated events of the boycott very briefly: Mrs. Rosa Parks was arrested on December 1, 1955, for refusing to give up her seat in a city bus to a white passenger. Less than 36 hours later, Montgomery's black community had organized a boycott of the buses to protest not only her arrest but the laws which required segregation. Once organized, the boycott seemed in many respects consistent with ordinary group theory analysis. The political interest group that Dr. King led, the Montgomery Improvement Association (hereafter the M.I.A.), focused its initial efforts on the specific issue of bus desegregation. At the least, by making the issue too dramatic to ignore, the M.I.A. helped speed a favorable decision through the federal courts. It thus widened the scope of conflict (Schattschneider, 1960, p. 19); in McConnell's terms, it effectively appealed to a much enlarged constituency. Moreover, the M.I.A.'s active minority (primarily black ministers) used such resources as formal education, their recognized social position, and organizational skills to maintain both rank and file support and (as Truman would stress) their own cohesion. Externally, the group secured "access" to a variety of strategically placed political authorities to build alliances with other groups, including white sympathizers, and coordinated their activities with such likely allies as the NAACP. The resulting process of persuasion, bargaining, and conflict produced outcomes, particularly beyond the immediate issue of the buses, that were indeed processual in the sense that no actor could entirely anticipate them with full certainty. Moreover, as Dahl might well point out, these successes in the 1960s partly reflected the impact of friendly presidential leadership. In turn, this leadership reflected both electoral calculations and a recognition that southern blacks were appealing directly to fundamental norms of the American regime. One result in the next decade was the Civil Rights Acts of 1964 and 1965.

This familiar group theory interpretation of the boycott and its consequences is attractive, partly because it can simultaneously account for both the blacks' specific victories and, once we turn to the formidable resources of opposing groups, the limited success in the 1950s and 1960s of their overall campaign for racial equality. The boycott thus illustrates the way the group theory approach facilitates empirical research in complex situations, particularly through the formulation of clear, empirically grounded, if not always quantitatively exact, propositions.

The boycott is particularly interesting, however, because it involved the sudden political activation of such large numbers of Montgomery blacks, even though, as measured by their *activity*, they had not previously been notably united either by any comprehensive organization or an agreed set of specific public policy goals. Equally to the point, the very "style" of the civil rights movement—particularly its rapid spread and enthusiastic support—seems entirely inexplicable apart from the shared values, aspirations, and patterns of social communication and religious experience among black Americans. Support for the protest over bus segregation spread with remarkable speed to presumably middle-class non–bus riders in the black community and to northern blacks, whose own buses were not segregated, even though neither group could expect significant gains from the boycott's success.[38]

Clearly, the boycott evoked such important support because it was in part a symbolic attack on segregation and more broadly on the entire social system of black inequality, North and South, which appealed to many blacks who had previously been politically inactive. It is this appeal on the one hand and this widespread social support on the other which surely account for the melange of sometimes cooperative, sometimes conflicting civil rights–oriented groups, which many observers and participants at the time took to be part of a larger movement.

In sum, the M.I.A. and several other civil rights groups became *politically* important at a rate far faster than the black community's economic and social gains, which were acquired over a number of decades. As in Dahl's metal houses controversy, we have, if not the intervention of an entire social group, at the least the vast increase in the proportion of black residents of Montgomery who were no longer politically quiescent. It is in such cases that group theorists can turn to the stability-disruption model. In terms of the introduction to this essay use of this model is necessary because the data to be explained include not simply the change in the proportion of all political activists who are black, but the massive change in the number and thus proportion of blacks who became activists. But it is in terms of such an issue—how a traditionally quiescent group turns to massive political protest in cases like the boycott—that the applicability of the model becomes most questionable.

Stability, Protest and Social Transformation

Rothman maintains (1960) that Truman's approach is generally inadequate in analyzing issues such as an American race relations. Although we have seen that the group theories perspective can illuminate many particular aspects of the boycott, it does seem clear that the Montgomery protest failed to conform to the critical assumption in the stability-disruption-protest model which the group theories approach must use to explain such developments. Specifically, the boycott does not seem to conform to the model's expectation that *existing* private goals and activities are transferred to politics. Neither the M.I.A. nor other civil rights groups of the period can reasonably be seen as an attempt to prevent or reverse some *disadvantageous* development disrupting a stable pattern of ongoing social activities—a pattern which their protest then sought to restore. To be sure, the previous pattern had many stable elements, since members of the black community had interacted with one another and with the city's whites for decades in relatively segregated ways. But that interaction confirmed the Negroes' inferior position. It was surely not those activities, and thus (following Bentley) the interests which those long-established *patterns of activity* reveal, that the boycott sought to protect. Rather, if we do take activity as a guide to their goals, we can see that the blacks' protest sought to *transform* the entire fabric of southern race relations.

There was in fact a social group which did turn to politics in the later 1950s to preserve and restore that same previously stable pattern of interracial activity. But it was a group of *white* southerners, reacting against black protest and demands for racial change.

This point may be generalized beyond American race relations. According to the stability-disruption model, new protesting political groups should seek to *restore* a social neighborhood against emerging threats, to *preserve* or reestablish an economic market against disruptions of "predator corporations," or to *secure* the labor movement's collective bargaining position against employer counterattacks. In each such case, the existing private (nonpolitical) activity—raising a family, residing in a particular neighborhood, making a living, or the like—continues to define the goal. The only difference is that political action has been chosen as the best instrument after suitable calculations of fear (repression) and advantage (the benefits as against the costs of establishing an organization).

Several considerations suggest that when a social group seeks a *new* goal, a *new* line of activity, which involves the change or elimination of its own ongoing social activities, these new activities fall outside the scope of the stability-disruption model. For one thing, instead of trying to reestablish the existing situation, these new interests often seek to transform the very context which makes such existing, ongoing activities possible, e.g., the entire cultural pattern of racial inequality underpinning black-white relations. In the second place, unlike the interests in food, sport, worship, sex, and occupation, the transforming interests in question here are *intrinsically* political, at least in the American regime. The changes they call for are sufficiently sweeping so that they can be won only through political action, because they often have immediate implications for the regime itself. Instead of being originally private and subsequently becoming political, these transforming interests, at least in societies like the United States, necessarily involve appeals to politics. In this sense, they are political from the beginning. In the third place—although this point raises tangled theoretical issues—there is some reason to believe that in such situations calculations of organizational costs and indeed the entire "economy of incentives" may temporarily lapse, in part because the hoped-for benefits cannot be meaningfully compared with the known costs. As Aristide Zolberg suggests, there appear to be certain highly charged times, when everything seems possible and ordinary "rational calculations" are forgotten (1972).

This problem, it must be stressed, is limited in scope; many protests in

American political history can be handled by the stability-disruption-protest model. Nevertheless, resolving this problem does require a break with Bentley's subjective interest approach which in turn mean the identification of political groups by their observable activity. To put it another way, although later group theorists abandoned Bentley's processual view of reality in part by recognizing the relevance of social groups in cases of sudden protest, they failed in certain cases to take the analogous step with respect to the concepts of group and political interest.

Subjective Interests and the Costs of Political Protest

Given the limitations of the stability-disruption-protest model, we shall shortly turn to the objective interest approach to account for suddenly emergent social protest. First, however, we shall briefly examine another approach, which, like the stability-disruption model, relies exclusively on subjective interest, but which differs from the model because it does not assume the disruption of on-going social activities. Rather, this view holds that the desire to change an existing social situation may exist for many years before protest develops. The protest in this view emerges as the result of a sufficient change in the social group members' economy of incentives, so that the costs of the protest no longer exceed the benefits. On this view, many of Montgomery's blacks had a long-recognized interest in ending racial inequality.[39] Their failure to act before 1955 can therefore be readily accounted for by a combination of organizational costs, fear of reprisals, and the greater attractiveness of nonpolitical activities, all of which fit easily into the group theory approach. The sudden emergence of the boycott in 1955 thus reflects not the disruption of a previously stable and satisfactory situation, which we have seen to be implausible, but the increased probability of success and decreased probability of severe reprisals after the Supreme Court's rulings in the school segregation cases.

But precisely because so many Montgomery blacks *did* nothing for many years prior to 1955 to protest segregation, this interpretation, in effect, must consider as subjective preferences such elements as merely verbal or even non-verbal expressions of discontent. Since group interests cannot be identified as *behaviorally* revealed preferences, this view actually rejects Bentley's equation of interest, group, and activity.[40] The consequence is a mare's nest of epistemological issues, which Bentley's interest-activity equation sought to avoid. In particular, we must now rely on the group members' verbal assertions about the content of the interest, which are subject to a raft of pretensions, confusions, and consciously or unconsciously self-serving distortions. This reliance in turn creates difficulties in identifying group members. For example, there were undoubtedly some blacks in Montgomery or elsewhere who articulated pro–civil rights sentiments in the early 1950s but, perhaps because they profited economically from continued segregation, remained inactive when the issue became acute, as it did in the boycott. Yet there were very probably other traditionalist blacks who verbally opposed civil rights aspirations before the boycott but in the heat of the crisis supported Dr. King. This situation creates a serious difficulty. To consider as group members all those—but only those—blacks who express discontent means including in the group some who ought to be excluded, i.e., blacks with merely verbal commitments. Yet it also excludes those inarticulate or verbally anti–civil rights blacks who ought to be included since they would—and did—participate in the actual boycott.

Equally important, this approach, unlike the stability-disruption model, fails to define the group in terms of race and thus moves away from the linkage between social life (here race relations) and political activity (the boycott), which the group theories tradition sought to establish. What animated the boycott, after all, was the *differential* response of individual blacks to their *common* situation and *shared* experiences in a white-dominated society.

By contrast, Bentley's original interest-activity equation does not suffer from a dependence on primarily verbal expressions of preference or interest. Nor does Bentley's approach require us to divide Montgomery blacks—as this alternative, broader subjective interest approach must—into two distinct groups: a political interest group of active blacks (and their white allies) and a social group of all other blacks. A strict Bentleyan, after all, would *define* the relevant group as only those visibly and actively interested in securing a given goal. Unfortunately, however, if only the politically active are considered, it becomes very difficult to ask a central question: How did a relatively small number of civil rights activists so suddenly acquire so much active support, during the boycott, from their previously quiescent fellow blacks?

Objective Interests: An Alternative Approach

There is a further difficulty confronting *any* exclusively subjective interest view, which in turn illuminates the rationale for an objective interest analysis. To take the Montgomery situation once again, there were some blacks who for decades before 1955 demonstrated by words and deeds an opposition to racial inequality. Yet even these individuals indicated by their *social* activity—their continuing participation in segregated unequal relationships at work, on the bus, in personal interaction—at least some acceptance of or cooperation with the prevailing racial system. Given this simultaneous political opposition and social accommodation, a consistently applied subjective interest view would necessarily say that these individuals' goals (i.e., subjective interests) were contradictory. And the same judgment would have to be made of those many boycotters who at the time of their boycott accepted and participated in other segregated or unequal relationships.

Intuitively, this point may seem forced if not tendentious, since it relies on "merely" behavioral indicators of interest. Thus, it can be argued, the "contradiction" is spurious. Since the boycotters were so clear in their insistence on change, this argument might run, their *real* interest was in securing racial equality. But why should the protesting political behavior, even if accompanied by heated verbal protestations of sincerity, be taken more seriously than the accommodating social behavior? To answer this question by referring to "real" interests (or their equivalent) in fact means that the *observer is asserting his own judgment* about the situation—precisely the step which the subjective interest analysis seeks to avoid, but which an objective interest approach explicitly undertakes.[41]

At any rate, it is by explicitly involving observer judgments through the framing of certain explicit hypotheses that the objective interest approach can describe situations of simultaneous political conflicts and social accommodation, and do so without violating its own assumptions. Indeed, we shall see that the objective interest approach sees such behavior not as contradictory but as closely interconnected, since it is the unsatisfactory character of the ongoing cooperative behavior that leads to the protests which seek major change. These observations are possible, in other words, once we distinguish very clearly between an *objective* (unrecognized) interest in some beneficial social policy or other good, and the *subjective* recognition of that interest as revealed in an individual's or group's behavior.[42] In this view, Montgomery's black community had an objective interest in ending the existing segregated pattern of race relations, which it did not recognize (as an action orientation) until late 1955 with the arrest of Mrs. Parks. At that point, the interest became subjective (recognized), and the black community acted on the now-recognized interest through the M.I.A.[43]

An objective interest thus specifies what is "good for" the given social group (Flathman 1966, p. 22), and for purposes of the present discussion, this benefit can often be the implementation (or rejection) of a specific public policy, e.g., the desegregation of municipal buses. Generally, the content of the objective interest is derived from the social group's social *location,* the way its stable relationships with others can be improved. Thus, to continue with the relatively clear example of black Americans, their subordinate or socially subjected position indicates an objective interest in protesting against and changing existing race relations, whether or not they act on it at any given time. More specifically, Montgomery's blacks had an objective (if behaviorally unrecognized) interest in ending segregated buses before the boycott—that is, transforming (abolishing) this particular pattern of activity and indeed the larger social context which supported it.

Clearly the use of objective interests severs Bentley's equation of interest and activity. Members of a group are said to have the interest—a particular policy is said to be "good for" them—whether or not they seek it through political activity (or indeed any other kind of behavior). And given this lack of activity as a criterion, the objective interest approach has the problem of specifying other warrants for attributing some particular objective interest to a given group. It is for this reason, among others, that Bentley and Truman explicitly reject any such imputation of objective interests by outside observers. Such imputations leave to these observers, with all their political biases and theoretical commitments, rather than to the group members' own behavior, the determination of what is in the group's interest, i.e., "good for" its members, and thus what political activity the group *should* undertake.

As Bentley himself observed, however, this objective-subjective interest distinction is rooted in and consistent with our ordinary linguistic usage. At least in English, it is just as appropriate to say that the (objective) interest of Mary is to change jobs (it will be good for her whether she thinks so or not) as it is to say she is *interested in* making the change (prefers to do so). Contemporary English would be clearly impoverished if it could not, for example, distinguish a relatively durable objective interest in some economically profitable public policy from preferences about that policy which may vary quite rapidly with changes in the individual's own moods, rhetorical arguments of politicians, or the type of available information.

My purpose, however, is not to dwell on the many linguistic and philosophic arguments invoking, explicating, and endorsing this objective interest usage (Barry, 1965; Flathman, 1966; Pitkin, 1967; Balbus, 1971; Connolly, 1972; Peterson, 1970).[44] Rather, my concern is to show in what ways objective interests can help develop the group theory approach. In this connection it is important to note that the objective interest approach does resemble the stability-disruption-protest model in some important respects. First, as used here, subjective interest parallels Bentley's equation of interest and activity. Subjective interest in this view is a political action orientation rather than just an abstract or verbal preference.[45] Second, the stability-disruption model and the objective interest approach both try to connect the character of a group's social situation to the content of its political demands. For example, each would describe the emergence of peak associations like the NAM as efforts to protect the business community against the incursions of powerful trade unions or undesirable government regulation. In the case of the stability-disruption model, this political activity is designed to protect the businessmen's shared activities which define their social group. For the objective interest approach, these new groups would be organized to foster common, if not hitherto fully recognized, interests in curbing union and government power. For both approaches the attitude about the desirable change—if and when it emerges—has no relevance or meaning apart from the social situation of the group. Third, the expectation that an objective interest will be acted on, given favorable conditions, closely parallels the idea of slack resources in the stability-disruption model—that is, situations where political activity is not undertaken and potential resources are not "spent" because there has been no disturbance in a satisfactory social situation, or where the likely benefits to be gained from the protest are smaller than the likely costs. In these cases of slack resources, where the social group is not yet a political interest group, it is necessary for the stability-protest model to specify the conditions which change the relative costs and benefits of protesting. Similarly, an objective interest analysis must specify the conditions under which a subjective interest is recognized and protest occurs.

When it comes to specifying the content of the interest, however, we reach a decisive difference. We can *observe* the stable ongoing social activity in the stability-disruption model and assume that the group members desire a given goal, which they then seek politically. But the "existence" of an objective interest—the *fact* that a given policy would actually benefit (be good for) these social group members—cannot be observed in the same way. To put it another way, for the stability-protest model, the content of the group's interest is already present in the social, nonpolitical activity which defines the group: Businessmen indicate their shared interest before turning to politics by their common concern for profits. They form the NAM only when it seems that making profits will be helped by organized political activity. So far as it goes, the objective interest approach can easily adopt this analysis. The emergence of protests against perceived threats to existing social activities can be described as the subjective recognition of an objective interest in benefiting the group. But in those cases where the social group members intervene politically to transform rather than preserve the existing situation, where the stability-disruption model breaks down, the objective interest approach does not and cannot rely on *direct* observation to establish the group's objective interest. To be sure, we can empirically observe those aspects of the social group situation which would be changed by a particular policy (e.g., racial desegregation), even though the members of the group are not actively trying to change it. We can only *hypothesize,* however, that under certain conditions the individuals will in fact find these costs unacceptable and then actively demand change. The group's behavior—in effect, its behaviorally revealed preferences, such as ending segregation—are thus related to the social situation of its members (segregated and inferior status) — but only in a *contingent* way. The behavior seeking the change emerges only where certain other conditions hold. Accordingly, attribution of an objective interest means hypothesizing that the subjective interest will be recognized, since it is clear that this subjective interest cannot be observed before the group becomes politicized. On the other hand, it is possible, at least in principle, to test these hypotheses empirically, by seeing whether the protest follows, once the conditions obtain.

Such a step, however, is by no means easy. In fact, neither the objective interest approach or the stability-disruption model has frequently specified these relevant conditions and thus successfully predicted future protests with any precision. In my view accurate *predictions* of this sort are extremely difficult, if not impossible, given the great importance of additional variables outside the scope of either approach. (In effect, we cannot sufficiently randomize the occurrence of these suddenly emergent protests to control for such outside influences and thus develop reliable predictive hypotheses.) The best one can expect, in my view, is postdiction—accounting for the course of events that have happened in the past—or more generally, an attempt to understand the emergence of such protest by identifying its sources (conditions) once it occurs. And the issue here is whether a concern with objective interests helps us formulate our propositions in ways which permit analyses of this sort.

Even if we state the goals of objective interest analysis this modestly, however, it remains unclear whether this approach can in fact illuminate developments that are more complicated than southern black protests against legal segregation. In order to examine this point, and more generally the value of objective interest analysis, we can usefully return to the work of Theodore Lowi.

Group Interests and Social Movements: Lowi's Account of Major Political Change

Lowi's discussion of social groups intervening to demand new public policies specifically includes those social movements, such as civil rights protests, which seek to transform rather than preserve or restore established patterns of social life. But Lowi's analysis of such emergent, protesting social movements does not formulate the issue in terms of previously objective (i.e., unrecognized) interests. On the contrary, at every stage a social movement is a collectivity with clear and observable policy-related action orientations (Lowi, 1971, pp. 50–51). Indeed, membership in these social movements is defined by these policy orientations rather than by the social attributes which characterize the members of such nonpolitical groups as classes, races, or religions. Lowi's arenas article (1964b), to be sure, does refer to social classes. Yet there, as in the 1971 discussion of social movements, he does not extensively analyze the stable, unequal situation of any social group as the continuing source of an objective interest in a change, which may or may not be subjectively recognized.

It does not follow, however, that the perspective Lowi adopts is unable to offer an account of the emergence of protesting social movements. Evidently, because the social movements he discusses often demand major changes, Lowi cannot, in such cases, embrace the stability-disruption-protest model (although we have seen that he does apply it to other groups, such as farmers and businessmen). It is entirely consistent with Lowi's 1971 discussion of social movements, however, to see black southerners before 1955 as recognizing an interest in ending their inequality but lacking the means to act or fearing the costs which such action would entail. The emergence of a protesting social movement could thus be seen as the result of the decline of likely repression or other obstacles—and it remains only to specify the conditions under which these obstacles diminish. We have seen, however, that this interpretation means that subjective group interests would include verbally asserted as well as behaviorally revealed preferences. As noted earlier, there would therefore be no clear way to avoid the problems inherent in merely verbal descriptions of one's goals.

Indeed, Lowi does not specify very clearly whether membership in a social movement is defined by political activity or by other attributes, such as race or occupation. We are not told, for example, if politically inactive blacks and those active in the civil rights movement belong to the same group (or movement).[46]

It would be possible, of course, for Lowi to resolve these problems by adopting an objective interest approach, so that race, class, religion, etc., would define membership in a social group movement. Insofar as the group had a socially deprived or unequal position, it could be said to have an objective interest in social change. And once the interest is subjectively recognized, a social movement is formed. Lowi does not explore this possible line of analysis at length, however, even though, I believe, it might in fact avoid certain difficulties in his interpretation.

Lowi's writings taken as a whole are certainly far less focused on the precise criteria for group membership than, say, on the contrast between organized political interest groups and social movements. Yet even on this issue the question of objective interests has its relevance. Given his belief in the conservatism of organized interest groups, Lowi sees social movements as the only force likely to produce major social change. But at this point, Lowi differs very sharply from an objective interest perspective. As already noted, attributing an objective interest which calls for major social change means hypothesizing that, given appropriate conditions, the desirability of change will be recognized and acted on, whether or not the group is already organized.[47]

In objective interest terms, then, if members of an organized group, such as blacks or hourly workers, remain unequal after the group is formally organized, their *objective* interest in change will continue. However conservative the group's officials become, the possibility remains that its rank and file or its leaders, anticipating their members' future demands, may once again become militant, that is, subjectively recognize the interest and actively seek change. In fact, if the appropriate conditions do obtain, so that the members are likely to see the benefits to be secured by change, the "logic" of the group's (unequal) social situation makes it profitable for group leaders to make militant appeals in order to retain the rank and file's loyalty.[48] But such developments are inconsistent with Lowi's assertion of an "iron law" of group deference.

This difficulty with Lowi's iron law suggested by an objective interest view is much more than a speculative possibility. There is considerable evidence, some of which Lowi himself reports, suggesting that long-established American interest groups do not always conform to the "iron law" of decadence. While depicting the organizational conservatism of the American labor movement, Lowi notes the existence of such "counter-currents" as the auto workers (UAW) (1971, p. 17). In many respects, the UAW did indeed press for much more change than other unions during the 1960s; at least at the national level it continued to support black demands for racial equality and even political demands to strengthen government attempts to eliminate air and water pollution. Yet the union is too long established, too large, and on occasion—e.g., the presidential election of 1972—too widely supported by other unions to be adequately discussed simply in terms of a "remnant of militancy" (1971, p. 18 n). Nor are the auto workers unique. The still longer established NAACP has continued to make integrationist demands for decades, and many environmentalist organizations, such as the Sierra Club, have consistently asserted the same broad goals for many years.[49]

It is true, of course, that even the UAW makes compromises, settles for limited gains, and remains very far from a socialist organization. Its efforts and those of like-minded groups have by no means eliminated the pattern of interest group liberalism that Lowi and McConnell so trenchantly describe. Nevertheless, the union's behavior (and that of some of their allies) is consistent with the proposition that at the least its members' interest in changing (improving) their social and economic positions somewhat offsets the conservative tendencies of its organization. Indeed, the fact that their union has varied in the level of its militancy over time conforms to the assumption that the level of subjective recognition of this objective interest rises and falls over time.

Objective Interests and the Arenas of Power Typology

The issue of organized group decadence is not the only point at which the objective interest approach is relevant to Lowi's work. There is at the heart of Lowi's typology of the arenas of power an important ambiguity about the character of intergroup conflict, which can be resolved only by systematically considering objective interests and in consequence considerably revising his original conception—and, in a way, the concept that he outlined recently (1970).

Lowi's 1964 article indicates that, among other attributes, the three arenas he had then identified vary considerably in their typical levels of group conflict. Most obviously, the distributive and regulatory arenas differ in the extent to which there are private negotiations between the elites—as opposed to direct public conflicts in which the two sides evidently recognize and act on opposing interests, and accordingly use most of their available resources. The first pattern certainly characterizes the distributive arena where the full House and Senate mainly ratify the quietly arranged decisions of their committees. By contrast, regulatory politics involves open floor fights between unstable coalitions (1964b, p. 679), a pattern, as Lowi observes, which is consistent with Truman's (1953) discussion of congressional politics. If the Montgomery boycott and similar cases offer any guide, these differences in levels of conflict are likely to be clearly related to the subjective recognition or nonrecognition of objective group interests. Thus those groups which recognize an interest in transforming (substantially improving) their basic social situation are likely to precipitate highly conflictual politics. Conversely, conflict seems much less likely if such broad interests in change are unrecognized, as is necessarily true in distributive politics, where the focus on certain individuals and very small groups obscures the interests of such groups as races or classes.

In fact, however, Lowi's views on conflict in the regulatory arenas appear to have changed so that his 1969 discussion appears rather similar to McConnell's discussion of rather muted conflict. The government, for example, only ratified "the *agreements* and *adjustments* worked out among the competing leaders." Lowi appears to attack interest group liberalism as the ideology of organized group politics, because it helps make regulatory politics resemble the distributive arena, by solving "the problem of enhanced conflict and how to avoid it" (Lowi, 1969, p. 71, emphasis supplied; p. 76) .[50]

Even more significant, the 1964 arenas article is itself ambiguous about the extent of overt conflict in redistributive politics. On the one hand, redistributive issues divide "bourgeoisie and proletariat" or "the haves and the have nots" (1964b, p. 692) in conflicts of "shared interests" which "are sufficiently stable and clear and consistent to provide the foundations for ideologies" (1964b, p. 711). As Lowi himself says, these remarks parallel a Marxist or quasi-Marxist understanding of class conflict. Yet he observes that redistributive issues are not usually resolved through dramatic public clashes on the House or Senate floor, as is typical of regulatory politics. Rather, Congress ratifies decisions privately negotiated in a "public opinion and interest group vacuum" (1964b, pp. 679, 680) by the peak associations and other elites. And as Lowi rightly points out, these observations are consistent with the elite cooperation view of C. Wright Mills, rather than with a class conflict perspective. In fact, Lowi recognizes differences between Marx and Mills on this question of cooperation and conflict in redistributive politics but explicitly refuses to choose between them (1964b, p. 681 n5).

Lowi's evident awareness that the level of conflict can vary in both the redistributive and regulatory arenas seems well warranted. Many American policies in the foreign, military, and domestic fiscal area have been initiated and decided in relative privacy, even when their consequences indivisibly affected very broad groups. American entrance into the Vietnam war offers only one case in point. That war, however, evoked the bitter overt conflict in later years. Again, the Wagner Act, which appreciably if not radically redistributed economic power between employers and workers, taken as classes, was also a matter of open conflict in the 1930s.[51] More recently, there has been open conflict, including crucial floor votes on federal income tax legislation, a policy Lowi himself singles out as redistributive.[52]

If on these issues there is open political conflict between the subjectively recognized interests of classes or other broadly defined groups, with the one side seeking substantial social or economic change, it is also consistent with objective interest analysis to expect that recognition of some of these interests will not occur. Lowi is quite right in at least implying that the levels of conflict will vary from case to case. The recognition of such broadly defined interests may vary over time, e.g. unions may become less militant, less insistent on a given redistributive policy. But—and here the objective interest approach diverges from Lowi's stress on the iron law of group decadence—it is equally possible that organizations whose members belong to socially deprived groups may also, at times, increase their insistence on militant conflict-producing political action. Now if this level of conflict—and thus the level at which such objective interests come to be subjectively recognized—is taken as a dimension independent of the aggregability (indivisibility) of a policy's outputs, the three arenas Lowi identified in 1964 can be located in a six-fold table (see Table 1).[53]

This expansion of Lowi's typology suggests the usefulness of the objective-subjective interest approach, provided that we assume that these different levels of conflict can be interpreted as the recognition (or nonrecognition) of opposed objective interests rather than assuming an iron law of increasing conservatism. We can try to specify empirically testable propositions about the occurrence of conflict in both the regulatory and redistributive arenas, by indicating the conditions under which social groups will recognize their interests in actively securing change.

The Content of Objective Interests: Cultural Meanings and Political Action

However desirable it may be for group theorists to adopt an objective interest approach, they must in the course of doing so, resolve important difficulties which can only be sketched out here. First, there are many groups, defined in regional, religious, economic, ethnic, racial, sexual, or other terms, which suffer from some important inequality. Yet many such groups remain quiescent for long periods of time; some have never engaged in protest at all. To which of these groups, then, is it empirically useful to attribute objective interests? In what way, in other words, apart from the observers' own preferences or theoretical commitments, can we account for the fact that some groups do recognize and act on such interests, while other groups do not?

TABLE 1   A two-dimension revision of Lowi's arenas of power[54]

Amount of policy output divisibility	Level of conflict (subjective recognition of interests)	
	Low	High
High	Lowi's distributive politics	Civil litigation
Medium	Cooperative interest group relations—decentralization of policy influence, as in McConnell	Open conflict among interest groups—unstable alliances, as in Truman
Low	Cooperative "power elite" politics, as in Mills	Conflictual redistributive politics, as in class or race conflict

To some extent this issue may be resolved by examining the extent of inequality in each case, together with the sequence of political developments that makes one group or another a relevant category for its members so that they engage in protest. But such comparisons among inequalities are difficult to make; in large part they depend on properly assessing the character of the *culture* in which the group lives. For example, it was in large part the set of *meanings* that Americans attached to class differences and their emphasis on individual self-help, that account for the relatively (as compared with Europe) belated and nonsocialistic political activism of industrial workers in the United States.

Since the objective interest approach can be interpreted as focusing retrospectively on understanding rather than prospectively on prediction, this problem may be less perplexing than a second, in which the cultural element must play at least as prominent a role—this is, specifying the *content* of the objective interest once a group is expected to protest. The observation that a group is unequal or otherwise deprived in some way does not by itself unequivocally designate the content of what it will seek politically. In what *particular* direction, in other words, should the observer assume that the group will seek to transform its social situation? At this point, of course, the stability-disruption-protest model has a clear advantage, for by its own terms we know that the protesting group will seek to preserve or restore its previous pattern of activity. But precisely because the objective interest approach accounts for efforts to transform such patterns, it is not possible in these cases to specify the content of the interest in this way.

The extent of this difficulty, to be sure, varies considerably. For those social groups which have been clearly subordinate or unequal to another group, at least some of the goals the group seeks may be relatively clear. Workers seeking more money, control over working conditions, fringe benefits comparable to those of their supervisors, and protection against discharge and the like—or blacks seeking desegregation of public accommodations—are relatively straightforward cases in point. More generally, the policy content of the objective interest can be deduced relatively easily, provided that the observers and the members of the social group see the inequality in the same way. Even here, however, there may be considerable uncertainty, once we move beyond the most immediately pressing grievances. To take the most historically prominent example, working-class groups have supported a wide variety of political demands from limited pro-union reforms to utopianism, anarchism, communism, and social revolution. It seems clear that designating the conditions under which a group begins to protest will not by itself indicate which set of goals will be sought.[55]

The issue becomes still more complicated, however, when we turn to relationships, or aspects of relationships, where inequality is less clear (so that the relevant attributes are not transitively ordered). Public interest issues often involve the protests of upper-middle-class environmentalist groups against the polluting activity of corporations. Again, although American blacks have been socially unequal in many respects, there are other situations where the prevailing cultural views as to which group is inferior are very complex, e.g., religious practice or cuisine; and there are still other areas, notably the development of an indigenous musical culture, where blacks are widely thought to be superior. The 1960s for example saw the rise of environmentalist and black nationalist groups which sought to transform the character of American social and economic life. In fact, black nationalism poses the problem in a particularly perplexing way, since demands for community control, nationalist cultural developments, and indeed the separation of black institutions from white society depart rather sharply from the integrationist civil rights tradition. In sum, the content of black demands a decade after the Montgomery boycott cannot be deduced by simply observing this historical pattern of racial discrimination and segregation.

This set of problems is obviously too complicated and intractable to be resolved in the present discussion. I would simply maintain: *First,* the group theories tradition must incorporate an objective interest analysis into its intellectual framework if it hopes to account for, or even satisfactorily describe, the political intervention of previously quiescent political groups demanding major changes. *Second,* this objective interests approach must specify the content of the social group's interest, that is, what it will demand when and if it is politicized. *Third,* this content can be attributed successfully only if one examines the precise cultural setting in which that group operates. In other words, it is the *specific meaning* of blackness in America, in the culture generally and among blacks in particular, to take the case of race relations, that accounts for the nationalist turn in black protest in the late 1960s.[56] Similarly, to understand why recent protests against the activities of large corporations have focused on specific ecological and consumer issues, we must ask how Americans have in fact culturally defined their social and political situation. We must look particularly at the place of progressivism rather than socialism as a traditional form of protest in America, and at our historically ambivalent attitude toward "nature" in a society seeking for many generations to "conquer" its frontier.[57] Only by looking at these cultural elements—an issue which, admittedly, Bentley himself did not emphasize—will the group theories tradition continue the work of recent decades in developing and improving on Bentley's initial formulation of the political activity of social and economic groups. Yet the task is far from simple; it must somehow spell out—and much more precisely than heretofore—the interconnections between political ideologies understood as programmatic, policy-related sets of demands, and what Geertz (1964) so brilliantly terms ideologies as "cultural systems."

CONCLUSION: POLITICAL REALITY AND EMPIRICAL CONCEPTS IN THE GROUP THEORIES TRADITION

In reviewing the work of five major group theorists, this essay has emphasized the divergence among later theorists from Bentley's view of political reality, together with their continuing use of two crucial concepts—group and interest—in very much the way he did. My argument, very simply, is that these concepts and Bentley's political perceptions were well suited for each other. As a result, when later theorists quite rightly viewed political life less processually, they created difficulties that could be fully resolved only by modifying his use of group and interest as well—in effect, by describing political developments in objective interest terms. This step, however, they have not as yet taken.

At least implicitly, Truman, Dahl, McConnell, and Lowi all see Bentley's emphasis on a moving political process of diverse groups continuously seeking social and economic goals as empirically unrealistic. Some of the most important elements of political life do not appear to be continuously in flux but in fact relatively stable, and each of these writers singles out structured patterns of political activities—institutions, customs, and organizations. On the other hand, although these political constraints narrow the range of group political behavior, it is still possible to show that, within these politically set limits, the group process continues. Policy-oriented groups animated by economically and socially relevant goals still shape political decisions in the course of interacting with one another.

These post-Bentleyan group theorists, however, did not limit themselves to identifying mainly political structural elements. They also recognized that important elements of social and economic activity combine in comparably stable repetitive patterns, exemplified in the normal routine behavior of such social groups as classes, neighborhoods, religions, and races. But determining the political influence of these stable social and economic groups presents certain difficulties if one employs the group theories understanding of "interest." Since these social groups are defined in terms of their members' political activity, only a portion of their members could be expected to become active politically on any issue. Thus, to return to the formulation in the introduction to this article, the question becomes not the social economic composition of those already politically active, but the proportion of the politically active among a given social group—and why this proportion might suddenly increase or decrease.

At the same time, though, because these later group theorists, like Bentley, remain concerned with the flow of group activity that produces policy decisions, they reach a question that Bentley's formulation largely avoided: How is this *changing* flow of policy-related activities—the group *process*—to be explained by these *stable* social groups, that is, social and economic *structures* whose activities are distinguished by their repetitive regularity? Bentley avoids this problem because he insists on viewing politics as a processual flow and on identifying groups in terms of their activities. If, as Bentley wished, the groups' economic and social interests can be defined in terms of political activities which seek to influence policy decisions, then social and economic influences are as fluid as the policy process they were designed to account for. Indeed, behaviorally revealed social and economic group goals were but different parts of that policy-making process itself.

Since later group theorists identify social groups apart from this political process, they have sought to resolve the problem in terms of the stability-disruption-protest model by assuming that the goals of the social group remain stable but that its activity on behalf of these goals becomes politicized. Stable groups, in other words, are seen as influencing a changing political process by intervening in the process when, and only when, politics is important in achieving the groups' stable goals. Here again Dahl's metal houses case illustrates the point. The "Hill" neighborhood had stable goals, and its residents intervened politically only when necessary. Dahl's account here "works." From the standpoint of New Haven politics, their suddenly emergent demands were only one temporary set of goals in a changing situation.

In arguing for an objective interest approach, however, I have tried to show that there are cases in which it is the behaviorally revealed goals of the stable social groups that change. Group politics cannot be fully analyzed if we identify groups only in terms of behaviorally revealed subjective interests. In order to satisfactorily describe such socially stable groups that change the content of their interest, it is necessary to sever the group's activity from its interest, i.e., the thrust of what it routinely *does* socially from what it will, in some situation, *demand* politically. Only such an approach, I have argued, can begin to delineate successfully that fateful connection between the stable elements which pattern our social life and those particular sets of political activities which seek to transform it.

NOTES

1. There have been a number of general discussions with quite different perspectives on the development of this group theories tradition. See among others, Dowling (1960), Golembiewski (1960), Hagan (1958), MacKenzie (1955), Monypenny (1954), Rothman, (1960), and Truman (1960). I have chosen to concentrate on five authors in the present essay precisely because these analyses have in fact so thoroughly covered the general field at least through the 1950s.

2. Some contemporary observers have suggested that these ethical disagreements are more limited than they initially appear, at least by comparison with those radical or socialist critiques of American society which reemerged in the late 1960s. Although I agree with part of this critique, the burden of this essay is to show where it is well taken—and where it is not. See Balbus (1971), Haupt and Leibfried (1972), and Balbus (1972).

3. See also Mahood (1967), Salisbury (1970), Zisk (1969), Kessel, Cole, and Seddig (1970), and Roche and Levy (1964). For a comprehensive and often brilliant summary of the entire pluralist literature as it relates to political power, which includes considerable work on pressure groups, see McFarland (1969).

4. As examples, consider Eckstein on Norway (1966), and Britain (1962), Beer (1956 and 1966), LaPolombara (1964), and Lijphart (1968). The group theories approach has also clearly influenced the functionalist view of comparative politics articulated by Almond (1960) and Almond and Powell (1966), and it at least parallels the neo-corporalist view of group activity typified by Schmitter (1971).

5. For examples, see Key (1964), Lubell (1956), Wilson (1960).

6. This view of political reality also affects Bentley's estimate of other scholars. For example, he dismisses Goodnow's celebrated distinction between science and administration as too fixed a formula, insisting that "always and everywhere there is action" (1967, p. 327).

7. The antiformalist character of Bentley's group theory approach might seem inconsistent with assertions about its typically "American" analytic perspective, since the emphasis on individual rights so prominent in American social thought had in fact nourished the political formalism that Bentley and others attacked. Yet this same concern for rights is also very congenial to the political process approach. To assert an individual right to engage freely in a certain activity is in fact to assert a correlative "no right," which prescribes that others shall not—denies them the right to—interfere in the pursuit of that activity. In the American case, where "no rights" most overtly limit the constraining power of the government, the effect is to endorse a pattern of activity in which no actor can, legitimately, force others to conform to his expectations about what the outcome would or should be.

A concern with rights thus produces the tension within American political thought comparable to the tension produced by process and social change which Smith observes, or the tension growing out of the instrumentalism-moralism dichotomy considered by Rogin (1967).

8. Although some limited interest groups can be expected to pursue their interests over long periods, provided the issue remains salient, an emphasis on multiple-interest groups would almost certainly lead us to expect repetitive rather than shifting group patterns.

9. As we shall see, Bentley considers the impact of regime in his consideration of potential activity, but the effects considered here are continuous and, over time, involve groups already actively pursuing their own goals. We are not concerned with the activities of the uninvolved who may arouse themselves to contain unacceptably intense conflict among the parties who previously entered the lists.

10. Nine chapters later, Truman can accordingly treat the public interest as a propaganda tool which, when plausibly asserted by one side in a debate, may enhance that faction's position.

11. As Truman says at another point, "Under the influence of events, the direction and intensity of overlapping [of group memberships] and conflict are constantly shifting. These shifts necessarily affect the claims of groups and relative influence that various groups are able to exercise." (1953, p. 161)

12. "Even where a shared trait is the basis of the group (defines eligibility for membership) it is the interaction which is crucial . . . not the shared characteristic" (Truman, 1953, p. 24).

13. This equilibrium also applies to the group's individual members: "when one speaks of a disturbance in an institutional pattern, one refers as well as to a disturbance in the individual organism" (Truman, 1953, p. 29).

14. Significantly, Truman places this discussion of equilibrium between the section on "groups in general," i.e., "The Group Concept" and the section on "Interest Groups" (1953, Chapter 2).

15. For similar observations on trade unions, see Truman (1953), p. 66ff.

16. Indeed, such disturbances can include "the potential groups representing separate *minority* elements" (Truman, 1953, p. 512, emphasis supplied).

17. The result, at least in comparison with other polities, was clearly a democracy or polyarchy as Dahl defined it in *A Preface to Democratic Theory,* (1972, p. 145) that is, a system with "a high probability that an active and legitimate group . . . can make itself heard effectively; . . . by 'effectively' I mean that one or more officials are not only ready to listen to the noise, but expect to suffer in some significant way if they do not placate the group, its leaders or most significant members."

18. Dahl recognizes that these objective differences "are frequently so great that they largely explain why subjective differences [in political demands] arise." Nevertheless, it is usually true that "everyone in the 'same' objective situation does not happen to respond in the same way" (1961, p. 275).

19. McConnell's work, of course, is part of a larger intellectual enterprise which, particularly during the 1960s, vigorously criticized group politics and political democracy in America. To these critics, the group process has not only discriminated against the socially and economically deprived—and to a greater extent than Dahl or Truman ordinarily emphasize—but also ignored or subverted the interests of the general public. Connolly, for example, charges that "the prevailing system inhibits some segments of society from efficacious involvement in the [group] balancing process" (1969), p. 17).

See E. E. Schattschneider, who recognizes many factors other than interest group activity but stresses the bias of the group process: "The business or upper class bias of the pressure system shows up everywhere" (1960, pp. 31-32). (See also Engler, 1961, *passim,* but especially p. 4; Kariel, 1961, p. 68; Foss, 1960, *passim;* Selznick, 1953, p. 387.)

20. In terms somewhat similar to Polsby's, McConnell observes, "in the large pattern of American politics, the really persistent thread of conflict has been among units smaller than class" (1966, p. 26).

21. McConnell suggests that this will in any event "always carry large uncertainties of meaning" (1966, p. 368).

22. Indeed, he makes this argument about the American labor movement, which does continue to exclude many unorganized workers, with somewhat more force than I believe to be justified (McConnell, 1966, Chapter 9; cf. Greenstone, 1969, *passim*).

23. Lowi first formulated the arenas perspective in a preliminary and less elaborate way at the end of his excellent study of patronage in New York City, *At the Pleasure of the Mayor* (1964a). He subsequently (1970) added a fourth type, constituent politics, which is briefly considered below.

24. Lowi argues convincingly that a policy *proposal* can be redistributive even if no redistributive *decision* is made because those favoring the status quo prevail. The decisive question is not how redistributive a program is but how redistributive it can be *if* finally implemented (1964b, pp. 691-2).

25. As we shall see presently, Lowi's view of the intensity of conflict in redistributive cases is a complex matter.

26. Partly for this reason it is not entirely clear whether the three types identified in 1964 cover all possible domestic policies or, alternatively, represent the categories that are empirically observed most frequently. Lowi himself has more recently emphasized variations in coercion, not aggregability, as the decisive criteria, and the precise connection between the two is not made explicit. We have not been told, as yet, whether certain levels of coercion empirically covary with certain levels of aggregability, whether the one conceptually or definitionally entails the other, or whether they are not connected. Such matters will presumably be discussed more fully in Lowi's forth-

coming major work on the arenas. In the meantime, since Lowi's very suggestive discussion of constituent politics and coercion as yet remains incomplete and appears to take his typology in a very different direction from the main thrust of the group theories tradition itself (toward a theory of state rather than of group activity), the present essay will concentrate on the strengths and deficiencies of the 1964 typology and its connection with Lowi's most important later writings (1969, 1971).

27. Of the four stages of collective political activity which Lowi considers in *The Politics of Disorder*, three involve the "expression," "articulation," and "definition" of political issues—that is, policy goals—and the fourth stage depends on the integration of "these goals" by the group members (1971, pp. 50–51).

28. Lowi sees the emergence of trade unions as an effort to ensure "union control of the labor market" and thus forestall attacks on their members' normal economic position (1971, p. 18). To be sure, Lowi never entirely embraces this equilibrium view, pointing out in particular the dynamic character of capitalist enterprise. Nevertheless, formal interest groups representing businesses are also a "reaction to these disequilibria" imposed by economic competition and other factors (Lowi, 1971. p. 22).

29. In attacking decentralization to local elites, Lowi also powerfully illustrates McConnell's concerns by describing the methods public officials in a southern city used in administering federal programs in order to resegregate what had been a residentially scattered black community (Lowi, 1969, p. 251).

30. I am indebted to Mark Solomon for making this point as well.

31. Indeed, Lowi himself may overstate these differences; in one article he seems to criticize American political scientists in general and (presumably) group theorists in particular for "trying to make a science out of a stateless politics" (1970, p. 323). Lowi undoubtedly has a point, but the previous sections of this paper have made clear the extent to which Bentley's followers have themselves emphasized institutional factors.

32. "Many colleagues," Lowi himself reported on the reactions to *The End of Liberalism,* believed "that I was looking to the Supreme Court to solve all our problems" (1971, p. 58).

33. Of course, some political interest groups, especially those with elaborate formal organizations, can also be very stable, exercising great influence for many decades on behalf of relatively consistent policy goals. Membership in such groups, however, is primarily defined in terms of commitment to these interests—what Truman calls claims on other groups. These groups, moreover, are continuously concerned with selecting the best tactics and strategies to achieve their goals, as social groups typically are not.

34. Group theorists, of course, also recognize that there are intrinsically political activities animated by political rather than "primary" private purposes. Dahl used the term *homo politicus* to designate that small minority of individuals, including professional politicians, whose political activities reflect a concern with political life for its own sake.

35. For an illuminating and creative discussion of these issues see Robert Salisbury, "Interest Groups" in this *Handbook,* Volume 4.

36. Among other factors, they cite the entrepreneurial role of organizational leaders who successfully show potential supporters the self-interested rationality of making limited contributions to organized activity, provided others also agree to do so. In that way each individual contributes support in exchange for the increased probability that a skillfully led organization will in fact secure the collective good.

37. For example, all workers in an industry may benefit in roughly the same way from recognition of an industrial union (a collective good), but those in larger factories may be more likely to strike because management control and reprisal are more difficult to make effective, and thus probable repression costs are lower.

38. In considering national issues of this sort, it may seem that Truman's typology in which members of social group interact with each other is not fully applicable. American blacks, for example, do not seem to fit his criteria of a group all of whose members interact with one another, given their large numbers and wide geographic dispersion. This point, however, does not seem to be a very significant criticism. Indeed, it seems more sensible, in reading *The Governmental Process*, to focus not on the *mutual* interactions of all social group members but on their *similar* behavioral interaction with similar significant others (even if in different geographic contents). Such interactions might well lead to that shared frame of reference which in the case of American blacks has meant both a distinctive life style and a distinctive subculture.

39. As Wolfinger quite rightly points out, "At least some Negroes were discontented and tried to do something about it" (1971, p. 1078).

40. It is just this difficulty, we may note, which the stability-protest approach avoids, since the group is defined by (first) social or nonpolitical activity before the disruption and by its political or protest activity afterward. The break with the group-interest-activity equation is thus minimized. To be sure, the activity changes, but the basic interest and thus the group identity remain the same, since in each case there is an attempt to secure the same interest through political rather than earlier nonpolitical means.

41. Nor is it clear that such judgments—in effect, the observers' hypotheses about which attributes of a given individual group or situation will prove decisive—can be avoided by any method. Any empirical analysis involves some abstractions from the myriad of data that confront the observer.

42. Although I have elsewhere (Greenstone, 1969; Greenstone and Peterson, 1973) used Ralf Dahrendorf's latent-manifest interest terminology, I will remain with the more conventional and subjective-objective interest usage in order to avoid an extended digression comparing the two sets of terms.

43. We can also speak of the recognition of a previously subjective interest for existing political interest groups if the group has been relatively inactive and then is dramatically revivified. There is here implicitly the notion of *degrees* of subjective recognition (or of manifestness), an issue discussed in Greenstone and Peterson (1973). Thus the simultaneous accommodation that continues along with the protest, e.g., continued participation in some unequal race relations during the boycott, can be interpreted as a partial recognition of the interest in a total change or transformation. Complete—behaviorally revealed—recognition would mean total noncooperation with such unequal institutions and thus represent the limiting case. But it is a level of recognition which few except full-time revolutionaries reach.

44. Nor will I reproduce in total here the arguments for the usefulness of imputing objective or latent interests in empirical research, which I have made elsewhere, particularly with Paul Peterson (Greenstone and Peterson, 1973, chapters 2 through 5).

45. Of course, this view is not the only possible interpretation one can have of subjective interest, although it seems to be Marx's as well as Bentley's. But if we were to view subjective interest as simply a preference, without reference to activity, the objective-subjective distinction would lose much of its usefulness, since the recognition of the interest would not necessarily account for the eruption of the protest movement with its vigorous activity.

46. Nor are we told if unions in the denomination stage, where charisma is fully routinized (such as the conservative building trades), are in the same movement as unions in stage 2, which remain more dynamic (and presumably include the UAW). (See Lowi, 1971, pp. 39, 18.)

For the objective interest approach, on the other hand, the political interest group making the protest is that subgroup within a social group (defined by one or more criteria unrelated to a policy interest, such as race, occupation, income, or whatever) who recognize a goal and adopt the consequent political action orientation.

47. From the objective interest perspective, the fact that the group in question is already organized may be one of the conditions negatively affecting the *probability* that the interest is recognized, but it by no means *forecloses* that outcome.

48. Such indeed seems true of the AFL-CIO's recurrent efforts to secure a more progressive tax structure, an issue which Lowi himself indicated is clearly redistributive.

49. Indeed, as this essay is being written, the UAW and some other industrial unions have begun to demand further limits on management authority in the areas of involuntary overtime, production rates, health and safety regulations, and the routine or boring quality of the work itself.

50. Lowi makes clear that interest group liberalism does refer to regulatory politics with its concern for somewhat but not completely disaggregable (indivisible) policy outputs. He lists as one prime example the 1962 tariff law which dealt with "broad categories of goods, rather than single items" (1969, p. 81).

51. Although the Wagner Act was a regulatory measure insofar as it established the National Labor Relations Board to regulate union management relations, the law was openly "tilted" by its sponsor to favor the establishment of labor unions. The fact that *only* employers could be charged with unfair labor practices until passage of the Taft-Hartley Act a decade later is but one case in point (see Edelman, 1957).

52. For example, the Gore amendment to the Tax Reform Act of 1969, which was approved on the Senate floor, substantially changed the provisions approved by its Finance Committee. Although the amendment was not the most progressive possible form of tax reduction, it did concentrate reductions far more heavily among low-income individuals than did the committee version, which reduced the percentage tax rates and thus rather significantly favored individuals in the highest brackets. Similar observations, of course, can be made about regulatory politics, where open conflict is endemic on labor issues but much less frequent on utility regulation.

53. In the distributive arena, with its highly divisible benefits, Lowi's belief that conflict is quite muted appears well founded, at least with respect to legislative politics. Conflicts between individuals may be primarily resolved in the American system through private law suits in civil litigation, as indicated in Table 1.

54. In his 1970 revision of the 1964 typology, Lowi himself suggests the two dimensionality of the arenas typology, considering first the probable immediacy (or remoteness) of governmental coercion on behalf of a given policy, and second the policy impact on either individual behavior or the broader environment of conduct. Distributive politics, he mantains, affects individual conduct but not through direct coercion; regulatory policies also affected individual behavior but through immediate coercion. By contrast, redistributive politics, which also relied on immediate coercion, did affect the environment of conduct. Lowi also suggests that "constituent" politics affects the environment of conduct but without using immediate coercion, but he does not discuss this arena in any detail in the 1970 article.

Although Lowi's discussion of coercion is typically suggestive (see also 1971, pp. 57 ff), it alters rather than builds upon his earlier view of the arenas of power. By arguing that regulatory and distributive politics both affect individual behavior, Lowi seems to abandon the key attribute of policy divisibility (disaggregability) by which he had distinguished the arenas in 1964, for in that version regulatory politics involved rather general rules affecting entire economic sectors, not individuals or firms. Nor does this 1970 revision consider the varying levels of conflict in politics discussed here.

55. I am indebted to Brian Barry for pointing out to me this difficulty in specifying

the precise policy goals groups adopt when they recognize a previously objective interest.

56. This point is discussed in some detail in Greenstone and Peterson (1973, especially chapters 3 and 10), which in turn draws heavily on the landmark work of Harold Cruse (1967).

57. To put the same question in a comparative framework, what elements in American political orientations supported political protest movements, which in turn secured strict automobile safety laws sooner than other industrialized countries, and defeated proposals to build a supersonic transport, when the USSR, France, and Britain—all of whom have had more "politicized" working classes or socialist traditions— did in fact build such planes?

REFERENCES

Almond, Gabriel (1958). "A comparative study of interest groups and the political process." *American Political Science Review* 52:270–82.

_____ (1960). "Introduction: a functional approach to comparative politics." In Gabriel Almond and James S. Coleman (eds.), *The politics of Developing Areas.* Princeton: Princeton University Press.

Almond, Gabriel A., and G. Bingham Powell, Jr. (1966). *Comparative Politics: A Developmental Approach.* Boston: Little, Brown.

Bachrach, Peter, and Morton Baratz (1962). "Two faces of power." *American Political Science Review* 56:947–52.

_____ (1963). "Decisions and nondecisions: an analytical framework." *American Political Science Review* 57:632–42.

_____ (1970). *Power and Poverty: Theory and Practice.* New York: Oxford University Press.

Bagehot, Walter (1900). *The English Constitution.* New York: Appleton.

Balbus, Isaac D. (1971). "The concept of interest in pluralist and Marxian analysis." *Politics and Society* 1: 151–77.

_____ (1972). "The negation of the negation." *Politics and Society* 3:49–63.

Barnard, Chester I. (1938). *The Functions of the Executive.* Cambridge, Mass.: Harvard University Press.

Barry, Brian (1965). *Political Argument.* New York: Humanities Press.

Bauer, Raymond A., Ithiel de Sola Pool and Lewis Anthony Dexter (1963). *American Business and Public Policy.* New York: Atherton Press. (Second edition, 1972)

Beam, George D. (1970). *Usual Politics.* New York: Holt, Rinehart and Winston.

Beer, Samuel H. (1956). "Pressure groups and parties in Britain." *American Political Science Review* 50:1–23.

_____ (1966). *British Politics in the Collectivist Age.* New York: Knopf.

Bentley, Arthur F. (1926). *Relativity in Man and Society.* New York: Putnam's.

_____ (1935). *Linguistic Analysis of Mathematics.* Bloomington, Ind.: The Principia Press.

_____ (1954). *Inquiry into Inquiries: Essays in Social Theory.* Edited and with an introduction by Sidney Ratner. Boston: Beacon Press.

_____ (1967). *The Process of Government*. Cambridge, Mass.: Harvard University Press.

Beer, Samuel H., and John Dewey (1949). *Knowing and the Known*. Boston: Beacon Press.

Blaisdell, Donald (1957). *American Democracy under Pressure*. New York: Ronald Press.

Bone, Hugh A. (1958). "Political parties and pressure groups." *The Annals of the American Academy of Political and Social Science* 319: 73–83.

Bryce, James (1895). *The American Commonwealth*. New York: Macmillan.

Clark, Peter B., and James Q. Wilson (1961). "Incentive systems: a theory of organizations." *Administrative Science Quarterly* 6:129–66.

Connolly, William E. (1969). "The challenge to pluralist theory." In William E. Connolly (ed.), *The Bias of Pluralism*. New York: Atherton.

_____ (1972). "On 'interests' in politics." *Politics and Society* 2:459–78.

Crenson, Matthew (1971). *The Un-politics of Air Pollution*. Baltimore: Johns Hopkins University Press.

Crick, Bernard (1959). *The American Science of Politics*. Berkeley: University of California Press.

Cruse, Harold (1967). *The Crisis of the Negro Intellectual*. New York: Morrow.

Dahl, Robert A. (1958). "A critique of the ruling elite model." *American Political Science Review* 52:463–9.

_____ (1961). *Who Governs?* New Haven: Yale University Press.

_____ (1967). Democracy in the United States. Chicago: Rand McNally.

_____ (1970). *After The Revolution*. New Haven: Yale University Press.

_____ (1971). *Polyarchy: Participation and Opposition*. New Haven: Yale University Press.

_____ (1972). *A Preface to Democratic Theory*. Chicago: University of Chicago Press.

_____ (1973). *Regimes and Oppositions*. New Haven: Yale University Press.

Dahrendorf, Ralf (1959). *Class and Class Conflict in Industrial Society*. Stanford, Calif.: Stanford University Press.

Dewey, John (1927). *The Public and Its Problems*. New York: Holt.

Disraeli, Benjamin (1845). *Sybil*. London: Colburn.

Dowling, R.E. (1960). "Pressure group theory: its methodological range." *American Political Science Review* 54:944–54.

Downs, Anthony (1957). *An Economic Theory of Democracy*. New York: Harper.

Dye, Thomas R. (1965). "Malapportionment and public policy in the states." *Journal of Politics* 27:586–601.

_____ (1969). *Politics, Economics and the Public Policy Outcomes in the American States*. Chicago: Rand McNally.

Easton, David (1953). *The Political System*. New York: Knopf.

_____ (1965). *A Systems Analysis of Political Life*. New York: Wiley.

Eckstein, Harry (1962). *Pressure Group Politics: The Case of the British Medical Association*. Stanford, Calif.: Stanford University Press.

_____ (1966). *Division and Cohesion in Democracy: A Study of Norway*. Princeton: Princeton University Press.

Edelman, Murray (1957). "Sensitivity to labor." In Milton Derber and Edwin Young (eds.), *Labor and the New Deal*. Madison: University of Wisconsin Press.

Engler, Robert (1961). *The Politics of Oil*. Chicago: University of Chicago Press.

Erhmann, Henry W., ed. (1958). *Interest Groups on Four Continents*. Pittsburgh: University of Pittsburgh Press.

Flathman, Richard (1966). *The Public Interest*. New York: Wiley.

Foss, Phillip O. (1960). *Politics and Grass*. Seattle: University of Washington Press.

Frolich, Norman, Joe A. Oppenheimer, and Oran R. Young (1971). *Political Leadership and Collective Goods*. Princeton: Princeton University Press.

Garceau, Oliver (1959). "Review of Bernard Crick's: *The American Science of Politics*." *The American Political Science Review*, 53:1117–9.

Golembiewski, Robert T. (1960). "The group basis of politics: notes on analysis and development." *American Political Science Review* 54:962–71.

Greenstone, J. David (1969). *Labor in American Politics*. New York: Knopf.

Greenstone, J. David, and Paul E. Peterson (1973). *Race and Authority in Urban Politics*. New York: Russel Sage Foundation.

Gross, Bertram M. (1953). *The Legislative Struggle*. New York: McGraw-Hill.

Hagan, Charles (1958). "The group in political science." In Roland Young (ed.), *Approaches to the Study of Politics*. Evanston, Ill.: Northwestern University Press.

Hale, Myron Q. (1960). "The cosmology of Arthur F. Bentley." *The American Political Science Review* 54:955–61.

Hartz, Louis (1955). *The Liberal Tradition in America*. New York: Harcourt, Brace.

_____ (1964). *The Founding of New Societies*. New York: Harcourt, Brace.

Haupt, Heinz-Gerhard, and Stephan Leibfried (1972). "Marxian analysis of politics or theory of social change: toward a Marxian theory of the political domain." *Politics and Society* 3:33–47.

Herring, E. Pendleton (1929). *Group Representation Before Congress*. Baltimore: Johns Hopkins University Press.

Holtzman, Abraham (1966). *Interest Groups and Lobbying*. New York: Macmillan.

Jacobson, Norman (1964). "Causality and time in political process: a speculation." *American Political Science Review* 58:15–22.

Kariel, Henry S. (1961). *The Decline of American Pluralism*. Stanford, Calif.: Stanford University Press.

Kessel, John H., George F. Cole, and Robert G. Seddig (1970). *Micropolitics: Individual and Group Level Concepts*. Hinsdale, Ill.: Dryden.

Key, V. O., Jr. (1964). *Politics, Parties and Pressure Groups*. New York: Crowell.

Key, V. O., Jr., and Frank Munger (1959). "Social determinism and electoral decision: the case of Indiana." In Eugene Burdick and Arthur J. Brodbeck (eds.), *American Voting Behavior*. New York: Free Press.

Kress, Paul F. (1970). *Social Science and the Idea of Process: The Ambiguous Legacy of Arthur F. Bentley.* Berkeley: University of California Press.

La Palombora, Joseph (1964). *Interest Groups in Italian Politics.* Princeton: Princeton University Press.

Latham, Earl (1952a). "The group basis of politics: notes for a theory." *American Political Science Review* 46:376–97.

——————— (1952b). *The Group Basis of Politics.* Ithaca: Cornell University Press.

Lijphart, Arend (1968). *The Politics of Accommodation: Pluralism and Democracy in the Netherlands.* Berkeley: University of California. Press.

Lineberry, Robert, and Edmund P. Fowler (1967). "Reformism and public policies in American cities." *American Political Science Review* 61:701–16.

Lowi, Theodore J. (1964a). *At the Pleasure of the Mayor.* New York: Free Press.

——————— (1964b). "American business, public policy, case studies and political theory." *World Politics* 16:676–715.

——————— (1969). *The End of Liberalism: Ideology, Policy and the Crisis of Public Authority.* New York: Norton.

——————— (1970). "Decision making vs. policy making." *Public Administration Review* 30:314–25.

——————— (1971). *The Politics of Disorder.* New York: Basic Books.

Lubell, Samuel (1956). *The Future of American Politics.* Garden City, N.Y.: Doubleday.

Lundberg, George A. (1939). *Foundations of Sociology.* New York: Macmillan.

McAdams, Alan K. (1964). *Power and Politics in Labor Legislation.* New York: Columbia University Press.

McConnell, Grant (1953). *The Decline of Agrarian Democracy.* Berkeley: University of California Press.

——————— (1960). *The Steel Seizure of 1952.* Birmingham: Alabama University Press.

——————— (1963). *Steel and the Presidency.* New York: Norton.

——————— (1966). *Private Power and American Democracy.* New York: Knopf.

McFarland, Andrew S. (1969). *Power and Leadership in Pluralist Systems.* Stanford, Calif.: Stanford University Press.

MacKenzie, W. J. M. (1955). "Pressure groups: the conceptual framework." *Political Studies* 3:247–55.

Macridis, Roy C. (1961a). *The Study of Comparative Government.* New York: Random House.

——————— (1961b). "Interest groups in comparative analysis." *Journal of Politics* 23:25–45.

Mahood, H. R., ed. (1967). *Pressure Groups in American Politics.* New York: Scribner.

Mansfield, Harvey, Jr. (1970). "Disguised liberalism." *Public Policy* 18:605–28.

Michels, Robert (1958). *Political Parties.* New York: Free Press.

Mills, C. Wright (1956). *The Power Elite.* New York: Oxford University Press.

Monypenny, Philip (1954). "Political science and the study of groups." *Western Political Quarterly* 7:183–201.

Muir, William K., Jr. (1955). *Defending "The Hill" Against Metal Houses*. University, Ala.: University of Alabama Press.

Odegard, Peter H. (1928). *Pressure Politics: The Politic of the Anti-Saloon League*. New York: Columbia University Press.

Olson, Mancur (1965). *The Logic of Collective Action*. Cambridge, Mass.: Harvard University Press.

Peterson, Paul E. (1970). "Forms of representation." *The American Political Review* 64:491–507.

Pitkin, Hanna (1967). *The Concept of Representation*. Berkeley: University of California Press.

Polsby, Nelson W. (1963). *Community Power and Political Theory*. New Haven: Yale University Press.

Roche, John P., and Leonard W. Levy, eds. (1964). *Parties and Pressure Groups*. New York: Harcourt, Brace and World.

Rogin, Michael Paul (1967). *The Intellectuals and McCarthy: The Radical Specter*. Cambridge, Mass.: M.I.T. Press.

Rothman, Stanley (1960). "Systematic political theory: observations on the group approach." *American Political Science Review* 54:15–33.

Salisbury, Robert H. (1969). "An exchange theory of interest groups." *Midwest Journal of Political Science* Vol. 1–32.

———— (1970). *Interest Group Politics in America*. New York: Harper and Row.

Schaar, John, and Sheldon S. Wolin (1963). "Review essay: *Essays on the Scientific Study of Politics,* a critque." *American Political Science Review* 57:125–50.

Schattschneider, E. E. (1935). *Politics, Pressure, and the Tariff*. New York: Prentice-Hall.

———— (1942). *Party Government*. New York: Holt, Rinehart and Winston.

———— (1960). *The Semi-Sovereign People*. New York: Holt, Rinehart and Winston.

Schmitter, Philippe C. (1971). *Interest Conflict and Political Change in Brazil*. Stanford, Calif.: Stanford University Press.

Schumpeter, Joseph (1962). *Capitalism, Socialism and Democracy*. New York: Harper and Row.

Selznick, Philip (1953). *T.V.A. and the Grass Roots*. Berkeley: University of California Press.

Sharkansky, Ira (1971). "Economic development, representative mechanisms, administrative professionalism and public policies." *Journal of Politics* 33:112–32.

———— (1972). *The Maligned States*. New York: McGraw-Hill.

Smith, David G. (1964). "Pragmatism and the group theory of politics." *American Political Science Review* 58:600–10.

Taylor, Richard W. (1952). "Arthur F. Bentley's political science." *Western Political Quarterly* 5:214–30.

Tocqueville, Alexis de (1956). *Democracy in America,* edited by Richard D. Heffner. New York: Mentor Books.

Truman, David B. (1953). *The Governmental Process.* New York: Knopf.

_____ (1959). *The Congressional Party.* New York: Wiley.

_____ ed. (1965). *The Congress and America's Future.* Englewood Cliffs, N.J.: Prentice-Hall.

_____ (1960). "On the inventions of systems." *American Political Science Review* 54:494–5.

Walker, Jack L. (1969). "Diffusion of innovations among the American states." *American Political Science Review* 63:880–99.

Weinstein, Leo (1962). "The group approach: Arthur F. Bentley." In Herbert J. Storing (ed.), *Scientific Study of Politics.* New York: Holt, Rinehart and Winston.

White, Morton (1957). *Social Thought in America.* Boston: Beacon Press.

Wildavsky, Aaron B. (1962). *Dixon-Yates: A Study in Power Politics.* New Haven: Yale University Press.

Wilson, James Q. (1960). *Negro Politics.* Glencoe, Ill.: Free Press.

_____ (1962). *The Amateur Democrat.* Chicago: University of Chicago Press.

Wolfinger, Raymond E. (1960). "Reputation and reality in the study of 'community power'." *American Sociological Review* 25:636–44.

_____ (1971). "Nondecisions and the study of local politics." *American Political Science Review* 65:1063–104.

Wolfinger, Raymond E., and John O. Field (1966). "Political ethos and the structure of city government." *American Political Science Review* 60:306–26.

Zeigler, Harmon (1961). *The Politics of Small Business.* Washington: Public Affairs Press.

_____ (1964). *Interest Groups in American Society.* Englewood Cliffs, N.J.: Prentice-Hall.

Zisk, Betty H. (1969). *American Political Interest Groups: Readings in Theory and Research.* Belmont, Calif.: Wadsworth.

Zolberg, Aristide (1972). "Moments of madness." *Politics and Society* 2:183–208.

INTRODUCTION

Organization theory is both a subfield of public administration—generally treated by political scientists under the rubrics of bureaucracy, small-group behavior, and management theory—and a vast, multidisciplinary domain that includes contributions from economics, mathematics, sociology, psychology, information and computer science, and business administration. According to James March, the field as a more or less identifiable cluster of research interests within a number of social sciences dates from a group of books written between 1937 and 1942 (March, 1965, p. xiii). Since then, many diverse studies have been generated in a number of disciplines. Although considerable progress has been made in recent years in finding a common vocabulary for the field, organization theory is still a field in search of an identity.

This is not to say that there aren't any common elements in organization theory, for there are. A number of more or less standard topics are covered in most textbooks. They include formal structure, small groups, leadership, interpersonal relations, bureaucracy, communications, innovation and change, organizational development, authority and control, decision making, and evaluation (Rubenstein and Haberstroh, 1966; James Thompson, 1967; Carzo and Yanouzas, 1967, Negandhi, 1973). What is lacking in the field is a common conceptual framework. There are a number of competing models of analysis in existence. Some emphasize concepts of rational choice taken from economics,

I am indebted to Fred I. Greenstein and Nelson Polsby for excellent comments and criticisms on an earlier draft of this chapter. I also owe a special debt to Martin Landau, who not only first interested me in the topic but also contributed excellent comments on earlier drafts; pages 323–25 draw on a rough first draft prepared by Martin Landau and me.

some focus on psychological variables, and still others build on sociological or political concepts.

In his excellent application of organization theory to the Cuban missile crisis, Graham Allison (1971) concluded that he could not summarize the vast literature of organization theory and referred his readers instead to the 1247 double-column pages of *The Handbook of Organizations* (edited by James March), in which a large part of the literature has been summarized. I will not attempt to compress this literature into a single conceptual scheme here. Nor shall I provide a comprehensive, bibliographical essay. Instead, I will focus on the major theories and concepts underlying most of the existing literature, and therefore the chapter will be relatively abstract. I will not describe actual organizations, attempt to classify them, or discuss specific variables and how they are interrelated. Questions dealing with organizational structure, decentralization, and the fact-value dichotomy are dealt with at the end of the chapter. For lack of space and time, however, I shall not get into the following topics, normally covered in organization theory: bureaucracy, leadership, interpersonal relations, communications, innovation, and planned change. Given the need to choose what to cover, I believe that it is better to focus on the major theories of organizational behavior than on structures, institutions, and processes. My main purpose will be to show how organization theory can help us understand politics, and vice versa.

The predominant theory used by most analysts to explain organizational behavior is rational choice. Organizational theories of rational choice, which will be described in this essay, can help us understand more about the role of consensus, multiple goals, self-interest, and motivation in decision making. Public choice theory, a fairly new addition to the field (also described below), can help us appreciate the problems involved in measuring and evaluating the goals of public policy. Decision and game theory, which will be considered here, can teach us about the role of uncertainty and risk in achieving goals. Small-group theory can tell us something about legitimacy and coercion as aspects of power; I will discuss some of the major findings of this literature later in the chapter. And finally, structural factors in organizations can help us understand constraints on goal achievement. When we combine these developments, we can begin to see the outline of a fruitful theory of decision making and therefore of politics as well, for what is political theory about if not public choice and decisions?

Although the predominant theory used in the field is rational choice, not all organizational behavior can be or has been explained in terms of rational choice. Other theories that have been used to describe organizational behavior include cybernetic (Ackoff and Emery, 1972; Emery, 1969; Ashby, 1956; Newell, Shaw, and Simon, 1959), system (Carzo and Yanouzas, 1967; Seiler, 1967), political (Allison, 1971; Zald, 1970; Harvey and Mills, 1970), exchange and technology (Perrow, 1972; Negandhi, 1973), game (Schelling, 1960; Allison,

1971; Farquharson, 1966), and decision theories (Bower, 1965; Crecine, 1969; Luce, 1959; Raiffa and Schlaifer, 1961; Menges, 1968). I cannot deal in detail with all these theories here. Instead, I will focus on rational choice theories and consider others, particularly political, system, game, and decision theories, only in terms of how they modify rational choice.

Political science models of organizational behavior are primarily prescriptive. A number of theorists have contended that the political process—sometimes called the "science of muddling through" (Lindbloom, 1959)—is a better way to make decisions than rational choice. But then, all models are both prescriptive and descriptive at the same time. Of course, no theory should claim to describe empirical organizations; the function of theory is to explain and predict rather than to describe. The rational choice model, for example, explains organizational behavior in ideal form. It also prescribes how to make good decisions. In this sense, most models are not meant to be descriptions of actual organizations, but tendencies which the analyst sees as possibly becoming or which he would like to see become actuality. A model is both a lens through which we view empirical organizational behavior more clearly and a prescription for making better organizational decisions. We shall deal with both descriptive and prescriptive elements of organization theory in this chapter.

There has been considerable fruitful cross-fertilization between organization theory and political science. Rational choice theories of politics have begun to proliferate, particularly in formal and mathematical political theory (see the chapter by Michael Taylor in Volume 3 of this *Handbook*), and organizational theorists have come to use the concepts of power and conflict rather liberally. But neither group has fully adopted the concepts and theories of the other as its own. In fact, there has been decided resistance to such adoption. Most rational choice theories of politics are economic in the sense that assumptions made about utility maximization of economic man have been applied to political man, and the various conditions under which rational individual and social choice is possible have been extensively analyzed (Downs, 1957; Taylor, 1971; Riker, 1962; Sen, 1970; Rabushka and Shepsle, 1972). But more prevalent in political theory is the view that political decision making deals with values and is distinctly different from rational choice. And although power and conflict are becoming more common in organizational theory, they are not the mainstay. Instead, the basic theme that runs through the literature of organization theory is economic efficiency. Economists have tended to impart the connotation of "scientific" to these questions and reserved the connotation "political" to value questions. The general conclusion seems to be that the latter are not amenable to scientific consideration, that questions dealing with values and ideology are not subject to rational choice or scientific analysis. We shall argue that this distinction is no longer valid. (See the chapter by Barry and Rae in Volume 1 of this *Handbook* for further consideration of these questions.) I will begin by contrasting the political and rational choice models of decision making.

THE POLITICAL VERSUS RATIONAL-CHOICE MODELS OF ORGANIZATIONAL BEHAVIOR

Political scientists have for some time contended that administrative behavior can best be understood as a political process (Wildavsky, 1968; Braybrooke and Lindbloom, 1963; Crecine, 1969). Much of the writing of political scientists has been an attack on the classical politics-administration dichotomy, and it has been confined mostly to analysis of public agencies. In recent years, organizational theorists also have begun to use political concepts (Zald, 1970; Hickson *et al.*, 1971; Perrow, 1970; Pondy, 1970). More significantly, they have applied political concepts to analysis of private or quasi-private organizations, such as hospitals, business firms, and factories. The behavior of these organizations, it is beginning to appear, can also be understood in political terms, not simply as rational instruments for the achievement of goals.

The blurring of the distinction between public and private organizations and the application of the same analytical model to all organizations constitute one of the more fruitful developments in organization theory. Of course, which model should be used to analyze organizational behavior is not an unimportant question. The choice of assumptions one makes when describing organizations is crucial; conceptual schemes are not neutral. Graham Allison (1971) has demonstrated quite convincingly that a single event (the Cuban missile crisis of 1961) looks very different when viewed by the rational choice model than when viewed by a political or an administrative model. The way the event is explained, the kinds of behavior we focus on, the importance of various actors, and how we finally evaluate the decisions—all depend on the theoretical model we bring to the task.

In addition, there is the question of which model is better. Several organization theorists have in recent years shown signs of dissatisfaction with the pure theory of rational choice (Simon, 1945; Pondy, 1970; Cyert and March, 1963; Bower, 1965; Harvey and Mills, 1970; Zald, 1970; Burns, 1966). Each theorist has modified the rational choice model in a different way. I will consider some of these in this chapter. There is considerable question, however, about whether it is possible to *modify* rational choice theory by adding political (or other) concepts to it, or whether it should be given up in favor of a better model. The two models—rational choice and political—are distinctly different in many ways, and they are often in direct conflict in their major assumptions.

The political model of organizational behavior has been applied to a wide variety of empirical organizations (Cyert and March, 1963; Harvey and Mills, 1970; Zald, 1970; Perrow, 1970; Bucher, 1970; Allison, 1971). Each analyst emphasizes different aspects of the model, but when organizations are viewed as political systems, they all have common aspects: Different power groups exist and compete; ruling coalitions are formed; and if we look hard enough, we may find within them even party systems or their functional equivalents. All organizations exhibit the phenomenon of demand aggregation; they possess constitutions (written and unwritten rules of the game) ; they are marked by the problem of transfer of power and succession; and they have characteristics not unlike those of modern states. Zald adds that some are best described as gerontocratic oligarchies, others as modernizing democracies, and that in his study of the YMCA, he "was driven to notions of pluralistic and dual politics" (Zald, 1970, p. 233).

When organizations are viewed as political systems, budgets become annual treaties (V. Thompson, 1969), reorganizations are indicators of ruling coalition changes, and decision rules reflect existing internal alliances. There is even an analog to international relations in that much interorganizational contact is directed toward the "forging of alliances," which not only furthers the interests of the participants but also creates a powerful "network of influence" (Zald, 1970). Such alliances may be open; they may also be secret. The key to organizational behavior, then, lies in a description of the processes which attend the distribution of power and the actors involved. Within a medical school, the contest frequently occurs between physicians and researchers (Bucher, 1970) ; in a corporation, between production and sales (Perrow, 1970) ; in a health agency, between health officers, nurses, and sanitarians (Palumbo, 1969a).

This political model of large-scale formal organization is quite different from the classical model of rational choice. In the rational choice model, organizations are assumed to have single goals, decision makers have sufficient information about alternative means to achieve goals, they act always to optimize goal attainment, and there is complete consensus among members about these goals. (Rationality is defined more rigorously in the section on decision theory below.) This model presents us with an "administrative man" who is able to order (rank) the consequences of each course of action open to him (March and Simon, 1958). When faced with a competing set of alternatives, $A,B,C,D,\ldots,N$, he not only can rank them in order of preference (i.e., $A>B$, $B>C$, $A>C$) but can determine whether his preference for A over B is greater than his preference for B over C (i.e., all the axioms of the number system apply). What this requires is the ability to develop a cardinal utility function: rational man can perform linear transformations (e.g., multiply each by 4) of the values associated with each alternative which preserve both the rank of each and the interval distance between them. He then is in a position to make an optimal choice, given the stated goals of the organization. If the condition he faces is certain, there is one best decision; if it is risky or uncertain, he will pick the alternative that maximizes expected utility or minimizes expected regrets (Luce and Raiffa, 1957; Savage, 1954; Hurwitz, 1951).

If we take the classical model as descriptive of actual organizations, we will predict that actors always behave so as to maximize the stated or manifest goals of the organization. And if we take it as normative, then the ideal way of behaving is equivalent to the ideal maxims of scientific inquiry. There is no hint in this model that decision issues or policy questions may be the result of the play of opposing forces and may therefore require a political solution.

The political model, on the contrary, implies that actors will treat stated goals as problematical and will seek to control the grounds which are used to legitimize goals. Nor will the clientele located in the organization's task environment remove themselves from this effort. Ideology, therefore, can in no way be discounted; it is continually at issue, profoundly affecting doctrine and decision, and providing a "covert representation of interests" in the setting of goals (Selznick, 1957). In fact, the struggle extends beyond goal setting, for each partisan group seeks to control the criteria by which goal attainment is measured. The ability to determine criteria of performance is obviously a source of great power (Goldner, 1970). In the political model, the question is not whether goals have been optimized, but *what* goals are to be considered legitimate. A challenge to existing goals invariably signals a power struggle, and a change in goals means that status and power relationships have been altered. In short, the crucial point is that behavior in the political model is a function of system politics which turns on the quest for power (Wildavsky, 1970).

When power is used as the independent variable, decision makers cannot be treated as rational, administrative men. They are not bent on realizing stated organizational goals, and they do not and cannot order their preferences. Nor are they actors, who, motivated by the desire to reduce or eliminate performance gaps, constantly probe their task environment in order to enlarge their repertoire of response. On the contrary, such ordering as is undertaken and such learning as does occur are directed toward strategies necessary to ensure survival and maintain power (Stein, 1952; Etzioni, 1964). In the political model, actors impose their ideology on the world, ignore the facts, and sift the environment only for information that supports their biases (Barnett, 1972). The principal criterion for rewarding people or for selecting a course of action is accessibility. How accessible will the person be and to whom? Will this course of action improve access to elites? These are the principal questions asked. On the other hand, the principal criterion for evaluating people and action in the rational model is technical and administrative competence. The major questions here: How capable is the person? Does the action achieve goals?

Access and technical competence are quite different criteria. And the two are not necessarily related. In the political model, individuals spend their time and effort devising strategies to improve access to the right people and information, not perfecting their skills. They are concerned not with achieving goals but with gaining access to the right people.[1]

In this game, decision makers have hidden or covert goals, pursue a policy of opportunism, and abandon the principle of transitivity of values. Performance gaps excite behavior changes only if they are perceived as liabilities by ruling elites. Thus organizational actors do not learn through probes of their task environment. Improvement in performance is not a result of training. And changes in goals and preferences are not the result of "rational" considerations; either they occur because they are forced, or they occur as the result of a bargain. Threat, sanction, and negotiation loom large in organizational life (Perrow, 1970; Allison, 1971).

The existence of bargaining means that organizations are not fully directed or controlled systems. They are polycentric institutions and therefore require workable consensus among their members. This need constrains both the ruling elite and those groups, lower in the hierarchy, who compete for power. The elite, always facing the danger of schism and competing groups, are themselves marked by internal disagreement. Differences in opinion exist among them about what organizational goals should be accepted (Gordon, 1945). This conflict can be detrimental because policy issues may not come to the top; when they do, they often take the form of concealed compromises that reflect the special interests of actors at the lower levels of the hierarchy (George, 1972). Furthermore, although conflict and coercion are frequently present in organizations, they may not constitute the major factor in producing change. A group must reach a high level of consensus on goals before change is feasible (Palumbo and Styskal, 1974). The need for change may give rise to power brokers whose function it is to manage consensus. They survive at the expense of those who cannot perform that function successfully.

The struggle for power within organizations is similar to the conflict between political parties in the United States. Uncertainty about what ideas are most efficacious for the success of the organization encourages diversity of views and goals to exist, just as uncertainty permits different party ideologies to exist in society at large (Downs, 1957). The functional equivalent of a party system in organizations consists of the groups and coalitions that form in support of particular goals; each group champions goals in the hope of advancing its own interests within the organization (the equivalent of winning an election for a political party). But of course, there must be some correspondence between the goals advanced by particular groups and the survival of the entity itself. In the rational choice model, the criterion by which leadership can be tested is achievement of organizational goals. There is no parallel for this in the political model. Growth and survival of political organizations are usually equated with bureaucratic power, which in most political philosophy is considered bad.

Several important differences can be seen between the political and rational-choice models. Actors in the rational-choice model are purposeful; they are concerned with achieving the organization's goals as efficiently as possible, and the interests of each member complement those of the organization. Actors in the political model also are purposeful, but they are concerned with achieving power for themselves, and the interests of each member of a political system do not necessarily complement those of the organization. In fact, in some normative democratic theory, the self-interests of individuals (power) and those of the organization (public interest) are often at odds. Attempting solely to advance one's own self-interest is considered unethical.

The lack of correspondence in the political model between the goals of individuals and those of the organization is due to a second important difference between the two models: the rational-choice model assumes that organizations have a single goal. "If multiple goals are allowed, means appropriate to one may block attainment of another; hence no unique course of action can be charted for a rational decision maker to follow" (Downs, 1957, p. 25). Therefore, in the rational model of politics, a political party must be defined as a team whose members agree on all their goals instead of just a part of them. Every member of the team has exactly the same goal as every other. The political model, in contrast, assumes that organizations have multiple goals, that the goals are often likely to be in conflict, and that achieving consensus among those who support the various goals is the chief objective of political action. Thus the management of conflict, rather than goal attainment, is asssumed to be the chief end of politics. Graham Allison (1971) summarizes these points in saying that the political model has many actors who have a number of different objectives, varying concepts of national, organizational, and personal goals and who make decisions by pulling and hauling, rather than by rational choice.

A third important difference between the rational-choice and political models is that the latter does not require the assumption of logical consistency. Consensus can be maximized without a cardinal or even an ordinal utility function. In fact, transitivity of choice is not desirable in political bargaining, since it works to exacerbate conflict by promoting intransigence among groups supporting particular goals. Where preferences are ambiguous, compromises are more easily reached and consensus more easily attained (Lindbloom, 1959).

A fourth difference between the two models of decision making is the question of whether rationality should be viewed as a process as opposed to a substantive result. In politics, rationality is most often viewed as a process of making decisions rather than achieving a substantive end. A rational political actor is one who attempts to maximize his own power; he is not interested in the substance of policy, only in how his position on a policy question can help him attain power (Downs, 1957). In organizations, rationality is usually viewed as success in achieving goals. In short, political man is interested in power; administrative man wants to achieve goals. This question is important to warrant more extended consideration.

RATIONALITY AS PROCESS INSTEAD OF
SUCCESS IN ACHIEVING GOALS

Political scientists often hold that politics is nonrational and cannot be explained very well through a theory of rational behavior. Nevertheless, a great deal of political behavior has been explained by the premise that individuals act rationally. A very familiar scenario shows politicians as rational individuals who, in an attempt to maximize votes, cleverly manipulate information, reward their friends through patronage and spoils, and punish their opponents. Their sole aim is to win votes and, once in office, to increase their margin of support. Voters have also been depicted as rational individuals who attempt to promote their own interests through the act of voting. They will vote for candidates of their own ethnic background, believing they will thus get more effective representation. They will exchange votes for favors, jobs, and fixed traffic tickets. Those with more at stake in politics, such as government workers, turn out to vote in higher proportion than the population in general (Lipset, 1963). People tend to stay away from elections that do not give them meaningful choices. And an increasing proportion of voters claim to be independents, apparently basing their voting decisions on rational considerations of the issues in an election (Pomper, 1968).[2]

But notice that rational choice does not have a single meaning. On the one hand, it refers to processes of action, to means, rather than to success in achieving goals. Anthony Downs, for example, contends that whether these processes outperform a nonrational man is not part of the rational-choice model (Downs, 1957). Downs develops two major rational man axioms based on a process definition of rationality. (1) Politicians seek to maximize votes so as to win office, and (2) voters cast their votes for the party they believe will provide them with the most benefits. Politicians never seek office as a means of carrying out particular policies; their only goal is to attain their private ends, which they can reach only by being elected (Downs, 1957, pp. 28–36).

In organizational behavior, on the other hand, a rational man is one who is more successful in achieving his goals than one who only follows "hunches" or "intuition." In the theory of private business, for example, the goal to be maximized is profits, and all organizational behavior is measured in relationship to how successful an organization is in achieving this goal. In the theory of consumer choice, a rational man attempts to maximize his satisfactions; his goal is defined clearly in terms of his own subjective feelings. For organizations in general, a rational actor attempts to maximize the output function E, under conditions of (1) certainty, where there is one best alternative for the organization, and (2) risk, where there isn't one best solution, but it is possible to assign probabilities to the states of nature and select the alternative that maximizes E. In all cases—the firm, consumers, and organizations—rationality is defined in terms of success in achieving goals, not simply as a process of making decisions. The same definition of rationality has been applied by Simon and Stedry to quasi-rational behavior; they define it as behavior in which satisfactory levels of goal attainment are defined, and a reward function, dependent on the goal attainment, is to be maximized (Simon and Stedry, 1969, p. 279).

This definition of rationality presents some difficult problems in analyzing public policy. It requires that we define the goals that are to be maximized by public agencies. So far, no one has been able to do this satisfactorily, and the result has been an acute dilemma for policy analysis. On the one hand, the process definition of rationality is not appropriate for analyzing public policy because it cannot be assumed, as it is with regard to economic behavior (Bergson, 1938), that the sum of the individual self-interests of government officials is the public interest. The public interest certainly is more than the sum of the power of all political and administrative officials in government.

But when we define rationality as success in achieving goals, we face difficult theoretical and measurement problems. Should we assume that public agencies have only a single goal (i.e., the public interest)? Can this be defined specifically enough to enable us to measure degrees of goal achievement? Is it theoretically fruitful to treat members of public agencies as members of a team who all agree on the goal of the agency? If not, as a compromise, is it possible to reduce all goals to a single dimension?

Clearly, the possibility of using rational-choice theories for analyzing public decisions depends on the way we answer questions such as these. If we cannot treat public agencies as having a single goal, it is necessary to modify the definition of rationality so that it can accommodate situations where multiple and possibly competing goals exist. Or alternatively, we can accept the process definition of rationality and somehow try to accommodate it with normative theories about the public interest. These normative theories tell us that we must consider the substance of rationality as well as the process. Some of the difficulties involved here can be illuminated by considering the economist's method for evaluating public policy choices: cost-benefit analysis.

INCOME DISTRIBUTION EFFECTS AND COST-BENEFIT ANALYSIS

Public-choice theory is one of the newer additions to the literature of decision making and organizational theory. It has been developed and fairly well dominated by economists (Buchanan and Tollison, 1972). One of the more important techniques used in public-choice theory for evaluating public policy is cost-benefit analysis.

In cost-benefit analysis, the goals of public policy are measured in strict dollar terms. The overwhelming majority of cost-benefit studies fail to take into account who the recipients of public policy are, how rich they are, what their party affiliation is, and similar important questions. Thus a dollar in benefits received by a rich man is given the same weight as a dollar in benefits received by a poor man (Zeckhauser and Schaefer, 1968; Weisbrod, 1968; Rothenberg, 1961; Foster, 1966). The existing wisdom is cost-benefit analysis decrees that a project that gives a million dollars to one rich man is to be preferred to one that gives $900 each to 1000 poor men, given that they both have the same cost, because its cost-benefit ratio is higher.

This conclusion has offended the sense of social justice of many economists. There consequently have been a number of attempts to take the income level of recipients of public services into consideration. But all these attempts have run into a serious problem: it is not possible to make interpersonal utility comparisons. The question is: Does the marginal value of a dollar received by individual A (or group A) equal the marginal value of a dollar received by individual B? If it does, the approach to social welfare is straightforward; we can simply add together the welfare of all individuals to get total social welfare (Bergson, 1938; Little, 1960; Foster, 1966; Zeckhauser and Schaefer, 1968). Empirically, however, in actual public choices, we know that government officials do not, and perhaps cannot, consider each group's welfare to be the same (or more precisely, the marginal value of a dollar received by each member of group A is not considered to be the same as the marginal value of a dollar received by each member of group B).

Consider, as an example, an area where cost-benefit analysis has been most successful: water resources decisions. In one study addressed to this question it was shown that the Congress has approved water resource projects that have lower benefit-cost ratios over other projects, simply because they are located in the districts of the more powerful Congressmen (Haveman, 1965). In these cases, the Congress has accorded more weight to each dollar received by people in the areas receiving the project than it does to those in the other areas. Decisions of this kind are made on the basis of bargaining and logrolling rather than on the basis of cost-benefit calculations.

This question has both normative and empirical components that cannot be resolved. To illustrate this I will use the following simplified example. Suppose that the people who will benefit by a particular project can be neatly divided into two classes: rich and poor. Should the marginal value of a dollar provided by a government project to the rich be given the same weight as the marginal value of a dollar provided to the poor? Many readers will say no. But if not, what weights should be given to the dollar benefits received by the rich?

One approach to this question is to begin with empirical observations and make normative inferences from them. In this approach, the definition of optimum distribution of welfare does not result from any value judgment made by the analyst. He is an observer of citizens' value judgments and opinions, just as he is an observer of their tastes on consumer goods. From these data he may deduce the optimal distribution of wealth. Some economists believe that useful normative economics is therefore a positive science because it is based on objective observation of subjective opinions (Kolm, 1969, p. 148).

But let us see what happens when we attempt to infer weights from empirical observations. We use the following simple example. Assume that there are two competing housing projects, Project A and Project B, and that the government must choose between them. Assume that Project A yields total benefits of $250, consisting of the following: 200 poor people receive $1 each, and five rich people receive $10 each. Assume that the cost of this project is $200; the benefit-cost ratio, therefore, is 1.25. Assume now that Project B will provide a total benefit of $150, consisting of the following: 50 poor people each receive $1 and 10 rich people each receive $10. If the cost of Project B is the same as Project A, i.e., $200, then its benefit-cost ratio is 0.75. By a strict cost-benefit comparison, the government should prefer Project A.

But now suppose that the government approves Project B rather than A. If we can assume that the only reason it preferred Project B is its income distribution effects, we can make interpersonal utility comparisons. In this hypothetical example, the government considered the marginal value of one dollar received by the rich to be more than three times as desirable as the marginal value of each dollar received by the poor. Thus, if we multiply each dollar received by the rich by 3, the total benefits of Project B will equal that of Project A. But the government, of course, must have used a higher weight than 3. Just how much higher a weight is used cannot be determined empirically. Any number larger than 3 will produce greater total benefits for Project B than for Project A and thus a higher benefit-cost ratio for B. We have no way of telling what weight actually was used. Of course, one might say that it is sufficient to know that the weight was greater than 3. But this does not mean that the government will always use precisely that amount. Thus, not only does the empirical method fail to tell us what weight was used in a specific case, but it cannot tell us what weight should be used in the future.

An attempt to solve this problem was made by Kaldor and Hicks, who maintain that if those who gain from a change can compensate the losers in such a way that everybody is better off, and if the Pareto criterion is satisfied (no further exchanges are possible without harming someone), the project should be approved (Zeckhauser and Schaefer, 1968). Their solution does not require that the compensation actually take place, because the government can redistribute income by other methods, such as progressive income taxes. The problem with this solution, however, is that rational choice theory does not tell us why public officials will compensate the losers; in fact, if their goal is to maximize their own power, there is every incentive for them to avoid redistributing income in favor of the poor after a certain point is reached (Foster, 1966). In any event, public choice theory does not provide a reason why public officials should compensate the losers of any specific government project.

An increasing number of economists believe that public-choice theory can no longer avoid this problem (Kolm, 1969; Rothenberg, 1965; Weisbrod, 1968; Elkin, 1974). Government officials are more concerned with the distribution effects of their decisions than with efficiency effects. Neither politicians nor bureaucrats make decisions in urban renewal, health, education, law enforcement, or welfare by means of criteria associated with maximizing efficiency. They are concerned with who gets what benefits. Public choice theory can make meaningful contributions to these decisions only when it includes measurements of how the benefits of public policy are distributed.

But that day may be a long way off, for no one yet has been able to provide an acceptable measure of the distribution effects of public policy. In fact, it is not possible to do so in some cases. For example, in the case of services that provide indivisible benefits, such as national defense, it is not possible to measure how they are distributed, because they are by definition indivisible. In other cases, such as tax policy, the benefits of one group may equal the losses of another, yielding a sum of zero benefits and thus no benefit-cost ratio at all. Finally, the theory does not tell us why the public officials *should* try to achieve an ideal distribution of benefits, even if the ideal can be defined.

These difficulties are formidable enough to cause the prudent theorist to seek to modify the theory of rational choice rather than mechanically to perfect cost-benefit measurements.

THE LIMITS TO OMNISCIENT RATIONALITY

At one extreme in our treatment of rationality, writes Herbert Simon (1945), are the economists who attribute to economic man a "preposterously omniscient rationality." Economic man, he continues, has a complete and consistent set of preferences, is aware of all alternatives open to him, can perform the most complex computation in order to find the best alternative, and is unafraid of risky and uncertain situations. Simon believes that in its extension to competitive game situations and in the realm of decision making under uncertainty, decision theory had ". . . reached a state of Thomistic refinement that possesses considerable normative interest, but little discernible relation to the actual or possible behavior of flesh and blood human beings" (Simon, 1945, p. 23; 1957, p. 202). For the study of politics, such heroic models appear to be "desperate enterprises."

These theoretical observations are supported by empirical findings that show that political man seldom is rational. Campbell *et al.* (1961), for example, have observed that nonrational factors frequently determine the outcome of elections. Those who weakly identify with parties, and who are least knowledgeable about issues, frequently shift their vote on the basis of such things as candidate image, and it is their behavior that determines the outcome of elections. Moreover, businessmen's attitudes toward such key issues as trade policy are by no means entirely rational. Their decisions involve more than self-interest and are based on nonrational premises, such as ideology, social role, background, etc. (Bauer, De Sola Pool, and Dexter, 1963). Pure expressions of rational self-interest are hard to come by even in large-scale formal organizations.

However, it is not necessary to abandon the concept of rationality entirely (Harsanyi, 1969; Simon, 1945; Landau, 1969; Diesing, 1962). Administrative man is not wholly rational, only intendedly rational. He attempts to "satisfice" rather than maximize. This is Simon's concept. He defines it as looking for a course of action that is "good enough" (Simon, 1945, p. 25). A satisficer searches for alternatives sequentially from those developed by the organization he belongs to. From this restricted range he selects a course that satisfies his aspirational level. His aspirations, of course, change over the course of time. Moreover, the decision maker greatly simplifies the environment of decision making. It may even be necessary, at times, for him to be inefficient and uneconomical in order to be rational. Landau has pointed out that redundancy in a system, contrary to the extreme strictures of Taylorism and scientific management, actually increases system reliability, especially when the system faces a high degree of uncertainty. Redundancy, duplication, and overlap are ways of avoiding error, and as such they are rational (Landau, 1969; Braybrooke and Lindbloom, 1963). Ferejohn and Fiorina note that a voter who follows the principle of minimizing his maximum expected regrets (this is explained later) is rational even though he is not maximizing (Ferejohn and Fiorina, 1974).

Rather than abandon the concept of rationality, therefore, we might try to modify it. A number of modifications of the model have been suggested since Simon first made his two major modifications of rational choice theory in his classic, *Administrative Behavior*, in 1945. The modifications frequently originate in work done in other theories—in psychology, systems, cybernetic, information, or decision and game theories. We will discuss several such modifications in this section.

Consider first the assumption of complete information. A majority of decisions in organizations involve situations in which there is less than complete information and in which decision makers have less than complete control over the variables affecting them. A large and growing part of decision theory deals with decision making under risk, where the decision maker must assign probabilities to alternatives on the basis of incomplete information.

(We shall describe this in more detail in the next section.) Nor is it rational for an individual to invest sufficient resources and time to obtain complete information if the payoff to him does not justify this expenditure. Practically all political decisions involve situations like this. A voter, for example, does not receive a high enough return to become completely informed about all the issues in an election. It is rational for him to use a number of shortcuts when making his decision. He may rely on specialists to provide the information he needs for better decisions (e.g., newspapers), and he sometimes uses ideology as a way of screening information coming from the environment. He reduces his uncertainty to the point where the marginal return for his vote exceeds the marginal cost of obtaining information, but no more than that. It even is rational for him to abstain from voting, particularly if the alternatives offered are practically indistinguishable, or if he perceives that the election will have little impact on public policy or his own fortunes. It is rational for specialized actors, such as newspapermen, to obtain complete information because they earn their living by analyzing elections, but voters in general do not get enough return for their votes to justify obtaining complete information. When an individual stops his search for information at the point where the marginal return just exceeds the marginal cost, he is not trying to optimize; he is, in Simon's concept, "satisficing." He searches his environment as a way of improving his chances of making a correct decision, not of ensuring that he does.

Another major modification of the theory of rational choice concerns incentives. Government decision makers must be motivated by noneconomic and nonegoistic factors, as well as by self-interest (Harsanyi, 1969; Rawls, 1971). In situations where the personal interests of public officials are not strongly affected, they may be willing to let their behavior be governed by general social welfare considerations. If there is a conflict, with each individual judging the issue from his own one-sided point of view, a third person, not directly affected can try to maximize social welfare (e.g., an ombudsman). Why will public officials sometimes make altruistic decisions? Because of their personal commitments to the organization and to society. Most individuals have a large enough stake in the continuation of an organization to cause them to put aside their proximate or immediate self-interest in some decision situations. Sunk costs (i.e., money already invested) traditions, family considerations, and nationalistic feelings are part of these (Harsanyi, 1969; Downs, 1967). Finally, a person's behavior can be explained somewhat in terms of a desire for social acceptance, as well as by a desire for economic gain.

Although it is possible to modify the theory of rationality in the two ways outlined above, there are other, more complex aspects of organizational behavior that make the prospects of salvaging rational choice much more bleak. One concerns the problem of competing goals. We said above that sometimes goals held by individuals may conflict in that the means appropriate for the attainment of one may block attainment of another (he is subject to "cross pressures"). The definition of rationality in this situation is extremely difficult, because we do not have a metatheory to tell us which goal the individual should prefer. Where the actor is a voter, one possible solution is to assume that each voter simplifies the problem by comparing the distance of each alternative from his optimum position in each dimension separately, then combining the differences in a simple linear way (Rae and Taylor, 1971). However, this solution does not work for organizational decision making, especially if we assume that there are several decision makers in an organization, as well as several goals (i.e., an organization is not a strict hierarchy with a single head). The various positions cannot be combined because some of the goals —and therefore interests—of groups may be in conflict. There does not seem to be any way to modify the theory of rational choice to solve this problem. The only alternative may be to turn to a different model of decision making.

Rationality, even in a limited sense of choosing a satisfactory rather than a maximum course of action, requires that feedback occur concerning the relationship between organizational action and the goals of the organization. Systems, cybernetic, and information theory have contributed to our understanding of this process. From the perspective of the decision makers, their rewards depend heavily on the extent to which goals are achieved and the ways in which information about their achievement is transmitted throughout the organization. If the alternative selected by a decision maker fails to achieve goals or is perceived to have failed, those who support the goals, as well as the alternative chosen, may be removed or demoted. This is not to say that feedback, even in profit-making firms, is accurate. There is empirical evidence that the correlation between management rewards and company profits is low (Gordon, 1945; Cooper, 1951). But feedback is essential to organizational survival, for the outputs of the system are a means of garnering support (Easton, 1965). Until recently, rational choice theories did not include analysis of how much impact a particular policy had and thus how information about goal achievement is recirculated throughout the system.

Although systems and cybernetic theories have helped us understand the importance of feedback loops to organizational decision making, there has been little success so far in applying these theories to empirical data. In regard to public decisions, it is particularly hard to do because of the difficulty of defining the goals of public choice. This, of course, has a number of important pragmatic as well as theoretical repercussions. For example, because the goals of public agencies tend to be stated in the most general and vague terms, it is extremely difficult to tell whether they have been achieved, and thus, it is also very difficult to hold public executives accountable for achievement (or nonachievement). One important theoretical ramification is that when goals cannot be specified and measured, the feedback loop in public decision making will be weak, and it may not be possible to reduce uncertainty to manageable dimensions. In the terminology of decision theory, this means that public choice decisions most often will be made under conditions of uncertainty. And as we shall show in a moment, it may not be possible to be rational under conditions of uncertainty. Rather than simply modify rational choice, we may have to completely abandon it. Decision theory is not perfectly clear on this point, but most existing theoretical logic leans heavily in this direction.

DECISION THEORY AND UNCERTAINTY

Decision theory has been classified in a number of ways. One classification is that of Duncan and Luce, who distinguish between decision making under conditions of certainty, risk, and uncertainty (Luce and Raiffa, 1957) : (1) Under conditions of certainty, the decision maker has complete information about the decision situation, and he can apply determinate models (such as linear and dynamic programming) to find optimum solutions. (2) Under conditions of risk, the decision maker does not have complete information about the variables related to his decision; he does not know what outcome will occur, but he is able to assign probabilities to each "state of nature" (defined below) and then select the outcome that will maximize his expected utility. (3) Under conditions of uncertainty, the decision maker is completely ignorant about what states of nature will occur; he cannot assign probabilities to them; the best he can do is select one decision rule from a number of different rules, such as maximum, minimax regret, and Hurwitz's $\propto$. (These rules are also defined below) . Which one is most appropriate depends on a number of factors unassociated with rational choice.

The crucial point for the theory of rational choice is the distinction between risk and uncertainty. As Luce and Raiffa have defined it, uncertainty involves complete ignorance about the consequences of action. Obviously it is not possible to be rational under these circumstances. And many theorists believe that most organizational behavior takes place under conditions of uncertainty. It follows that organizational behavior cannot be rational. Of course, not all theorists believe that uncertainty implies complete ignorance; many contend that it is just a special case of risk, or that it can be handled by the subjective approach to probability. Because the distinction between uncertainty and risk and the meaning of uncertainty have such important consequences for the theory of rational choice, I shall give it detailed consideration in this section.

The distinction between risk and uncertainty was probably first made by Frank Knight in 1921; but in recent years most economists have ignored the distinction because it does not seem to serve any useful purpose for them. Some tend to view the presence of risk and of uncertainty to be identical: each case presents a situation where the outcome of an action cannot be predicted with certainty, but where we can specify the set of all possible outcomes and assign probabilities to each. Once we assign probabilities to alternatives no matter how they are arrived at, there is no need for a distinction between risk and uncertainty (Borch and Mossin, 1968, p. 13). Ackoff has suggested that the distinction is unnecessary because it is possible to reduce all uncertainty to risk. If a decision maker has enough information to formulate his decision problem, he has enough information to assign probabilities to various alternatives (Ackoff, 1962). Moreover, the probabilities do not have to be "objectively" true. If the decision maker has some information about the decision situation, no matter how imperfect, he should be able to assign judgmental probabilities to the various states of nature. A judgmental, or subjective, probability will enable him to apply the same methods that are applied in decision making under risk. The problem of objective versus subjective probability is complicated and important enough to require careful exposition, and we shall do so in a moment. Let us first describe decision making under each condition—certainty, risk, and uncertainty—then discuss the distinction between objective and subjective probabilities, and finally, show the relevance of all this to organization theory.

The case of decision making under certainty covers a large area. Not only a large part of operations research but a considerable amount of formal theory in economics, political science, psychology, and management science can be classified under this heading. In a typical situation in business administration, a company has several factories and warehouses; it has to ship products from the factories to the warehouses; and it knows with certainty the shipping costs, factory output capacity, and warehouse requirements. Its job is to determine what material should be shipped and which warehouse will receive goods from which factories. This is a complicated mathematical problem, but there is no uncertainty or risk involved.

The mathematical tools for analyzing decisions of this kind are more highly developed than for decisions under risk or uncertainty. They involve the calculus to find maxima and minima (i.e., linear programming), the calculus of variations to find functions, production schedules, and inventory schedules (dynamic programming), and in political science and sociology, a number of causal modeling techniques. In all these applications, the decision maker has full information about the possible outcomes for all the alternatives (or acts, as they are often called) and complete control over the variables that affect the outcomes; he is dealing with closed systems. He can pick the optimal act and know with certainty that it will occur. Decision making under certainty is deterministic. The decision maker is not taking a risk, nor is he uncertain about the consequences of his action.

There is also a category of decision making under certainty in game theory. Game theory, an important part of decision theory, was first developed by the mathematical economists Von Neumann and Morgenstern (1947). It has since blossomed into a powerful science with an extensive technical literature and applications in many diverse areas. (See the bibliography in Luce and Raiffa, 1957). It will be useful to discuss how game theory approaches certainty, risk, and uncertainty.

Those parts of game theory that involve determinate and certain solutions are zero-sum games with a saddle point. A saddle point is that situation in which the larger of the row minima is equal to the smaller of the column maxima. Rational actors should select a strategy leading to this solution because any other strategy would produce a worse situation (Palumbo, 1969c, pp. 315–16). In such games, there is only one best strategy for each actor: the minimax strategy. Zero-sum games with a saddle point are strictly determined games. The only difference between them and the case of certainty in decision theory is that for the latter the opponent is "nature," whereas in game theory the opponent is another rational actor trying to outdo the decision maker and force him into his worst choice.

Decision making under certainty is relatively rare in politics. Consequently there has been relatively little chance to apply linear and dynamic programming or zero-sum game models in political science. To date, the theory of zero-sum games has found application almost exclusively in the study of military engagements (Taylor, 1971, p. 368). Of course, this does not mean that there is no place for deterministic models in politics; causal models have been used extensively in political science in recent years (Blalock and Blalock, 1968; Alker, 1969). However, deterministic models do not appear to be as useful as probabilistic models for building theories of organizational behavior.

In decisions under risk, as we said earlier, the decision maker does not have complete information about the outcomes of each alternative available to him. He is not certain what "state of nature" will occur. He must pick an alternative, A_1, A_2, . . ., A_n, depending on the probability of the various states of nature, S_1, S_2, . . ., S_n. For example, assume that the problem is a decision to appeal for financial support for a new political cause. To simplify the illustration, we will assume that the appeal must be made on television. Various numbers of one-minute spots can be purchased at a cost of $700 per minute. Acts A_1, A_2, . . ., A_n are therefore various lengths of television time to be purchased. The campaign manager does not know beforehand how many minutes to buy; but he has experience in raising funds for political causes and therefore estimates probabilities for how many people are likely to respond to a TV campaign. The states of nature, S_1, S_2, . . ., S_n, can be depicted as various numbers of contributors, such as 100, 200, 300, etc., that might respond for each alternative. Assume that the campaign manager has enough experience to know that the pattern of probabilities for different numbers of contributors closely resembles a Poisson distribution. A Poisson distribution is a family of distributions for discrete events in which p, the probability of success, and q, the probability of failure, are very small (Palumbo, 1969c, 92). See Table 1.

TABLE 1   Poisson probability distribution for
$m = 300$*

Event: Number of contributors x	Probability $p\,(x)$
0	.050
100	.149
200	.224
300	.224
400	.168
500	.101
600	.050
700	.024
800	.008
900	.003
	1.000

* m is the expected mean number of successes for the
event.

The data in Table 1 constitute a kind of betting model of reality. The most likely number of contributors to respond to a TV appeal is either 200 or 300, but it could be as low as zero or as high as 900. A decision maker faced with the data in Table 1 might be tempted to buy just enough minutes of TV time to reach 200 or 300 contributors because these are the most likely response levels. But of course, the decision also depends on the cost of TV time and on the amount each person will contribute. If TV time were free, he should ask for sufficient time to reach at least 900 contributors, the maximum number possible that can be reached via this medium (in our hypothetical example). But TV time is not free, his budget is not unlimited, and the decision therefore cannot be made on the basis of probabilities alone.

In order to include costs and benefits in our decision, a payoff matrix must be computed. We said above that the cost of TV time is $700 per minute (in this hypothetical example). Assume that each person responding will contribute $10, and that there is a limit to how many responses can be expected for each number of minutes of TV time purchased, so that a one-minute slot can be expected to reach 400 people at the most, two minutes can be expected to reach an upper limit of 500 people, and so on. The payoffs for these assumptions are depicted in Table 2. Thus, if the campaign manager buys three minutes of TV time and 300 contributors respond, his total contribution will be 300 × $10 (the amount contributed) − 3 × $700 (his total cost) = $900.

Table 2 shows that the action the campaign manager should take depends on his attitude toward risk. If he decides to buy one minute of time, he is guaranteed a return of $300, no matter what. This is the least risky decision, and a conservative decision maker would opt for it. If he buys five minutes,

TABLE 2 Payoff matrix

Events: Number of contributors responding	Actions: Number of TV minutes purchased				
	1	2	3	4	5
0	$ − 700	$ −1400	$ −2100	$ −2800	$ −3500
100	300	− 400	−1100	−1800	−2500
200	1300	600	− 100	− 800	−1500
300	2300	1600	900	200	− 500
400	3300	2600	1900	1200	500
500	3300	3600	2900	2200	1500
600	3300	3600	3900	3200	2500
700	3300	3600	3900	4200	3500
800	3300	3600	3900	4200	4500
900	3300	3600	3900	4200	4500

he runs a high risk because he could lose $2500, but he could also make as much as $4500. A speculative decision maker might opt for this decision. Which action should be selected? One decision criterion is to select an alternative depending on the personality of the decision maker. Obviously this is not the rational approach. A rational decision maker would include the probabilities of various levels of contributor response in his decision calculations, as well as the cost of each alternative.

To show how he could do so, we must compute the expected total contribution for each alternative. Table 3 illustrates the computations for the event "Buy two minutes of TV time." The column labeled "Total payoff" in

TABLE 3 Expected total contribution for alternative: Buy two minutes

Event: Number of Contributors Responding (x)	Probability $p(x)$	Total payoff π	Expected total payoff $\pi \cdot p(x)$
0	.050	$ −1400	$ − 70.00
100	.149	− 400	− 59.60
200	.224	600	134.40
300	.224	1600	358.40
400	.168	2600	436.80
500	.101	3600	363.60
600	.050	3600	180.00
700	.024	3600	86.40
800	.008	3600	28.80
900	.003	3600	10.80
			$1469.60

Table 3 is the amount that would result if two minutes of TV time were bought (see Table 2). The maximum expected contribution that would result for this alternative is $436.80. The expected total contribution (ETC) is $1469.60. This value is interpreted in the same way as the expected value of a random variable. It is the average contribution that would result if the decision were repeated many times and each time the decision maker chose the same alternative (in this case, to buy two minutes of TV time). Note that his total contribution will never be $1469.60. It is possible that he could buy two minutes of TV time and have as many as 500 contributors respond; his total payoff would then be $5000.00 − $1400.00 = $3600.00. But the probability that this will happen is low ($p = .101$).

To be able to make a rational decision, it is necessary to compute an expected total contribution for each possible alternative (Table 4). The alternative with the highest expected total contribution is to buy one minute of TV time. A rational actor would pick this alternative. (It is only coincidental that the rational solution is also the conservative solution.)

As we can see, a lot hinges on the values given to the three variables; two are known (the cost of TV time and the amount each contributor will give), whereas the third is unknown (how many persons will respond to each number of minutes of TV time bought). Once probabilities are established for the unknown variable, the alternative a rational actor should select is not in doubt. It is a "risky" decision in that he does not know for certain what his payoff will be; it is possible for him to lose as much as $3500 on his decision to buy one minute of TV time or make as much as $4500. The probabilities for these outcomes are low, but rare events, such as the run of 26 black in a row on a roulette wheel (gambler's ruin) or a perfect hand in bridge have been known to occur. The decision maker, however, knows exactly how much risk he is taking and therefore can make a rational decision.

Suppose, however, that the decision maker does not have enough experience to be able to assign probabilities to the states of nature on some "objective" basis (defined rigorously below), such as the relative frequencies of responses to past campaigns of this type. Can he still make a rational decision?

TABLE 4   Expected total contribution for each alternative

Action: Number of TV minutes purchased	Expected total contribution
1	$1818.30
2	1469.60
3	842.20
4	175.60
5	−501.50

The answer is not perfectly clear. Some believe so, providing that we are able to reduce the decision maker's uncertainty to a level of risk. If he has no "objective" basis for assigning probabilities to the various levels of viewer response, he may assign "subjective" probabilities to each. If he does so, he can treat all uncertainty as cases of risk. But some do not believe this is possible, particularly those who subscribe to the objective positions concerning probability. To make this problem clear, let us first consider the difference between uncertainty and risk more precisely.

The distinction between uncertainty and risk can be illustrated with the following example. Assume that you have a choice between two different wagers:

> W1—You receive $1000 if the next president of the United States is a Democrat; $0 if he is not.
>
> W2—You receive $1000 if the top card drawn from an ordinary, well-shuffled deck of playing cards is red, $0 if it is black.

Which wager would you prefer to take? In experiments involving wagers of this kind, most individuals prefer W2 because there is a definite probability that can be assigned to the alternatives, whereas there is none for W1 (Ellsberg, 1961; MacCrimmon, 1968). The second wager is a case of risk, the first is a case of uncertainty. Why? Because there are no objective probabilities that can be assigned to whether the next president will be a Democrat. Of course, the reader may respond that we can assign some intuitive, or subjective, probabilities to W1; for example, we might say that, based on past electoral behavior, the probability that the next president will be a Democrat is $p = .60$. But this is not the same as the basis we would use to assign a probability for drawing a red card from an ordinary deck of playing cards ($p = 0.50$). The election of a president is not an event which can be repeated an infinite number of times, nor is it an event for which we can assign a mathematical probability, because we do not know all the characteristics of every member of the set (as we do with the playing cards). But still, the probability we did pick *is* a probability; it is based on historical knowledge and political analysis rather than relative frequencies or enumeration of members of the set. Of course, the accuracy of the probability defined this way is more questionable than that for drawing a red card, because we do not have enough information to compute precise mathematical probabilities. But, you may argue, for the purpose of decision theory, it is sufficient to have probabilities. Decision theory, as such, is not concerned with how accurate probabilities are. Moreover most probabilities for decisions under risk need not be objectively true. For example, empirical evidence indicates that subjects do not maximize objective utility even where the stakes are clear and the probabilities stated (Edwards, 1953; MacCrimmon, 1968). This much is true. But remember that, as we said above, the organizational definition of rationality requires that our decisions have some degree of success in achieving goals; this is how we distinguish it from the process concept of rationality. It is worth emphasizing at this point that no matter how we assign probabilities to alternatives, objectively or subjectively, it is important that they be empirically accurate; otherwise it is not possible to measure degree of goal achievement and, therefore, to be substantively rational.

In game theory, zero-sum games that do not have a saddle point are similar to decision making under risk. In these games, the decision maker alternates between strategies, playing one with greater frequency than others. He determines the best mix and the probabilities with which he should play each strategy in the mix. These games have a minimax solution. They involve an element of risk in that all the decision maker can do is pick the strategy with the highest probability of success. He does not have a single, best course of action, only a risky course. However, since he can compute probabilities of picking the correct strategy, he can be rational.

There is also a category of decision making under uncertainty in game theory. In uncertain games, the winnings of one player do not equal the losses of another (they are thus "non zero-sum" games), the decision maker is ignorant about what strategy his opponent might play, and he does not have one best strategy. The strategy he should play is influenced by a number of factors, such as whether he can make side payments, whether he can expect his opponent to cooperate, and a host of variables related to his opponent's possible behavior (Taylor, 1971; Farquharson, 1966). In regard to a United States–Soviet arms control agreement, for example, we are not involved in a zero-sum game, because both sides can win if arms control is adopted, and the policy of each player is constrained both by their alliances and by their internal politics. The players thus are not free to adopt the single best strategy available to them, even if they are able to reduce uncertainty sufficiently to tell what it is.

Not many decision rules have been developed for uncertain games. The two that are most widely known are maximim and minimax regret. The first directs a decision maker to select that course of action that offers the highest security level (Luce and Raiffa, 1957). Thus, in the example given in Table 5, the decision maker should select A_1 because it guarantees him a payoff of at least 3. But this course of action is justified only if we assume that nature is

TABLE 5   Uncertainty matrix

Actions	States of nature	
	S_1	S_2
A_1	3	5
A_2	8	1

not malevolent (her every gain is his every loss), and that nature does not always know the decision maker's choice before making her own.

The criterion of minimax regret focuses attention on the opportunity loss of an incorrect decision. The loss is measured by the difference between an achieved payoff and the payoff that would have been attained if the decision maker had known what the state of nature would be. In the example above, the minimax regret for A_1, S_1 is the difference $A_2 - A_1 = 8 - 3 = 5$. The minimax regret criterion says that one should choose the course of action which minimizes the expected regret for *any* strategy selected by nature.

The weakness of these two criteria as aids for decision making is that they look only at outcomes and do not consider how likely the corresponding states of nature are. Compare this with the example of decision making under risk discussed above. If we could assign probabilities to the states of nature in the example in Table 5, we could reduce uncertainty to risk. If we did this, there would be a best choice. If we cannot, there is no way to determine which decision rule is a valid criterion for rational behavior under conditions of uncertainty (Arrow, 1951). Decision making under uncertainty, therefore, is not a modified case of rational choice, at least not so long as it is not possible to reduce uncertainty to risk. We do not know how to make a rational choice under uncertainty, because we do not have a criterion that will tell us what decision rule is best. Michael Taylor (1971) has concluded that the applications of cases of uncertainty, such as those contained in the classic problem of Prisoner's Dilemma, "raise a host of interesting questions about cooperation and conflict, about the applicability of game theory (and, indeed, all rational choice theories) to such situations, and about the meaning of 'rationality' itself" (Taylor, 1971, p. 371; Rapoport and Chammah, 1965).

There are many empirical situations that seem to resemble conditions of uncertainty, especially in politics. In many political situations, the decision maker is ignorant about what action his opponent may take, or he cannot assign reasonable probabilities to the alternatives, even if he can specify them. For example, in United States—Soviet diplomatic relations, the United States cannot specify all the alternatives the Soviet Union may take, and it cannot assign reasonable probabilities to those it can identify. It does not know enough about Soviet decision making structures, Russian national character, or the personalities of the principal actors. Therefore, the United States cannot predict how the Soviet Union may react to a particular action it takes. This was illustrated well in the Cuban missile crisis of 1962. During a television interview concerning the crisis, Kennedy said that the decision to blockade Soviet ships bound for Cuba had much greater impact on the Soviet Union than he had originally expected. The Russians were very reluctant to have the United States board Soviet ships and get a close look at their secret missiles. This reaction was something Kennedy had not considered in his original decision. The same was true, Kennedy said, of the decision to order low-level, intensive photography of the missile sites already set up in Cuba. The flights greatly upset Castro, but he could not shoot them down, because that would give the United States a reason to invade Cuba. Castro, thus, unexpectedly helped the United States by putting pressure on the Soviet Union to have the missiles removed. Graham Allison (1971) stresses that startling results were produced by the blockade of Cuba, and he describes the many miscalculations, misunderstandings, and uncertainties that occurred. In such decisions, the potential reaction of the opponents is not predictable. If the reaction does not follow any known probability distribution, the situation does not fit our definition of risk. The decision maker may not be completely ignorant in these situations, but he is close to it—at least close enough to make the assumption of ignorance fairly realistic.

Situations like these best fit our definition of decision making under uncertainty. The decision maker cannot assign *objective* probabilities to the alternative states of nature. If we agree that the majority of political decisions fall into this category of decision making (i.e., where it is not possible to predict the reaction of an opponent), it also follows that most political decisions cannot be rational. This is of course a rather important theoretical conclusion. Because of its importance, let us consider the meaning of objective and subjective probability in some detail.

An objective probability can be defined in two ways. (1) The first definition makes it a relative frequency: the ratio of those cases that fit the definition of an event to all those that fall into the general class. For example, we can compute objective probabilities of dying at age 45 of lung cancer; of getting into an auto accident for a 21-year-old male driver; and of having an I.Q. greater than 120. These events and many others like them are repeated a great number of times under very similar circumstances; the relative frequencies of their occurrence are used as probabilities. (2) The second definition of objective probability is mathematical: the ratio of all members of the set conforming to our definition of an event to all possible events in a *finite* sample space. The events and sample space must be finite and countable. Thus we may define the sample space as all possible outcomes of selecting a sample of three beads from a population of three black and two red beads, and the event as the selection of a sample containing at least two black beads. Or we may define a sample space as all the possible outcomes of selecting three cards from an ordinary playing deck, and the event as the selection of three aces. A definite probability can be assigned to each of these events.

Most political events do not come close to either definition of objective probability. Whether the Soviet Union will engage in an atomic war over the Middle East, whether the Congress will pass a national welfare law, or whether a particular individual (e.g., Ted Kennedy) will be elected president in 1980— these are events that are not (and cannot be) repeated a large number of times, and they are not events in a finite and countable sample space. They are, in fact, events in an infinite sample space and, by definition, cannot be assigned an objective probability. The last point is important enough to warrant emphasizing and repeating. It is not possible to assign objective probabilities to events in an open and infinite set, because probability requires that we identify and enumerate all possible outcomes (i.e., combinations and permutations) of events. Because decision making under uncertainty always involves an open set, it cannot be analyzed through the objective approach to probability.

We said above that one possible way to deal with cases of uncertainty is to try to reduce them to conditions of risk. There are several ways to do this. One is to arbitrarily compress the sample space we are concerned with into a finite and countable one. For example, we might assume that we have identified all the relevant variables, even if we haven't. We make such an assumption when we make causal inferences in nonexperimental research design; we assume that variables not in our system of equations are exogenous predetermined). We take these exogenous variables as "givens" (Blalock and Blalock, 1968; Simon, 1957). We then use the same procedures for uncertainty as we do for risk. But this may involve premature closure of the set and lead to erroneous results, particularly if we have not identified all the relevant variables.

Another and perhaps better way to deal with uncertainty is to use the subjective approach to probability, which treats probability as a question of judgment or belief that exists only in the decision maker's head rather than something that occurs "out there." Philosophically, in fact, according to the subjective approach, there are no "objectively true" probabilities at all. All probabilities are to be interpreted as true only in our minds, reflecting the degree of confidence we have that various states of nature will occur. Probabilities are always based on the incomplete knowledge we have. This approach opens up vast new areas of application formerly closed, and it leads to very powerful and interesting theoretical questions. It behooves us, therefore, to take a little time to describe how decisions would be treated from this approach.

I will begin with an example. Assume that there is a public health agency that rents hospital rooms by the month from a private hospital. If in any particular month it rents too many rooms, it will lose money on those it cannot use. If it rents too few rooms, it will have to turn away needy people. To make a decision, the agency must estimate future demand and assign probabilities to each level. For example, it might be able to use 6, 7, 8,. . ., n rooms a day, and each level must be assigned a probability, $p_1, \ldots, p_n$, such that

$$\sum_{i=1}^{n} p_1 = 1.00.$$

How does the agency decide what probability to assign to each possible level of demand? If it takes the objective approach, it will construct relative frequencies of each level of demand for each day in the same way insurance agencies do, and it will use them to assign probabilities to various levels of demand. If it takes the subjective approach, the agency will use someone's judgment about the probabilities of various levels of demand. In the latter case, probability represents the degree of confidence the decision maker has in the person's judgment about each level of demand, and he can arrive at them strictly on hunch, logic, or intuition. If the decision maker revises these subjective judgments in accordance with each day's actual experience, he is using the Bayesean approach to decision making. This approach will bring him to the same conclusion as the objective approach wherever the objective approach is applicable—that is, where he can repeat his decision a large number of times under similar circumstances (Churchman, 1961). In those cases where he can revise subjective probabilities on the basis of objective experiences, the two approaches come to the same conclusions.

The subjective approach to probability might be said to be superior to the objective approach because it can be used where the objective approach can be used, as well as where it cannot. In the former cases, the subjective approach is not in conflict with the objective approach; the subjective approach merely formalizes the use of judgment by expressing subjective judgments in the form of explicitly stated utilities and weights and can be thought of as a formal completion of the objective approach (Raiffa and Schlaifer, 1961, 16). Where the objective approach cannot be used, that is, in decisions that cannot be repeated or counted, the subjective approach adds a totally new dimension of possibilities to decision making. However, there is a question as to whether this is really an advantage. It might be that where there are no known objective probabilities, the probabilities used by the decision maker will be widely different from the empirical events he is trying to influence. Then the subjective approach is no advantage but actually a disadvantage, because it binds us to the use of a decision making procedure that may yield very erroneous results. There have been several attempts to resolve this problem.

Von Neumann and Morgenstern (1947) developed the subjective approach in the following way. We might ask the decision maker to compare a gamble involving a state of nature whose probability is unknown with a gamble involving known probabilities. If he turns out to be indifferent between a lottery that offers him a valuable prize if the state of nature occurs and a lottery that offers him the same prize if he draws a red ball from an urn containing 35 red and 65 black balls, then we say, by definition, that he attaches a personal probability of 0.35 to the state of nature. These personal probabilities are then used to calculate the expected utility of each alternative, and the one that offers the highest expected utility is selected. This reduces uncertainty to risk. It does have one drawback, however, when we try to apply it: the decision maker may refuse to make the probability judgment that would be necessary, or his judgment may be completely wrong. The solution obviously does not work in these instances.

In theory, the subjective approach eliminates the need for decision making under uncertainty, at least in the sense that probabilities can be assigned to various states of nature, regardless of whether they are "objectively" correct or true. And if a decision maker can formulate a problem with probabilities, he has succeeded in reducing his problem to a case of risk. But even though the problem of whether all uncertainty can be reduced to risk is solved in theory, there still remain difficult empirical and practical questions about the usefulness of the subjective approach. So far, the subjective approach has not been tested sufficiently for us to reach any conclusion about whether it will work in actual cases.

IMPLICATIONS FOR THE THEORY OF RATIONAL CHOICE

There are a number of important conclusions that flow from the discussions of the last two sections. In decisions under certainty and risk there is an optimum solution, but it can be found only because we know all possible outcomes or can assign probabilities to them. It is not possible to do this where there is more than one goal for an organization—that is, in cases of uncertainty. There is no metatheory to tell us which goal to prefer if two or more goals are in conflict. If we could put all goals on a single scale, so that m units of achievement of goal 1 could be compared to n units of loss of goal 2, we could tell which goal to prefer. But to date, decision theorists have not developed such a metatheory.

A second major conclusion concerns the question of consensus among members of an organization. We said above that in the theory of rational choice, actors must be assumed to be a single team of individuals whose members agree on all their goals, not just a part of them. This means that we cannot consider the cost of achieving consensus or the problems associated with multiple strategies of action (Pondy, 1970). It is only the theory of decision making under uncertainty that allows us to consider conflict and consensus. For example, whether we should follow a maximum or a minimax regret rule depends on whether we assume our opponent will compromise or try to defeat us. There still is some cause to doubt whether decision theory will find a solution to these situations, using the axioms of rational choice (Taylor, 1971).

A third point to emphasize is that the subjective approach to probability enables us to reduce uncertainty to risk and thus use rational choice in many cases where it is not possible to use the objective probabilities. However, the problem of how accurate these probabilities are has not yet been solved. The theory of "satisficing," of course, does help here because it enables the decision maker to limit the set of alternatives he will investigate; he can compress the sample space into a finite and countable one. But some ambiguities remain. There are advocates of the maximizing model who say that satisficing is no different from what they have advocated all along; they never believed that the objective of a maximizing analysis was to find the best of all possible courses of action (Raiffa and Schlaifer, 1961, p. viii). Satisficing is just another way of saying that we should include the cost of searching in our decision model. And most economists agree that the costs of searching for information should be included in the model (Zeckhauser and Schaefer, 1968, 92). But there is nothing in the principle of satisficing that tells us when the decision maker's search has gone far enough. A decision maker's aspiration level changes as the state of the world changes; it rises as opportunities improve. Changes in aspiration level are partly perceptual and psychological, and it is difficult, if not impossible, to place a hard dollar value on these factors. Moreover, when a decision maker stops his search once he has found a satisfactory alternative, he has not considered many other possible options, even if they are costly. And one of these unconsidered options may be very much better than the satisfactory one. It is hard to see how this can be called rational behavior (Barry and Rae, Volume 1 of this *Handbook*). Thus, with regard to the question of satisficing, we may conclude with Zeckhauser that: "A general economic theory of information acquisition and optimal decision making under imperfect conditions has yet to be developed. Without such a development, the concept of optimal choice can be defined in principle, but not always in practice" (Zeckhauser and Schaefer, 1968, 96).

The fourth point to emphasize concerns the distinction between "nature" as an opponent and a "rational actor" as an opponent. Decision situations in which the opponent is "nature" are usually defined as demand in economics or the null hypotheses in statistical hypothesis testing. We are not sure what nature will do, and we use probability theory as a way of outwitting nature. But we do not assume that nature will always present us with the worst possible alternative. In fact, the maximum likelihood method of making statistical inferences assumes that the most typical (favorable) value will turn up in random sampling. In statistical decision theory, nature is not considered to be a rational and calculating opponent (Menges, 1966, p. 141). Moreover, nature cannot be changed. The probabilities assigned to states of nature do not depend on the state of mind of the decision maker; rather they reflect some objective "fact" about reality (Churchman, 1961, p. 139).

Game theory introduces an entirely new dimension to decision making because it involves situations in which the opponent is a rational individual who is attempting to outwit the decision maker; this actor may be malevolent and force the decision maker to select his minimum, or poorest, strategy. Rationality in game theory has two sides to it: the decision maker, who is trying to maximize his self-interest, is rational; and his opponent, who also is trying to maximize his self-interest, is rational. If it is a zero-sum situation, the opponent will always keep the decision maker's gains to a minimum. In non zero-sum games, the players are not always in direct conflict, and it may be rational for them to bargain and compromise. In both cases, however, it is essential that the decision maker know something about his opponent's motives and intentions. It is also essential in games under uncertainty for him to communicate with and attempt to change the behavior of his opponent. This, of course, greatly expands the concept of rationality. It introduces the element of compromise, which seems essential in politics.

In empirical political situations, the ability of one participant is dependent on the choices of other participants. A decision maker cannot always win or optimize and must bargain: "Viewing conflict as a bargaining process," writes Schelling (1960, pp. 5–6), "is useful in keeping us from becoming exclusively preoccupied either with conflict or the common interest." In bargaining, there is a powerful common interest in reaching an outcome that is not enormously destructive to values on both sides. It seems rational for an individual to bargain and accept less than his optimum alternative when he is faced with an opponent who can reduce his gains to a lower level if he insists on his optimum. For example, on the assumption that the decision maker's optimum is 20, it is rational for him to accept a choice of action that yields him only 15 if he cannot get 20.

The compromise model of decision making allows a great deal of flexibility in decision making. It sees organizational behavior as a struggle for power—one in which there are not necessarily clear-cut victories, absolute levels of achievement, or final solutions to problems. A good example is arms control. A decision maker does not know what weapons system his potential enemy might use if negotiations break down and conflict ensues. He must therefore develop a weapons system based on subjective judgment, i.e., "contingency plans." But it is rational for him to continue to bargain, avoid conflict, and attempt to reach agreement on limiting armaments.

In the compromise model, there is no objectively real situation "out there" other than what the decision maker himself constructs out of the billions of bits of information he receives from his decision environment (Simon and Stedry, 1954). He may—erroneously—construct the environment and misread his opponent's intentions. But he does not always lose when he makes such errors. In this model, not only is it possible for decision makers (or organizations) to have multiple goals, but it is essential, because they are best conceived of as coalitions of groups, each with its own goals and each attempting to maximize its power in the organization. The organization itself does not have a goal (Simon, 1964; Cohen, March, and Olsen, 1972; Etzioni, 1964). But it is questionable whether rational choice is possible under these conditions. Decisions in the compromise model are the results of outputs of various actors that are determined primarily by routines established in these organizations prior to that instance (Allison, 1971, p. 68). Since behavior in the model is not directed at substantive goals, it is not rational in accordance with the definition given above.

I conclude that it may be possible to expand and improve the theory of rational choice in such a way as to make it more useful in public choice and political situations. But there still remain a large number of problems to be solved. Moreover, it seems that in expanding it, we have in effect rejected the rational model. In particular, the assumptions that organizations have multiple goals or perhaps no goals at all, that there is no consensus among members of an organization, that opponents are likely to be malevolent, and that most decisions are made under conditions of uncertainty do not seem to be compatible with any theory of rational choice.

The problem is whether we should view the modifications of rational choice discussed in this section as part of a new definition of rationality (i.e., a theory of "limited" rationality), or whether they are best conceived of as part of a completely different theory of choice. To make some of them (i.e., multiplicity of goals, uncertainty) part of the definition of rationality requires that we abandon some of the fundamental axioms of the theory of rational choice, particularly those concerning goals and consensus. But then a theory of rational choice modified as drastically as this is not really a theory of rational choice any longer. On the other hand, if we view some of the ideas concerning multiplicity of goals, uncertainty, and the need for compromise as constraints on rational behavior rather than as part of the definition of rationality, we may still retain the assumptions of rational choice, providing, of course, that we apply the theory only to those limited cases where the model is a reasonably good approximation of empirical reality. It is correct to require a theoretical model to be a good fit for empirical events. But in that case, the choice may not be a happy one, because very few aspects of organizational behavior may adequately conform to the strict and even the limited theory of rationality. The great bulk of organizational behavior seems to fit a nonrational, psychological model better, as Simon and others have been trying to persuade us for a long time now.

The solution to these problems is not easy. Before we can reach final conclusions about them, however, it is necessary to explore a few additional important questions in organization theory. One of the more important concerns the structure of decision making.

THE ANATOMY OF DECISION MAKING

In classical administrative theory, the formal structure of decision making is viewed as the institutional embodiment of purpose that constrains individual choice (Selznick, 1957), whereas the informal structure frequently is viewed as a nonrational constraint. It prevents decision makers from rationally directing the behavior of individuals toward the goals of the organization. In its most simplified form, the informal group is seen as embodying human feeling and as being nonrational, whereas the formal organization is concerned only with the optimum realization of tasks.

The formal structure pertains to the rules and regulations in organizations, the formal roles provided in organizational charts—who has what kind of authority, what their sanctions are, how centralized an organization should be, what the best span of control is, and so on.

Under the strictures of scientific management, concern with the formal structure focused on the best way to perform a given task, including even the body movements one should make so as to waste the least time and effort (Gross, 1964; Willoughby, 1927; Gulick and Urwick, 1937). Ideas about specialization, unity of command, span of control, and organization by purpose, process, clientele, and place were developed by traditional theorists into principles that were assumed to be scientifically verifiable. But the human relations movement that began in the Westinghouse studies in 1929 and the revolution that came with developments in decision theory, role theory, and, finally, the computer revolution upset these "scientific principles" and showed they were nothing more than proverbs (Simon, 1945, Chapter 2; Roethlisberger and Dickson, 1947). With these developments the formal structure was found to be less and less important, and the informal group was discovered.

Chester Barnard, in his classic, *The Functions of the Executive* (1938), developed the concept of informal organization as "the aggregate of . . . personal contacts and interactions and associated grouping of people." The informal organization, Barnard discovered, is not always in conflict with the formal; it is essential to the formal organization as a means of communication, source of cohesion, and a means of protecting the integrity of the individual. But ever since theorists made a distinction between formal and informal organization, they have assumed that legal and constitutional specifications do not adequately describe the system. Informal organizations weaken, modify, and rearrange decisions of the formal system. In this respect, political parties can be seen as informal organizations and, depending on the circumstances, can sometimes constitute an invisible government in which the "real decisions" are located. They prevent, in any case, a directed rationality.

The same distinction exists in the political system as in organizations: there are formal and informal rules. Indeed, with developments in behavioral science, it seemed for quite some time that political science had consigned inquiry about formal rules to the lawyers and taken for itself the task of describing only the informal. Research tells us that every agency of government is marked by sets of informal rules, and the mastery of them, notwithstanding formal constraints, not only is the key to understanding systemic processes but is critical to the success of political actors. Consider these informal rules of Congress with their unique and interesting names: logrolling, senatorial courtesy, patronage, trial balloons, inner clubs, and plea bargaining. Political style—whether of the president or the Senate floor leader—is a part of informal decision rules. A president's style may be idiosyncratic, but it leaves its effect in a striking manner on the dictionary of informality.

It is the recognition that such informalities pervade decision structures that has prompted recent efforts to devise effective formal rules. The attempt to find effective formal rules, of course, is a part of prescriptive theory, but such attempts frequently are based in empirical description of actual decision structures. Prescriptive theory takes as its prime task the job of devising rules that will cause men to maximize desired goals. This is a task that focuses not only on rules of representation, but also on the structure of decision making. The effort is an exercise in organizational design, an attempt to fashion a rational, determined system that will efficiently carry out sets of stated preferences (Bennis, 1969; Galbraith, 1973). Prescriptive theorists, in this sense, are similar to rational choice theorists. In both cases, decision rules are formulated so that they lead "to a previously defined goal, every element in this series . . . receiving a functional position and role." The phrase is Mannheim's and it defines formal or functional rationality (Mannheim, 1941; Weber, 1947).

The problem posed by organizational constraints on rationality, both formal and informal, extends to the question of substantive rationality. Although much of rational policy analysis searches for decision rules that will enable selection of alternatives, little is concerned with the selection of goals. There is no doubt that political culture, ideology, class, status, and ethnic factors constrain selection of goals as well as selection of alternatives. Alternatives and goals are interrelated, as is expressed by the very important concept of "nondecision." Those who have developed this concept argue in substance that the elements of the set which finally become a part of the formal organizational system are determined by those who benefit by the system. Not making a decision obviously is a way to support the status quo. A choice not to make a decision is just as much a decision as positive policy action is.

But there is more to nondecision making than restricting the choice set. The concept of nondecision has to do with substantive rationality. Those who are concerned with nondecisions are concerned more with the substantive results and ends aimed at than with the means used (Lowi, 1969; Bachrach and Baratz, 1962). Their most frequent point of departure is Mannheim's thesis that in modern societies, functional rationality displaces substantive rationality. In highly complex and technical situations, the capacity of decision makers to carry out goals is reduced. This leads to ever increasing centralized decision making in which the role of the individual is minimized and that of structure is inflated.

But rationality that deals only with processes tends to result in irrationality. Goals cannot be evaluated in terms of instrumental power alone; they also involve a relation to absolute values (Weber, 1947). A good part of the dispute over properties of decision systems is in fact a controversy over goals, not over the process of making decisions. The concern with goals and their evaluation, however, is often carried on without concern for the practical problem of power. What can be accomplished with given means, even if we include entire political systems in the meaning of that term, is limited by the fact that power is not an infinite and unlimited commodity.

POWER IN ORGANIZATIONAL THEORY

Only in recent years have organizational theorists begun to focus on the concept of power. It is becoming apparent that a good theory of organizational behavior will have to include some consideration of power. But the concept is illusive and ambiguous, even though there is an extensive literature on it as well as on its synonyms: authority, influence, and control. I will deal here only with some of the more recent developments of this literature.

Traditionally, power in organizations has been conceived of as vertical, and this concept most often refers to the control of operational employees by superiors (ostensibly to see that they work toward the goal of the organization). In some ways this view of power relations was a way of ignoring the problem of power by transferring it to the domain of authority relations. The "science of management" would enable organizations to make individuals work for the achievement of organizational goals. Authority, in the traditional view, results from position and refers only to the formal structure. Power derives from informal relations in the organization. Although traditional theorists recognized the existence of power, they considered it an obstacle to be overcome. Thus authority, in the classical view, is an asymmetrical relationship that always moves from the top down. The power of those lower down in the hierarchy and the ability of subordinates to gain independence from superiors have only recently been dealt with. It is unique and refreshing to learn that bureaucratic rules can be viewed as a means by which subordinates protect themselves from arbitrary action by superiors (Crozier, 1964). More recently, the horizontal dimensions of power have been studied. This includes the power of one group in an organization, such as the salespeople, over another group, such as production (Perrow, 1970). Bucher describes the conflict between the basic science faculty and clinicians in a medical school and finds that the source of power of each group depends on their stature as well as their formal authority (Bucher, 1970). Dubin contends that the power of a group is related to the number of other functionaries in an organization capable of performing the group's function (Dubin, 1963). James Thompson (1967) relates degrees of power to uncertainty: those units that have to deal with a more uncertain environment have greater power. Crozier suggests that ". . . the predictability of one's behavior is a sure test of one's own inferiority" (1964, p. 168).

It is apparent that power does not have a standard meaning in organization theory. A complete history of the concept has not yet been written, but when it is, we will probably find that it has been used almost invariably as a synonym for coercion. "Power," writes Max Weber, "is the probability that one actor within a social relationship will be in a position to carry out his own will despite resistance, regardless of the basis on which this probability rests." (Weber, 1947, p. 152). Those relations in which "severe sanctions are expected to be used or are in fact applied to sustain a policy against opposition" are called power by Lasswell and Kaplan (1950).

Coercion, whether or not it involves the use of force, always involves control over rewards and punishment (Cyert and MacCrimmon, 1954, p. 589). It also involves a conflict of wills; i.e., actor A wants to achieve some end but is blocked by actor B (Dahl, 1957, 1968). Because B stands in the way of his achieving his ends, he must try to get B to help him. To the extent to which he succeeds, he has coercive power.

But it is possible for A to get B to do his bidding without the use of coercion. B may help A of his own volition because he feels it is the right thing to do. Can we say that power is not involved when B helps A achieve his ends even if coercion has not been used? Obviously not, because that would reduce the concept of power to an excessively narrow realm. Application of aspects of role theory can help us solve this problem. Cases where B cooperates with A, without coercion, can be labeled "legitimate power" (Collins and Raven, 1954; Apter and Andrain, 1972). The word "legitimate" conveys the notion that B's cooperation occurs regardless of whether he is being observed by A. B behaves in the expected way because he accepts it as part of the legitimate definition of his role. He will do it willingly, even eagerly, because he believes it is the right behavior. Coercive power, on the other hand, always involves the use of surveillance. Because A is consciously trying to get B to behave in a particular way, he must watch him to see whether he does; otherwise he cannot use his sanctions.

The distinction between coercive and legitimate power helps solve problems posed by the concept of nondecisions. We can view the distinction between actual decisions and nondecisions as synonymous with the distinction between coercive and legitimate power. Actual decisions, such as laws, ordinances, administrative rulings, court decisions, and the like, generally involve the use of coercive power (i.e., orders, commands, threats, use of sanctions) because once a matter becomes a part of the public arena, there usually are opposing sides and interests as well as supporters. Seldom is a decision completely unanimous. Laws, ordinances, administrative rulings, and the like result in changes in the definition of roles and in the goals of key actors. Because such changes may imply loss of status, those affected may oppose them. Although some of the participants involved in a particular decision supporting actor A may do so because they believe it is the right thing to do (legitimate power is involved), there may also be actors opposing A and attempting to block him. These opposing actors can be persuaded to help A only through the use of coercive power.

Coercive and legitimate power are best seen as two mutually exclusive domains whose boundaries do not overlap. By definition this must be true because the use of coercive power is not necessary if A can rely on legitimate power alone. This does not mean that all decisions involve only coercive power. Some actors may support the decisions because they feel they are the right decisions. But unless there is complete unanimity, any decision will involve some use of coercive power.

It seems useful to think of legitimate power as being more extensive than coercive power, even though each may expand and contract at various times. The greatest portion of decision-making behavior is legitimate behavior in the sense that decision makers usually do not have many alternatives from which to choose, given the premises and the structure of decision making they face. For example, Ted Sorenson concluded that "Presidents rarely, if ever, make decisions—particularly in foreign affairs—in the sense of writing their conclusions on a clean slate. . . . The basic decisions, which confine their choices, have all too often been previously made" (Sorenson, 1967). This, of course, is true at each level in an organization, not just for the top person. And although the issue of what rules will be used to make a decision in a particular case may itself become a subject for coercive power, once they are formed, the rules are internalized and serve to direct behavior in most decision situations. This is simply another way of saying that role prescriptions are a part of legitimate power; a person accepts a given role specification and will not change his behavior unless confronted with new information (Simon, 1945).

Power can therefore be used to describe role behavior when we mean legitimized power rather than coercion. This is a broad conception of power—too broad, perhaps, to be of much use in organization theory. F. L. Bates (1970) concludes in this regard: "Unless some concept of deliberate control or intentional determination of alter's actions by ego is implied in the definition of power, all interaction between ego and alter becomes power behavior, and power becomes a veiled synonym for behavior itself" (Bates, 1970, p. 204). It is true that such a definition includes almost all behavior and therefore is not very useful. But it is also true that coercive power is but one aspect of power, and distinguishing legitimate power is one way to call attention to this fact. The distinction also seems to be better than the traditional distinction between authority and power.

When power is the most important variable in organizational behavior achievement of goals is not a cucial factor. When power is involved, "individuals have no chance of being materially rewarded or even of gaining in status by their personal achievements. Personal achievements are not even measurable" (Crozier, 1965, p. 139). Each group in an organization is autonomous and has little to gain by teamwork. Because successful performance is not required, power behavior, in contrast to rational behavior, does not promote achievement of organizational goals. The principal question in organizations is how much freedom and independence each group is able to achieve. This is not to say that there is no concern whatsoever for goal achievement. Societal norms about the limits of conflict and power behavior, and expectations about performance, require some constraint and attention to achievement of goals. An organization must take account of its errors and attempt to correct them, particularly in the public realm in a democratic setting. The pressure to make an organization accountable to its clientele and to the public at large keeps it from becoming concerned exclusively with problems of power. The important emphasis from the standpoint of this chapter is that when power is a factor in organizational behavior, substantive rationality is not possible.

The problem of verifying these hypotheses is that, to date, no one has succeeded in measuring power in organizations; thus far no good typology, let alone operationalization, of the concept has been achieved. Such a typology, when it is developed, will have to apply to nondecisions. In other words, it must be used in those cases where no action is taken at all, for the choice to take no action has power consequences.

CENTRALIZATION AND DECENTRALIZATION IN ORGANIZATION

Centralization and its obverse, decentralization, have always been a leading concern in debates about how organizations should be structured. How can we tell when an organization has been decentralized if we cannot measure power? One way is to look at the kinds of decisions involved. Probability concepts turn out to be very useful here. In this study of decentralization in bureaucracies, Blau concluded that executives tend to decentralize decision-making responsibility over those kinds of decisions that are subject to standardized treatment and to keep "risky" decisions to themselves (Blau, 1970, p. 169; J. Thompson, 1967). They are able to do so because they can designate the procedures to be followed by subordinates in risky decisions. If the majority of decisions in an organization are programmable, the organization will have the appearance of being decentralized when in fact it is not. The outcomes of decisions are strictly determined, and the only discretion subordinates have is over what program to apply (i.e., linear or dynamic programming; strategy A or B; pricing policy X or Y, etc.). Programmed decisions of this kind are made under conditions of certainty, and a mistake in program application by subordinates is easily detected. Because the solution to the decision problem is strictly determined, it cannot be said that there actually has been any decentralization of power.

It is sometimes logical for superiors to try to program as many decisions as possible, since doing so greatly eases their supervisory task. This pressure explains the tendency for functional rationality (concern with processes) to replace substantive rationality (concern with goals) and the proportion of programmed decisions to increase under political modernization (Landau, 1973). Nevertheless, there are very few organizations, even in modern societies, where the majority of decisions can be programmed: "Conditions of certainty or near certainty, appear to be rare facts in the life of a public agency, and when they exist, their scope is likely to be severely restricted." (Landau, 355, 1969)

Decisions involving risk and uncertainty cannot be decentralized as easily. The best design for an organization depends on the degree of uncertainty in an environment. An "organic" design is better in an uncertain environment, and a "mechanistic" design may be better where conditions are certain (Galbraith, 1973; Bennis, 1969; Palumbo, 1969a; Burns and Stalker, 1961). The mechanistic model is one in which there is a high degree of role specificity, formal rules, and strong hierarchical authority. An organic model is one in which there is greater decentralization, broad participation by lower-echelon employees in decision making, and flexibility in roles. The greater the uncertainty in the environment, the greater the amount of information needed during execution of decisions. The organic model may be the best design under these conditions (George, 1972). Put in the form of a hypothesis, this prescription states that as conflict within an organization increases, so does constructive thought and action, and this is what is needed in uncertain decision environments (Bower, 1965). Empirical evidence supports the hypothesis that there is more innovation in organizations which are more decentralized and in which there is greater participation in decision making. But this is not invariably true; it depends on the technology involved (Palumbo, 1969a; Hage and Aiken, 1969).

There is some ambiguity concerning these hypotheses. It seems logical that there should be greater actual centralization under conditions of uncertainty. Under uncertainty, a substantial amount of judgment is needed to estimate probabilities of various states of nature or possible strategies of opponents. Judgment also is involved in determining the value to be assigned to the payoffs of each alternative and the cost of searching for possible courses of action. In these cases, superiors cannot designate what procedures should be followed by subordinates. They must keep subordinates under surveillance to see that they attempt to achieve the goals desired by superiors. It also follows that decisions under uncertainty are more likely to involve coercive than legitimate power.

The need for substantive rationality also helps promote centralization in organizations, as well as in society at large, for in order to be able to achieve desired ends, it is necessary to have a directed structure. If the organization is to achieve given goals, subordinates cannot be allowed to substitute their own ends for those of the organization, and power cannot be decentralized except under strict accounting procedures, for there will be no mechanism to ensure that they attempt to achieve the organization's goals. There are a number of empirical examples of how centralization is brought about by a desire for substantive rationality. Pondy, for example, found that if cooperation in organizations is strictly voluntary, each department will be motivated to overestimate its externalities and welch on its output agreement (Pondy, 1970).

Ostrom found that without central interference, each landowner sitting over a common pool of water will have an incentive to pump out excessive amounts, thus wasting resources both in the short and in the long run (Ostrum, 1971, p. 124). These defections from an optimum solution can be overcome only through the use of hierarchical authority (Arrow, 1958; Downs, 1957). Thus it may be that an optimum solution and the achievement of desired ends is possible only if all power is lodged in a single source which imposes a solution on the rest. Otherwise goal displacement may occur. It also follows that it is more difficult to find an optimum solution in cases where power is equally divided among actors in an organization. If we conceive of this hypothesis in continuous terms, we find that under conditions of risk and uncertainty, the more polycentric an organization, the less likely it is to find a way to achieve desired goals. An organic model, therefore, seems most appropriate where the principal concern is to determine which of a number of competing goals is most desirable. The mechanistic model is more appropriate where goals are not in doubt, and achievement is the main concern.

But as we said above, there is some ambiguity here. Power in most organizations is distributed in the form of a *J* curve; it is relatively centralized with few actors having a great deal of power and most having very little power (Shapley and Shubik, 1954). The reason may be that uncertainty is more characteristic of organizational environments than certainty. But a large part of prescriptive writing on organizational design recommends an "organic" and decentralized model for organizations that face uncertain environments (George, 1972; Bennis, 1969). There is little empirical evidence about whether the organic model is likely to perform better than a centralized policy-making system. The question frequently hinges on the style of the chief executive and on values and ideology.

FACTS AND VALUES IN DECISIONS

The view in a large part of the organization theory literature, when the question is considered at all, is that the distinction between facts and values corresponds, roughly, to the distinction between rational and nonrational elements of decision making. Facts, in the traditional logical positive view, are knowable, subject to empirical verification (Simon, 1945, p. 46). Values are not. They may often be in conflict. It is not possible to compare values quantitatively, and decisions involving values are more likely to resemble a zero-sum situation (gains in one value mean a loss of another). It is not possible to make a rational choice about values in these cases. Consider, as an example, a possible conflict between two values: equality and quality. Assume that the more equality there is in the distribution of a given output, such as health services, the less quality there is. Some may believe that equality is more important than quality, or that we should give up a large amount of quality of services for a small increase in equality. Another person may not agree. It is not possible to tell empirically if one of these values is better than another, or to decide how much equality is equal to a given amount of quality (Simon, 1945, p. 50). Thus the standard position in the organizational theory literature is that values should be treated as givens (Simon, 1945; McKean, 1958; Hitch and McKean, 1961). Science cannot deal with values, only with means of achieving them.

This line of reasoning, unfortunately, has produced a number of complex, unresolvable theoretical problems; it now appears to be a rather unfruitful approach to the problem. First of all, the traditional view that facts are empirically verifiable is questionable. Not only do theoretical models determine what facts we observe, but also facts may be facts only in the context of a given theory. They do not have meaning or empirical existence outside of a theory (Allison, 1971). A growing part of philosophy of science, which we cannot consider in detail here, has questioned whether a theory can be disproven by contrary facts alone, and even whether there are "facts" independent of a theory (Lakatos and Musgrave, 1970; DiRenzo, 1966). It is also questionable whether empirical methods can and should be used to try to "prove" laws of human behavior (Palumbo, 1973).

These rather complex philosophical and methodological problems cannot be considered here. All that is possible is to outline what appear to be the most promising developments as they pertain to organization theory. First, it should be emphasized that the fact-value dichotomy is better seen as a continuum. An important point to note is that both facts and values are present in every decision. Some decisions may contain a larger value component than others, but the distinction between facts and values is analytical rather than empirical. In actual organizations, every decision has both factual and value components. Second, empirical methods can be used to determine whether a goal is desirable. For example, sampling and statistics can be used to determine how poorly services (health, welfare, justice) are distributed. Of course, there isn't much dispute over this. But empirical methods also can be used to help select goals. There is more dispute about this unless, of course, empirical methods are considered to involve more than data collection and analysis. And they do; they also involve deductive reasoning, and this is essential in ethical problems as well as in empirical problems. "Formal modeling" or mathematical political theory has shown that empirical theory involves more than making inferences from data. And this form of theory can and should be expanded.

It is of course not possible to derive value propositions from empirical observations. As we demonstrated above, the decision as to how much weight should be given to a dollar received by a poor man as compared with that received by a rich man can be made only on nonempirical grounds (i.e., ideology, ethics). For example, it is possible to determine empirically what impact various distributions (of income, health services, welfare, etc.) will have on spending and thus on economic growth. And whether economic growth is a desirable goal also contains both factual and value elements. To be able to assign a decision to the category "good" requires a great deal of both factual and ethical knowledge. All decisions have an empirical component concerning what impact selecting certain goals may have, as well as an ethical component concerning how desirable a goal is. And the two cannot be separated empirically. To value a decision requires knowledge that permits us to fit decisions to problems as we fit data to curves.

Without opening the elusive question of ultimate value, it should be apparent that the development of science and technology, whatever difficulties they generate, does not necessarily result in the subordination of ends for means, or in the dichotomization of facts and values. On the contrary, such developments increase the number of choice sets available, as well as the range of alternatives in each. This growth of knowledge bestows on us a greater freedom of choice by providing us with an ever increasing fund of relevant goal alternatives to select from. By expanding the set from which we select alternatives, we help explicate goals, even if we do not provide a rule to tell us how to select goals. And the elevation of factual premises in our decision systems increases the probability that those we select are relevant and satisfactory solutions (Landau, 1973).

The proposition that it is possible to be rational and scientific about selecting values assumes, of course, that we broaden the definition of a rationality to include the search for goals as well as the selection of means. One of the more interesting criteria that have been proposed as a way of dealing with this problem is social equity (Rawls, 1971; Frederickson, 1974). Those who advocate using it as the standard by which to evaluate the output of organizations couple their proposal with an attack on rational choice. The latter tends to elevate the values of economy and efficiency while, at times, claiming to be ethically neutral. Thus, runs the argument, since value choices must be made, we should pick more democratic values as the primary goal of public choice.

However, since selection of goals in organizations occurs most often under conditions of uncertainty, it is to be emphasized that approximations to empirical reality are never complete. New problems arise, unanticipated consequences occur, change takes place, and these require adjustments in judgments about what is desirable, as well as about what states of nature are most likely to occur. In any event, it seems fruitful to abandon the fact-value dichotomy and the logical impasse it entails, in favor of a language that enables us to deal rationally with values as well as with facts. But as with other developments in organization theory, although it is possible to deal rationally with values in theory, it has not yet been worked out in practice.

CONCLUSIONS

The assumptions of the theory of rational choice are powerful and elegant in their simplicity, and the theory has provided exciting and interesting explanations for a large range of behavior, especially in economics, where it originated.

It has been most successfully applied to problems which involve individual decision makers (microeconomics) and in which value is unidimensional and expressible in dollars. But these conditions are not characteristics of large-scale organizations (Bower, 1965). Hence most of the assumptions of the pure theory of rational choice prove to be a bad fit for organizational behavior. Individuals in organizations are motivated by more than self-interest; they are more likely to satisfice than maximize; organizations have more than one goal; choice involves a search for goals as well as for means; it seldom is possible to find objective probabilities for the alternatives faced by the organization; feedback concerning decisions is likely to be vague and incorrect; and the cost of achieving consensus is a major part of most organizational decisions.

Many—perhaps most—decisions in organizations cannot be understood in terms of rational choice, strictly defined. They involve a great deal of uncertainty; individuals do not always do the correct thing; and the most logical choices, even the most satisfactory ones, are not invariably made. Many decisions, therefore, can best be understood in terms of nonrational choice.

When we deal with public choice, there is an added complication. The goals of public agencies are stated in general and abstract terms. Stated goals of public agencies frequently are symbols to disguise the multiple goals public agencies actually have. These goals usually involve situations that are uncertain; in other words, they have to do with infinite and uncontrollable behavior sets. Cause and effect cannot be identified in these cases, and therefore public officials responsible for these decisions cannot be held accountable. They can be held accountable only for their *positions* on various issues, not for their actual performance. This means that public choice involves ideology as much as it involves performance.

Organizations learn, adapt, compromise, and continuously search for ways of legitimating new goals, for their very lives depend on the successful quest for consensus on a set of goals. Decisions, therefore, frequently depend on the distribution of and changes in that vague quantity called power. Organizational behavior can be explained as well—if not better—by changes in power in organization as by conscious attempts to achieve goals. There are, of course, psychological factors dealing with personality and learning that are important in organizational behavior. We have not been able to consider them extensively here, but on the surface it seems that they can be more easily incorporated into a political model than the rational choice axioms. This is not to say that the quest for power, for self- actualization, and for need fulfillment are unrelated to task achievement; there is a wide gap in our knowledge about just how the two are related. It is to conclude only that a political model of organizational behavior seems to be a better way to explain the empirical world of organizational behavior than the pure theory of rational choice.

NOTES

1. Very little has been written on the question of access as a factor in organizational behavior. One interesting application in urban politics is Oliver P. Williams, *Metropolitan Political Analysis: A Social Access Approach,* New York, Free Press, 1971.

2. There are some who believe that voters are not at all rational and that it isn't rational for a person to vote, given the small return he or she receives. For example, see Donald Stokes, "Some dynamic elements of contests for the Presidency," *American Political Science Review,* Vol. 60, no. 1, March 1966. And compare John A. Ferejohn and Morris P. Fiorina, "The paradox of not voting: A decision theoretic analysis," *American Political Science Review,* Vol. 68, no. 2, June 1974, 525–37. There is also some evidence that politicians do not always reward the voters who helped them win elections. See Andrew Glassberg, "The linkage between urban policy outputs and voting behavior: New York and London," *British Journal of Politics,* 3, 1973.

REFERENCES

Ackoff, Russell (1962). *Scientific Method; Optimizing Applied Research Decisions.* New York: Wiley.

Ackoff, Russell, and Fred E. Emery (1972). *On Purposeful Systems.* Chicago and New York: Aldine-Atherton.

Alker, Haywood (1969). "Statistics and politics; the need for causal data analysis." In S. M. Lipset (ed.), *Politics and the Social Sciences.* London: Oxford University Press.

Allison, Graham (1971). *Essence of Decision.* Boston: Little, Brown.

Apter, David, and Charles Andrain (1972). *Contemporary Analytic Theory.* Englewood Cliffs, N.J.: Prentice-Hall.

Argyris, Chris (1957). *Personality and Organization.* New York: Harper and Row.

Arrow, Kenneth (1951.) "Alternative approaches to the theory of choice in risk-taking situations." *Econometrica* 19.

_____ (1958). *Social Choice and Individual Values.* New York: Wiley.

_____ (1973). "Social Responsibility and Economic Efficiency." *Public Policy* 21:303–19.

Ashby, W. Ross (1956). *An Introduction to Cybernetics.* London: Chapman and Hall.

Babilot, George (1966). "Basic problems in taxation and welfare theory." In Paul L. Kleinsorge, (ed.), *Public Finance and Welfare Essays in Honor of C. Ward Macy.* Eugene: University of Oregon.

Bachrach, Peter (1967). *The Theory of Democratic Elitism.* Boston: Little, Brown.

Bachrach, Peter, and Morton Baratz (1962). "The two faces of power." *American Political Science Review* 57:947–52.

Barnard, Chester (1938). *The Functions of the Executive.* Cambridge: Harvard University Press.

Barnes, Louis B. (1957). "Organizational change and field experimental methods." In Victor H. Vroom (ed.), *Methods of Organizational Research.* Pittsburgh: University of Pittsburgh Press.

Barnett, Richard (1972). *The Roots of War.* New York: Atheneum.

Bates, F. L. (1970). "Power behavior and decentralization." In Mayer Zald (ed.), *Power in Organizations*. Nashville: Vanderbilt University Press.

Bauer, Raymond, Ithiel De Sola Pool, and Lewis A. Dexter (1963). *American Business and Public Policy*. New York: Atherton.

Bauer, Raymond, and K. J. Gergen, eds. (1968). *The Study of Policy Formation*. New York: Free Press.

Bennis, Warren (1969). *Organizational Development: Its Nature, Origins and Purposes*. Reading Mass.: Addison-Wesley.

Bergson, Abram (1938). "A reformation of certain aspects of welfare economics." *Quarterly Journal of Economics* 52:314–44.

Blalock, Hubert, and Ann Blalock (1968). *Methodology in Social Research*. New York: McGraw-Hill.

Blau, Peter (1970). "Decentralization in bureaucracies." In Mayer Zald (ed.), *Power in Organizations*. Nashville: Vanderbilt University Press.

_____ (1972). "Interdependence and Hierarchy in Organizations." *Social Science Research* 1.

Borch, Karl, and Jan Mossin (1968). *Risk and Uncertainty*. New York: St. Martin's Press.

Bower, Joseph (1965). "The role of conflict in economic decision making groups." *Quarterly Journal of Economics* 79.

_____ (1968). "Descriptive decision theory from the administrative viewpoint." In R. Bauer and K. J. Gergen (eds.), *The Study of Policy Formation*. New York: Free Press.

Braybrooke, David, and Charles E. Lindbloom (1963). *A Strategy of Decision*. New York: Free Press.

Buchanan, James, and Robert Tollison (1972). *Theory of Public Choice*. Ann Arbor: University of Michigan Press.

Buchanan, James, and Gordon Tullock (1962). *Calculus of Consent*. Ann Arbor: University of Michigan Press.

Bucher, Rue (1970). "Social process and power in a medical school." In Mayer Zald (ed.), *Power in Organizations*. Nashville: Vanderbilt University Press.

Bucher, Rue, and H. G. Nutini (1969). *Game Theory in the Behavioral Sciences*. Pittsburgh: University of Pittsburgh Press.

Burns, Tom (1966). "On the Plurality of Social Systems." In J. R. Lawrence (ed.), *Operational Research and the Social Sciences*. London: Tavistock.

Burns, Tom, and G. M. Stalker (1961). *The Management of Innovation*. London: Tavistock.

Campbell, Angus, Philip Converse, Warren E. Miller, and Donald Stokes (1966). *Elections and the Political Order*. New York: Wiley.

Carzo, Rocco, and John Yanouzas (1967). *Formal Organization: A Systems Approach*. Homewood, Ill.: Dorsey.

Churchman, C. West (1961). *Prediction and Optimal Decision*. Englewood Cliffs, N.J.: Prentice-Hall.

_____ (1968). *The Systems Approach*. New York: Delacourte Press.

Cohen, Michael D., James G. March, and John Olsen (1972). "A garbage can model of organizational choice." *"Administrative Science Quarterly* 17:5.

Collins, Barry, and Berthran Raven (1969). "Group structure, attractions, coalitions, communications, and power." In Garner Lindzey and Elliot Aronson (eds.), *The Handbook of Social Psychology,* 2nd edition. Reading, Mass.: Addison-Wesley.

Coombs, C., and D. Beardslee (1954). "On decision making under uncertainty." In R. M. Thrall, C. H. Coombs, and R. L. Davis (eds.), *Decision Processes.* New York: Wiley.

Cooper, W. W. (1951). "A proposal for extending the theory of the firm." *Quarterly Journal of Economics* 65:

Crecine, John (1969). *Governmental Problem Solving.* Chicago: Rand McNally.

Crozier, Michel (1964). *The Bureaucratic Phenomenon.* Chicago: University of Chicago Press.

Cyert, Richard M., and K. R. MacCrimmon (1954). "Organizations." In Garner Lindzey (ed.), *The Handbook of Social Psychology.* Reading, Mass.: Addison-Wesley.

Cyert, Richard M., and James March (1963). *A Behavioral Theory of the Firm.* Englewood Cliffs, N.J.: Prentice-Hall.

Dahl, Robert (1957). "The concept of power." *Behavioral Science* 2:201–15.

_____ (1968). "Power." In David L. Sills (ed.), *International Encyclopedia of the Social Sciences.* New York: Crowell-Collier-Macmillan.

Diesing, Paul (1962). *Reason in Society.* Urbana: University of Illinois Press.

DiRenzo, Gordon J., ed. (1966). *Concepts, Theory and Explanation in the Behavioral Sciences.* New York: Random House.

Downs, Anthony (1957). *An Economic Theory of Democracy.* New York: Harper and Row.

_____ (1967). *Inside Bureaucracy.* Boston: Little, Brown.

Dubin, Robert (1963). "Power, function, and organization." *Pacific Sociological Reveiw* 6:16–24.

Easton, David (1965). *A Framework for Political Analysis.* Englewood Cliffs, N.J.: Prentice-Hall.

Edwards, Ward (1953). "Probability preference in gambling." *American Journal of Psychology* 66:349–64.

Elkin, Stephen L. (1974). "Political science and the analysis of public policy." *Social Policy.*

Ellsberg, Daniel (1961). "Risk, ambiguity, and the savage axioms." *Quarterly Journal of Economics* 75:643–69.

Emery, James (1969. *Organizational Planning and Control Systems.* New York: Macmillan.

Etzioni, Amitai (1964). *Modern Organizations.* Englewood Cliffs, N.J.: Prentice-Hall.

Farquharson, Robin (1966). "The application of game theory to committee procedure." In J. R. Lawrence (ed.), *Operational Research and the Social Sciences.* London: Tavistock.

Frederickson, H. George, ed. (1974). "Symposium on social equity in the public service." *Public Administrative Review,* Jan.–Feb. 1974.

Ferejohn, John A., and Morris P. Fiorina (1974). "The paradox of not voting: a decision theoretic analysis." *American Political Science Review* 68: 525–37.

Foster C. D. (1966). "Social welfare functions in cost-benefit analysis." In J. R. Lawrence (ed.), *Operational Research and the Social Sciences*. London: Tavistock.

Galbraith, Jay (1973). *Designing Complex Organizations*. Reading, Mass.: Addison-Wesley.

George, Alexander (1972). "The case for multiple advocacy in making foreign policy. *American Political Science Review* 56: 751–96.

Goldner, Fred H. (1970). "The division of labor; process and power." In Mayer Zald (ed.), *Power in Organizations*. Nashville: Vanderbilt University Press.

Gordon, R. A. (1945). *Business Leadership in the Large Corporation*. Washington: Brookings Institute.

Green, Philip, and Sanford Levinson, eds. (1970). *Power and Community*. New York: Knopf-Vantage Books.

Gross, Bertram (1964). *The Managing of Organizations*. New York: Free Press.

Gulick, Luther, and Lyndall Urwick, eds. (1937). *Papers in the Science of Administration*. New York: Institute of Public Administration.

Hage, Jerald, and Michael Aiken (1969). "Routine technology, social structure, and organizational goals." *Administrative Science Quarterly* 14:366–76.

Harsanyi, John C. (1969). "Rational choice models of political behavior vs. functionalist and conformist theories." *World Politics* 21:513–38.

Harvey, Edward, and Harvey Mills (1970). "Patterns of organizational adaptation: a political perspective." In Mayer Zald (ed.), *Power in Organizations*. Nashville: Vanderbilt University Press.

Haveman, Robert (1965). *Water Resource Investment and the Public Interest*. Nashville: Vanderbilt University Press.

Hicks, J. R. (1940). "The valuation of social income." *Economica*.

Hickson, D. J., *et al.* (1971). "A strategic contingencies theory of inter-organizational power." *Administrative Science Quarterly* 16:216–29.

Hitch, Charles J., and Roland McKean (1961). *The Economics of Defense in a Nuclear Age*. Cambridge: Harvard University Press.

Hurwitz, Leonid (1951). *Optimality Criteria for Decision Making Under Ignorance*. Cowles Commission Discussion Paper, Statistics, No. 370.

Kolm, S. (1969). "The Optimal production of social justice." In Julius Margolis and H. Guitton (eds.), *Public Economics*. New York: St. Martin's Press.

Lakatos, Imre, and Alan Musgrave (1970). *Criticism and the Growth of Knowledge*. Cambridge: Cambridge University Press.

Landau, Martin (1961). "The concept of decision making in the field of public administration." In Sidney Mailick and E. Van Ness (eds.), *Concepts and Issues in Administrative Behavior*. Englewood Cliffs, N.J.: Prentice-Hall.

—————— (1969). "Redundancy, rationality, and the problem of duplication and overlap." *Public Administration Review* 29:346–58.

—————— (1973). "The self-correcting organization." *Public Administration Review* 33:533–42.

Lasswell, Harold, and Abraham Kaplan (1950). *Power and Society; A Framework for Political Inquiry.* New Haven: Yale University Press.

Lawrence, Paul R., and J. W. Lorsch (1967). *Organizations and environment.* Cambridge: Harvard University Press.

Likert, Rensis (1961). *New Patterns of Management.* New York: McGraw-Hill.

Lindbloom, Charles E. (1959). "The science of muddling through." *Public Administration Review* 19:79–88.

Lipset, Seymour M. (1963). *Political Man.* New York: Doubleday.

Little, I.M.D. (1960). *A Critique of Welfare Economics:* London: Oxford University Press.

Lowi, Theodore (1969). *The End of Liberalism.* New York: Norton.

Luce, Duncan (1959). *Individual Choice Behavior.* New York: Wiley.

Luce, Duncan, and Howard Raiffa (1957). *Games and Decisions.* New York: Wiley.

MacCrimmon, Kenneth (1968). "Descriptive and normative implications of the decision theory postulates." In Karl Borch and Jan Mossin (eds.), *Risk and Uncertainty.* New York: St. Martin's Press.

Mannheim, Karl (1941). *Man and Society in an Age of Reconstruction.* New York: Harcourt, Brace, Jovanovich.

March, James (1962). "The business firm as a political coalition." *Journal of Politics* 24:662–78.

_____, ed. (1965). *Handbook of Organizations.* Chicago: Rand McNally.

March, James, and Herbert Simon (1958). *Organizations.* New York: Wiley.

Marini, Frank, ed. (1971). *Toward a New Public Administration.* New York: Chandler.

Marschak, T. A. (1965). "Economic theories of organization." In James March (ed.), *Handbook of Organizations.* Chicago: Rand McNally.

McCoy, Charles A., and John Playford, eds. (1967). *A Political Politics.* New York: Crowell.

McKean, Roland (1958). *Efficiency in Government Through Systems Analysis.* New York: Wiley.

Menges, Gunter (1966). "The suitability of the general decision model for operational applications in the social sciences." In J. R. Lawrence (ed.), *Operational Research and the Social Sciences.* London: Tavistock.

_____ (1968). "On some open questions in statistical decision theory." In Karl Borch and Jan Mossin (eds.), *Risk and Uncertainty.* New York: St. Martin's Press.

Michalos, Alex. "Rationality between the maximizers and the satisficers." Unpublished manuscript, n.d.

Mott, Paul (1972). *The Characteristic of Effective Organizations.* New York: Harper and Row.

Nedd, Albert (1971). "The simultaneous effect of several variables on attitudes toward change." *Administrative Science Quarterly* 16:258–69.

Negandhi, Anant R., ed. (1973). *Modern Organizational Theory: Contextual, Environmental, and Socio-Cultural Variables.* Kent, Ohio: Kent State University Press.

Newell, Allan, J. C. Shaw, and H. A. Simon (1959). *A Variety of Intelligent Learning in a General Problem Solver.* Santa Monica, Calif.: Rand Corporation.

Ostrom, Vincent (1971). "Policentricity." Paper delivered before the American Political Science Association Meeting.

Palumbo, Dennis (1969a). "Power and role specificity in organization theory." *Public Administration Review* 29.

_____ (1969b). "A systems analysis of local public health." *American Journal of Public Health* 59:673–79.

_____ (1969c). *Statistics in Political and Behavioral Science*. New York: Appleton-Century-Crofts.

_____ (1973). "Comparative analysis: quasi-methodology or new science?" *Comparative Urban Studies*.

Palumbo, Dennis, and Richard Styskal (1974). "Professionalism and receptivity to change." *American Journal of Politics*.

Perrow, Charles (1970). "Departmental power and perspective in industrial firms." In Mayer Zald (ed.), *Power in Organizations*. Nashville: Vanderbilt University Press.

_____ (1972). *Complex Organizations: A Critical Essay*. Glenview, Ill.: Scott, Foresman.

Pomper, Gerald M. (1968). *Elections in America: Control and Influence in Democratic Politics*. New York: Dodd, Mead.

Pondy, Louis (1970). "Toward a theory of internal resource allocation." In Mayer Zald (ed.) *Power in Organizations*. Nashville: Vanderbilt University Press.

Rabushka, Alan, and Kenneth A. Shepsle (1972). *Politics in Plural Societies: A Theory of Democratic Instability*. Columbus, Ohio: Merrill.

Rae, Douglas, and Michael Taylor (1971). "Decision rules and policy outcomes." *British Journal of Political Science* 1.

Raiffa, Howard (1970). *Decision Analysis: Introductory Lectures on Choices Under Uncertainty*. Reading Mass.: Addison-Wesley.

Raiffa, Howard, and Robert Schlaifer (1961). *Applied Statistical Decision Theory*. Cambridge: MIT Press.

Rapoport, Anatol, and Albert Chammah (1965). *Prisoner's Dilemma: A Study in Conflict and Cooperation*. Ann Arbor: University of Michigan Press.

Rawls, John (1971). *A Theory of Justice*. Cambridge, Mass.: Harvard University Press.

Riker, Willeman (1962). *The Theory of Political Coalitions*. New Haven: Yale University Press.

Rivlin, Alice M. (1971). *Systematic Thinking for Social Action*. Washington.: Brookings Institute.

Roethlisberger, F. J., and W. J. Dickson (1947). *Management and the Worker*. Cambridge: Harvard University Press.

Roos, Noralou P. (1974). "Influencing the health care system: policy alternatives." *Public Policy* 22: 139–67.

Rothenberg, Jerome (1961). *The Measurement of Social Welfare*. Englewood Cliffs, N.J.: Prentice-Hall.

_____ (1965). "Urban renewal programs." In Robert Dorfman (ed.), *Measuring Benefits of Government Investments*. Washington.: Brookings Institute.

Rubenstein, Albert, and Chadwick Haberstroh (1966). *Some Theories of Organization*. Homewood, Ill.: Dorsey.

Savage, Leonard J. (1954). *The Foundations of Statistics.* New York: Wiley.

Schelling, Thomas (1960). *The Strategy Conflict.* London: Oxford University Press.

Schultze, Charles L. (1968). *The Politics and Economics of Public Spending.* Washington.: Brookings Institute.

Seiler, John A. (1967). *Systems Analysis in Organizational Behavior.* Homewood, Ill.: Dorsey.

Selznick, Philip (1957). *Leadership in Administration.* Evanston, Ill.; Row, Peterson.

Sen, Amartya (1970). *Collective Choice and Social Welfare.* San Francisco: Holden-Day.

Shapley, L. S., and Martin Shubik (1954). "A method for evaluating the distribution of power in a committee system." *American Political Science Review* 48:787–92.

Shephard, Herbert (1965). "Changing interpersonal and intergroup relationships in organizations." In James March (ed.), *Handbook of Organizations.* Chicago: Rand-McNally.

Simon, Herbert (1945). *Administrative Behavior.* New York: Macmillan.

_____ (1957). *Models of Man.* New York: Wiley.

_____ (1964). "On the concept of organizational goal." *Administrative Science Quarterly* 9:1–22.

Simon, Herbert, and Richard Stedry (1969). "Psychology and economics." In Garner Lindzey and Elliot Aronson (eds.), *The Handbook of Social Psychology,* 2nd edition. Reading, Mass.: Addison-Wesley.

Sorenson, Ted (1967). "You get to walk to work." *New York Times Magazine,* March 19.

Stein, Harold, ed. (1952). *Public Administration and Policy Development.* New York: Macmillan.

Taylor, Michael (1971). "Review article: mathematical political theory." *British Journal of Political Science* 1.

Thompson, James (1967). *Organizations in Action.* New York: McGraw-Hill.

Thompson, Victor (1969). *Bureaucracy and Innovation.* Tuscaloosa: University of Alabama Press.

Verba, Sidney (1961). *Small Groups and Political Behavior.* Princeton: Princeton University Press.

Von Neumann, John and Oskar Morgenstern (1947). *Theory of Games and Economic Behavior.* Princeton: Princeton University Press.

Wallace, Anthony F. C. (1961a). *Culture and Personality.* New York: Random House.

_____ (1961b). "The psychic unity of human groups." In B. Kaplan (ed.), *Studying Personality Cross-Culturally.* Evanston, Ill.: Row, Peterson.

Weber, Max (1947). *The Theory of Social and Economic Organization.* Translated and edited by A. M. Henderson and Talcott Parsons. New York: Oxford University Press.

Weisbrod, Burton (1968). "Income redistribution effects and benefit-cost analysis." In Samuel B. Chase (ed.), *Problems in Public Expenditure Analysis,* Washington.: Brookings Institute.

Wildavsky, Aaron (1968). "The political economy of efficiency: cost-benefit analysis, systems analysis, and program budgeting." In Austin Ranney (ed.), *Political Science and Public Policy*. Chicago: Markham.

_____ (1970). "Rescuing policy analysis from PPBS." In Robert Haveman and Julius Margolis (eds.), *Public Expenditures and Policy Analysis*. Chicago: Markham.

Willoughby, W. L. (1927). *Principles of Public Administration*. Baltimore: Johns Hopkins University Press.

Zald, Mayer N. (1960). "Organizations as polities: an analysis of community organization agencies." *Social Work* 2.

_____ (1962). "Organizational control structures in five correctional institutions." *American Journal of Sociology* 68:335–45.

_____, ed. (1970). *Power in Organization*. Nashville: Vanderbilt University Press.

Zeckhauser, Richard, and Elma Schaefer (1968). "Public policy and normative economic theory." In Raymond Bauer and K. J. Gergen (eds.), *The Study of Policy Formation*. New York: Free Press.

INDEX

INDEX